I0362116

Rabbi Abraham Isaac Hakohen Kook

Commentary to The Legends of Rabbah bar Bar Ḥannah

Introduction, Translation and Notes

By Bezalel Naor

With 15 Original Illustrations by Tamar Odenheimer

KODESH PRESS

אורות
OROT

Orot/Kodesh

5779/2019

Commentary to the *Legends of Rabbah bar Bar Ḥannah*
Rabbi Abraham Isaac Hakohen Kook

Introduction, Translation, Appendices and Notes
© Bezalel Naor 2019

Illustrations by Tamar Odenheimer

The English translation of Talmud *Bavli, Bava Batra* 73a-74a
is based on that of Rabbi Adin Even-Israel Steinsaltz in the
William Davidson Talmud, Sefaria Library,
www.sefaria.org with slight modifications.

Painting on cover:
Joseph Mallord William Turner, *Aldborough, Suffolk* (1827-1829)

Cover design by Rivka Serebrowski

All rights reserved. No part of this publication may be reproduced, distributed, or transmitted in any form or by any means, including photocopying, recording, or other electronic or mechanical methods, without the prior written permission of the publisher, except in the case of brief quotations embodied in critical reviews and certain other noncommercial uses permitted by copyright law.

For permission requests, write to the publisher.

Published and distributed exclusively by:

Kodesh Press L.L.C., New York, NY
www.kodeshpress.com

Orot, Inc., Monsey, NY
www.orot.com

Layout, design and typesetting by
Dynagrafik Design Studio, Monsey, New York

ISBN: 978-1-947857-11-7 hardcover

Printed in the United States of America

Table of Contents

Introduction 9

The Manuscript of Rav Kook's Commentary 13

Précis of Rav Kook's Commentary to the Legends of Rabbah bar Bar Ḥannah 23

The Fifteen Legends of Rabbah bar Bar Ḥannah

1. The Wave that Threatens to Sink the Ship 27
2. The Littlest Star and the Secret of the Sand Bar 39
3. Hurmin son of Lilith, Demon of Cupidity 51
4. The Aesthetic Antelope 57
5. Of Frog, Serpent and Raven 65
6. Piscine Bones to Palatial Beams 73
7. The Cookout that Was Washed Out 83
8. The Two-Finned Fish (*Dipterus*) versus the Single-Finned Fish (*Monopterus*) 91
9. The Seabird *"Ziz Sadai"* 99
10. The Grievance of the Goose 109
11. Divining for Water and Souls 117
12. The Generation of the Desert 135
13. The Scorpions of Sinai 149
14. Koraḥism and the Love Beyond Love 155
15. A Breadbasket Circling the Earth 167

Conclusion 173

Appendices

1. "*Barukh ha-Ba, Señor*": Rav Kook and the *Dybbuk* in Jaffa 179
2. Man and Time: The Vilna Gaon on the Three Levels of the Soul 184
3. Rabbi Ḥayyim Hirschensohn's *Motsa'ei Mayim* and Rav Kook 192
4. A Kabbalistic Theory of Personality 198
5. Luzzatto's *'Adir ba-Marom* and *KaLaḤ Pitḥei Ḥokhmah* 209
6. Rav Kook's Critique of the Mussar Movement 214
7. Letter of Rabbi Mordechai Gimpel Jaffe on the Wisdom of Kabbalah 222
8. Rabbi Samuel of Kalvaria's *Darkhei No'am* 226
9. A Kookian Midrash on the Name "David" 230
10. Rav Kook, the Messiah, and the Vatican 235
11. The Mysterious *Nunim* of Psalm 107 240

Kabbalistic Chart 249

Lexicon of Kabbalistic Technical Terms 251

Bibliography of Works Cited by Rav Kook 253

General Biblography 255

Indexes 275

Hebrew Text of *The Legends* and Rav Kook's Commentary 1-36

Illustrations for the Legends of Rabbah bar Bar Ḥannah

(Based on *Talmud Bavli, Bava Batra* 73a-74a)

1. A huge wave threatening to sink the ship is held back by a wooden staff upon which is carved the name of *Ehyeh Asher Ehyeh.*
2. A huge wave lifts the ship all the way up to a small star in the sky.
3. A demon runs on top of the city wall and a horseman below is unable to catch up to the demon.
4. A giant antelope (*Re'em*). In the background, the Jordan River.
5. A giant frog, swallowed by a serpent; in turn, swallowed by a raven. In the background, a huge, branched tree.
6. A giant fish washed up on shore destroys sixty cities.
7. Sailors mistake a huge fish for an island. They land on it and start to make a camp fire to cook.
8. A ship travels for three days and three nights just to reach from the front fin to the back fin of a giant fish.
9. Seafarers observe a giant bird (*Ziz Sadai*) standing just up to its ankles in the deep, turbulent waters of the sea.
10. Rabbah bar Bar Ḥannah sees in the desert geese whose wings are so fat that they droop down and rivers of oil flow beneath them.
11. In the desert, Rabbah bar Bar Ḥannah encounters a Bedouin who by picking up a clump of dust and smelling it, can tell how far away is the water.
12. That same Bedouin shows Rabbah bar Bar Ḥannah the Hebrews who died in the Desert (on the way out of Egypt to the Promised Land). They are so huge that one of these dead is lying on its back with its knee raised, and a Bedouin riding a camel under the knee with his spear upright is unable to reach the knee arched overhead.
13. That same Bedouin shows Rabbah bar Bar Ḥannah Mount Sinai surrounded by scorpions large as white donkeys.
14. That same Bedouin shows Rabbah bar Bar Ḥannah the place in the desert where the congregation of Koraḥ were swallowed by the earth. Two geysers of smoke issue from the earth. Rabbah bar Bar Ḥannah places a damp woolen cloth on the end of a spear and holds it over the fissure and the heat is so intense that the cloth is singed.
15. That same Bedouin shows Rabbah bar Bar Ḥannah the place where heaven and earth "kiss" one another.

Introduction

Rabbah bar Bar Ḥannah has been referred to as the Jewish Sinbad the Sailor.[1] His tall tales, fifteen in all, are recorded in the Babylonian Talmud in Tractate *Bava Batra* (73a-74a). The particular chapter in which they are situated is named "The Seller of the Ship" ("*Ha-Mokher et ha-Sefinah*"). Appropriately, these tales of seafarers (*neḥutei yama*) were inserted in that legal discussion, as is the wont of the Talmud to mix *Aggadah* with *Halakhah*, thus tempering law with lore and legend.[2]

Rabbah bar Bar Ḥannah's narratives take us beyond the "comfort zone" of the rational to an alternate reality where imagination runs riot. The psychological stress brought on by prolonged periods of isolation at sea (scene of the earlier legends in the series) or the desert (scene of the later legends), produces fantastic imagery. The hypnotic motion of the ocean waves conjures up aquatic creatures of mythic proportions; and the shifting sands of the Sinai Desert, stretching as far as the eye can see, expose the unsuspecting wanderer to visions and voices of the ghosts of the generation of the Exodus from Egypt. And in that case, Rabbah bar Bar Ḥannah is accompanied by the canny *tay'a*, a guide who has all the makings of a shaman, initiating his charge into the spiritual unknown.[3] In these liminal zones at the frontier of credibility (medieval Kabbalist Rabbi Menaḥem Ziyyoni threw in the Norwegian tundra for good measure),[4] the mysteries of man's being are revealed: layers of soul; forces of chaos and cosmos, destruction and creation. Not for naught does Rav Kook conclude his rendition of the legends with the verse from Proverbs 20:5 (once invoked in regard to Rabbah bar Bar Ḥannah): "Counsel in the heart of man is like deep water; and a man of understanding will draw it out."

The Legends of Rabbah bar Bar Ḥannah enjoyed immense popularity, catching the imagination of commentators throughout the ages. Rabbi Moshe Zuriel, the indefatigable scholar of B'nei Berak, compiled a bibliography of no less than fifty-five commentaries to the *Legends*. Perhaps the most famous of these commentaries is that of the Vilna Gaon, Rabbi Elijah Kramer (1720-1797).[5] In this regard, we would be remiss not to mention that one of the very few *haskamot* or formal approbations written by the Vilna Gaon was that to Samuel ben Eliezer of Kalvaria's *Darkhei No'am* (Koenigsberg, 1764), a commentary to the Legends of Rabbah bar Bar Ḥannah, employing the quadrivial method of *Pardes* or *Peshat*, *Remez*, *Derush*, *Sod*, with a heavy concentration of Lurianic Kabbalah.[6]

An English version of *The Tales of Rabbah bar-bar Ḥannah* was published by Judah David Eisenstein (New York, 1937).

Rav Kook's commentary to the *Legends* first appeared in print in Jerusalem in 1984 in the second volume of his collected essays, *Ma'amrei ha-Rayah*. In this early work (written at age twenty-five), Rav Kook yet cites sources.[7] Later, when his style of writing switched to "stream of consciousness," sources were eliminated.[8] For this very reason, the commentary to the Rabbah bar Bar Ḥannah legends is of extreme importance. Here, Rav Kook divulges the many and varied Kabbalistic sources that informed his view. We see him equally at home in the world of the Vilna Gaon and of his rival Rabbi Shneur Zalman of Liadi (founder of Ḥabad Ḥasidism).[9] A great influence upon Rav Kook's thought was the earlier Italian mystic, Rabbi Moses Ḥayyim Luzzatto.[10]

In *Ma'amrei ha-Rayah*, Rav Kook's commentary was provided by Rabbi Shlomo Aviner with brief summaries as well as an index.[11] These are certainly helpful to the reader.

The present edition is the first time in any language that the commentary of Rav Kook is presented complete with much needed explanatory notes.

In the English translation I have adhered as closely as possible to Rav Kook's original Hebrew. In places where Rav Kook's presentation deviated from the sequence of the Talmudic text, I rearranged sentences to restore the flow of the Talmudic narrative.[12]

*

In many of the stories, we find Rav Kook in his commentarial capacity engrossed in the spiritual work of "*tikkun neshamot*" (mending souls). Toward that end, I thought fit to append to this work the "real-time" report of the exorcism that Rav Kook performed in Jaffa, as recorded by the Rav's only son Tsevi Yehudah (whom I had the privilege of knowing).

Rabbi Yosef Leib Zussman heard from his master Rabbi Ya'akov Moshe Ḥarlap (eminent disciple of Rav Kook) that Rav Kook engaged in "*tikkunei neshamot*" (mending souls). Many times, Rav Kook would discuss great men from the World of Truth (i.e. the Afterlife) who stumbled in some matter and whose souls required mending. Rav Kook would point out that they were present in the room. The method of mending these souls consisted in revealing the inner root of holiness in that very failing. In this way, the Rav would mend them. "So I heard explicitly from his [i.e. Rabbi Ḥarlap's] holy mouth."[13]

In one of his journals, Rav Kook wrote:

> The mending of souls (*tikkunei neshamot*) is one of the most exalted visions of the hidden world. A healthy soul—accustomed to the theoretical visions,

while provided with a powerful ethical education and a lucid intellect—takes interest in it with a pure passion.

The actions are but the outer signs of a corrupted or corrected soul. True, deeds do play a part in correction or corruption, but the main corruption is essential, just as the main correction is essential.

The soul essence can be in a pure, bright state, ready for life and eternity; or it can be in a dark, somber state, whereby the living, enlightened world will be the opposite of its essence. In that case, the soul longs to destroy, to break and ruin everything, because all that is good is opposite her, and this opposition stabs her from every side. And the more her essence is revealed in her midst—the more her pain grows; the more she sees with an open eye that all opposes her and goes in a direction opposite her own.

This is the lot of a castaway soul, whose pain is unending.

And the pure heart, revealed in the best of humans, is aroused to take pity on her. This very arousal already extends to her an essential, spiritual, psychic current. The current proceeding from a source of strong life, from a spring of freedom and good choice, mixes with the torn essence, sinking in the maelstrom of iniquity, in the depth of pain and *Weltschmerz*, and calms her churning waves, mollifies and comforts her, arousing in her the sparks of light hidden in her midst—until she acquires a new existence, and returns to the days of her youth, days before sin clouded her countenance.

The desire to mend souls advances and expands in the pure heart full of the mysteries of purity; it breaks down all the barriers, broadens the borders, and ascends to the Great Sea of the collective soul of the nation, suffering from the evil habits that darkened her beauty.

The desire [to mend souls] turns to the collective soul of humanity, and to the soul of the beast, and to the living soul of the World of Action. In the very place where there is revealed freedom—there lies in wait the serpent of destruction and obliteration.

And the pure spirit longs to do good to all, to make all pleasant.

> And the longing arouses a powerful will, hidden and concealed. Stealthily it penetrates, turning eternities of desert and desolation to the Eden of God's Garden.[14]

Finally, in a heartfelt letter to a friend of long standing, Rabbi Pinḥas Hakohen Lintop of Birzh, Rav Kook called upon his fellow Kabbalist to engage in "*'avodat ha-tikkun shel ha-neshamot*" (the work of mending the souls):

> I seem to recall that in one of our conversations we shared the secret of the work of mending the abused and lost souls of past generations, that is worthy of, and incumbent upon the righteous of the generations. This holy work should not be neglected at the End of Days, for "the souls of the wicked are the damagers of the world (*mazikei 'alma*),"[15] and once they are mended, the world is reconstructed in its glory.[16]

BN

5779/2019

The anecdote related in Appendix 10 ("Rav Kook, the Messiah and the Vatican") was confirmed in a telephone conversation on the evening of Thursday, December 27, 2018 (20 Tevet, 5779). Wishing to hear from Rabbi Nota Greenblatt directly, the present writer placed the call to the Rabbi's home in Memphis, Tennessee. As soon as Rabbi Greenblatt heard Rav Kook's name mentioned, he interjected: "I received a *berokho* [blessing] from him."

He fleshed out a bit the setting of his late father's conversation with Rav Kook by saying that they were not alone in the room at that time. There were other people present when that conversation took place.

In his recollection, "The *Rov* [i.e. Rav Kook] said: 'We cannot talk about *Mashiaḥ* until the Vatican is uprooted, for the Church is the source of *sin'at Yisrael* [antisemitism].'"

The Manuscript of Rav Kook's Commentary

As I was readying the book for publication, I had the good fortune, thank God, to inspect the manuscript of Rav Kook's commentary, which differs in some respects from the printed version of *Ma'amrei ha-Rayah* (1984).

Description of the Manuscript

Embedded in one of Rav Kook's many journals, the commentary extends for 39 pages, numbered in the journal 124b-143b. The journal is oblong-shaped; the pages are 7¾ inches wide by 6 inches high. There are 15 lines per page.

The title reads: *"Derushim le-Be'urei RBBH de-P[erek] ha-Sefinah." Derushim* are homilies. As opposed to *Ma'amrei ha-Rayah*, where the Editors presented the work as a *Perush* or Commentary, Rav Kook himself termed his work *Be'urim* or Explanations.[17]

Adjacent to that title, a later title was squeezed in: *"Tov Re'iyah Bava Batra."* Written in the hand of the author's son, Rabbi Tsevi Yehudah Hakohen Kook, this is clear evidence that the heir thought to include these explanations of his father in a future work on the Talmud to be titled *"Tov Re'iyah."*[18]

In the manuscript, Rav Kook provided the text of the legend (or at least a significant portion thereof) before presenting his commentary on that particular legend. At the very end of the commentary, comes Rav Kook's conclusion: "I bless the Lord who has counseled me and helped me thus far to commence and conclude my thoughts . . ."

Rav Kook's version of the text of the legends does not adhere strictly to that of the Talmud or *'Eyn Ya'akov*.[19] What is the explanation for that? It is conceivable that Rav Kook, who was renowned for his phenomenal memory, quoted the text from memory—which has a way of playing tricks. Less likely is the possibility that Rav Kook set out to consciously create an eclectic text of his own.

Variants

Most of the deviations of the printed version of *Ma'amrei ha-Rayah* from the manuscript version are negligible in nature—with one major exception.

In the commentary to the sixth legend, there is a discussion of the difference between *halakhot* that are immutable and those that are subject to revision based upon the judgment of the authority of the day.[20] In the original Rav Kook wrote:

> In Torah, there are these two categories: Things that are worthy of enduring forever, so there are found many *halakhot* that will not change from their fixed state, for thus were they established, to be an eternal covenant. [Then] there are *halakhot* that change in their rulings from one generation to the next, depending on its leaders and what seems appropriate to the "judge who is in your days."
>
> Everyone who toils in Torah and develops Torah novellae, has a portion in both of the categories.

Evidently, because of the extreme sensitivity of the issue and concern lest Rav Kook's remarks be misinterpreted by those seeking to reform *Halakhah*, the editors of *Ma'amrei ha-Rayah* saw fit to reword the passage:

> In Torah, there are these two categories: *Halakhot* (laws) that will never change, for they were established as an everlasting covenant; and *halakhot* (laws) that change <u>in the *hora'ot sha'ah* (*ad hoc* rulings) of the *ḥakhmei ha-Torah* (Torah sages)</u>, the leaders of the generation, "the judge who is in your days."
>
> Everyone who toils in Torah and develops Torah novellae, <u>from the source of eternal life that the Lord planted in our midst and showed Moses on Sinai</u>, has a portion in both of the categories.

The previous year (1983), Rav Kook's book *'Arpalei Tohar* was also subjected to such "remedial reading." A passage concerning *hora'at sha'ah* (*ad hoc* legislation) read in the original:

> Only when prophecy rests upon Israel is it possible to correct this through a *hora'at sha'ah* (*ad hoc* ruling); then it is done in a permissible manner and [by] a revealed commandment. As a result of the stopping up of the light of prophecy, this correction comes about by a *long-lasting* breach [of the law] that saddens the heart *by its external aspect*, but gladdens it [i.e. the heart] *by its internal aspect.*[21]

In the doctored version the final sentence was made to read:

> As a result of the stopping up of the light of prophecy, this correction comes about by a breach [of the law] that saddens the heart *by its essence*, but gladdens [the heart] *by its end.*[22]

The word *long-lasting* was dropped. *External aspect* was replaced with *essence* and *internal aspect* with *end.*

As much ink has already been spilled concerning the doctored passages in the 1983 edition of *'Arpalei Tohar*, we need not belabor the point.

Unfortunately, in some places the photocopy I consulted was faded, preventing me from doing a comparative analysis of each and every word of the manuscript. I noted deviations wherever I spotted them. Again, with the exception of the singular instance of doctoring, the deviations I detected were truly minor and certainly incapable of recasting the commentary in a different light.

As was to be expected, the overwhelming majority of *mar'ei mekomot* or "addresses" of Rav Kook's quotes were provided by the editors, rather than by the author himself. In this edition, I have presented Rav Kook's commentary in its pristine state. The references with their exact coordinates (whether book, chapter and verse of the Bible, or folio of the tractate of the Talmud) have been relegated to the notes.

ABBREVIATIONS

RAYH = Rabbi Avraham Yitsḥak Hakohen [Kook]

RZYH = Rabbi Zevi Yehudah Hakohen [Kook]

[1]Raphael Patai wrote: "We are told that Rabba bar Bar-Hana, the well-known author of many fantastic tales of the sea, used the picture of a mast as his signum instead of signing his name" (R. Patai, *The Children of Noah: Jewish Seafaring in Ancient Times* [Princeton, 1998], p. 30). The reference is to *b. Gittin* 87b and *Bava Batra* 161b. Unfortunately, Patai confused Rabbah bar Rav Huna with Rabbah bar Bar Ḥannah.

[2]Concerning the inclusion of *aggadot* in an otherwise halakhic discussion, see Maimonides' Introduction to his *Commentary to the Mishnah* (Kafaḥ ed., p. 19): "And the fourth [objective], sermons (*derashot*) that fit the topic of the chapter."

In the Ḥasidic school of thought of Izbica-Radzyn-Lublin great significance was attached to these juxtapositions of *Halakhah* and *Aggadah*, whether it be on the specific level of a particular chapter within a tractate (as per Maimonides), or even on the general level of the tractate of the Talmud. See Rabbi Yeruḥam Leiner, *Tif'eret Yeruḥam* (Brooklyn, NY, 1967), *Shabbat Ḥazon* (pp. 95-96); Sarah Friedland Ben-Arza, *"Shekhenut ve-Korat Gag,"* in *Me'at la-Tsaddik*, ed. Rabbi Gershon Kitsis (Jerusalem, 2000), pp. 269-288. To the many references provided in Ben-Arza's article, one should add Rabbi Zadok Hakohen [Rabinowitz] of Lublin, *Komets ha-Minḥah* (Lublin, 1939; photo offset B'nei Berak, 1967), 37a.

[3]See our appendix "A Kabbalistic Theory of Personality."

[4]See below note 96.

[5]Rabbi Aharon Feldman translated the Gaon's comments into English. See A. Feldman, *The Juggler and the King: The Jew and the Conquest of Evil: An Elaboration of the Vilna Gaon's Insights into the Hidden Wisdom of the Sages* (Israel, 1990). Recently, there appeared in print the super-commentary of Rabbi Moshe Shapiro to the Gaon's commentary. See Rabbi Moshe Shapiro, *"Be'urim ba-Aggadot Rabbah bar Bar Ḥannah," Yeshurun* 37 (Elul 5777/2017), pp. 439-509.

One notices that on some points Rav Kook's commentary coincides with that of the Vilna Gaon, but these may be random rather than indications of intellectual indebtedness. In the third legend, both the Gaon and Rav Kook understand the verse in Psalms 107:26, "They mounted up to the heavens, they went down to the depths," as referring to the day of death. Wicked Hurmin is unrepentant to the end. In the fourth legend, both the Gaon and Rav Kook present the *orzila* or antelope as a boastful, pretentious Torah sholar. And in the fifth legend, both commentators relate the *pushkantsa* or female raven to the Torah scholar who exhibits seemingly cruel behavior towards his children.

An important commentary to the *Aggadot Rabbah bar Bar Ḥannah* from the school of the Vilna Gaon, is that by Rabbi Yitsḥak Eizik Ḥaver, in *Afikei Yam* (Jerusalem, 1994), vol. 2, pp. 347-392.

[6]The Vilna Gaon's *haskamot* can be counted on one hand. They include an approbation to an unnamed work of Rabbi Aryeh Leib Epstein of Koenigsberg (*"Ba'al ha-Pardes"*). Actually, the approval is more of the author than of the book, which the Gaon never read, as he was incapacitated by illness. Rabbi Epstein is most famous for his Kabbalistic prayer book, but again, there is no way of knowing which work was presented to the Gaon. The Gaon's *ad hominem* approbation was published in Rabbi Epstein's work *Halakhah Aḥaronah ve-Kuntres ha-Re'ayot* (Koenigsberg, 1759), 9a.

Another endorsement was ostensibly written to uphold the Kabbalistic *kame'ot* or amulets that Rabbi Jonathan Eybeschuetz had dispensed while serving as Rabbi of Metz. (Rabbi Eybeschuetz had been accused by Rabbi Jacob Emden of being a crypto-Sabbatian. According to Emden, Eybeschuetz's amulets contained veiled references to the Messianic role of Shabtai Tsevi.) The letter from Rabbi Elijah of Vilna was published in Rabbi Eybeschuetz's collection of testimonies, *Luḥot 'Edut* (Altona, 1755), 71b. Of late, Prof. Leiman has cast aspersions on the authenticity of this letter of defense. See Sid Z. Leiman, "When a Rabbi is Accused of Heresy: The Stance of the Gaon of Vilna in the Emden-Eibeschuetz Controversy," in *Me'ah She'arim: Studies in Medieval Jewish Spiritual Life in Memory of Isadore Twersky,* ed. Fleischer, Blidstein, Horowitz, Septimus (Jerusalem, 2001), pp. 251-263.

(In a footnote, Leiman mentions the pride that the Gaon's biographer, Rabbi Joshua Heschel Levin, took in the Gaon's letter to Rabbi Eybeschuetz, which was written at the tender age of thirty-five. See Leiman, p. 262, n. 22. Rabbi Tsevi Yehudah Kook was told in private conversation by his father that *"Gedolei Yisrael"* did not hold Rabbi Levin, the author of *'Aliyot Eliyahu*, to be authoritative. Rabbi Tsevi Yehudah conjectured that Rav Kook had received this advice from Rabbi Naftali Tsevi Yehudah Berlin [Netsiv] of Volozhin. See Ḥayyim Avihu Schwarz, *Mi-Tokh ha-Torah ha-Go'elet*, vol. 2, Jerusalem 1989, p. 252. It should be mentioned, however, that there was a power struggle between Rabbis Levin and Berlin as to who would preside over the Volozhin Yeshivah. Rabbi Berlin was the son-in-law of Rabbi Isaac of Volozhin, while Rabbi Levin was married to Rabbi Isaac's granddaughter. As Rabbi Berlin emerged victorious, Rabbi Levin was ousted from the Yeshivah, and eventually relocated to Paris, where he ministered to the newly formed community of Russian-Jewish immigrants.)

An aside: A later Kabbalist who evidently was convinced of the legitimacy of Rabbi Eybeschuetz's amulets was Rabbi Ya'akov Tsevi Yolles. In his monumental lexicon of the Kabbalah, *Kehillat Ya'akov*, Rabbi Yolles cites approvingly Rabbi Eybeschuetz's explication of an amulet in *Luḥot 'Edut*. See Rabbi Ya'akov Tsevi Yolles, *Kehillat Ya'akov*, Part Two (Lemberg, 1870), end s.v. *Malkhut* (II) (2c).

In light of the above, there is reason to believe that in truth, the only *haskamah* written by the Vilna Gaon to a specific title is that to Rabbi Samuel of Kalvaria's *Darkhei No'am*! See Dov Eliach, *Ha-Gaon* (Jerusalem, 2002), vol. 3, pp. 1253-1261. In Eliach's reckoning, the Gaon wrote only two *haskamot*, both *ad hominem* rather than of the actual book. Ibid., p. 1253. Eliach reiterates this in regard to the approbation of Rabbi Epstein. Ibid. pp. 1258-1259, n. 5. I have no idea why Eliach finds the *haskamah* to *Darkhei No'am* to be purely *ad hominem*. A simple reading would tell us that the Gaon approved the contents of the book as well. Ben-Zion Katz certainly understood that the Gaon approved the contents of *Darkhei No'am*. See Ben-Zion Katz, *Rabbanut, Ḥasidut, Haskalah*, Parts 3-4 (Tel-Aviv, 1958), 48ff. (The quote from the *haskamah* is somewhat imprecise. The precise text of the *haskamah* to *Darkhei No'am* is found in Eliach, pp. 1257-1258.) Concerning the exact number of *haskamot* written by the Vilna Gaon, see Katz, p. 255, n. 53.

[7]One is tempted to construe the commentary to the Legends of Rabbah bar Bar Ḥannah as a contribution to the *'Eyn Ayah* project, Rav Kook's commentary to the *'Eyn Ya'akov* legends of the Talmud, commenced during his tenure as Rabbi of Zoimel (Zeimelis), Lithuania. See Rabbi Moshe Tsevi Neriyah, *Tal ha-Rayah* (Tel-Aviv, 1993), p. 117. For more on the *'Eyn Ayah* project, see my introduction to *Of Societies Perfect and Imperfect: Selected Readings from Eyn Ayah, Rav Kook's Commentary to Eyn Yaakov Legends of the Talmud* (New York: Sepher-Hermon, 1995).

However, one must admit that the tenor of the commentary to the Legends of Rabbah bar Bar Ḥannah is totally different from that of the *'Eyn Ayah* commentary. The former is explicitly Kabbalistic in nature; the latter approximates the language and perhaps even the method of Maharal of Prague. Clearly, the Kabbalistic commentary to the Legends of Rabbah bar Bar Ḥannah was intended for a select audience conversant with that idiom. On the other hand, the rationalist presentation of *'Eyn Ayah* recommends it to a wider audience.

We can establish with near certainty the *terminus a quo* for our composition. In his commentary to the fourteenth legend of Rabbah bar Bar Ḥannah, Rav Kook cites the Kabbalistic work *Beit 'Olamim* by Rabbi Yitsḥak Eizik Ḥaver. As that work was first published in Warsaw in 1889, Rav Kook could not have penned his commentary before that date. According to Rabbi Neriyah, the commentary to the Legends of Rabbah bar Bar Ḥannah was written in Zoimel in the year 1890. See Neriyah, *Tal ha-Rayah*, p. 124. (Born in 1865, Rav Kook was twenty-five when he penned this profound work of Kabbalah!)

In the recently released manuscript *Metsi'ot Katan*, Rav Kook recorded an apercu of his father Rabbi Shelomo Zalman Kook to the Rabbah bar Bar Ḥannah cycle of legends:

> … as my master, my father, may he live, wrote to me, regarding the intention of the Sages, of blessed memory, in [the legends of] Rabbah bar Bar Ḥannah in [Tractate] *Bava Batra*, that "a fish" [Legends 6-8] is what the wicked man is called, because this world is referred to as a tempestuous sea, and the wicked

> is at home there, just as the fish is at home in the sea. This is not the case of the righteous man. He knows that he is a passing guest; he is called a "sea voyager" [Legends 1-2].
>
> (Rabbi Abraham Isaac Hakohen Kook, *Metsi'ot Katan* [Israel: Maggid, 2018], par. 66 [p. 97])

Though *Metsi'ot Katan* too was written during those early years in Zoimel, this interpretation of Rav Kook's father did not find its way into our present work. In his commentary to the Legends of Rabbah bar Bar Ḥannah, Rav Kook charts a course entirely his own, suffused with Kabbalistic symbolism. The sea voyagers are the souls who appear to Rabbah bar Bar Ḥannah to reveal to him mysteries of existence, and the fish are various types of Torah scholars.

For yet a third way to approach the symbolism of the sea and the ships, see our appendix "Rabbi Samuel of Kalvaria's *Darkhei No'am.*"

[8]See Rabbi Moshe Tsevi Neriyah, *Tal ha-Rayah*, p. 123.

[9]Biologically, Rav Kook was of mixed parentage. His father's family were distinguished students of the Volozhin Yeshivah, founded by Rabbi Ḥayyim of Volozhin, prime pupil of the Vilna Gaon. Rav Kook's paternal great-grandfather Rabbi Dov Baer Jaffe of Turetz (later Rabbi of Utian) was one of the first ten students of the Volozhin Yeshivah; his son, Rav Kook's great-uncle, Rabbi Mordechai Gimpel Jaffe, Rabbi of Ruzhany (in Belarussian, or Rozhinoy in Yiddish) and author of *Tekhelet Mordekhai*, a supercommentary on Naḥmanides' commentary to the Pentateuch, was an illustrious student of the founder's son, Rabbi Isaac of Volozhin.

Rav Kook's mother, on the other hand, was the daughter of Rabbi Raphael Felman, a Ḥabad Ḥasid. Rav Kook's maternal grandfather established the Kopyster synagogue in Grieva (a suburb of Dvinsk, Latvia), Rav Kook's birthplace, and ensconced there the famed Kopyster *Mashpi'a*, Rabbi Yeḥezkel Yanover. (Kopyst was a branch of Ḥabad Ḥasidism. The Rebbe of Kopyst, Rabbi Shelomo Zalman Shneurson, author of *Magen Avot*, was a grandson of Rabbi Menaḥem Mendel Shneurson of Lubavitch, author of Responsa *Tsemaḥ Tsedek.*)

Thus, Rav Kook was an intellectual heir to both Kabbalistic legacies, that of the Vilna Gaon and his disciple Rabbi Ḥayyim of Volozhin, on the one hand, and that of Ḥabad, on the other hand.

[10]In his commentary, Rav Kook references two Kabbalistic works of Luzzatto: *'Adir ba-Marom* (on the *Idra Rabba* section of the *Zohar*) and *KaLaḤ Pitḥei Ḥokhmah.* For Rav Kook's thoughts on Luzzatto's literary *oeuvre*, see our Appendix "Luzzatto's *'Adir ba-Marom* and *KaLaḤ Pitḥei Ḥokhmah.*"

Rav Kook had a deep psychological identification with the Paduan mystic. See *Igrot ha-Rayah*, vol. 1 (Jerusalem, 1961), p. 42 (Letter 43). According to Rav Kook's biographers, Luzzatto's allegorical drama *La-Yesharim Tehillah*, which young Avraham Yitsḥak discovered in his father's library, exerted an early influence upon the development of his Hebrew literary style. See Neriyah, *Tal ha-Rayah* (Tel-Aviv, 1993), pp. 16, 19, 204-205. In private conversation with a young *protégé,* Yitsḥak Hutner, Rav Kook confided: "I think that I am the reincarnation of Rabbi Moshe Ḥayyim Luzzatto" (quoted in Neriyah, *Tal ha-Rayah*, p. 122).

This period of the 1890s seems to have been a time of intense engagement with the Kabbalah of Luzzatto, as witnessed by the numerous explicit references to his works in Rav Kook's *pinkasim* produced in that period, namely *Pinkas 15* and *Pinkas 16*. See *Pinkesei ha-Rayah*, vol. 3, ed. Rabbi Levi Yitsḥaki (Jerusalem, n.d. [2011]), 15:3 (p. 35), 15:9 (p. 41), 15:23 (p. 60), 15:27 (p. 66), 15:34 (p. 78), 15:35 (p. 80), 15:40 (pp. 88-89), 15:43 (p. 90), 15:46 (p. 94), 15:53 (p. 100), 15:68 (p. 117), 15:71 (p. 120), 16:2 (p. 134).

For the most part, the references are to the works *'Adir ba-Marom* and *KaLaḤ Pitḥei Ḥokhmah* (the two works of Luzzatto cited in our present work). The one exception is the reference in 15:71 (p. 120) to Luzzatto's work *Pitḥei Ḥokhmah ve-Da'at* (Warsaw, 1884). In 16:27 (p. 188) and 16:31 (p. 195) we find comments to Luzzatto's *Mesillat Yesharim* (*Path of the Just*), but that is a work of ethics, not Kabbalah.

*

In a letter written from Jaffa on 12 Kislev, 5667 [1906] to a Jerusalemite zealot, Rabbi Yesh'ayah Orenstein, Rav Kook advocates for the study of works of Ḥasidism, on the one hand, and the works of the Vilna Gaon and Rabbi Moses Ḥayyim Luzzatto, on the other. See *Igrot ha-Rayah*, vol. 1, p. 41 (Letter 43). The recipient was a Ḥabad Ḥasid.

Rav Kook's "triangulation" of Rabbi M.Ḥ. Luzatto, the Vilna Gaon and Rabbi Shneur Zalman of Liadi (founder of Ḥabad Ḥasidism) parallels that of his older colleague and fellow Kabbalist, Rabbi Pinḥas Hakohen Lintop, Rabbi of Birzh, Lithuania. In an article that appeared in Isaac Suvalsky's annual *Knesset ha-Gedolah*, Year 1 (Warsaw, 1890), Rabbi Lintop mentioned approvingly the works of the *Ba'al ha-Tanya* [i.e. Rabbi Shneur Zalman of Liadi], and the recently published works of the Gaon Rabbi Elijah of Vilna and Rabbi Moses Luzzatto. In an unpublished manuscript, Rabbi Lintop remarked that the Gaon Rabbi Elijah follows the lead of Rabbi M.Ḥ. Luzzatto. See *Kana'uteh de-Pinḥas*, ed. Bezalel Naor (Spring Valley, NY, 2013), p. 122, note 74. Regarding the first encounter between Rabbi Lintop and Rav Kook in Zoimel, and their ensuing friendship, see ibid. p. 108, n. 30. Concerning Rav Kook's eclectic approach to the study of Kabbalah, see ibid. p. 117, n. 63; and p. 121, n. 73. (To the latter note, one should juxtapose now the criticism of the exclusive study of Ḥabad Ḥasidism expressed in *Pinkas 5*; see *Kevatsim mi-Ketav Yad Kodsho*, ed. Boaz Ofen, vol. 3 [Jerusalem, 2018], 5:9 [p. 24]. This was published earlier in *Pinkesei ha-Rayah*, vol. 3, p. 319, under the rubric, *"Ma'amarim 'al Ḥovat Limmud Miktso'ot ha-Aggadah."*)

Rabbi Tsevi Yehudah, son of Rav Kook recounted this charming anecdote:

> The Gaon Rabbi Pinḥas Lintop, of blessed memory, Rabbi of Birzh, came to Zeimel to make the acquaintance [of Rav Kook] and borrowed the manuscript of the book [by Rav Kook] *'Eyn Ayah*, on the legends of the Talmud, *'Eyn Ya'akov*. Rabbi Lintop returned the manuscript with the binding beat up, explaining that it had died "because of work," in the course of his studying it in great depth.
>
> (Additions [*Hosafot*] taped in at the end of Rabbi Tsevi Yehudah Hakohen Kook, *Li-Sheloshah be-Elul* [Jerusalem, 1978], par. 2 [To the Zeimel Chapter])

The *halakhah* states that if one borrowed an animal and it "died because of work" (*"metah me-ḥamat melakhah"*), the borrower is exempt.

[11] In the 1984 edition of *Ma'amrei ha-Rayah* these form a separate loose fascicle of 8 pages to be inserted in the book.

[12] This was especially the case in the eighth legend.

[13] *Mi-Beḥirei Tsadikayya: Ma'amarim ve-igrot, reshamim ve-zikhronot … Harav Yosef Leib Zussman* (Jerusalem, 2007), p. 149.

Regarding the method of *"tikkun neshamot"* (mending souls), it is told of the Ba'al Shem Tov that the *tikkun* consists in "connecting *nefesh* to *nefesh*, *ru'aḥ* to *ru'aḥ*, *neshamah* to *neshamah*." (The context is the Ba'al Shem Tov's unsuccessful attempt to mend the soul of the failed Messiah, Shabtai Tsevi, who came to the Ba'al Shem Tov seeking a *tikkun*.) See Dov Baer of Linitz (Illintsi), *Shivḥei ha-Besht*, ed. Avraham Rubinstein (Jerusalem, 2005), pp. 133-134.

[14] *Kevatsim mi-Ketav Yad Kodsho*, vol. 2, ed. Boaz Ofen (Jerusalem, 2008), *Pinkas ha-Dappim* 1, par. 39 (pp. 74-75); *Pinkesei ha-Rayah*, vol. 4, ed. Z.M. Levin and B.Z. Kahana-Shapira (Jerusalem, 2017), par. 73 (pp. 177-178).

[15] *Zohar* III, 70a. Cf. *Zohar* III, 25a.

[16] *Igrot ha-Rayah*, ed. RZYH Kook, vol. 1, p. 143 (Letter 112).

If need be, Rav Kook would impart a smattering of the esoteric discipline to contemporary rabbinic luminaries who by disposition and training were far from the "mysteries of Torah." Such was the case in the response to Ridbaz:

> Whoever is prepared to engage in the inwardness (*penimiyut*) of the mysteries of the Torah, is filled with the light of love (*ḥesed*) of the "Torah of Love" [Proverbs 31:26; *b. Sukkah* 49b], and there devolves upon him the obligation to engage in the mending of the fallen (*tikkun nefulim*) and bringing close the distant. In the language of the Sages of the Secret, this is called "gathering sparks of holiness from the husks (*kelipot*)."
>
> (*Igrot ha-Rayah*, vol. 2 [Jerusalem, 1961], p. 186 [Letter 555]; and see earlier p. 153 [Letter 522])

[17]For the difference between *perush* and *be'ur* in Rav Kook's lexicon, see his Introduction to *'Eyn Ayah*, ed. Rabbi Ya'akov Filber, vol. 1 (Jerusalem, 1987).

[18]The literal translation of the title is "Good of Sight." Of course, there is a double entendre here for the letters *Re'iyah* are the initials of the author's name: **R**abbi **A**vraham **Y**itsḥak **H**akohen.

[19]*'Eyn Ya'akov* is a collection of the *aggadot* or legends of the Talmud compiled by Rabbi Ya'akov ibn Habib. It was first printed in Salonika in 1516. In Eastern Europe in Rav Kook's day, *'Eyn Ya'akov* enjoyed immense popularity.

[20]See Maimonides, *MT*, *Hil. Mamrim* 2:1-4.

[21]*Shemonah Kevatsim* 2:30.

[22]*'Arpalei Tohar* (Jerusalem, 1983), p. 15. The original undoctored version is available in *Shemonah Kevatsim* 2:30. For a discussion of this controversial passage, see my introduction to *Orot* (2015), pp. 74-75.

Précis of Rav Kook's Commentary to the Legends of Rabbah bar Bar Ḥannah

by Bezalel Naor

1. The debasement of Israel in exile enabled the Christian interpretation of history that the Lord had rejected His people Israel (God forbid) together with the Pauline doctrine that the practical commandments of the Torah have been abolished. In truth, the phenomenon of exile is part of the divine plan, the Secret of Unity (*Sod ha-Yiḥud*), whereby the oneness of God is revealed precisely through the opposition, the negativity, the darkness—and its conversion to light.

2. The souls of Israel—even the smallest soul—are exceedingly precious. The *kelipot* (literally "husks" or "shells," i.e. the forces of impurity) latch on to them in order to derive sustenance from their holiness. The rescue of these souls hinges on their embodiment. Only in the state of embodiment is there free will, which allows them to extricate themselves from the *kelipot*.

3. There are people so attached to their material possessions that they live in fortified cities ("gated communities") and make sure that not a single drop of their largesse trickles down to the poor. Even the prospect of imminent death cannot serve as a "wakeup call."

4. One whose study of Torah is ulterior-motivated, so as to achieve fame, tends to study in a haphazard fashion. Also, since his Torah study is not *li-shemah* (for its own sake), it does not translate into character refinement. The *ḥillul ha-shem* (desecration of the Name) that results from the combination of Torah scholarship (however shoddy) and weak character, stands in direct opposition to the principle of "*'Arevut*" (mutual responsibility) to which Israel bound themselves at the Jordan River.

5. The governing principle of the Torah is *ḥesed* (love). On rare occasions, love calls for seemingly cruel behavior. When a Torah sage acts in such way, an outside observer finds it unfathomable that those actions stem from love, but that is truly the case.

6. The saga of a big fish that rotted is symbolic of a Torah sage who has strayed. His soul may yet be saved on account of the power of Torah absorbed in his "bones." After a twelve-month process of catharsis, this great soul may be rehabilitated.

7. There are great souls such as Rabbi Shim'on ben Yoḥai and his companions who sometimes engage in material pleasures. When lesser souls emulate their behavior, the results prove disastrous. They fail to realize that even when those exalted souls engage in the material, they are rapt in *devekut* (cleaving) to the divine. Lesser beings will simply drown in the sea of materialism.

8. On the level of "smallness" (*katnut*) there is a hiatus between the practical and the theoretical. However, on the level of "greatness" (*gadlut*) there is no bifurcation of the theoretical and the practical. All is theoretical—even the practical.

9. Though the spiritual giant has his sights set primarily on the heavenly secrets of the Torah, and "wings of love and fear" carry him aloft, his study of the earthly, practical aspects of the Torah is of great profundity and not to be underestimated.

10. Oil dripping from the wings of fattened geese symbolizes an abundance of worldly wisdom. Should Israel make good use of the "seven [worldly] wisdoms," the benefit derived therefrom would be twofold: Vis-à-vis the nations of the world, it would bring honor to the People of Israel. Internally, studied for the sake of heaven, those wisdoms would provide "wings of love and fear" to soar heavenward. Israel's failure to seize the initiative would be reprehensible.

11. There are two types of wise men: the sedentary "agriculturalist" (*ḥakla'i*) and the peripatetic "merchant" (*soḥer*). The latter type, symbolized by the Bedouin, takes up the wanderer's staff and is forever on the way. He searches out the wisdom of the Torah as visible in man and the world. His specialty is the uncanny ability to read souls through physiognomy (*ḥokhmat ha-partsuf*). Even more remarkable, by "sniffing" the body, the wandering wise man can penetrate beyond deeds and characterology to the *"shoresh ha-neshamah"* ("root of the soul"). He has such a keen sense of "smell" that it is well-nigh impossible to fool him.

12. The spiritually exalted nature of the Generation of the Desert actually prevented them from entering the Promised Land and condemned them to stay behind in the wilderness. Their way of serving the Lord is not for us to emulate. Ultimately, it is beyond our comprehension. Their method—both in terms of wisdom and works—remains a mystery.

13. The Nations of the World appear as "scorpions" poised to sting Israel. Their resentment goes back to the time of Israel's acceptance of the Torah at Mount Sinai.

The Nations are forever bristling at the yoke of Judaic morality imposed on the human race. But they have the potential to be turned into "white donkeys," a symbol of love. Their *tikkun* or rectification depends on that of Israel itself. Redemption need not be delayed because of the divine "oath." God looks to man to abolish the oath of Exile that He has taken.

14. The antinomianism of Koraḥ and his congregation need not necessarily result in the abolition of the commandments. Even if technically the commandments should be retained by these rebels against normative Judaism, their "commandments" are of no redeeming value, for all has been subordinated to a mystical level of love (*Ḥesed de-'Atik*) that transcends this-wordly earthbound existence. Since it is Earth that suffers from this corruption, it is she who exacts revenge on Koraḥ's band by swallowing them.

15. There is overlap of collective needs and individual needs. Individual fulfillment (*tikkun ha-perat*) can actually come about through the perfection of the collective (*tikkun ha-kelal*), but the route it takes is circuitous. This cosmic cycle does not provide instant gratification the way self-absorption does. The spiritual results will be found, but after a time delay.

The Wave Threatening to Sink the Ship

1

R[abbah] said: Seafarers related to me that **this wave that sinks a ship appears with a ray of white fire at its head, and we strike it with a club upon which is inscribed *Ehyeh asher Ehyeh* ("I shall be that I shall be")[Exodus 3:14], *Yah*, the Lord of Hosts, *Amen, Amen, Selah*. And** the wave **subsides.**

THE WAVE THAT THREATENS TO SINK THE SHIP AND THE STAFF OF "*EHYEH*": BATTLING SUPERSESSIONIST THEOLOGY

It is possible to interpret that the voyagers on the Sea of Divine Wisdom[23] are referred to as "seafarers" (*neḥutei yama*). Essentially, it appears to me that they are the souls that would appear to Rabbah bar Bar Ḥannah to teach him novel thoughts and mysteries of the Torah regarding the divine governance. Alternatively, the ministering angels are the voyagers on that sea.[24]

They imparted to him the nature of the power of impurity that would "sink the ship"; that would sink, God forbid, the People of the Lord.[25] That corresponds to the power of impurity of Jesus.[26] The essential heresy [of Christianity] was [the claim] that though the Lord began to raise up Israel, He later spurned them, God forbid.[27]

In truth, if that were so, does not the Lord know the future? And then, all the greatness bestowed upon us would, God forbid, amount to evil, being as the greatness did not remain permanently ours, but rather brought upon us the hatred and enmity of the nations. In the rash opinion [of Christianity], it only appears as love on the outside, but truly the essence of the thing was punishment.

But Christianity's perspective is based primarily on the visible fact that the Lord abandoned us to the peoples of the earth. We know that in truth, the final goal of the revelation of the Lord's glory will result precisely from the fact that Israel have been dispersed among the nations (until the time that sin will be concluded).[28] Thereby, there will become famous the Lord's supervision over His people—even in exile.

Exile is necessary for another reason as well: in order to include this world [as opposed to the World to Come—BN] in holiness. When the Redemption comes about, the focus will be on spirituality. As the Sages, of blessed memory, said: "'There will arrive years when you will say: I have no desire in them'—These are the Days of Messiah in which there is neither merit nor demerit."[29] Since the Lord desires that this mundane world as well achieve perfection, He subjected us to the state of the "Hiding of the Face" [of God],[30] and thus it comes about that we observe His commandments pertaining to this-worldly matters.[31]

These two [objectives]—His divine supervision over His people in exile (whereby precisely exile paves the way for redemption); and the combination of this world and the World to Come[32]—make up the "Secret of Unity" (*Sod ha-Yiḥud*) of His name, which includes all the attributes.[33] In this way, there is revealed His glory, how He produces the legion of existents. And through this, His name is established (*mit'ammen*) on all sides, whether it be judgment or compassion; material or spiritual. It is also clarified that His rule is eternal, for everything that could possibly pose as opposition or contradiction on the part of the Other Side (*Sitra Aḥera*), has already been actualized—and [despite that] it is seen that all are His servants.[34] So when this wisdom is revealed, "the deceit of the deceitful is no longer of avail,"[35] and it *subsides*.

This is what is meant by **this wave that sinks a ship,** for in truth it desired to sink the ship, for wisdom is the water,[36] the waters of the sea, but to us [Israel] there was transmitted [the ability] to navigate the multitudinous waters[37] by way of vessels, which are the commandments. He who desires to abolish the practical commandments (*mitsvot ma'asiyot*),[38] ipso facto desires to sink the ship in the sea. For the most part, the commandments are predicated upon the election of Israel and remembrance of the Exodus from Egypt. So this impure wave comes along and **appears with a ray of white fire at its head,** as if to say that only at the beginning was it white, [symbolic of divine] governance that tends to the whiteness of love,[39] but truly it was a burning fire,[40] because there was no perfection, no eternal sanctity, for we fell into a deep pit and were dispersed among the nations to be subjugated by them.

But **we strike it with a club upon which is inscribed *Ehyeh asher Ehyeh*** (**"I shall be that I shall be").**[41] [This is the response,] that for the most part, the divine sanctity is revealed through the Lord's supervision over us in exile.[42] In this way, judgment and compassion are synthesized, and darkness is transformed to light.

Yah, symbolizes the two worlds, this world which was created with the letter *hé*, and the World to Come, created with the letter *yod.*[43] ***Yah*** requires that we unite the two worlds, and that is impossible [to achieve] other than by exile.

Afterwards, there is mentioned the full name [of YHVH], to say that only through ***Ehyeh asher Ehyeh*** and ***Yah***—namely, divine supervision over us in exile, and the purpose of exile, which is to unify heaven and earth; this world and the World to Come—does there come about the secret of the full name, that glories in its branches[44] and is comprised of all the sanctities.

And through this, there is revealed His dominion over all the hosts above and below, ***Tseva'ot*** **[Lord of hosts],** and there is made known His faithfulness (*ne'emanut*) in this world and the next, ***Amen, Amen.***[45] There is also made known His eternity, whereby His will does not change, God forbid. Rather, His word endures forever.[46] And when this impure power is smitten with this rod of God, it **subsides** and is incapable of doing evil. But "a little more and there will be no wicked man,"[47] and "the righteous shall inherit the earth."[48]

[23]Rav Kook employs the term "Sea of Wisdom" (*Yam ha-Ḥokhmah*) with great frequency in his commentary. (Cf. *Pinkesei ha-Rayah*, vol. 3, *Pinkas* 16:12 [p. 161].) A Kabbalistic term, it occurs already in Gikatilla's *Sha'arei Orah*. See Rabbi Joseph Gikatilla, *Sha'arei Orah*, ed. Joseph Ben Shlomo, vol. 1 (Jerusalem, 1970), First Gate (p. 62). An Aramaic version of the term ("*Yama de-Ḥokhmeta*") occurs in *Zohar* III, 58a; 137b (*Idra Rabba*).

[24]Rabbi Yom Tov ben Abraham (Ritba) of Seville (13th-14th centuries) wrote in his commentary to *Bava Batra* that some of the spectacles in the legends of Rabbah bar Bar Ḥannah are very feasible, such as the enormous size of the fish or the height of the waves. Other things were not actually witnessed but beheld in a dream:

> When the wise men travel upon the ocean and see there the wonders of the Lord—especially when they meditate and cogitate upon those awe-inspiring and wonderful matters—at the time of sleep there appear to them wondrous visions derived from their [diurnal] thoughts.
>
> The *Ge'onim* wrote that whenever Rabbah bar Bar Ḥannah says "I have seen," he refers to a dream when he was voyaging the ocean.

Ritba's explanation of the legends of Rabbah bar Bar Ḥannah was printed in the Vilna edition of the Talmud, Tractate *Bava Batra*, following the novellae of Maharam Schiff. For a critical edition, see *Ḥiddushei ha-Ritba, Bava Batra*, ed. Rabbi Moshe Yehudah Hakohen Blau (New York, 1977).

[25]In Hebrew, "*Knesset 'Am Hashem*." *Knesset Yisrael* is the Kabbalistic term for the Jewish People. It has been translated into English as "*Ecclesia Israel*." In Kabbalah, it symbolizes the *sefirah* of *Malkhut*.

In his writings and also in his oral teaching, Rav Kook would employ this term of "*Knesset Yisrael*," rather than the more standard "*Kelal Yisrael*." The term "*Knesset Yisrael*" became the hallmark of Rav Kook's teaching. The Torah that Rav Kook dispensed at the Third Meal of the Sabbath was referred to by one of his admirers in Jerusalem, Rabbi Shimshon Aharon Polonsky ("Tepliker Rav"), as the "*Knesset Yisrael Torah*." Rabbi Isaac Hutner recalled that when Rav Kook would pronounce the words "*Knesset Yisrael*," he would become overcome with emotion, as if these words embodied the essence of his vitality and his soul's striving. See Rabbi Moshe Tsevi Neriyah, *Likkutei ha-Rayah* (Tel-Aviv, 1990), p. 185.

In *Tikkunei Zohar*, the ship ("*sefinah*") serves as a trope both for the body of the individual Jew and of the collective Jewish nation. See *Tikkunei Zohar* (Vilna, 1867), *tikkun* 21 (f. 60), and the commentary of Vilna Gaon, ad loc., s.v. *de-sa'arat gufa de-bar nash de-'inun Yisrael.*

[26]Rav Kook wrote that *Yeshu* (Jesus) has the same numerical value as *kefirah* (denial). "Jesus is the general root of heresy and denial." *Pinkesei ha-Rayah*, vol. 3, ed. Levi Yitsḥaki (Jerusalem, n.d.), p. 375, par. 12.

Elsewhere, it seems as if Rav Kook is almost engaging in a sort of *"tikkun ha-neshamah"* or correction of the soul of Jesus. In the recently released *Metsi'ot Katan* (par. 180 on pp. 187-188) Rav Kook writes: " ... with all of his sinking in evil, the good sparks shall be salvaged; the proof being that he [i.e. Jesus] praised Israel and is better than the wicked Bil'am." The reference is to the passage in *b. Gittin* 57a.

In his classic work, *Orot* (1920), Rav Kook would write:

> ... the exalted Masters of the Foundation ... will raise up all the descents, whether their own, those of the Jewish People, or those of the fallen giants, who stood to be messiahs, but fell, were trapped and broken. Their [i.e. the fallen giants'] sparks were scattered and seek a living and enduring *tikkun* (correction) in the foundation of David, King of Israel.
>
> (*Orot*, Lights of Renascence, chap. 70; Naor ed., pp. 416-417)

That chapter would appear to be inspired by a passage in *Tikkunei Zohar*, *tikkun* 30, *netiv tinyana*.

Earlier, the Paduan Kabbalist Rabbi Moshe David Valle, a member of the circle of Rabbi M.Ḥ. Luzzatto, presented a nuanced perception of Jesus. See Rabbi Moshe David Valle, *Sefer ha-Likkutim*, ed. Rabbi Yosef Spinner (Jerusalem, 1998), vol. 1, pp. 83 and 242.

For Rabbi Israel Ba'al Shem Tov's attempt to mend the soul of Shabtai Tsevi, see *Shivḥei ha-Besht*, cited above note 13. (Jesus is mentioned tangentially in that connection.)

During his tenure as Rabbi of Jerusalem, Rav Kook was maligned by the city's *kanna'im* or zealots for having a decade earlier published in the journal *Ha-Nir* (1909) that Jesus possessed great personal charisma, though he lacked academic training. See *Orot*, ed. Naor, pp. 67-68; *"Derekh ha-Teḥiyah"* in *Ma'amrei ha-Rayah*, vol. 1, ed. Elisha Langenauer and David Landau (Jerusalem, 1980), pp. 5-6; "The Way of Renascence" in Bezalel Naor, *When God Becomes History* (New York: Kodesh Press, 2017), p. 71.

[27]Rav Kook elaborates on this point in his responsum to the communal leaders of Klausenberg or Cluj, Romania, in defense of their Rabbi Moshe Shmuel Glasner. Once again, he points out that the fundamental heresy of Christianity consists in this notion that "Israel are a people from whom the Lord has turned his face away." The reference is to a dialogue (conducted in sign language) between an early Christian and Rabbi Joshua ben Ḥananiah in Imperial Rome. See *b. Ḥagigah* 5b in the uncensored version of *Ḥisronot ha-Shas* (Tel Aviv, 1966; photo offset of Cracow, 1894). In that instance, Rav Kook invokes the authority of Maharal of Prague in his work *Netsaḥ Yisrael* (Eternity of Israel) [chap. 11] that the divine election of Israel is essential and not subject to revocation. See Rav Kook's responsum in *Yashuv Mishpat* (Cluj, 1922); later anthologized in *Ma'amrei ha-Rayah*, vol. 1 (Jerusalem, 1980), p. 59 (where it is re-titled *"Perek be-Hilkhot Tsibbur"*). See my note to the Koren/Maggid edition of *Orot* (2015), pp. 477-478,

note 206. A Kabbalistic interpretation of the encounter between the Christian and Rabbi Joshua ben Ḥananiah may now be found in *Metsi'ot Katan*, par. 295 (pp. 451-452).

Rav Kook would brook no compromise and mince no words when it came to supersessionist or replacement theology. In another work, entitled by its editor *Li-Nevukhei ha-Dor* (*For the Perplexed of the Generation*), Rav Kook writes:

> The opinion rooted in the literature of those religions—Christianity and Islam—that the value of Israel is already void, God forbid—must cease to exist.
>
> (Rabbi Abraham Isaac Hakohen Kook, *Li-Nevukhei ha-Dor*, ed. Rabbi Shaḥar Raḥmani [Tel-Aviv, 2014], p. 56)

It should be noted that though Ritba earlier interpreted allegorically various legends of Rabbah bar Bar Ḥannah as alluding to the superpowers of Edom and Ishmael (i.e. Christendom and Islam), Rav Kook is rather unique in the respect that he engages with the historical development of Christianity and its break with Judaism. Thus, his focus is not eschatological but theological. This goes not only for the present work but other works as well. Many passages in Rav Kook's seminal work *Orot* are repartees to the *Minim* (Sectarians), the rabbinic term for the early Christians.

[28]The reference is to Daniel 9:24. See Rav Kook's commentary to the thirteenth legend and note 374.

[29]Ecclesiastes 12:1; *b. Shabbat* 151b. Quoted in Naḥmanides' commentary to Deuteronomy 30:6 (Chavel ed., p. 480).

[30]In Hebrew, *hester panim*. See Deuteronomy 31:17-18.

[31]Cf. Rabbi Shneur Zalman of Liadi, *Torah 'Or*, *Vayyeshev*, s.v. *Shir ha-ma'alot be-shuv...hayinu ke-ḥolemim* (28c-29a).

[32]In an entry to a Jaffa journal (1904-1914), Rav Kook would flesh out this idea:

> The wise of heart truly recognize the nothingness of this world in and of itself, and they elevate their thought and *Weltanschauung* to the level of the World to Come and its bliss. And since they view all of existence as one continuum, *ipso facto* this world too becomes beautified by them. And as a result, they seek to correct and improve it. And from this, comes the desire of the righteous (*tsaddikim*) of the civilization of life in this world; a civilization that will surpass in mightiness of spirit all that the spirit of man revealed as a result of its superficial love for this world in and of itself....
>
> (*Shemonah Kevatsim* 1:468)

[33]The *Hanhagat ha-Yiḥud* (the Governance of Unity)—as opposed to the *Hanhagat ha-Mishpat* (the Governance of Justice)—is the central teaching of the Kabbalah of the great Paduan mystic

Rabbi Moses Ḥayyim Luzzatto or Ramḥal (1707-1746). According to Ramḥal, these two tracks run throughout history. The Governance of Unity is a rather straightforward, short-term approach whereby good is rewarded and evil punished. The Governance of Justice, on the other hand, is a rather circuitous route. Its long-term goal is the revelation of God's unity. There are times in the history of the world that immediate reward and punishment are subordinated to this far-reaching plan that comes under the rubric of the Governance of Unity. That interest is served by the ongoing tension between good and evil, and the eventual realization that evil itself was good in disguise! This is Ramḥal's solution to the problem of evil or theodicy. See Rabbi Ḥayyim Friedlander's introduction to his edition of Luzzatto's *Da'at Tevunot* (B'nei Berak, 1975), pp. 19-20; and Yosef Avivi, *Zohar Ramḥal* (Jerusalem, 1997), p. 99 ff. (Avivi exchanges Friedlander's *"Hanhagat ha-Mishpat"* for *"Hanhagat ha-Gemul."* The difference is purely semantic.)

[34]Cf. *Orot, Yisrael u-Teḥiyato*, chap. 9 (Maggid edition, p. 171): "The Lord makes peace and creates evil, *and all are His servants*." And see my note thereto on pp. 477-478, note 206. The chapter is now available in *Shemonah Kevatsim* 5:36.

In the section of Luzzatto's *'Adir ba-Marom* that serves as commentary to the passage of the *Idra*, *"Palguta de-Sa'arei"* ("The Part of the Hair"), referenced by Rav Kook in the present work (see note 406), we read:

> The lights being the root of the *Sitra Aḥera* (the Other Side) ... is not a blemish on their honor, for to the contrary, the power of the Emanator, blessed be His name, is known by this, after all the worst evil has been returned to good.
>
> (*'Adir ba-Marom*, ed. Rabbi Mordekhai Chriqui [Jerusalem, 2018], p. 299)

In another book, attributed to Luzzatto, *KaLaḤ Pitḥei Ḥokhmah* (it too referenced by Rav Kook in the present work, see note 386), this theme is spelled out in more striking terms:

> ... then the evil itself shows the great honor of the unity of the King, saying: "This is what the King vanquished!"
>
> (*KaLaḤ Pitḥei Ḥokhmah*, ed. Rabbi Yosef Spinner [Jerusalem, 1987], *petaḥ* 49 [p. 168])

See also Rav Kook's notes to *KaLaḤ Pitḥei Ḥokhmah* in *Pinkesei ha-Rayah*, vol. 3, *Pinkas* 15:35 (p. 81, par. 2). (The paragraph rebuts the supersessionist theology of the *Minim* or Christians, while alluding to a work by the *Ḥasid* [i.e. Luzzatto] *à la* the thirteen principles of faith of Maimonides.)

And finally, in a passage from Luzzatto's *oeuvre* that might very well have served as the basis for Rav Kook's statement regarding the purpose of the Exile, the author engages in moral exhortation:

> Behold, this is a firm peg for the faith of the Children of Israel. Let their heart not grow faint from the length of the Exile and its bitterness, for on the contrary, the Holy One, blessed be He, permitted and allowed evil to do all that it is capable of doing ... And at the end of everything, the heavier the burden imposed by evil on people, the more there will be revealed the power of His unity, may He be blessed, and his powerful rule, as He is omnipotent.
>
> (*Da'at Tevunot*, chap. 40; Friedlander edition, p. 26; Spinner edition, p. 45)

Da'at Tevunot was first published by Rabbi Samuel Luria in Warsaw in 1889, so while not referenced in our work, there is no reason that Rav Kook could not have availed himself of the book.

Rabbi Yitsḥak Eizik Ḥaver, influenced by Rabbi Moses Ḥayyim Luzzatto, wrote of the "Secret of Returning the Evil to Good" (*Sod Haḥzarat ha-Ra' le-Tov*) in *Ginzei Meromim*, his commentary to *Masekhet 'Atsilut*. See *Masekhet 'Atsilut 'im Be'ur Ginzei Meromim*, ed. Yonatan Meir (Jerusalem, 2000), pp. 38, 42. Initially printed in Johannisburg in 1864, this was the first of Rabbi Yitsḥak Eizik Ḥaver's original Kabbalistic works to be published by his son after his passing. While the pseudepigraphic work *Masekhet 'Atsilut* (attributed to "Eliyahu ben Yosef") reads like a medieval Kabbalistic text, today scholars call into question whether this is truly so. One of the disturbing facts is that no manuscripts survive. (It was published from a manuscript in the possession of the Vilna Gaon after his passing by his son Rabbi Abraham.) See Yehuda Liebes, *"Masekhet 'Atsilut: Ḥibbur Kabbali Psevdo-Epigraphi me-'et ha-Ga'on mi-Vilna bi-Tse'iruto?"* in idem, *Li-Tsevi u-le-Ga'on* (Tel-Aviv: Idra, 2017), pp. 87-92.

*

In a sermon delivered on Rosh Hashanah 1933 in the Ḥurvah synagogue in Jerusalem, Rav Kook referred to the newly elected *Fuehrer* of Germany, Hitler, as an "impure *shofar*" of the Messiah. (The *shofar* is the horn blown on Rosh Hashanah, preferably a ram's horn.) The import of the sermon was that Hitler's rise to power was a wake-up call to the Jews of Europe to return to their ancestral Land of Israel. See *Ma'amrei ha-Rayah*, vol. 1, ed. Elisha Langenauer and David Landau (Jerusalem, 1980), p. 269.

[35]*b. 'Avodah Zarah* 11b.

[36]Cf. Maimonides, *MT*, end *Hil. Mikva'ot* (11:12): *"mei ha-da'at"* ("the waters of knowledge"). Other texts have *"mei ha-de'ot"* ("the waters of opinions"). Cf. end *Mishneh Torah* (*Hil. Melakhim* 12:5), quoting the verse in Isaiah 11:9: "For the earth shall be full of the knowledge of the Lord, as the waters cover the sea." Rav Kook himself quotes the verse in Isaiah in his commentary to the second legend; see below note 61.

For the Kabbalistic term *"Yam ha-Ḥokhmah"* ("Sea of Wisdom"), see above n. 23.

[37]Hebrew, *"la'asot melakhah be-mayim rabim,"* a paraphrase of Psalms 107:23.

[38]An oblique reference to Paul (Saul of Tarsus). Pauline Christianity abolished actual performance of the commandments, circumcision being the most blatant example.

[39]See Rabbi Moses Cordovero, *Pardes Rimonim*, Gate 10 (*Sha'ar ha-Gevanim*), chap. 1.

[40]See *Ra'aya Mehemna* in *Zohar* III, 175:

> This commandment of *tsitsit* (ritual fringes) includes *tekhelet* (blue) and white; judgment and compassion. In a flame, the white fire does not consume; the blue consumes and destroys.

See Rabbi Aaron Hakohen of Apta, *Keter Shem Tov*, Part Two (Zolkiew, 1795), s.v. *eikhah yashvah vadad*; in the Kehot edition, Brooklyn, 1981, par. 342 (50c). In his notes (97a), Rabbi Immanuel Shochet points out that the wording of *Keter Shem Tov* differs slightly from that of its source in Rabbi Jacob Joseph of Polnoye, *Toledot Ya'akov Yosef*, *Devarim*, end chap. 1. Where *Toledot Ya'akov Yosef* has *"esh okhlah"* ("a consuming fire"); *Keter Shem Tov* has *"isha tikhla"* ("blue fire").

In *Zohar* I, 51a we are shown that in a flame there are two lights: above, a shining white light; and below it, a black or blue (*tekhelet*) light. Whereas the white light is constant and unchanging, the blue-black light is subject to change and given to destruction.

[41]Exodus 3:14.

[42]In the Rabbinic reading, the name *Ehyeh asher Ehyeh* ("I shall be that I shall be") refers obliquely to the exile of the Jewish People. See *b. Berakhot* 9b:

> "I shall be that I shall be" [Exodus 3:14].
>
> The Holy One, blessed be He, said to Moses: Go tell Israel, I was with you in this subjugation and I shall be with you in [future] subjugations to the kingdoms.
>
> [Moses] said to Him: Let the present trouble suffice. (Rashi: "Why worry them now with ill tidings?")
>
> [Thereupon] the Holy One, blessed be He, said to him: Go tell them "*Ehyeh* ('I shall be') sent me to you" [Exodus 3:14]. [The words "that I shall be" were omitted.]

In a letter written from Jaffa in the year 1907, Rav Kook's son, Tsevi Yehudah, quotes this passage from the Talmud to Shem Tov Geffen. Tsevi Yehudah decries those who "ignore eternity, the flash of the future, *Ehyeh asher Ehyeh*, that is engraved together with *'Yah Adonai Tseva'ot'*—the breadth and the depth—on the club with which we strike the wave of the sea" (*Tsemaḥ Tsevi: Letters of Rabbi Tsevi Yehudah Hakohen Kook*, vol. 1, ed. David Landau, Ze'ev Neuman and Shaḥar Raḥmani [Jerusalem, 1991], p. 6). It is difficult to glean the writer's exact meaning.

[43]*y. Ḥagigah* 2:1; *b. Menaḥot* 29b; *Genesis Rabbah* 12:10; *Midrash Tehillim*, ed. Buber (Vilna, 1891), Psalm 114 (pp. 471-472).

[44]Hebrew, *ha-mitpa'er ba-'anafav*. An allusion to the fact that the Tetragrammaton (YHVH) symbolizes the *sefirah* of *Tif'eret*, which in turn, has two meanings: glory (*pe'er*), and branches (*p'orot*) as in Ezekiel 31. See Rabbi Moses Cordovero, *Pardes Rimonim*, Gate 23 (*Sha'ar ha-Kinnuyim*), s.v. *Tif'eret*.

[45]"*Amen*" occurs twice, corresponding to the two worlds. *Amen* is interpreted as "*ne'eman*" (faithful). See *b. Shabbat* 119b.

[46]Cf. Psalms 119:89.

[47]Psalms 37:10.

[48]Psalms 37:29.

The Little Star

2

R[abbah] b[ar] B[ar] Ḥ[annah] said: Seafarers related to me that **between** one **wave and** the next **wave** there are **three hundred parasangs,**[49] **and the height of a wave is three hundred parasangs. One time,** seafarers recounted, **we were traveling along the route and a wave lifted us up until we saw the resting place of a small star which was the size of the area needed for scattering forty *se'ah* of mustard seeds. And if it had lifted us higher, we would have been scorched by the heat** of the star.

And the wave raised its voice and shouted **to another** wave: **My friend, did you leave anything in the world that you did not wash away, that I may come and destroy it?** The second wave **said to it: Go out** and **see the greatness of your Master,** God, for even **the width of a strand of sand** on the land **I cannot pass, as it is stated: "Will you not fear Me, said the Lord; will you not tremble at My presence? I have placed the sand for the boundary of the sea, an everlasting law, which it cannot pass"** (Jeremiah 5:22).

THE LITTLEST STAR AND THE SECRET OF THE SAND BAR: THE UNCOMPROMISING LAW OF FREE WILL

We have already said that the waves that desire to sink the ships voyaging in the sea; that seek to destroy the world, are the forces of impurity that break loose of their masters. Now, "this opposite this made God,"[50] and just as the forces of holiness are particularized, so too the forces of impurity opposing them. An example would be the twelve tribes of Israel and the twelve princes of Ishmael.[51] As it is written, "He erects the borders of peoples according to the number of the Children of Israel."[52] Now the Camp of Israel in the Desert was three parasangs.[53] That would be on the Kabbalistic level of *'Asiyah*. It is known that the World of *'Asiyah* is symbolized by ones; the World of *Yetsirah* by tens; and the World of *Beri'ah* by hundreds.[54] [The principle is:] The more things approach their root above, the greater their light and more multiplied their splendor. So in the World of *Beri'ah*, which is the place of the souls of Israel,[55] the "Camp of Israel" measures three hundred parasangs. If so, the antipode too, the *Sitra Aḥera* (Other Side) and its powers are three hundred parasangs high. **And the height of a wave is three hundred parasangs.** This is its height at its supernal root.

However, it is known that the wicked are divided.[56] As it is written concerning Esau, "souls" in the plural.[57] "All those who do evil shall be divided."[58] The Holy One, blessed be He, will not allow them to come together. So between their various aspects, there intervenes a power of holiness, to prevent them from joining together to wreck the world.[59] This is alluded to by their saying that **between** one **wave and** the next **wave** there are **three hundred parasangs.** The general sanctity of the Camp of Israel intervenes between those "waves," preventing them from achieving success. "The deceitful shall not succeed in grilling his prey."[60]

Now the powers of evil wish to snare the souls of Israel. When the souls of the sinners fall into their hands, the powers of evil derive thereby bounty and sustenance.

One time, seafarers recounted, **we were traveling along the route.** [Note that] they did not say "we were traveling by boat," for that would have implied that they traversed the Sea of Wisdom. To analyze the matters of the Other Side, one need not have recourse to the Sea of Wisdom. For those matters are extreme lowliness in comparison to holiness; their aspects begin where the degrees of holiness end. Their region is not full of knowledge "as the waters cover the sea."[61] **We were traveling along the route,** in a dry river bed,[61*] to know the powers of evil.

We saw the resting place of a small star. Israel are likened to stars.[62] He apprehended the level of the soul of one of the least of Israel taken captive by the *kelipot* (literally "husks" or "shells," i.e. the forces of impurity), and he saw that from that one soul the forces of impurity derive bounty and sustenance for all their aspects.

It is known that the evil forces are likened to bees. As it says, "They chased you as do the bees."[63] Similarly it says, "They surrounded me like bees."[64] And just as the Sages said that the bee dies after having bitten,[65] so too in regard to the powers of evil, it is said, "When man rules over man to his own hurt."[66] For in so doing, "they stumbled and fell."[67] But the forces of evil rejoice in their temporary success.[68]

Mustard is the food for bees, as the Sages said: "Keep your bees far away from my mustard, for they come and eat my mustard flowers."[69]

As a rule, the forces of evil divide into four levels, corresponding to the four worlds[70] of *Atsilut, Beri'ah, Yetsirah* and *'Asiyah*; and corresponding to [the four *sefirot* of] *Ḥokhmah* and *Binah, Tif'eret* and *Malkhut*, as is known.[71] He beheld how through the soul of the least of Israel, the forces of evil have abundance for all their camps: **the size of the area needed for scattering forty *se'ah* of mustard seeds. Forty** corresponding to all four of their aspects, each comprised of ten.

Though previously he spoke in terms of hundreds, now that he is speaking about the *nefesh* (lower soul) that falls into their hands [he speaks of tens].[72] The *neshamah* (higher soul), situated in [the World of] *Beri'ah*, does not fall [into their hands]; the hand of strangers does not reach there. This is the Secret of the Guarded Wine (*yayin ha-meshumar*).[73] Only [lower in the World of] *Yetsirah*—which is the Secret of Good and Evil—can the forces of evil nest and cast a net. This is the Secret of the Palace of the King,[74] for the "King" symbolizes [the *partsuf* of] *Ze'ir Anpin* that nests in [the World of] *Yetsirah.*[75]

[There is another reason why the numerology has shifted from hundreds to tens:] The forces of evil desire to capture the soul for their food. [In the food chain,] the nourishment is always one step less than the one nourished. (It is the way the author of *'Akedah* wrote in *Parashat ha-Man* [the Portion of the Manna], that the nourishment is one level less than the nourished.)[76] The forces of evil wish to swallow [the soul] alive, as it says, "Then they would have swallowed us alive."[77] The forces of evil do not suck the flow in a way that the one nursing remains superior to the suckling. Rather they engage literally in "swallowing," turning the soul [which is their provider] into their "bread." So truthfully, when the forces of evil are busy in their state of *Beri'ah* [symbolized by hundreds], they lower [the soul] to the [reduced] value of *Yetsirah* [symbolized by tens]. Thus, the food of the forces of evil amounted to **forty *se'ah* of mustard seeds.**

But it is only a place *prepared* for sowing "gall and wormwood,"[78] not ready made sustenance. That is because the soul that falls into their hands, provides them with vitality only if the soul adds impurity and sins which are the bitter food that sustains them; or if the soul has become so absolutely evil that even the *mitsvot* (good deeds) performed are handed over to the forces of evil, adding to their power "in the right hand of falsehood."[79]

The seafarers came to see the impure picture in order to understand the matter of the forces of evil and how to beware of them. In doing so, one must be careful that those forces of evil not adhere to one, God forbid. So the Sages, of blessed memory, explained that one must pass quickly through the place of the spectacle of the *kelipot*, so that they not adhere to one. Now first the seafarers saw how they snare souls, and all that they do with the oppressed [souls] if the souls do not attempt to escape from their prison. But the seafarers figured that they best not gaze upon them overly much, so as "not to turn to the idols,"[80] for a strange fire from their bad breath burns and consumes. **And if it had lifted us higher, we would have been scorched by the heat (*hevel,* literally "breath").** This is the secret of the verse "There is a vanity (*hevel*) that takes place on earth,"[81] for their entire matter is but vanity. *Hevel* or breath is merely the preparation for speech, for their speech was never completed. The forces of evil came about because they were never completed by the sanctity of the Sabbath.[82] It is known from the words of the Sages that the demons were created on the Eve of the Sabbath at twilight [before the actual arrival of the Sabbath].[83] Thus, they were never perfected; they are defective and remain arrested in the [preverbal] state of "breath."[84]

And the wave raised its voice and shouted **to another** wave: **My friend, did you leave anything in the world that you did not wash away, that I may come and destroy it?** The second wave **said to it: Go out** and **see the greatness of your Master,** God, for even **the width of a strand of sand** on the land **I cannot pass.**

It is known that even the souls that have fallen into the hands of the forces of evil do not come totally under their control as long as the souls yet reside within the body, for they may yet avail themselves of *beḥirah* (free will).[85] One may sincerely repent at a moment's notice,[86] retrieving from the forces of evil all that they robbed.[87] Truthfully, it is wondrous that with all their might and brazenness—which allow them to vanquish and injure great things that are stripped of corporeality—the powers of evil have no ability to injure those residing within the body.

Now the body is compared to the visible shore. So when the wave of impurity was asked if it had left anything which it had not flooded—"overflowing … shall reach even to the neck"[88]—it had to admit that it could not surpass the sand, symbolic of the body. Not because of the strength of the body *per se*, which being sand and dirt "is of little account,"[89] but because of the strength of the Lord.

As it is stated: "Will you not fear Me, said the Lord; will you not tremble at My presence? I have placed the sand for the boundary of the sea, an everlasting law, which it cannot pass" (Jeremiah 5:22). While the verse speaks of the physical sea, it also alludes to higher matters. The main reason that people fall is *ye'ush* (despair). The Evil Inclination tells one that it is impossible to fix that which was corrupted.[90] But in truth, **I have placed the sand for the boundary of the sea, an everlasting law.** That law is the power of *beḥirah* (free will). Free will is forever the general law.[91] "It cannot pass." So one must always be strong in the fear of the Lord, even if one has sinned much, for as long as one lives, there is yet hope of escaping to dry land, where the waves of the raging sea cannot seize one. One must escape to seek shelter in *beḥirah* (free will), over which the forces of evil were not given power and control.

[49]Rabbah bar Bar Ḥannah quoted his teacher Rabbi Yoḥanan as saying that the average man can walk ten parasangs in the course of a day. See *b. Pesaḥim* 93b-94a. Estimates for the length of a Talmudic parasang vary between 3.65 and 3.84 kilometers or 2.27–2.39 miles.

[50]Ecclesiastes 7:14.

[51]Genesis 25:16.

[52]Deuteronomy 32:8.

[53]*b. Sanhedrin* 5b.

Parenthetically, none other than Rabbah bar Bar Ḥannah attested that he witnessed the site of the encampment of Israel in the Desert and its size was three parasangs. See *b. 'Eruvin* 55b; *Yoma* 75b; and Rashi's recension in *Berakhot* 54b, s.v. *Maḥaneh Yisrael kamah havei? Telata parsei.*

[54]

> In *Atsilut* is the mystery of thousands; and in the World of *Beri'ah* is the mystery of hundreds; and in the World of *Yetsirah* is the mystery of tens; and in the lowest world, which is the World of *'Asiyah*, ones.
>
> (Rabbi Shabtai [Sheftel] Horowitz, *Shefa' Tal* [Hanau, 1612], unpaginated introduction, *"Ben Me'ah Shanah"*)

And see ibid. 1:5 (11d).

In the Kabbalistic scheme, reality is divided into four worlds (from top down): *Atsilut* (Emanation), *Beri'ah* (Creation), *Yetsirah* (Formation) and *'Asiyah* (Making). (See our Kabbalistic Chart.) The source of this schema is the verse in Isaiah 43:7: "Every one that is called by My name and for My honor I created him (*berativ*), formed him (*yetsartiv*), even made him (*'asitiv*)."

In another instance, Rav Kook utilized the correlation between hundreds and the World of *Beri'ah* to explain the *notarikon* of *madon—me'ah dinei* (*b. Sanhedrin* 7a). See *Metsi'ot Katan*, par. 271 (top page 424).

[55]The souls of Israel are carved out from under the *Kisse ha-Kavod* or Throne of Glory (*Zohar* III, 29b). See Rabbi Joseph Karo, *Beit Yosef, Orah Ḥayyim*, chap. 224, s.v. *ha-ta'am she-be-ḥakhmei Yisrael 'omer she-ḥalak.* The original text read: "Since the souls of Israel are carved out from under the Throne of Glory, they are like a portion (*ḥelek*) of the Lord." (In later editions, this phrase was censored; see Rabbi David Cohen, *Tikkunim be-Sifrei ha-Tur*, Brooklyn, 1995, p. 19.)

The Throne of Glory, in turn, is located in the world of *Beri'ah.*

For Kabbalistic explanations, see Rabbi Karo's disciple, Rabbi Moses Cordovero, *Pardes Rimonim*

31:2; idem, *Shi'ur Komah* (Warsaw, 1883), s.v. *Torah*, chap. 37 (22b); and Rabbi Shabtai (Sheftel) Horowitz, *Nishmat Shabtai Halevi* (Prague, 1616), Gate 12 (*Ḥillukei Mekorei Neshamot*), 25d-26a. Cf. *b. Shabbat* 152b.

[56]Aramaic, *be-piruda*. This is likely a reference to the saying of the *Zohar* II, 95 (*Saba de-Mishpatim*): "[It] begins in unity and ends in division" (*"Sharei be-ḥibbura ve-siyyem be-piruda"*). Rav Kook understands divisiveness to be the essential character of evil, as opposed to holiness, whose essential nature is unity. See *Orot ha-Kodesh*, vol. 1, p. 15 [=*Shemonah Kevatsim* 5:61]; and vol. 2, pp. 440-441 [=*Shemonah Kevatsim* 7:69].

[57]Genesis 36:6. See Rashi, Genesis 46:26, quoting *Leviticus Rabbah* 4:6: "Esau had but six souls, yet Scripture refers to them as the 'souls of his household' in the plural, since they worshiped many gods. Jacob had seventy [souls], yet Scripture refers to them as 'soul' [singular], since they worshiped one God."

[58]Psalm 92:10.

[59]Hebrew, *"letashtesh ha-'olam."* In the Aramaic of the Zohar: *"metashtesh 'alma."* See *Saba de-Mishpatim* in *Zohar* II, 108b, 112a; and *Zohar* III, 170b.

[60]Proverbs 12:27.

[61]Isaiah 11:9.

[61*]Cf. Job 14:11.

[62]*Numbers Rabbah* 2:13.

[63]Deuteronomy 1:44.

[64]Psalms 118:12.

[65]*Midrash Tanḥuma,* ed. Buber (Vilna, 1881), *Shelaḥ,* 42b. (Rome ms. comment on Deut. 1:44.)

[66]Eccles. 8:9; Rabbi Ḥayyim Vital, *Sefer ha-Gilgulim* (Frankfurt, 1684), chap. 2 (2d), cited in Rabbi Jacob Lorberbaum of Lissa, *Ta'alumot Ḥokhmah* to Eccles.; Rabbi Shneur Zalman of Liadi, *Tanya* IV, 25 (140b). Rav Kook's images of "bounty" (*shefa'*) and "food" (*mazon*) come from *Sefer ha-Gilgulim,* ibid. (2a-b).

[67]Psalms 27:2.

[68]In the Commentary to Psalm 107 attributed to the Ba'al Shem Tov, at verse 23, s.v. *yoredei ha-yam ba-'oniyot*, we read:

> Sometimes a great soul descends from a lofty place to the *kelipot*, and the *kelipot* rejoice that the soul has descended among them. And this is the meaning of "those who go down to sea in boats." It refers to the soul that descends into the sea of *kelipot*, as explained in the *Saba* [portion of *Zohar*], *Mishpatim*. (See there.) But the *kelipot* do not know that "they do work in many waters"

> [Psalm 107:23]. This means that these holy souls are active when they descend into "many waters." And these souls annihilate the *kelipot* and ascend from there to their rightful place.
>
> (*Siddur Tefillah Yesharah—Berdichev* [photo-offset Williamsburg, 1975], *Minḥah le-ʿErev Shabbat*, no pagination)

For variants, see Rivka Schatz-Uffenheimer, *"Peirusho shel ha-Besht le-Mizmor 107,"* *Tarbiz* 42 (1973), p. 167, lines 92-95. Instead of "And these souls annihilate (*mekhalim*) the *kelipot*," Schatz's version reads: "And raise up (*ma'alim*) souls from the *kelipot*." Both variants may be found in *Ba'al Shem Tov 'al ha-Torah*, ed. Shim'on Menaḥem Mendel [Wodnik] of Gowarczów (Lodz, 1938), *Yitro.*

[69]*b. Bava Batra* 25b.

[70]Rav Kook employs the Hebrew term *ma'alot* or "levels."

[71]See our Kabbalistic Chart.

[72]In the Kabbalistic framework, the three levels of the soul (from lowest to highest) *nefesh*, *ru'aḥ* and *neshamah*, correspond to the three worlds (again, from bottom up) *'Asiyah*, *Yetsirah*, *Beri'ah*, which are assigned numerical values of ones, tens and hundreds. The number forty (which comes under the rubric of tens) thus belongs to the World of *Yetsirah* and the middle level of soul, or *ru'aḥ*—not the lowest level of *nefesh*. It seems that a scribal error has crept in and the word *"nefesh"* in Rav Kook's commentary should be replaced with *"ru'aḥ."*

[73]*b. Berakhot* 34b.

[74]This may be an allusion to the verse in Proverbs 30:28: "A spider you can take with the hands, yet she is in a king's palaces (*be-heikhlei melekh*)."

[75]The term is *"Ze'ir Anpin (ha-)mekanen bi-Yetsirah."* See Rabbi Ḥayyim Vital, *'Ets Ḥayyim* 3:1. See our Kabbalistic Chart.

In *Pardes Rimonim* (Gate 23 [*Sha'ar ha-Kinnuyim*], chap. 13, s.v. *Melekh*) Rabbi Moses Cordovero writes that in general, without further qualification, *Melekh* symbolizes the *sefirah* of *Tif'eret*. Translated into Lurianic parlance, that would yield the equation of *Melekh* with the *partsuf* of *Ze'ir Anpin*. See e.g. Rabbi Ḥayyim Vital, *Peri 'Ets Ḥayyim*, beginning *Sha'ar ha-Tefillin*. (For the equation of *Melekh* with *Tif'eret*, see Rabbi Isaac of Acco, *Me'irat 'Eynayim* to Genesis 2:7 [Erlanger ed., 39b] and so too Recanati's interpretation of Naḥmanides, Numbers 30:3. See below note 193.)

[76]Rabbi Isaac Arama, *'Akedat Yitsḥak*, Exodus, beginning Gate 41.

[77]Psalms 124:3.

[78]Deuteronomy 29:17.

[79]Psalms 144:8, 11.

[80]Cf. Leviticus 19:4.

[81]Ecclesiastes 8:14.

[82]Cf. The Introduction of Rabbi Naftali Herz Halevi Weidenbaum to his commentary *Luḥot ha-Berit*, in Anonymous, *Berit 'Olam*, Part II (Jerusalem, 1937), pp. 9-12 (especially p. 10).

[83]*m. Avot* 5:6.

[84]The incomplete state of the demons is symbolized by "breath" (*hevel*), incomplete speech.

[85]Atypical of many rabbinic thinkers who were yet locked into the Cartesian mind-body dualism, Rav Kook held the body in very high regard. In *Orot* (1920), he advocated for *"hit'amlut"* (physical exercise). In the very beginning of *Orot ha-Teshuvah* (1925), he accorded status to *teshuvah gufanit* (bodily return) as a most basic, integral part of the process of *teshuvah*, or return to God. In our work too, early as it is (stemming from the days of Rav Kook's first rabbinic post in Zoimel) we are treated to a taste of this holistic thinking.

Though impossible to prove, it is possible that Rav Kook's focus on body was inspired by reading Rabbi Moses Ḥayyim Luzzatto's *Ma'amar ha-Ge'ulah*, first published by Samuel Luria in Warsaw in 1889. In that work, Luzzatto treats the importance of *tikkun ha-guf* (mending of the body) and the part it plays in the redemptive process. (An English translation of Luzzatto's treatise by Rabbi Mordechai Nissim is available under the title *Secrets of the Redemption.*) See also my comment in the *Koren Rav Kook Siddur* (2017), s.v. *u-va le-Tsiyon go'el u-le-shavei fesha' be-Ya'akov* (pp. 237-240).

*

A strong statement against mind-body dualism is made by the early Ḥasidic master Rabbi Menaḥem Naḥum of Chernobyl in his classic Ḥasidic text *Me'or 'Eynayim*. The Maggid of Chernobyl bases his remarks upon the religious disputation between an anonymous magus or Zorastrian priest and Amemar, recorded in *b. Sanhedrin* 39a. (See below note 96.) The Zoroastrian tried to prove from the division of the human body into upper and lower extremities the existence of two deities, Ahura Mazda and Ahriman. (See Rashi ad loc.) The Maggid comes back with a resounding reply:

> God forbid! The truth is that man is a complete unity (*aḥdut gamur*) in all 248 limbs and 365 sinews, as is known. And one must unite the two parts to cleave to the complete good, so that the material prove not overwhelming—even from the "half below"—for one God created them.
>
> (*Me'or 'Eynayim*, *Vayyetse*, s.v. *vayyisa Ya'akov raglav*)

In the course of the discussion, the Maggid invokes the verse "In all your ways acknowledge

Him" (Proverbs 3:6). Menaḥem Naḥum Twersky of Boston (a descendant of Rabbi David of Tolna, grandson of Rabbi Menaḥem Naḥum of Chernobyl) informs me that this verse is a leitmotif of his namesake's work *Me'or 'Eynayim.*

[86]See *b. 'Avodah Zarah* 17a: "There is one who acquires eternity in a single moment." Also, *'Avodah Zarah* 10b and 18a.

[87]Cf. *Orot*, *Yisrael u-Teḥiyato* (Israel and Its Renascence), end. chap. 6, where this thinking of "taking back stolen lights" is applied on the collective level vis-à-vis the nations of the world. In Naor ed., p. 165.

[88]Isaiah 8:8.

[89]Isaiah 2:22.

[90]Cf. Ecclesiastes 1:15.

[91]See Moses Maimonides, *Shemonah Perakim* (Eight Chapters), Introduction to the Commentary to the Mishnah, Tractate *Avot*, chap. 8; and idem, *MT*, *Hil. Teshuvah*, chaps. 5-6.

See too Rabbi Shneur Zalman of Liadi, *Likkutei Torah, Pinḥas*, s.v. *Tsav et B'nei Yisrael* II, chap. 1 (75b-d); Rabbi Menaḥem Mendel Shneurson of Lubavitch, *Derekh Mitsvotekha* (Poltava, 1911; photo-offset Brooklyn, 1953), *Mitsvat Vidui u-Teshuvah*, chap. 4 (39b-40b); and Rabbi Shelomo Zalman of Kopyst, *Magen Avot* (Berdichev, 1902), *Pinḥas*, s.v. *Tsav et B'nei Yisrael* (60d-61d).

Rabbi Shneur Zalman differentiates between the World to Come, referred to as "*'olam barur*" (*b. Pesaḥim* 50a; *Bava Batra* 10b), an already clarified world, and this world, which he deems "*'olam ha-birur*," a world yet in the process of clarification. He compares the World to Come to the body of the mature adult, whose respective limbs cannot be substituted one for the other; while this world is comparable to the body of the fetus, whose limbs are yet interchangeable. (Rabbi Shneur Zalman delivered this discourse in the Hebrew year 5565 or 1805. It seems that he anticipated the findings of embryonic stem cell research by about two centuries!)

In his youth in Grieva (a suburb of Dvinsk), Latvia, Rav Kook was exposed to the Ḥabad teachings of the Kopyster Rebbe. His *ma'amarim* were taught at the Third Meal of the Sabbath by none other than Rabbi Yeḥezkel (Ḥatskel) Yanover, the official *ḥozer* of the Kopyster Rebbe. Rav Kook's maternal grandfather, Rabbi Raphael Felman, who founded the local Kopyster *shtiebel*, brought Rabbi Yeḥezkel to Grieva and ensconced him in the *beit midrash*. See Rabbi Neriyah, *Siḥot ha-Rayah* (Tel-Aviv, 1979), pp. 49, 266.

Hurmin son of Lilith

3

R[abbah] b[ar] B[ar] Ḥ[annah] said: I have seen the one called **Hurmin, son of Lilith, when he was running on the pinnacles of the wall of** the city of **Meḥoza, and a cavalryman riding a horse below him was unable** to catch up to **him. One time, they saddled for him two mules and they stood on the two bridges of** the river **Donag, and he jumped from this one to that one, and from that one to this one. And he was holding two cups of wine in his hands and was pouring from this one to that one, and from that one to this one, and not a drop fell to the ground. And that day was** stormy, similar to the description in a verse dealing with seafarers: **"They mounted up to the heavens, they went down to the depths;** their soul melted away because of trouble" (Psalms 107:26). **They heard in the house of the king, and they killed him.**

WALLED CITIES AND GATED COMMUNITIES: JUGGLING FINANCES AND THE DEMON OF CUPIDITY

Rabbah bar Bar Ḥannah relates how he beheld the power of evil that comes from the hankering of the masses "to place their trust in gold."[92] Their entire hankering amounts to building walled compounds. They are tight-fisted when it comes to giving charity. They put their trust in erecting fortresses, fortifying the city in which they dwell with massive walls. But truly, this is the root of their destruction. The fortification will be of no avail in a time of emergency because the force of destruction was prepared precisely by their having misplaced their trust in the Lord. [Instead,] they put their trust in the might of their hands. It is known that among the wealthy men of Meḥoza,[93] there were found such types. As we say in [Tractate] *Rosh Hashanah*: "Their faces resemble the black of the pot. Said Rava: And those are the most beautiful sons of Meḥoza; they are called 'Sons of Gehinnom.'"[94]

Even though Lilith resides primarily in places of destruction and desolation, as it is written, "There shall Lilith repose,"[95] and she does not wish for the settling of the world—nonetheless, a settlement destined for destruction, is for all intents and purposes considered a ruin. In such a "settlement," Lilith rejoices.

Hurmin, son of Lilith. In other words, one of the authorized representatives of Lilith. [Hurmin] derives from the Aramaic word *hurmana* or authority.[96] **Was running on the pinnacles of the wall of** the city of **Meḥoza,** for he resides on top of the towering walls which the foolish inhabitants of Meḥoza erected, thinking that they were settlers of the world, when in reality they were *ḥaruvei karta* (destroyers of the city).[97] For in so doing, divine supervision and salvation was denied them. Not only were the fortresses [in and of themselves] of no avail, but even cavalry mounted on horseback were incapable of saving their souls. Whereas if they had not placed their trust in palaces and fortresses, they would have been protected by divine supervision. Now, even **a cavalryman riding a horse below him was unable** to catch up to **him,** which is to say that he was unable to drive out the disgusting power that resides specifically in those fortresses.

Rabbah bar Bar Ḥannah goes on to tell how there is unleashed destructive power both on a general level and on an individual level. There are those whose lust for money is so great that they have no other desire but the pointless acquisition of wealth, even if they should be childless, so that they needn't worry about the upkeep of their children after they die; and even if they are already so aged that they have one foot in the grave (so to speak), and can see that the time is near when they will have to transition to another world; and even if they are full of such abundance that they can no longer place all the wealth. Despite all that, such an individual will count every penny to make sure that no charity is disbursed to the poor of the planet. The power of impurity is so overwhelming that even on the day of death nothing will be left to charity, which might preserve the wealthy man's soul in the World to Come. Such people are the "chariot"[98] of **Hurmin son of Lilith.** Through them, Hurmin is empowered to build only to destroy, and to destroy that which was already built, increasing desolation and destruction.

Such people, when they are childless, should worry about their soul. If there has been no blessing from their bodies, then at least they should make sure that their soul is not barren of the fruit of the righteous.[99] But if they are lacking as well the fruits of good deeds, then the result is that both body and soul are sterile, like a mule that does not reproduce and lacks blessing, as the words of our Sages in the first chapter of [Tractate] *Kiddushin.*[100] **One**

time, they saddled for him, meaning that the individuals became "chariots" upon which the evil power of Hurmin might ride, **two mules,** i.e. childless persons, devoid of any good deed, rendering [not only the body, but] the soul as well a "mule" without offspring, **and they stood on the two bridges of** the river **Donag,** which is to say that the persons were about to transition from world to world, and both body and soul could sense as much: The powers of the body collapse, and the soul too—its shadow departs from it, as the words of the *Zohar*.[101] "And there is no power on the day of death."[102] They are full of wealth and abundance, which itself intoxicates with the wine of pride.

And he jumped from this one to that one, and from that one to this one. Hurmin's control extended over both body and soul. Sometimes he would strengthen the spell of miserliness by telling the person that the money must go to invigorate the body that is weakened with age; other times, he would convey that the funds must be expended upon singers, male and female, to gladden his depressed spirits.[103] Either way, why should one give to charity when the money is required for other disbursements?

[Despite the fact that death was imminent, since] they were full of wealth and abundance, they were drunk with power. This is symbolized by the fact that **he was holding two cups of wine in his hands,** an image of overabundance: twice as much as was truly necessary. **And was pouring from this one to that one, and from that one to this one.** He was juggling assets from one business to another. (Sometimes, the transfer of funds was quite ridiculous.)[104] **And not a drop fell to the ground.** No wealth trickled down to the poor of the planet; it was confined to his choicest cup.

And that day, the day of death, **"They mounted up to the heavens,"** the soul ascended to heaven, and the body "**went down to the depths,**" and despite all that, the miserliness could not be shaken off, since all his days he was accustomed to it and "was attached to it like heresy."[105]

Since he would not give charity to redeem his soul, **they heard in the house of the King,** meaning the heavenly King, **and they killed him.** Had he engaged in charitable works, they would have granted him additional years, as the Sages, of blessed memory, said: "'Charity saves from death' [Proverbs 10:2]—Not from a bizarre death, but from death itself!"[106] "True charity leads to life."[107]

[92]Job 31:24.

[93]For references to the legendary wealth of Meḥoza, see Rashi, *Bava Kamma* 119a, s.v. *li-v'nei Meḥoza*; and Rashbam, *Bava Batra* 36a, s.v. *be-tsavar Meḥoza*. And see *Ḥiddushei Aggadot Maharasha, Ta'anit* 21a, s.v. *di-nefishei b'nei ḥeila*.

[94]*b. Rosh Hashanah* 17a. Rashi explains that in life, the men of Meḥoza were self-indulgent and corpulent. The point is that their sojourn in Gehinnom gave their faces an emaciated look.

Concerning Rava's exchanges with the men of Meḥoza, see too *b. Bava Metsi'a* 59a: "Said Rava to the men of Meḥoza: 'Honor your wives in order that you become wealthy.'"

[95]Isaiah 34:14: "Yet there shall Lilith repose, and find herself a place of rest." Lilith is the name of a she-demon.

[96]The term *"hurmana de-malka"* (royal authority) occurs often in the Talmud. See *b. Berakhot* 58a; *Gittin* 57b; *Bava Metsi'a* 84a; *Ḥullin* 57b; and *Temurah* 4b (in variant of *'Arukh*, s.v. *Harman*).

In his commentary to our passage in *Bava Batra*, Rabbi Samuel ben Meir (Rashbam) records two variants:

> Hurmin—with a *nun*. This is the correct reading. So I heard from Father, my teacher. And I heard "Hurmiz" with a *zayin*.

Rashi has the reading Hurmiz with a *zayin*, while his grandson Rabbeinu Tam, a.k.a. Rabbi Jacob ben Meir of Ramerupt, has Hurmin with a *nun*. See Rashi and *Tosafot*, *Sanhedrin* 39a, s.v. *de-Hurmiz*; and *Tosafot*, *Bava Batra* 8a, s.v. *Ifra Hurmiz*. (Thus, the two brothers Rashbam and Rabbeinu Tam adopted their father Rabbi Meir's reading of Hurmin with a *nun*, over their maternal grandfather Rashi's reading of Hurmiz with a *zayin*. I have been preceded in this observation by Rabbi Ḥayyim Hirschensohn, *Motsa'ei Mayim* [Budapest, 1924], p. 56.)

The exchange between the magus and Amemar in *b. Sanhedrin* 39a has been treated recently by Eli Aḥdut, "Jewish-Zoroastrian Polemics in the Babylonian Talmud," *Irano-Judaica* IV (1999), Hebrew Section, p. 27. I find it curious that the author cites neither the medieval authorities Rabbeinu Ḥananel (*ad loc.* and copied by Rabbi Nathan ben Yeḥiel of Rome, *'Arukh*, s.v. *Hurmiz*) and Rashi (*ad loc.*), nor the modern scholarship of Alexander Kohut, *Aruch Completum* , vol. 1 (Vienna, 1878), s.v. *Ahurmin*; and vol. 3 (Vienna, 1882), s.v. *Hurmiz*. (Concerning the magus of Talmud Bavli as a Zoroastrian priest, see further below note 109.)

Leaving aside the question of orthography—whether the name is spelled with a *zayin* or a *nun*—the consensus among traditional commentators is that this being is a demon. So understood Rashbam and earlier Rabbeinu Gershom. (However, Rabbi Yom Tov ben Abraham Asevilli or Ritba has an alternative explanation that this is the name of a man who was extremely knowledgeable concerning demonology and magic.)

Ritba writes:

> Hurmiz bar Lilitha—Some say that he was a demon, and in the North, the demons are often revealed to men.

Cf. Rabbi Menaḥem ben Meir Ziyyoni:

> They [i.e. the demons] are found primarily in the extreme North, such as the country of *Norwegen* (i.e. Norway) and that *paysage* because of the cold.
>
> (*Sefer Ziyyoni* [Cremona, 1560], *Aḥarei*, s.v. *goral eḥad la-Hashem ve-goral eḥad la-'Azazel* [66c])

It is likely that both the Spanish sage Rabbi Yom Tov ben Abraham Asevilli and the Ashkenazic Kabbalist Rabbi Menaḥem Ziyyoni drew on sources of Ḥasidei Ashkenaz. (*Norwegen* is the German designation for Norway.) See Boaz Huss, "Demonology and Magic in the Writings of R. Menaḥem Ziyyoni," *Kabbalah* 10 (2004), pp. 55-72.

Some Arctic explorers describe having vivid hallucinations and even seeing "ghosts" when trekking through the environment. According to recent psychological studies, this effect is the result of sensory deprivation.

[97]See *y. Ḥagigah* 1:7 and *Lamentations Rabbah*, *Petiḥata* 2, where the opposition is between "*neturei karta*" (guardians of the city) and "*ḥaruvei karta*" (destroyers of the city).

[98]Hebrew *merkavah*. Cf. *Genesis Rabbah* 47:6: "The Patriarchs are the chariot." In the Kabbalistic tradition, the term "chariot" is employed whenever a human being has become a living embodiment of some celestial force, whether pure or, as in this case, impure.

[99]See Rashi, Genesis 6:9, quoting Midrash: "The main offspring of the righteous are their good deeds."

[100]*b. Kiddushin* 17a.

[101]See *Zohar* I, 217b, 227a; III, 13b; and Naḥmanides and Baḥya ben Asher to Numbers 14:9, s.v. *sar tsilam me-'aleihem.* According to Kabbalistic tradition, on the night of *Hoshana Rabbah*, someone slated to die during the course of the coming year has no shadow.

[102]Ecclesiastes 8:8.

[103]Maimonides wrote in Chapter 5 of the *Shemonah Perakim* (introduction to the Commentary to the Mishnah, *Avot*) that listening to music is one way to overcome depression.

[104]The Aramaic "*mehapekh matarata*" is an idiomatic expression for a needless exchange. See Rashi, *Ketubot* 110a, s.v. *hapukhei matarata lamah li.*

[105]*b. 'Avodah Zarah* 17a.

[106]*b. Shabbat* 156b.

[107]Proverbs 11:19.

The Antelope

4

R[abbah] b[ar] B[ar] Ḥ[annah] said: I have seen a day-old antelope (*'orzila*)[108] that was as large **as Mount Tabor. And how** large **is Mount Tabor?** It is **four parasangs. And the length of its neck** was **three parasangs, and the place where its head rests** was **a parasang and a half. It deposited feces and** thereby **dammed up the Jordan.**

THE AESTHETIC ANTELOPE AND THE ULTERIOR-MOTIVATED TORAH STUDENT

The foundation of Torah is to study it for its own sake and study it constantly, rather than casually. He who learns Torah constantly, learns it for its own sake; he whose motivation is impure studies Torah haphazardly, just enough to impress people with his knowledge.[109]

The Sages, of blessed memory, said that Torah study took place on Mount Tabor for but a fleeting moment in time, as stated in [Tractate] *Megillah*.[110] Now the method of the ulterior-motivated Torah student is to quickly check the four levels of Torah known as *Pardes* (*Peshat, Remez, Derush, Sod*),[111] as Rabbi Moses Cordovero wrote in *'Or Ne'erav*[112] concerning the class of sinners who haughtily assume that they are worthy of perfecting their knowledge of Kabbalah, the way they would any wisdom.[113] However, since their intention is merely to show off, it follows that while reading Torah they exclude the part of *Peshat* (the simple meaning). For *Peshat* is something common to all people; there is no opportunity there for showing off. So for the main part, such an individual's business is making a name for himself in the three portions of *Derush, Remez, Sod*,[114] while ignoring the *Peshat*. Not so the one engaged in Torah for its own sake. Since Torah itself is beloved, all the matters of Torah are equal in his eyes: *Derush* and *Peshat*, *Remez* and *Sod*.

[To go back to the "show-off,"] even when it comes to the three portions [of *Remez, Derush, Sod*], his reading is selective. As the Sages, of blessed memory, commented upon the verse "He who keeps company with harlots, wastes wealth" [Proverbs 29:3], "Whoever says this saying is beautiful and this is not beautiful—wastes the wealth of Torah."[115] This fellow whose sole motivation is to show off, engages with only those portions that he presumes will bring him glory and honor in the eyes of people. As a result, the Torah does not sanctify his deeds, causing desecration of the Name of Heaven. Not only does such an individual not sanctify the Name of Heaven, by improving others, but the contrary, others become worse when they see his corrupt ways.

At the time that Israel crossed the Jordan River, they accepted upon themselves the principle of *'Arevut*, namely, that they are guarantors responsible for one another, as the Sages, of blessed memory, stated in [Tractate] *Sotah*.[116] *'Arevut* implies that each must be concerned with correcting his fellow Jew. So the aforementioned individual whose Torah learning corrupts others—as the Sages, of blessed memory, said in [Tractate] *Yoma*: "What would be an example of 'desecration of the Name'? Someone who reads and studies, and assists scholars, but is dishonest in business, and does not speak pleasantly to people… In regard to such a person, Scripture says, 'And when they came unto the nations, whither they came, they profaned My holy name, in that men said of them: These are the people of the Lord, and are gone forth out of His land'"[117]—stands in direct opposition to the covenant of *'Arevut* that was contracted at the Jordan River.

Now the Sages, of blessed memory, said: "The antelope has beautiful horns but its strength is not great."[118] One who pursues pleasant conversation and beauty but does not see fit to strengthen the holiness of his soul with the true power of Torah and fear [of the Lord], is likened to an antelope. Such a person studies only that which is esthetically pleasing to people, not that which will add eternal strength to his soul and to the assembly above, as it is written, "Give might to God."[119]

There is a hint in the word **"'orzila"** that the light (*'or*) of Torah is cheap (*zila*) in his eyes. One who learns Torah for its own sake recognizes the excellence of the Torah and its precious value, and knows how Torah conveys man to the most wonderful wholeness. For that reason, everything in the Torah is beloved and precious in his eyes, and Torah scholars are dear in his eyes, for he knows their value and honor. Such an individual is himself a precious light on account of the divine Torah in his heart. But the fellow who learns to show off, reducing Torah to a superficial ornament to dazzle people, does not recognize the treasure of Torah and its holiness. So in his eyes, she is cheap, though he does know a bit of her light. Thus, ***'or-zila***, a "cheap light."

that was as large **as Mount Tabor.** He will quickly abandon the words of Torah because he does not cling to the holiness of the Torah. He is like Mount Tabor, which came to study Torah (at Mount Sinai) for a brief time,[120] but the sanctity does not permanently reside in it. He does not learn gradually by toiling in Torah (*ʿamel ba-Torah*). He does not fulfill the dictum that "a person should first recite the words of the text and after conceptualize."[121] First one studies *Peshat* and afterwards *Remez*, *Derush* and *Sod*. "He does not want understanding, but only that his heart reveal itself."[122] [His goal is to reveal] that he knows much Torah, and "in all of Torah (*tushiyah*) he is famous."[123]

And how large **is Mount Tabor?** It is **four parasangs.** Though he only learns occasionally, he jumps about, swallowing—without peace of mind and gradual growth—from all the four sections of the Torah (*Peshat*, *Remez*, *Derush*, *Sod*).

However, since his entire motivation is to find favor and honor in the eyes of the world, **the length of its neck,** meaning its voice, is only **three parasangs.** Its voice is used for only three sections of the Torah, namely *Remez*, *Derush*, *Sod*, by which he can proclaim himself a great savant. But *Peshat* he tosses away, for there is no glory in that. He will not know the text of Bible and Mishnah.[124] Whatever he does study of *Peshat* is merely a stepping stone to be able to boast of the other three sections (of *Remez*, *Derush*, *Sod*), in order to make a name for himself.[125]

Even in regard to those three sections, his reading is selective. As the pious author of *Ḥovot ha-Levavot* (*Duties of the Heart*) pointed out in his introduction, the fool engages only in those parts [of Torah] that increase his status among his contemporaries.[126] So our *ʾorzila* is focused on only half of the three sections that he has studied. **The place where its head rests** was **a parasang and a half.** His head is in only half of what he studied: the half needed to dazzle folks. He sized up that in each of the three parts of Torah, there is a half that will gain recognition in the eyes of people, and another half that is of value only to the true lovers and students of Torah.

If someone engages in Torah for its own sake, he does not differentiate. Even those things that are necessary for people, he will engage in for the sake of heaven. *Par contre*, the *ʾorzila* selects only that which is necessary for people; that is his goal. So the Torah will not put him on the right way; it will not sanctify his ways. His ways and character traits are corrupt. Not only does he not fulfill the *ʿArevut* contracted at the Jordan River, which would entail aiding one's fellow man in observance of the Lord's commandments—the contrary, **it deposited feces and** thereby **dammed up the Jordan.** When he is presented with some test [of character] and his shame revealed, all will witness the putridity of his character. That will cause people to sin, damming up the purpose[127] of the Jordan, for he who causes others to sin, opposes the *ʿArevut* of the Jordan.

[108]This legend of Rabbah bar Bar Ḥannah also turns up in *b. Zevaḥim* 113b. There, the text is more explicit: *orzila de-reima*. See the discussion in *Tosafot*, *Bava Batra* 73b, s.v. *hakhi garsinan*, and *Zevaḥim* 113b, s.v. *orzila de-reima*. (It is interesting that the discredited reading of Rabbeinu Shmuel, *"orzila de-yama,"* has evidently been expunged by copyists from our commentary of Rashbam to *Bava Batra*.)

[109]Rav Kook once remarked on Rashi's two conflicting accounts of how the mythic salamander comes into being. At the conclusion of Tractate *Ḥagigah* (27a, and also *Sanhedrin* 63b), Rashi attributes it to the constant burning of a fire in a single spot for seven years. This contrasts with Rashi's explanation in *Ḥullin* 127a that it is produced from the fire by magic. Rav Kook came up with two distinct types of salamander, symbolic of two types of Torah scholars. One applies himself assiduously to the study of Torah for "seven years." This is the sort of Torah scholar that the Talmud (end *Ḥagigah*) compares to the salamander which is impervious to fire. The other type of Torah scholar is compared to a deceptive "magus who chants and does not know what he is saying" (*b. Sotah* 22a). Quoted in Rabbi Tsevi Yehudah Hakohen Kook, *Li-Sheloshah be-Elul*, vol. 1 (Jerusalem, 1938), par. 86 (pp. 37-38).

For various attempts by *Aḥaronim* to reconcile the seeming contradiction in Rashi, see Rabbi Nosson Slifkin, *Mysterious Creatures* (Israel, 2003), pp. 85-87.

As for the "chanting magus," Saul Lieberman supposed (based on the Arabic usage of a Christian sect) that the reference is to a Zoroastrian priest who chants the *Avesta* but does not understand what he is saying. See S. Lieberman, *Tosefta Ki-Fshutah*, Part 7, *Seder Nashim* (Jerusalem, 2007), *Hosafot*, p. 588. Other instances of *magus* as Talmud Bavli's designation for a Zoroastrian priest, are cited above note 96.

[110]*b. Megillah* 29a.

[111]*Peshat* is the simple meaning, *Remez*—hints embedded in various codes; *Derush*—homiletics; *Sod*—the secret or mystery, i.e. the inner, esoteric content. The acronym of these four methods of interpretation is *Pardes*.

For the historical development of *Pardes* as the four levels of Biblical exegesis, see Gershom G. Scholem, *On the Kabbalah and Its Symbolism* (New York, 1970), pp. 50-62 (especially pp. 57-59).

[112]*'Or Ne'erav*, Part 1, chap. 6.

[113]In *'Or Ne'erav* (Venice, 1587), Part I, chap. 6 (17a), Rabbi Moses Cordovero decries those who "study it [i.e. Kabbalah] other than for its own sake; and in their eyes a portion of this wisdom is equal to the brief acquaintance that they have with medicine, astronomy, logic, mathematics, and other wisdoms."

[114]Rav Kook employs the intials DRS for *Derush*, *Remez*, *Sod* (to the exclusion of *Peshat*). He may be alluding to the connubial behavior of an *'am ha-arets* (ignoramus) who proverbially attacks

his bride the way a lion "tears apart" (*dores*) its prey; see *b. Pesaḥim* 49b. Torah is likened to a *kallah* or bride. (See *Zohar* II, 5b.) Perhaps Rav Kook is hinting that the ignoramus dispenses with the preliminary *Peshat* and ravages the *Derush*, *Remez* and *Sod* of Torah.

[115]*b. 'Eruvin* 64a.

[116]*b. Sotah* 37b. A more apposite reference is *b. Sanhedrin* 43b. See also *y. Sotah* 7:5.

[117]Jeremiah 36:20; *b. Yoma* 86a.

[118]*Sifré, Ve-Zot ha-Berakhah* 12: "'His horns, the horns of an antelope'—The strength of the ox is great but its horns are not beautiful; an antelope has beautiful horns but its strength is not great."

[119]Psalms 68:35. See *Zohar* II, 32b; and Rabbi Ḥayyim of Volozhin, *Nefesh ha-Ḥayyim*, I, 3.

[120]*b. Megillah* 29a.

[121]*b. Shabbat* 63a. See Rashi there, s.v. *de-ligmar inish*.

[122]Proverbs 18:2.

[123]Proverbs 18:1. *Tushiyah* is a synonym for Torah (*b. Sanhedrin* 26b). See Rabbi David Altschuler, *Metsudat Zion* ad locum.

This quote from Proverbs was applied to Rav Kook himself in a laudatory fashion by his great-uncle Rabbi Mordechai Gimpel Jaffe; see Rabbi Moshe Tsevi Neriyah, *Tal ha-Rayah* (Tel-Aviv, 1993), p. 79. (Facsimile of the manuscript on page 77.)

[124]In another writing of Rav Kook, it becomes apparent that he subscribed to the notion of the Vilna Gaon that the levels of *Peshat* and *Sod*—in other words, the simplest and most esoteric readings of a text, or the lowest and highest worlds—unite. See *Shemonah Kevatsim* 1:871 and my discussion of that passage in Bezalel Naor, *The Limit of Intellectual Freedom: The Letters of Rav Kook* (Spring Valley, NY, 2011), pp. 208-210. The context is the dissimilar realms of Joseph (*Peshat-Sod*) versus Judah (*Remez-Derush*).

In the following paragraph (*SK* 1:872), Rav Kook writes that the "body of man, which is so material and lowly, corresponds to the theory of *Peshat* in the Torah and the world; and his soul, which is so lofty [and] spiritual…is from *Sod*." He goes on to speak of "the real power" ("*ha-ko'aḥ ha-re'ali*") of the *Peshat*, which is to unite with the "supernal loftiness" ("*ha-'atsilut ha-'elyonah*") of the *Sod*. In Kabbalah, *Sod* corresponds to the World of *Atsilut*.

Clearly, these are applications of literary theory to macrocosmos and microcosmos.

See now Biti Roi, "'And They Were Watering the Torah': The Gaon of Vilna and his Affinity to *Tiqqunei ha-Zohar*" (Hebrew), *Da'at* 79-80 (5775/2015), p. 67ff. Roi calls this interconnectedness of *Peshat* and *Sod* a "circular relation" (*yaḥas ma'agali*). She writes: "According to this conception, the relation between the four parts of *Pardes* is not hierarchical, as generally accepted, and the connection between the first level of *Peshat* and the last level of *Sod*, turns out to be a circular relation" (ibid., p. 70).

[125]Aramaic, *negid shemeh*. Taken from *m. Avot* 1:13.

[126]"I saw that even he who did interest himself in the study of the Law, applied himself only to those things which would make him wise in the eyes of fools, or would make him seem learned to those who pretend to be scholars" (Baḥya ben Joseph ibn Paquda, *The Book of Direction to the Duties of the Heart*, trans. Menaḥem Mansoor [Oxford, 1973], Introduction, p. 92).

[127]In Rav Kook's manuscript (and so it was transcribed in *Ma'amrei ha-Rayah*, p. 428), the word is spelled *"to'elet"* or purpose. Without the *vav*, the word could read *"te'alat"* or channel (of water). In context, the latter reading might make more sense.

The Frog, the Serpent and the Raven

5

And Rabbah b[ar] B[ar] Ḥ[annah] said: I have seen a certain frog that was as large **as the fort of Hagronya. And how** large **is the fort of Hagronya?** It is as large as **sixty houses. A serpent came and swallowed** the frog. **A raven came and swallowed the serpent, and** flew **up and sat in a tree. Come** and **see how great is the strength of the tree,** which could bear the weight of that raven. **Rav Pappa bar Samuel said: If I had not been there, I would not believe** it.

A MATRYOSHKA DOLL OF FROG, SERPENT AND RAVEN: LEVELS OF LOVE—AND CRUELTY

The main attribute of Torah is *ḥesed* (lovingkindness), as is written in the formula of the prayer: "For with the light of Your face, You gave us [Lord our God] the Torah of life and the love of kindness."[128] However, the completeness of Torah and the root of faith [require] that all the attributes be included therein in the Secret of Unity. Even the attribute of cruelty, when utilized for holiness, is something that completes the Torah.

At its root, *ḥesed* (love) works first to love oneself.[129] This too is an act of lovingkindness, as the Sages, of blessed memory, said in regard to preserving the body: "Let us perform a kindness with this poor thing, as it is written, 'He that does good to his own soul is a man of kindness (*ḥesed*).'"[130]

But sometimes it happens that Torah dictates that one must sacrifice oneself to a cruel death in order to sanctify the Name of Heaven.[131] If someone is possessed of good character traits, it is easy to sacrifice oneself if need be. But to act cruelly toward others is much more difficult and stands in opposition to good character traits. Nonetheless, if this is what the occasion calls for, it is said in this regard: "Cursed be he who stops his sword from [shedding] blood."[132] [The classic example is] Saul who failed because he took pity on Amalek.[133]

And yet this is not so heavy when the cruelty is directed again other nations. It is much heavier when the occasion calls for acting cruelly towards the sinners of the Children of Israel, who are literally "children" in the estimation of all who fear the Lord.[134] In such a regard, it was said: "His brothers he did not recognize and his children he did not acknowledge."[135] This is the extreme of cruelty. Yet it is not impossible for the whole individual. Not only does such behavior not distance one from wholeness; it actually crowns one's wholeness. Thereby, one ascends the Tree of Life.[136] From this, we can recognize the power of the "holy rigors" (*gevurot kedoshot*) that are included in our holy Torah. "The Torah was given with rigor."[137]

In truth, if one beholds from afar a person behaving in a cruel manner, one is unable to imagine that essentially that person's intention is for holiness and for true love. Only one who [himself] arrives at this [spiritual] level and sees how such a person's entire thought is only of love, believes that [the supposedly cruel person] is connected to the Tree of Life, which is the source of love and compassion—by way of the trait of cruelty.

I have seen a certain frog. The frogs sacrificed their lives for the sanctification of the Name in Egypt. As we say in [Tractate] *Pesaḥim*, Ḥananiah, Mishael and Azariah learned from the frogs (by *a fortiori* reasoning) that they too should sacrifice their lives for the sanctification of the Name [by submitting] to the fiery furnace.[138] **That was** as large **as the fort of Hagronya.** Which is to say that it included all types of rigors (*gevurot*). ("Sixty are the queens." This is the secret of the "sixty rods of fire." This is the secret of the rigors which are included in the six extremities [*ketsavot*], each consisting of ten.)[139] The name "Hagronya" derives from the Hebrew word *"garon"* ("throat").[140] The throat symbolizes the judgments (*dinim*). For that reason, ritual slaughter consists in [cutting] the throat. Thereby, we extract from it the judgments, and then [the animal] is permitted [to be eaten].[141]

And how large **is the fort of Hagronya?** It is as large as **sixty houses.** This alludes to the "sixty courthouses."[142] ["Sixty are the queens."[143] This is the secret of the "sixty rods of fire."[144] This is the secret of the rigors which are included in the six extremities (*ketsavot*),[145] each consisting of ten.][146] The point is that this aspect is [regnant] in the soul, whereby all the spiritual attributes are fired up with rigors, and one treats oneself cruelly by sacrificing one's life for the sanctification of the Name.

Still, that is merely cruelty to oneself. More pronounced than that, is assuming the attribute of cruelty toward others, for the sake of sanctifying the Name: to exact revenge from the enemies of the Lord. **A serpent came and swallowed** the frog. The frog's cruelty toward itself was "swallowed" up or surpassed by the cruelty of the serpent which was directed to others.

And all of this was yet as nothing compared to the cruelty toward one's own children: **A raven came and swallowed the serpent.**[147] This is a female raven, judgmental (*mele'ah dinim*) and cruel toward her fledglings, for the raven is cruel toward its own offspring.[148] Thus, the cruelties toward oneself [symbolized by the frog] and toward strangers [symbolized by the serpent] were "swallowed" or surpassed by the cruelty of the raven.

And with all that, the raven flew **up and sat in a tree.** This is the Tree of Life that yields the fruit of love and goodness in the world. For this unique individual's entire objective was love and the benefit of the entire world, by eliminating the thorns from the vineyard.[148*]

Come and **see how great is the strength of the tree,** which could bear the weight of that raven. All of those judgments (*dinim*) were for the end result of love (*ḥesed*). We can learn [from this] how great is the power of love that all these judgments were subsumed by it, [to the point that] they too are accounted as the lot of love.

Rav Pappa bar Samuel said: If I had not been there, I would not believe it. If I would not have arrived at this spiritual station, whereby I myself am capable of such action, I would not have believed it possible that all this [cruelty] could be done from the side of love and holiness.

[128]Conclusion of *Shemoneh 'Esreh* or *'Amidah* prayer.

[129]See Rabbi Eliezer Papo, *Pele Yo'ets*, s.v. *ahavat 'atsmo.*

[130]The reference is to the Midrash *Leviticus Rabbah* 34:3:

> "He that does good to his own soul is a man of kindness [and he that oppresses his own flesh is cruel]" [Proverbs 11:17].
>
> This could be said of Hillel the Elder, for when he would depart from his disciples, he would walk with them part of the way. [Unbeknown to them, he was on his way to the bath-house.]
>
> They said to him: 'Rabbi, where are you going?"
>
> He said to them: "To perform an act of lovingkindness with a guest in the house."
>
> They asked quizzically: "Every day you have a guest?"
>
> He answered them: "Is this poor soul not a guest in the house? Today she is here, tomorrow she will not be here."

[131]Writing in a halakhic vein, Rabbi Isaiah Halevi Horowitz (*"SheLaH ha-Kadosh"*) determined that one who is about to die a martyr's death should first recite the blessing, "Blessed are You, O Lord, our God, King of the Universe, who has sanctified us by His commandments and commanded us to sanctify His name in public." The halakhist found earlier support for his ruling in the *Piskei Halakhot* of Rabbi Menaḥem Recanati (Bologna, 1538), chap. 70. See Rabbi Isaiah Halevi Horowitz, *Shnei Luḥot ha-Berit, Sha'ar ha-'Otiyot, 'Ot Aleph*. The source in *Shnei Luḥot ha-Berit* was pointed out to the encyclopedist Tovia Preschel by RZYH Kook. See Tovia Preschel, *"Berakhah 'al Kiddush Hashem," HaDo'ar*, no. 37 (24 Elul 5730/1970), note 4; available at: www.toviapreschel.com/he/

[132]Jeremiah 48:10.

[133]1 Samuel chap. 15.

[134]Rav Kook follows the opinion of Rabbi Meir in *b. Kiddushin* 36a:

> The phrase "You are children" [Deuteronomy 14:1], how do they interpret it?
>
> It was taught in a *beraita*:
>
> "You are children to the Lord your God." When you behave as children, you are called "children"; when you do not behave as children, you are not called "children." These are the words of Rabbi Yehudah.
>
> Rabbi Meir says: Either way, you are called "children."

See Rav Kook's famous response to the criticisms of Rabbi Jacob David Ridbaz, in *Igrot ha-Rayah*, vol. 2, p. 194. There, Rav Kook writes that the *halakhah* is in accord with Rabbi Meir's opinion. He cites as sources the *Seliḥah* or penitential prayer *"Yisrael 'Amekha,"* composed by the Tosafist Rabbi Isaac ben Meir, and the Responsa of Rabbi Solomon ben Abraham ibn Adret (Rashba), nos. 194 and 242. At the conclusion of the second volume of *Igrot ha-Rayah,* the editor Rabbi Tsevi Yehudah Hakohen Kook provides additional sources for his father's halakhic decision. See ibid., pp. 343-344.

[135]Deuteronomy 33:9.

[136]The Tree of Life is synonymous with Torah: "She is a tree of life to those who uphold her, and her supporters are fortunate" (Proverbs 3:18).

[137]Cf. *Zohar* I, 243a; III, 80b.

[138]

> Thaddeus Man of Rome interpreted:
>
> What [precedent] did Ḥananiah, Mishael and Azariah see that they sacrificed themselves for the sanctification of the Name by submitting to the fiery furnace? They applied to themselves *a fiorti* reasoning from the frogs. If it is written of the frogs, who are not commanded concerning sanctification of the Name, "And the river shall swarm with frogs, which shall go up and come into your house, and into your bed-chamber, and upon your bed, and into the house of your servants, and upon your people, *and into your ovens*, and into your kneading-troughs" [Exodus 7:28]—all the more so we, who are commanded concerning sanctification of the Name!
>
> (*b. Pesaḥim* 53b)

[139]In the manuscript, there occur here Rav Kook's remarks concerning the significance of the number sixty. Since they are obviously displaced, I have placed them here between parentheses and relocated them to their proper place below, where they are bracketed.

[140]Cf. Rabbi Naḥman of Breslov, *Likkutei Moharan* I, 3.

[141]See Rabbi Ḥayyim Vital, *Sha'ar ha-Pesukim*, *Vayyeshev* (chap. 39), s.v. *ve-Yosef hurad Mitsraymah.*

[142]I have yet to find the source for this expression. In Kabbalah, there are "twenty-four [celestial] courts." See *Zohar* III, 136b; 293a.

[143]Song of Songs 6:8. It is possible that a scribal error has crept into Rav Kook's manuscript. The more apposite reference would be Song of Songs 3:7: "[Behold the bed of Solomon] sixty strong men [*gibborim*] surround it." This would establish the connection between the number sixty and the attribute of *"gevurot."* See *Pinkasei ha-Rayah*, vol. 3, p. 370, par. 6; and *Kevatsim mi-Ketav Yad Kodsho*, vol. 3, *Pinkas* 5:76. Cf. *Likkutei Moharan* I, 5, s.v. *masga shitin parsei.*

[144]*b. Ḥagigah* 15a. Rashi *ad locum* translates *pulsei* into Old French as *bastinado* or caning. See also *Bava Metsi'a* 85b and the *'Eyn Ya'akov* version of *Yoma* 77a. And see *Zohar* II, 51b, 66b; III, 60a and 270b. In *Ra'aya Mehemna* (in *Zohar* III, 263b) there is a single "rod of fire" (*pulsa de-nura).*

[145]The term *"shesh ketsavot"* (six extremities) first occurs in *Sefer Yetsirah* 1:13 and 4:3. In this instance, the reference is to the six *sefirot* of *Ḥesed, Gevurah, Tif'eret, Netsaḥ, Hod* and *Yesod.* They may be visualized as the six sides of a cube. In that scenario, the seventh *sefirah* of *Malkhut* would be an invisible point at the center of the cube. See Rabbi Judah Löw (Maharal of Prague), *Gevurot Hashem* (Jerusalem, 1971), Third Introduction (pp. 18-19) and chap. 70 (321b); idem, *Tif'eret Yisrael* (Jerusalem, 1970); chap. 40 (122a); and idem, *Derekh Ḥayyim* (Jerusalem, 1971), *Avot* 5:15 (255b). See *Sefer Yetzirah*, ed. Rabbi Aryeh Kaplan (York Beach, Maine: Samuel Weiser, 1997), pp. 87, 163-165.

One might be tempted to wonder aloud why Rav Kook does not mention that in the windpipe there are *six* rings (*shit 'izkin de-kaneh*). The answer is obvious: Those six rings of the windpipe do not symbolize in Kabbalah *gevurot.*

[146]In the manuscript, the bracketed words occurred in the preceding paragraph. See above note 139.

[147]It should be pointed out that similarly in the seafaring tale of Rav Yehudah the "Hindu" (referring not to his religion but rather his land of origin, India), the *"tanina"* or serpent (in this case, a sea serpent) is vanquished by a *"pushkantsa"* or raven. See *b. Bava Batra* 74b. Rav Kook's commentary extends only as far as the Rabbah bar Bar Ḥannah cycle.

[148]*b. 'Eruvin* 22a.

Rav Kook adopts the interpretation of Rashbam whereby *"pushkantsa"* is a female raven.

According to recent research, *"pushkantsa"* is actually a Pahlavi word: *paskuč*. In Armenian, *paskuč* is the mythic griffin. See Reuven Kiperwasser, "Rabba bar bar Ḥana's Voyages" (Hebrew), *Jerusalem Studies in Hebrew Literature* 22 (2008), pp. 232-233, note 67; and p. 234, note 74.

[148*]Cf. *b. Bava Metsi'a* 83b.

The Fish that Washed Ashore

6

R[abbah] b[ar] B[ar] Ḥ[annah] said: One time, we were traveling in a ship and we saw a certain fish in whose **nostril a mud-eater [*akhla tina*],** i.e. a type of insect, **had sat** and killed him. **And the waters thrust** the fish **and threw it upon the shore.**[149] **And sixty districts were destroyed by** the fish, **and sixty districts ate from it, and** another **sixty districts salted its** flesh to preserve it. **And they filled from one of its eyeballs three hundred flasks of oil. And when we returned** there **after** the **twelve months** of **the year** had passed, **we saw that they were cutting beams from its bones, and they had set out to build those districts** that had been destroyed.

PISCINE BONES TO PALATIAL BEAMS: THE *TIKKUN* OF THE ALIENATED TORAH SCHOLAR

This story informs us of the fate of a Torah scholar who, though corrupted, can still be rehabilitated. Though the ruin of a Torah sage who has spoiled is enormous, nonetheless the Torah said: "We save Aḥer (i.e. Elisha ben Abuyah) in the merit of his Torah," just as "we save the outer case of the Torah scroll together with the Torah scroll."[150]

As it is said in [Tractate] *Ḥagigah*: "'Gold and glass cannot equal it [neither shall the exchange thereof be vessels of fine gold]' [Job 28:17]. – Just as vessels of gold and vessels of glass, though broken, can still be repaired; so a Torah scholar, though he has spoiled, can still be repaired."[151]

The repair of the Torah scholar is compared to that of broken glass to teach the enormity of the damage. Truthfully, gold too, once broken, can be repaired, so why the [additional] illustration of glass? The brokenness of gold does not detract so much from its excellence, for it is yet gold, but glass—its main perfection is its form, and when its form has been corrupted, then for the time being, it is a total loss. And despite that, through work and refining, it can be repaired.

This teaches that though [the Torah scholar was] extremely corrupted, nevertheless there is in the holiness of the Torah a wonderful power, capable of uplifting him [i.e. the Torah scholar] from the depths of the earth and returning him to holiness. Even Do'eg and Aḥitophel eventually enter the World to Come.[152] This is because the holiness of the Torah hovers [over him] and does not allow the corruption to take complete control over the soul to the point of extinction. Though one might strengthen the power of impurity's hold over oneself, God forbid—nonetheless, the inner holiness that has been absorbed in the soul from the light of Torah, works to offer one hope at the end. "Though the root thereof wax old in the earth, and the stock thereof die in the ground—yet through the scent of water it will bud, and put forth boughs like a plant."[153]

One time, we were traveling in a ship to survey the affairs of souls traversing the sea. But whereas souls within bodies are referred to as "passengers on ships,"[154] those souls that have already been stripped of the body are compared to fish: **and we saw a certain fish.** Rabbah bar Bar Ḥannah commences to speak of the condition of the soul of a Torah scholar whose ways were greatly corrupted.

It is known that the essence of man is in the nose upon which the vitality depends. In the words of the *Zohar*: "By the nose, the face is known."[155] In addition, the sense of smell is synonymous with the light of wisdom, for the olfactory sense is more spiritual than the other senses. As the Sages, of blessed memory, said: "What is something from which the soul derives pleasure, but the body does not derive pleasure? This is fragrance."[156]

It happened that a Torah scholar had an evil thought that invaded his intellect[157]: **in** whose **nostril a mud-eater [*akhla tina*],** i.e. a type of insect, **had sat** and killed him.

Thence his deeds were so corrupt that he was thrust from the holiness of the Torah.[158] **And the waters thrust** the fish. As stated in the *Zohar*, if someone is not worthy of the light of the holy Torah, there are several snakes and scorpions guarding the way to the Tree of Life, that sting him.[159] And if someone is much corrupted, one is pushed away from the Torah. And in turn, all his deeds are corrupted.

It is known that each tractate of the [sixty tractates of the] Talmud contains distinct deeds and a unique area of holiness. When a man learns Torah and observes her, he settles [the sector of] the world corresponding to the section of holiness of that tractate. [Contrariwise,] when one corrupts one's ways, then **sixty districts were destroyed.** A district is more comprehensive than a city. The *sefirah* of *Malkhut* is referred to as "the city of [our] God."[160] This is a reference to the literal sense of the Mishnah.[161] Now when one expands [upon the Mishnah] with *pilpul* (dialectic) and Torah novellae, each "city" develops into a "district." And all sixty districts were destroyed.

The many Torah novellae that one developed [fall into two categories.] Some are appropriate for a certain time. Others are eternal, appropriate in every generation. The latter are not perishable, but they may lose their vitality.

Sixty districts ate from it, meaning from the concepts of Torah that were time-sensitive. **And** another **sixty districts salted its** flesh to preserve it. The "salted flesh" refers to those words of Torah worthy of enduring throughout the generations.

In Torah, there are these two categories: Things that are worthy of enduring forever, so there are found many *halakhot* that will not change from their fixed state, for thus were they established, to be an eternal covenant. [Then] there are *halakhot* that change in their rulings from one generation to the next depending on its leaders and what seems appropriate to the "judge who is in your days."[162]

Everyone who toils in Torah and develops Torah novellae,[163] has a portion in both of the categories.

Now this is in the practical part of the Torah, summed up by the "six extremities" (*Ḥesed*, *Gevurah*, *Tif'eret*, *Netsaḥ*, *Hod*, *Yesod*) in the six orders [of the Mishnah], which then break down into sixty tractates, symbolized by "sixty districts."

However, the theoretical, intellectual part [of the Torah] is represented by the three *sefirot* of *Ḥokhmah* (Wisdom), *Binah* (Understanding) and *Da'at* (Knowledge), which are above the "six extremities." Even though [this renegade Torah scholar] removed one eye [from Torah] and beheld with it the pleasures of this world, nevertheless it is the natural inclination of the wise man to engage in intellectual pursuits,[164] so that eye too was of use: **They filled from one of its eyeballs three hundred flasks of oil.** The oil symbolizes the oil of wisdom,[165] which is full of the three aspects of *Ḥokhmah* (Wisdom), *Binah* (Understanding) and *Da'at* (Knowledge). These three aspects are expressed as three *hundreds*. When discussing the practical, the numerical expression was sixty or six *tens*. Now that the discussion focuses on the theoretical, the symbolic expression is hundreds.

Still, this entire discussion is restricted to the benefit that others derived from the renegade Torah scholar though he himself was corrupted. The prime example is Aḥer (i.e. Elisha ben Abuyah), from whose mouth Rabbi Meir nonetheless imbibed Torah.[166]

However, the holiness of the Torah availed the Torah scholar himself, ensuring that he would not be totally rejected. But only after he underwent a catharsis, could his inner essence[167] effect that he return in a reincarnation. Then, that essential power of Torah contained in him would act upon him in his reincarnated state, enabling him to fix all that he had destroyed [in his previous lifetime]. For in the final analysis, his powers are great. **And when we returned** there **after** the **twelve months** of **the year** had passed, **we saw that they were cutting beams from its bones, and they had set out to build those districts** that had been destroyed. They saw that twelve months after [the Torah scholar's passing], by which time he had been somewhat purified in the crucible of suffering, he returned to the world [reincarnated]. Or that above, the method of his *tikkun* (spiritual correction) was arranged: Through the essential holiness of Torah absorbed in him, he would strive to repair and rebuild all that he had destroyed.

But it seems that **twelve months** were required to break down the [spiritual] poison, in order that the holiness of the Torah be activated after the decomposition of the body.[168]

Either the Torah scholar returned in a body, or in several *nitsotsot* ("sparks"),[169] in conformity with the ways of the divine governance. Thus, he repairs all that he destroyed. An inexact analogy would be the Faithful Shepherd (i.e. Moses) returning to fix the Mixed Multitude.[170] Consult also the *Sefer ha-Gilgulim* (Book of Reincarnations), whereby a Torah scholar reincarnates many times over because he is not sentenced so much to Gehinnom.[171]

[149]Rabbeinu Gershom writes that the sea threw the dead fish to the shore "because the sea tolerates in its midst nothing disgusting (*shum mi'us*)." In Rashbam's transcription, this has become "a dead object" (*davar met*). The comment seems gratuitous.

With the passage of time, scholars increasingly come to appreciate the Persian or Zoroastrian background of these tales of Rabbah bar Bar Ḥannah. In the Zoroastrian religion, water *per se* is sacred. See Eli Aḥdut, "Jewish-Zoroastrian Polemics in the Babylonian Talmud," *Irano-Judaica* IV (1999), Hebrew Section, pp. 36-38 (discussing *b. Ta'anit* 5b). More recently, Reuven Kiperwasser wrote (regarding the third legend) that the King's ire was aroused by Hurmiz's sacrilege of the water when he juggled two cups of water. (Kiperwasser follows the reading of "water" found in manuscript. In our printed editions we have "two cups of wine." For variants, see Rabbi Raphael Nathan Nata Rabbinovicz, *Dikdukei Soferim*, *Bava Batra*, Munich 1881.) See Reuven Kiperwasser, "Rabba bar bar Ḥana's Voyages" (Hebrew), *Jerusalem Studies in Hebrew Literature* 22 (2008), p. 231.

Did Rabbeinu Gershom, a millennium ago, already suspect a Persian provenance to the Rabbah bar Bar Ḥannah legends recorded in the Babylonian Talmud? The third legend concerning Hurmin or Hurmiz (known to be Persian names referring to the Zoroastrian gods Ahriman and Ahura Mazda respectively) might have alerted Rabbeinu Gershom.

[150]*y. Ḥagigah* 2:1; *Ecclesiastes Rabbah* 7:8.

[151]*b. Ḥagigah* 15a. Found also in *Ecclesiastes Rabbah* 7:8 with slight variants. The wayward Elisha ben Abuyah (a.k.a. Aḥer) is credited (by Rabbi Akiva) with this interpretation of the verse.

[152]This is the opinion of anonymous *"doreshei reshumot"* in *y. Sanhedrin*, chap. 10, end *halakhah* 2; and *b. Sanhedrin* 104b-105a. Do'eg and Aḥitophel are examples of Torah scholars who turned bad. See Rabbi Shelomo Eliashov, *Hakdamot u-She'arim* (Piotrków, 1909), 6:9 (29d-30d). The Ḥasidic master Rabbi Zadok Hakohen (Rabinowitz) of Lublin wrote at length on the unique perception of the*"doreshei reshumot"*; see his *Maḥshevot Ḥaruts* (Piotrków, 1912), 45a-b, 85c; and idem, *Takkanat ha-Shavin* (Beit El, 1988), 55a, 218, 220b, 221b-222a.

[153]Job 14:8-9.

[154]Hebrew, *"holkhei ha-yam ba-'oniyot."* Cf. Psalms 107:23: *"yordei ha-yam ba-'oniyot."*

Zohar (II, 199a) likens the body of man to a ship. Jonah's embarcation upon the boat is symbolic of the soul's descent into the body.

> Jonah who descends to the ship, this is the soul of man that descends to this world to be in the body of man ....
>
> And then, man goes in this world as a ship in the midst of the Great Sea that threatens to be broken, as it says, "And the ship threatened to be broken" [Jonah 1:4].

So too in *Tikkunei Zohar* (*tikkun* 21). See *Tikkunei Zohar* (Vilna, 1867), f. 60, and comment of the Vilna Gaon there, s.v. *de-sa'arat gufa de-bar nash de-'inun Yisrael.*

In the Vilna Gaon's reading of the Book of Jonah (inspired by *Zohar*), Jonah's maritime adventure is a trope for everyman's spiritual journey in this world. Besides being the proper name of a man, *Yonah* in Hebrew is a dove, a symbol of the soul. The Gaon provides several rationales for this symbolism. See Rabbi Elijah of Vilna, *Peirush 'al Yonah* (Vilna, 1800), Jonah 1:1.

In *b. Berakhot* 3a, Rabbi Yosé hears a voice from heaven "cooing as a dove" (*menahemet ke-yonah*).

The *Zohar*'s own explanation for the soul being referred to as "*yonah*" (derived from the verse in Leviticus 25:17) is roundabout.

At the onset of his commentary to the Legends of Rabbah bar Bar Ḥannah, the Gaon references his commentary to the Book of Jonah, explaining that "this world is called 'the sea' and the body is called a 'ship,' and through it the soul descends into the sea of this world; and those who constantly engage in the affairs of this world are called 'seafarers' (*yordei ha-yam*) for they study the vicissitudes of this world." Rabbi Elijah of Vilna, *Peirush 'al Kamah Aggadot* (Vilna, 1800), 1a.

[155]*Zohar* III, 137b. (The source of this concept is *m. Yevamot* 16:3; *b. Yevamot* 120a.) In *Pinkas 15*, a journal written at approximately the same period as the commentary to the legends of Rabbah bar Bar Ḥannah, Rav Kook expands upon this theme:

> The spirit of life is in the nose. "By the nose, the face is known," for there is the residence of the *ru'aḥ*, which is the main level of man. For the *nefesh* is below man's level, and the *neshamah* above him, and his main interest is the *ru'aḥ*.
>
> (*Pinkesei ha-Rayah*, vol. 3, ed. Rabbi Levi Yitsḥaki [Jerusalem, n.d. (2011)], 15:73 [p. 122])

See further ibid. 16:37 (pp. 224-226).

On the centrality of *ru'aḥ* in Rav Kook's system (as in that of the Vilna Gaon), see below note 299 and our Appendix, "The Vilna Gaon on the Three Levels of the Soul."

[156]*b. Berakhot* 43b.

[157]The simple meaning of *akhla-tina* is a "mud-eater," name of a parasitic worm in fish. *Tina* in this context means "mud." However, Rav Kook plays with the word *tina*, ascribing to it its other meaning of an "impure thought." Cf. *b. Ḥagigah* 15b and *Sanhedrin* 75a.

[158]Though not spelled out, evidently Rav Kook relies on the rabbinic adage: "There is no 'water' but Torah" (*b. Bava Kamma* 17a). Thus, the fish cast away by the waters of the sea symbolizes the soul of the renegade Torah scholar rejected by the holiness of the Torah.

[159]*Zohar* II, 17b.

[160]Psalms 48:2; *Zohar* II, 235a; III, 5a.

[161]See *b. Beitsah* 28b: "*Matnitin malketa*" ("*Mishnah* queen"). Also *Numbers Rabbah* 18:21: "'Sixty are the queens' [Song of Songs 6:8]—Sixty tractates." And in *Canticles Rabbah* 6:8: "These are sixty tractates of *Halakhot*."

See Rabbi Shneur Zalman of Liadi, *Torah 'Or, Ḥayyei Sarah*, s.v. *vayyetse Yitsḥak lasu'aḥ ba-sadeh* (17b): "*Mishnah* is referred to as 'city' and *Beraita* is referred to as 'country.'"

[162]See Rashi, Deuteronomy 17:9, quoting *Sifré* and *b. Rosh Hashanah* 25b.

In *Ma'amrei ha-Rayah*, vol. 2 (1984) this sensitive passage was fleshed out by the editors so as not to allow an antinomian or Reform reading of Rav Kook's words. In *Ma'amrei ha-Rayah*, the sentence reads:

> *Halakhot* (laws) that will never change, for they were established as an everlasting covenant; and *halakhot* (laws) that change in the *hora'ot sha'ah* (*ad hoc* rulings) of the *ḥakhmei ha-Torah* (Torah sages), the leaders of the generation, "the judge who is in your days."

Rav Kook wrote much on the concept of "*hora'at sha'ah*" (*ad hoc* ruling) and the legitimate power of the *Halakhah* to adapt to changing situations. See Rabbi Abraham Isaac Hakohen Kook, *Li-Nevukhei ha-Dor*, ed. Rabbi Shaḥar Raḥmani (Tel-Aviv, 2014), chap. 13 (especially pp. 89-90); and idem, *'Arpalei Tohar* (Jerusalem, 1983), p. 15 = *Shemonah Kevatsim* 2:30.

For a crucial difference between the *hora'at sha'ah* of a prophet and that of a *beit din* (court), see idem, *Mishpat Kohen* (Jerusalem, 1937), no. 144 (p. 343), and *Shmu'ot Rayah: Bereshit—Shemot*, ed. Rabbi Yeshayahu Hadari (Jerusalem, 2015), *Va'era* 5692 (pp. 241-242).

Rabbi Mordechai Yosef Leiner of Izbica referred to the eternal laws of Torah as "*kelalim*" (generalities) and the ephemeral aspects as "*peratim*" (specifics). See *Mei ha-Shilo'aḥ*, Part One (Vienna, 1860), *Mas'ei*, s.v. *ken mateh b'nei Yosef doverim* (56a). (In *Mei ha-Shilo'aḥ*, Part Two [Lublin, 1922], *Beha'alotekha*, s.v. *'al pi Hashem yaḥanu* [29a], this thinking was applied to the practice of the Yehudi ha-Kadosh who did not adhere to the times of prayer set by the *halakhah*!) And see the expansion upon this teaching in the work of a student of Rabbi Isaac Hutner, Rabbi Yitsḥak Alster, *'Olat Yitsḥak*, Part Two (Jerusalem, 2005), *No'aḥ*, p. 11.

[163]In *Ma'amrei ha-Rayah* there were added these cautionary words: "from the source of 'eternal life that the Lord planted in our midst' and 'showed Moses on Sinai.'"

The former quote was adapted from the blessing recited after reading from the Torah. The latter quote is a a conflation of *y. Pe'ah* 2:4 ("Even that which a diligent student will in the future pronounce before his master, was already said to Moses on Sinai") and *b. Megillah* 19b ("The Holy One, blessed be He, showed Moses *Dikdukei Torah* and *Dikdukei Soferim*, and what the scribes will in the future innovate").

[164]Cf. Rabbi Shneur Zalman of Liadi, *Tanya* I, 15 (21a) regarding the natural proclivity of the scholarly type.

[165]Oil is a symbol of wisdom (*ḥokhmah*). In his commentary to the tenth legend, Rav Kook will adduce the verse in Proverbs 21:20: "There is desirable treasure and oil in the dwelling of the wise." For Kabbalistic sources, see Rabbi Moses Cordovero, *Pardes Rimonim* 23:21, s.v. *shemen*; Rabbi Shneur Zalman of Liadi, *Tanya* I, 53 (75a); Rabbi Menaḥem Mendel Shneurson of Lubavitch, *Derekh Mitsvotekha* (Brooklyn, 1973), *Mitsvat Ner Ḥanukkah*, chap. 1 (72a).

[166]*b. Ḥagigah* 15b. Though Elisha ben Abuyah became a heretic, his devoted disciple Rabbi Meir continued to study Torah at his feet. In justification of Rabbi Meir's behavior, it was said: "Rabbi Meir found a pomegranate; its inside he ate, its peel he threw away" (ibid.).

Rabbi Moshe Tsevi Neriyah heard from his master Rav Kook the following analysis of the parable. Why, asked Rav Kook, a pomegranate? Why not a citrus fruit? Citrus fruits also have a peel. Rav Kook's answer was that in addition to the thick outer husk, in the interior the pomegranate has a thin membrane separating the seed chambers. This requires greater discernment. Everyone is capable of separating the thick peel from the fruit on the inside, but only a Rabbi Meir possessed the discernment necessary to separate between the thin interior membrane and the fruit. (Transmitted by Rabbi Neriyah to Rabbi Ya'akov Fisher in oral conversation.)

[167]The Hebrew word for essence, "*'atsmut*," is related to the word for bone: *'etsem*. Momentarily, we shall see how the "bones" of the fallen Torah scholar contributed to the work of reconstruction.

[168]Hebrew, *'ikul ha-guf*. See *b. Shabbat* 152b that "after twelve months *the body is nullified*" ("*ha-guf batel*"). Earlier on that page of the Talmud the term employed is "*'ikul ha-basar*" ("decomposition of the flesh"). See further Rabbi Ezekiel Landau, *Tsiyun le-Nefesh Ḥayah* to *Berakhot* 18b, s.v. *shanei kevurah be-maḥatselet shel kanim*; and Rabbi Yeḥiel Ya'akov Weinberg, *Pinui 'Atsmot Metim* (Berlin, 1926), p. 15.

That "*'ikul ha-basar*" ("decomposition of the flesh") results in atonement for the deceased is implicit in *b. Sanhedrin* 46a. See Rashi ibid. s.v. *nit'akel ha-basar*. This theme is greatly expanded upon in *Zohar* II, 151a. See the note of Rabbi Reuven Margaliyot in *Nitsutsei Zohar* there.

[169]In the latter scenario, "sparks" of the Torah scholar's soul would be distributed in coming generations in *several* bodies.

[170]Rabbi Ḥayyim Vital, *Sefer ha-Likkutim*, *Va-'Etḥanan*, s.v, *Vayit'abber Hashem bi lema'ankhem* (II); Rabbi Joseph Ḥayyim of Baghdad, *Ben Yehoyada'*, *Bava Batra* 73b, s.v. *ve-khi hadran le-batar treisar yarḥei*.

[171]This is the passage in *Sefer ha-Gilgulim* (Frankfurt am Main, 1684), chap. 6 (6a):

> There is another [reason] why the wicked reincarnates but three times and the righteous thousands. It has to do with what they said about Elisha Aḥer: "Let us

> not judge him and let him not enter the World to Come" [*b. Ḥagigah* 15b]. The concept is what the Sages, of blessed memory, said: "The fire of Gehinnom does not rule over Torah scholars" [*b. Ḥagigah* 27a]. So what should they do to purge their sins? Therefore, the Holy One, blessed be He, chose for the righteous and the Torah scholars many *gilgulim* (reincarnations) rather than the punishment of Gehinnom. And corresponding to the number of their sins and their severity, is the number of reincarnations.
>
> Furthermore, they profit from the reincarnation, for every time they reincarnate, they add merits. So the result is that the reincarnation is beneficial, which is not the case in Gehinnom.
>
> However, the wicked over whom rules the fire of Gehinnom, enters there and purges his sins. And Gehinnom is better for him than entering into several reincarnations, because every time, on the contrary, he would add sin to crime, and would perish from the world without possibility of rehabilitation.

In the parallel passage in *Sha'ar ha-Gilgulim*, Introduction 4, Rabbi Ḥayyim Vital writes:

> We shall explain the reason for the aforementioned difference between the righteous and the wicked. It is to be understood based on what the Sages, of blessed memory, said concerning Elisha Aḥer: "We shall not judge him because he engaged in Torah" (*b. Ḥagigah* 15b). Behold, the righteous who engages in Torah—especially of the early ones—is not judged in Gehinnom, and since he is forced to have his sins purged before he enters the Garden of Eden, he has no correction other than *gilgul* (reincarnation) .... Therefore, he is reincarnated several times to atone for and correct his sins. This is not the case regarding a wicked man, who enters Gehinnom, where all his sins are cleansed together, so that he has no need to return in reincarnations.

Cf. earlier Rabbi Joseph Karo, *Maggid Meisharim* (Vilna, 1875), Job 32 (52d): "But the mystery of the matter [is] that a man who fears sin, reincarnates three times, to purify him, but one who does not fear sin, reincarnates only two times, so that he will not be corrupted the third time, which would be counterproductive...."

The Fish Mistaken for an Island

7

Rabbah b[ar] B[ar] Ḥ[annah] said: One time, we were traveling on a ship and we saw a certain fish upon whose back sand had settled, and grass grew on it. We assumed that **it was dry land and went up and baked and cooked on the back** of the fish, **but when its back** grew **hot, it turned over. And were it not for the fact that the ship was close by, we would have drowned.**

THE COOKOUT THAT WAS WASHED OUT: WHEN NOT TO EMULATE A HOLY MAN

In the first story concerning the wave that sinks the ship, I explained the symbolism of sinking the ship: the nullification of practical commandments. When one is immersed exclusively in intellect and thought, this is the beginning of sin. However, it is written in *Mikdash Melekh* that there are great souls engaged in thought, such as Rabbi Shim'on ben Yoḥai and his companions, who are exempt from the commandments,[172] as we say in the first chapter of [Tractate] *Shabbat*: "But individuals such as us must interrupt [Torah study] for reciting the *Shema'* and for prayer."[173] From this, we learn that there can be a great man whose level and ways we are not to emulate.

Now it sometimes happens that a person observes the behavior of the great man in regard to the material plane, and [unbeknown to the untrained observer, the great man] is navigating in his mind lofty matters. He does all for the sake of Heaven, and all his days his concern is only bringing pleasure to his Creator. All his days are as holy as the Sabbath,[174] so he may derive physical pleasure from this world, the way the Sages said: "Whoever wishes to pour a wine libation upon the altar, let him fill the throats of Torah scholars with wine."[175] But one must know that below the surface of the material plane, the great man is navigating a single thought; his thought is fixated on the Lord, blessed be He. Nothing comes between him and that thought.[176] Other people, when they derive pleasure from this world, are sullied by material affairs and cannot rise up.[177]

In *Likkutei Torah* by the Gaon Rabbi Shneur Zalman, you will find similar ideas regarding the level of such holy people. The author compares them to fish that swim without having to proceed gradually.[178] And see the *Saba* in the portion *Mishpatim*.[179]

This **fish** we should not emulate. It is apparent to all that his conduct is holy, but it is a difficult service that cannot be copied. Only on certain occasions, when he must learn with his disciples, does he lower his level a bit and exhibit some this-worldliness and materialism. In this way, a person who is not on his level might come to emulate him, [thinking] to perfect himself by adopting his customs, but then that person will sink into this-worldly matters.[180] He is also in danger[181] of losing his [level of] holiness, because he will become lax in his observance of practical commandments, while lacking the ability to grasp on to wisdom. Therefore one must return to one's [previous] level; to serve [God] physically according to the exoteric Torah, and to be punctual in the bodily observance of the commandments.

Once we were traveling on a ship, to examine the matters of wisdom while garbed in the material (as I have written several times).[182] **And we saw a certain fish,** namely a holy man, a [spiritual] giant, such as Rabbi Shim'on ben Yoḥai and his companions. **Upon whose back sand had settled.** There is the figure of the "front" and the figure of the "back." The "back" symbolizes the lowering [of the spiritual level] necessary to perfect the other. From the aspect of the "backside," Rabbah bar Bar Ḥannah observed in the great man's behavior some materialism. But in reality, the great man's thought was devoted to lofty matters, to perfect the holy service according to the wisdom revealed to him.

We assumed that **it was dry land,** and that the wise man was engaging in simple matters, and we copied his actions. **And went up,** we thought we ascended to a high [spiritual] level. **And baked and cooked on the back** of the fish. We engaged in material pursuits, and in emulation of the great man (whose main pursuit is Torah and wisdom), we did not engage that much in practical commandments. **But when its back** grew **hot,** and the fire in his bones[183] was aroused by the supernal sanctity in his heart, **it turned over.** He was immediately turned into another man, for this is the trait of these high holy beings. They have no need of gradual growth, for in all their deeds they cling to the Lord, blessed be He. Then we saw that we cannot emulate his behavior, because it is beyond us. We were lost, **and were it not for the fact that the ship was close by,** which is to say that we did not distance ourselves from the simple sense of the Torah and performance of the practical commandments through [bodily] service[184]—that shielded us from the flood of water—**we would have drowned** in the sea, for the high holy beings are compared to fish in the sea, who are in no need of sea vessels. They sail with their wisdom and their holiness, though their study of Torah and intellectual pursuits results in decreased performance of commandments—as was the case of Rabbi Shim'on ben Yoḥai and his companions.

But individuals such as us must perfect ourselves through the vessel of the body and its service. The body will act as a ship,[185] to "traverse the seaways."[186] Not drifting far from the ship is what spared our lives.

[172]The editors of *Ma'amrei ha-Rayah* refer the reader to *Mikdash Melekh*, vol. 1, f.179. *Mikdash Melekh* is a commentary to *Zohar* by Rabbi Shalom Buzaglo. It was first published in Amsterdam in 1750. In that edition, to *Zohar*, *Vayyeshev*, 179b, we find the following: "It is known that there are souls that come as an *'ibbur* ("impregnation") to aid the righteous. In regard to them it is written, 'The dead are free' [Psalms 88:6], for they are not subjugated to the evil inclination. They are not close to reward, but they are far from punishment."

Cf. the saying of Rabbi Yoḥanan in *b. Shabbat* 30a, 151b and *Niddah* 61b: "'The dead are free'—Once a man dies, he is freed of the commandments."

[173]*b. Shabbat* 11a. Whereas Rabbi Shim'on ben Yoḥai and his companions interrupt only for reciting *Shema'*, but not for prayer. *Ibid.* In *y. Shabbat* 1:2, Rabbi Yoḥanan quotes Rabbi Shim'on ben Yoḥai as saying: "The likes of us who are busy with the study of Torah, do not interrupt even for the recitation of *Shema'*."

In *'Arpalei Tohar*, Rav Kook wrote: "There are certain righteous (*tsaddikim*) who, according to their level, do not need to pray or to learn except at intervals [such as Rav Yehudah]." In the original, preserved in *Shemonah Kevatsim* 2:34, the words "Rav Yehudah" are missing. They were supplied (evidently for the sake of clarification) in the 1983 edition of *'Arpalei Tohar* (p. 16). As pointed out in Rabbi Shilat's endnotes to *Arpalei Tohar*, the reference is to *b. Rosh Hashanah* 35a: "Rav Yehudah would pray every thirty days." Rashi *ad loc.* explains that Rav Yehudah would complete his study of Talmud every thirty days (allowing free time to pray).

[174]See *Ra'aya Mehemna* in *Zohar* III, 29a: "The soul of the Torah scholar is called Sabbath Queen." Furthermore, there is a statement attributed to Rabbi Isaac Luria that the food consumed on the Sabbath does not corporealize; see Rabbi Jacob Zemaḥ, *Leḥem min ha-Shamayim* (Munkatsh, 1905), 21a, s.v. *kol mah*, and Rabbi Samuel Bornstein of Sokhatchov, *Shem mi-Shmuel*, *Koraḥ* 5670 [1910].

The indefatigable Torah scholar Rabbi Moshe Zuriel *shelit"a* shared with me that at the conclusion of the *Idra Rabba*, Rabbi Shim'on bar Yoḥai is compared to the Sabbath; see *Zohar* III, 145a. Furthermore, the numerical value of "*Shim'on bar Yoḥai*" (702) equals the numerical value of "*Shabbat*" (702). Finally, Rabbi Zuriel observed that the saga of Rabbi Shim'on bar Yoḥai is contained in the Tractate *Shabbat* (*b. Shabbat* 33b-34a).

[175]*b. Yoma* 71a.

[176]Cf. Maimonides, *Guide of the Perplexed* III, 52; quoted in the gloss of Rabbi Moses Isserles to *Shulḥan 'Arukh*, *Oraḥ Ḥayyim* 1:1.

It is told that during the year that Rav Kook studied in the Volozhin Yeshivah, the lamp by which he read at night in his room had written upon it the words from Psalms 16:8: "*Shiviti Hashem le-negdi tamid*" ("I have set the Lord before me always"). See Rabbi Moshe Tsevi Neriyah, *Siḥot ha-Rayah* (Tel-Aviv, 1979), pp. 100-101.

[177]Rav Kook does not point to any concrete examples from the annals of Jewish history. To this reader (BN), the description conjures up the image of the Ḥasidic master Rabbi Israel Friedman of Ruzhin (1796-1850). The Ruzhiner was legendary for his opulent courtly lifestyle which perplexed many of his contemporaries. To the outside observer, lacking the key to the inner sanctum of this enigmatic personality, the Ruzhiner's behavior would have been more appropriate for an Austrian aristocrat than a Ḥasidic Rebbe!

Inter alia, Rav Kook's only son, Rabbi Tsevi Yehudah, enjoyed excellent relations with several descendants of the Ruzhin dynasty, most notably Rabbi Israel Friedman of Chortkov, who held court in Vienna between the two world wars. The Rebbes of Ruzhin and Rav Kook saw eye to eye concerning the supreme importance of Erets Yisrael. See my introduction to *Orot* (Maggid, 2015); Rabbi Shelomo Aviner, *Tsevi Kodesh*, vol. 1 (Beit El, 2005), pp. 127-129 (concerning the Rebbes of Chortkov, Husiatyn, Boyan and Sadigora); *Rabbeinu: Harav Tsevi Yehudah Hakohen Kook* (pictorial album), ed. Rabbis Shelomo Aviner and Ze'ev Neuman (Jerusalem, 2004), pp. 118-119 (concerning Rabbi Moshe Friedman, Boyaner Rebbe of Cracow). A facsimile of RZYH Kook's letter to his father concerning his meeting with the Chortkover Rebbe in Vienna, is contained in Menaḥem Kempinski's biography of Rabbi Meir Yeḥiel Shapira, *Me-Ruzhin le-Tsiyon* (Har Berakha, 2010), p. 81.

[178]Rabbi Shneur Zalman of Liadi, *Likkutei Torah*, *Shemini*, s.v. *Livyatan zeh yatsarta lesaḥek bo*. The *Alter Rebbe* speaks there of the righteous who are likened to "*nunei yama*" ("fish of the sea"). The paradigm is Rabbi Shim'on bar Yoḥai. See Bezalel Naor, "Plumbing Rav Kook's Panentheism" in *From A Kabbalist's Diary* (Spring Valley, NY, 2005), pp. 127 and 131, n. 27. The essay appeared earlier in *Engaging Modernity: Rabbinic Leaders and the Challenge of the Twentieth Century*, ed. Moshe Z. Sokol (Northvale, NY, 1997), pp. 79-89.

See further Rabbi Shneur Zalman's primary disciple, Rabbi Aharon Halevi Horowitz of Staroselye, *'Avodat ha-Levi*, Genesis-Exodus-Leviticus (Lemberg, 1861), *Derushim li-Keri'at Yam Suf*, s.v. *lehavin 'inyan keri'at Yam Suf* (25d):

> There they are "fish of the sea" (*nunei yama*). As it is known, there are creatures whose vitality is the water, and it is not within their ability to be separated from there for even a moment because of their nature to unite with their [source of] vitality. Should they be separated on land, they would immediately die. This is the soul of Moses, who was on the level of "*Mah*" ("What") [Exodus 16:7], the essence of nullification (*bittul*) to his [source of] vitality, and so too, several righteous individuals (*tsaddikim*), such as Rabbi Shim'on ben Yoḥai and Rav Hamnuna Saba.

Moses was drawn from the water (Exodus 2:10). Rav Hamnuna's name was explained in punning fashion as "*Ḥam Nuna*" ("Hot Fish"). See *Kiddushin* 25a, *Tosafot*, s.v. *Hamnuna Karnuna* (quoting Rabbeinu Ḥananel). According to a tradition from the *"Gurei ha-Ari"* ("Lion Cubs"), i.e. disciples of Rabbi Isaac Luria, Rav Hamnuna Saba was a reincarnation of Moses! See Rabbi Ḥayyim Yosef David Azulai (ḤYDA), *Nitsutsei Orot*, *Zohar* III, 144b.

In *Metsi'ot Katan*, employing the imagery of Psalm 8:9, Rav Kook likens full-time students of Torah to "the fish of the sea," whose vitality is in the water—as opposed to part-time students of Torah who merely "pass through the paths of the seas." See *Metsi'ot Katan*, ed. Harel Cohen (Israel, 2018), par. 375 (p. 519).

[179]The reference is not clear. It appears that Rav Kook refers to *Zohar* II, 100b, where the *Saba* or Elder (unlike the more prudent Bar Yoḥai) plunges into the Great Sea without the rudiments of a sailboat: ropes and mast. Though initially upbraided for being so foolhardy, the *Saba* is finally encouraged to continue his sea voyage on his own terms. (See earlier *Zohar* 98b, and later 103b-104a.) See now Biti Roi, "'And They Were Watering the Torah': The Gaon of Vilna and his Affinity to *Tiqqunei ha-Zohar*" (Hebrew), *Da'at* 79-80 (5775/2015), p. 68.

[180]Rabbi Israel Ba'al Shem Tov expressed this very idea. His grandson, Rabbi Moshe Ḥayyim Ephraim of Sudylków writes:

> I heard from my grandfather, of blessed memory, that sometimes one comes to the *tsaddik* (righteous man) to learn from his deeds, and the *tsaddik* just then is in a state of *"katnut"* ("smallness"), and so he [i.e the observer] receives from him, not knowing to distinguish. So it happened that one came to the famous MOHaRaN, of blessed memory, and saw him just then drinking coffee while wearing *tallit* (prayer shawl) and *tefillin* (phylacteries). He [i.e. the observer] travelled home and also began to behave so.
>
> (*Degel Maḥaneh Ephraim*, *Bamidbar*, s.v. *ve-lo yavo'u lir'ot ke-vala' et ha-kodesh va-metu*)

One assumes that "MOHaRaN" of the anecdote is Ba'al Shem Tov's companion Rabbi Naḥman of Kosov.

See also Rabbi Dov Baer of Mezritch (successor to Ba'al Shem Tov):

> The *tsaddik*, not only when he is engaged in matters of holiness does he cleave to Him, blessed be He, but even when he is separated from matters of holiness and goes out to [engage in] secular matters, work or trade, he does not separate his thought from cleaving to God; it is just as it was when he engaged in learning [Torah] or some matter of holiness . . . "Rather the dung of the mules (*pirdotav*) of Isaac than the silver and gold of Abimelekh" [*Genesis Rabbah* 64:7]. This refers to someone who is constantly engaged in Torah and commandments, and then goes and wastes time. This comes about because he sees that sometimes

> the wholly righteous (*tsaddik gamur*) also takes time out from learning Torah, but he does not know that though [the *tsaddik*] is disengaged, nevertheless his thought is not separated from holiness. This observer compares himself to the *tsaddik* and in reality totally wastes his time . . .
>
> (Rabbi Dov Baer of Mezritch, *'Or Torah*, ed. Rabbi Isaiah of Dinowitz [Koretz, 1804], *Toledot*, s.v. *vayyigdal ha-ish*; [Brooklyn: Kehot, 1972], 13b-c)

[181]Hebrew, *mesukan*. Rabbi Menaḥem Mendel Morgenstern of Kotsk taught: "'All the ways are presumed dangerous' [*y. Berakhot* 4:4]—except for the way of the Torah." By "dangerous ways" (*"derakhim be-ḥezkat sakanah"*), the Kotsker may have been referring to the doctrine of *"'avodah be-gashmiyut"* (serving God through the corporeal) promulgated by Ḥasidism, though his grandson Rabbi Samuel Bornstein of Sokhatchov interpreted the warning differently. (See below note 191.) Historically, it is known that the Kotsker represented a revolution within Ḥasidism. Perhaps most telling in this respect is the Kotsker's psychic identification with the Vilna Gaon! "The Rebbe of Kotsk used to say that he has the soul of the Vilna Gaon, and though he was born during the lifetime of the Vilna Gaon, it came about through *'ibbur neshamah*." (As opposed to *gilgul* or reincarnation, whereby the soul of the deceased incarnates in the newborn, in the case of *'ibbur* or "impregnation," the soul of the deceased may enter the body of an already mature individual.) Rabbi Michael Forshlager of Baltimore heard this from the Kotsker's son-in-law Rabbi Abraham Bornstein of Sokhatchov (author of *Avnei Nezer*); it was transcribed by Rabbi Ya'akov Perlow of Novominsk (a descendant of the Kotsker) who interviewed Rabbi Forshlager in Baltimore. See *Mikha'el be-Aḥat*, ed. Ben Zion Bergman (Ashdod, 2013), p. 39.

[182]In the previous story, Rav Kook explained that souls within bodies are referred to as "passengers on ships," while souls stripped of the body are compared to fish.

[183]Aramaic, *eshata de-garmei*. In the context of *b. Berakhot* 32a it refers to a fever; see Rashi there s.v. *eshata de-garmei*: *"Maleveid* in OF." Rav Kook employs the expression figuratively to refer to an essential holiness. See too his remarks in *'Eyn Ayah* to *Berakhot* 32a (page 146, par 63).

[184]Though the word *"'avodat"* ("service of") was left hanging in the manuscript, one assumes that Rav Kook intended it to be followed by the word *"ha-guf"* ("the body").

[185]See *Tikkunei Zohar* (Vilna, 1867), *tikkun* 21 (60a).

[186]Hebrew, *"la'avor orḥot yam."* Cf. Psalms 8:9.

The Two-Finned Fish

8

R[abbah] b[ar] B[ar] Ḥ[annah] said: One time, we were traveling in a ship and the ship traveled between one **fin and** the other **fin of a fish** for **three days and three nights.** The fish was swimming in the opposite direction of the ship, so that **it** was swimming **upward** against the wind and the waves, **and we were** sailing **downward. And if you would say** that **the ship did not travel very fast, when Rav Dimi came** from Erets Yisrael to Babylonia **he said:** In the short amount of time required to **heat a kettle of water,** that ship can **travel sixty parasangs. And** another demonstration of its speed is that **a horseman shot an arrow, and** yet the ship was traveling so swiftly that it **outraced it. And Rav Ashi said: That** fish **was a sea *gildana*, which has two** sets of **fins.**

THE TWO-FINNED FISH VERSUS THE SINGLE-FINNED FISH: COLLAPSING THE PRACTICAL INTO THE THEORETICAL

Rabbah bar Bar Ḥannah reported that they were journeying upon the Sea of Wisdom when they observed in a soul the way in which its wisdom was distributed.

It is known that there are two types of intellect: theoretical and practical. After a soul has completed its portion of Torah and wisdom in this world, it is perfected in both the theoretical and practical.

The way that Rabbah bar Bar Ḥannah and his fellow travelers studied the soul was by observing the distribution of its wisdom from the theoretical to the practical, on all three levels of soul (*nefesh*, *ru'aḥ*, *neshamah*);[187] and furthermore, on each of those soul-levels in terms of the attainments of *Tif'eret* and *Malkhut*, which is to say, *Torah she-bi-Khetav* (the Written Torah) and *Torah she-be-'al Peh* (the Oral Torah).[188]

However, there is a general apprehension lacking specifics; and then there is a specific apprehension. There is an apprehension of the specific attributes of *Ḥesed* and *Gevurah* on their own. And then there is an apprehension of *Da'at* (Knowledge) which combines the attributes together. "And by knowledge (*da'at*) the chambers are filled."[189]

Now to truly understand on the specific level the *combinations* of the attributes, one must first understand specifically each attribute on its own. If one truly apprehends the combination of the specific attributes, this is positive proof that one succeeded earlier in apprehending each of the specific attributes *per se*. It is the *sefirah* of *Da'at* that subsumes the "six extremities" (of *Ḥesed, Gevurah, Tif'eret, Netsaḥ, Hod, Yesod*), and permeates all of them.

There is apprehension that comes from natural human intellect, through *pilpul* (dialectic) and the ways of reason; and attainment through divine inspiration.[190] But essentially the apprehensions subdivide into *a posteriori* apprehension, which is a gradual apprehension necessary for materialists; as opposed to essential *a priori* apprehension.[191] An example of the latter would be a wise man presenting to his disciple that which is known to him.

They **traveled between** one **fin and** the other **fin,** between the extensions of two types of intellect included in that soul, by virtue of which she (flies and) swims in the Sea of Wisdom. **Three days and three nights**. The number three represents the three soul-levels (*nefesh, ru'aḥ* and *neshamah*). Day symbolizes the Written Torah (corresponding to the *sefirah* of *Tif'eret*); night symbolizes the Oral Torah (corresponding to the *sefirah* of *Malkhut*).[192] Rabbah bar Bar Ḥannah and company observed how the three levels of the soul apprehended both Written and Oral Torah.

The fish was swimming in the opposite direction of the ship, so that **it** was swimming **upward** against the wind and the waves, **and we were** sailing **downward.** The apprehension of that soul—"that fish"—was from the top down; our apprehension was from the bottom up.

It is also possible to visualize it in the opposite manner: The fish was swimming upward and the boat was sailing downward. In other words, that soul came to the realizations on its own.[193] When Rabbah bar Bar Ḥannah and his shipmates observed the essence of that soul, there were revealed to them the realizations that were already "engraved" in her. When one innovates words of wisdom, one works from the bottom up. They, on the other hand, who lacked the ability to investigate the very root of the wisdoms "engraved" in her, but rather discovered them vicariously through her as an already finished product, worked their way from the top down, by observation of her entire edifice (*shi'ur komah*).[194]

And if you would say that **the ship did not travel very fast.** If you should say that the apprehension of Rabbah bar Bar Ḥannah and company was only a general apprehension (which is an inferior apprehension, as the *Zohar* states regarding knowledge of divinity, that the lesser level is general knowledge, while the greater knowledge is specific),[195] the response is:

In the short amount of time required to **heat a kettle of water.** Water symbolizes *ḥasadim* (love) and fire *gevurot* (rigors).[196] The heating of the water by the fire symbolizes the combination of *Ḥesed* and *Gevurah*[197]; the nexus of that combination is *Da'at* (Knowledge).[198]

That ship can **travel sixty parasangs.** This is the specialized knowledge of the "six extremities" (*Ḥesed, Gevurah, Tif'eret, Netsaḥ, Hod, Yesod*), represented by "three days and three nights."[199] Because each of the six attributes is apprehended in an individuated manner, the numerical representation is six tens or sixty. This is in regard to the quantity of knowledge. He went on to say that the quality of the knowledge was so great, so deep that **a horseman shot an arrow, and** yet the ship was traveling so swiftly that it **outraced it.** The horseman is a wise man who shoots the arrows of reason guided by human intellect, yet Rabbah bar Bar Ḥannah's crew was superior to the fastest intellect.

And Rav Ashi said: That fish **was a sea *gildana*, which has two** sets of **fins.** When it comes to apprehension, there is smallness (*katnut*) and greatness (*gadlut*). When one ascends to a very great level, there is no division between the theoretical and the practical—all is theoretical, for the source of the practical intellect is (also) the theoretical.[200] When one is accomplished in apprehension, the practical ascends to the theoretical source, and unites in a complete unity. When the soul is on such a level, it is beyond the comprehension of mere mortals. Only the **sea *gildana***—spiritual small fry (*katnut*)—**which has two** sets of **fins,** meaning that the theoretical and practical are divided into two aspects, was comprehensible to Rabbah bar Bar Ḥannah and company, because they were able to latch on to its practical intellect.

[187]See our Appendix, "The Three Levels of the Soul."

[188]In Kabbalah, the Written Torah is symbolized by the *sefirah* of *Tif'eret* and the Oral Torah by the *sefirah* of *Malkhut*. See below note 192.

[189]Proverbs 24:4; *Zohar* III, 136a, 289b, 296a. See *Yisrael u-Teḥiyato*, chap. 21, in *Orot*, ed. Bezalel Naor (Maggid, 2015), pp. 218-219. Cf. Rabbi Dov Baer of Mezritch, *Maggid Devarav le-Ya'akov*, ed. Rabbi Solomon of Lutzk (Brooklyn: Kehot, 1986), chap. 6 (6a); 88 (17a-b); and idem, *'Or Torah*, ed. Rabbi Isaiah of Dinowitz (Brooklyn: Kehot, 1986), chap. 396 (99a).

[190]Hebrew, *ru'aḥ ha-kodesh ve-shefa' elohi.*

[191]Cf. Abrabanel's distinction between prophecy and philosophy: "The essential distinction between the two is that intellectual prophecy is *a priori* knowledge whereas philosophic knowledge is *a posteriori*" (Alvin Jay Reines, *Maimonides and Abrabanel on Prophecy* [Cincinnati, 1970], p. lxxviii).

A disciple of Rav Kook, Rabbi Mordechai Gimpel Barg, devoted a chapter of his book, *Be'er Mordekhai* (Jerusalem, 1926) to the topic of "Understanding Life" (pp. 23-24). He writes that there are two ways to arrive at understanding what life is all about. One way is *a posteriori* (*min ha-me'uḥar el ha-mukdam*). By observing the Creation, one will eventually arrive at acknowledgment of the Creator. Barg quotes the verse in Isaiah 40:26: "Lift up your eyes on high, and see: Who created these?" This way is murky and veiled in a thick mist. But there is another way which is *a priori* (*min ha-mukdam el ha-me'uḥar*). Crystal clear, it was given at Mount Sinai.

The disciple is echoing what Rav Kook wrote in his commentary to the prayer book. There, Rav Kook explains that when we reckon by the creation of the world, evening precedes morning. When we reason from the world, darkness precedes illumination. But when we proceed from Mount Sinai—which is the principle in regard to sacrifices—day comes first; the light of understanding is immediate. See *Siddur 'Olat Re'iyah*, ed. Rabbi Tsevi Yehudah Hakohen Kook, vol. 1 (Jerusalem, 1939), pp. 109-110, s.v. *ashreinu she-'anaḥnu mashkimim u-ma'arivim*; and *The Koren Rav Kook Siddur*, ed. Bezalel Naor (2017), pp. 58-61.

Concerning Rabbi Mordechai Barg and his charming work of thought, *Be'er Mordekhai*, see now *Haskamot ha-Rayah*, ed. Rabbis Ari Shvat, Tsuriel Ḥallamish and Yoḥanan Fried (Jerusalem, 2017), no. 167 (p. 317).

*

These two sources of understanding—Reason versus Revelation—were the subject of an exchange between *Ha-Yehudi ha-Kadosh* ("the Holy Jew"), Rabbi Jacob Isaac Rabinowitz of Pshiskha (Polish, Przysucha), and his disciple, Rabbi Simḥah Bunim. One Sabbath night, the Holy Jew asked Rabbi Bunim: "Upon what do you base your apprehension of the divinity?"

Rabbi Bunim responded: "Lift up your eyes on high, and see: Who created these?" Rabbi Bunim's master, the Holy Jew, corrected him, saying: "That is a lower level. The higher level is 'I am the Lord your God who took you out of the Land of Egypt' [Exodus 20:2]." See Rabbi Abraham Joseph Igra, *Toledot Avraham Yosef* (Cracow, 1938; photo offset Brooklyn, n.d. [1980]), *Va'era*, 22c.

(See the earlier exchange between Rabbi Judah Halevi and Rabbi Abraham ibn Ezra, recorded in Ibn Ezra's commentary to Exodus 20:2. Ibn Ezra was asked by Halevi why the first commandment references the Exodus from Egypt and not the Creation of heaven and earth. Ibn Ezra replied that mankind are not equal when it comes to belief in God. The commandment must be universal. By marshaling proof for the belief in God from the miraculous events of the Exodus, *"Anokhi"* appeals to both the learned man and the common man. However, Ibn Ezra held that the scientific method, though limited to the learned class, is still prescribed by the Torah. "And from the ways of the Lord, the *maskil* [enlightened] will know the Lord.")

Into the next generation, Rabbi Bunim's disciple, Rabbi Menaḥem Mendel Morgenstern of Kotsk said: "'All the ways are presumed dangerous' [*y. Berakhot* 4:4]—except for the way of the Torah." The Kotsker's grandson, Rabbi Samuel Bornstein of Sokhatchov, interpreted "the dangerous ways" as those predicated upon observation of the Creation, such as recommended by Maimonides in chap. 2 of *Hilkhot Yesodei ha-Torah*. See *Shem mi-Shmuel, Sukkot* 5679 [1918], s.v. *ba-Midrash* (*Vayyikra Rabbah*).

[192]This association of the Written Torah with day and the Oral Torah with night originates with Moses' experience on Mount Sinai.

> "He was there with the Lord forty days and forty nights" [Exodus 34:28]. By day, the Holy One, blessed be He, would teach him the Written Torah, and by night He would teach him the oral Mishnah.
>
> (*Midrash Tanḥuma, Ki Tissa* 28)
>
> Rabbi Joshua ben Korḥah says: "Moses spent forty days on the mountain; reading Scripture by day and studying Mishnah by night." (*Pirkei de-Rabbi Eliezer*, chap. 46)

In Kabbalah, the Written Torah is associated with the *sefirah* of *Tif'eret*, while the Oral Torah is associated with *Malkhut*. See Rabbi Joseph Gikatilla, *Sha'arei 'Orah*, ed. Joseph Ben Shlomo (Jerusalem, 1970), vol. 1, p. 84, note 102 (First Gate), *Malkhut*=Oral Torah; p. 248 (Fifth Gate), *Tif'eret*=Written Torah. And Rabbi Moses Cordovero, *Pardes Rimonim*, Gate 23 (*Sha'ar 'Erkhei ha-Kinuyim*), chap. 22, s.v. *Torah*.

In the famous introduction to *Tikkunei Zohar* which begins *"Pataḥ Eliyahu"* ("Elijah Opened"), we read: "*Malkhut* is the mouth. We call it the Oral Torah."

[193]See Rav Kook's description of the creative process of Rabbi Abraham Bornstein of Sokhatchov as evidenced in his halakhic works *Avnei Nezer* and *'Eglei Tal*; in *Ma'amrei ha-Rayah*, vol. 1 (Jerusalem, 1980), pp. 203-204.

During his sojourn in St. Gallen, Switzerland (1915-1916), Rav Kook reflected on the difference between the *sefirot* of *Ḥokhmah* (seminal Wisdom) and *Binah* (derivative Understanding), and the tragedy that befalls an original thinker should he reduce himself to the level of *Binah*:

> If one whose soul is founded upon *Ḥokhmah* does not recognize his attribute, and descends to the attribute of *Binah*, removing his thought from *Ḥokhmah* out of a lack of self-awareness—he shall find himself destroyed and wretched.
>
> (*Shemonah Kevatsim* 7:147 = *Orot ha-Kodesh*, vol. 1, p. 57)

In that *pensée*, the term "*ḥayyei ha-Binah*" ("the life of *Binah*") may be traced back to Naḥmanides' commentary, Numbers 30:3 (Chavel ed., p. 323). After quoting the *Sifré*, which typifies a vow as "vowing by the life of the King" ("*noder be-ḥayyei ha-Melekh*"), Naḥmanides supplies the Kabbalistic interpretation whereby the *neder* or vow is situated in *Tevunah*. Rabbi Menaḥem Recanati explains that *Neder* = *Nun dar*: That which dwells at the fiftieth level or *Binah*. See the commentary of Recanati, Numbers 30:3. See also Naḥmanides' commentary to Genesis 2:7 and Rabbi Isaac of Acco's supercommentary, *Me'irat 'Eynayim* (Erlanger ed., pp. 39-40). Remarkably, Naḥmanides' Kabbalistic interpretation of the *Sifré* found its way into his Talmudic novellae. See *Ḥiddushei ha-Ramban* to Tractate *Shavu'ot* 29a (Hershler ed., p. 131). The version of Rabbi Isaac of Acco is vastly superior to that of Rabbi Hershler's edition.

Lastly, see Rabbi Ḥayyim Vital, *Peri 'Ets Ḥayyim*, beginning *Sha'ar ha-Tefillin*: " … the mystery of 'the life of the King' (*ḥayyei ha-Melekh*) who is *Ze'ir Anpin*, and his 'life' extends to Him from *Binah* and *Ḥokhmah*."

[194]Rav Kook's point is well taken. An original thinker swims upstream; latecomers swim downstream. A very popular biography of Rav Kook by Rabbi Shmuel Hakohen Avidor is entitled *Ha-'Ish Neged ha-Zerem* (*The Man Against the Current*). In response to the publication of the biography, Rav Kook's son, Rabbi Tsevi Yehudah, is said to have quipped: "I see the current, but I don't see the man." However, the foreword to the second edition tells a very different story, whereby Rabbi Tsevi Yehudah (the teacher of Avidor) was actually very fond of the biography and penned notes in the marginalia of his copy. See Rabbi Shmuel Avidor Hakohen, *Ha-'Ish Neged ha-Zerem* (Tel-Aviv, 2002), pp. 9-10. The marginalia are published at the end of the edition.

[195]*Ra'aya Mehemna* in *Zohar* II, 25a. The *Ra'aya Mehemna* differentiates between knowing God in a general way (*be-'oraḥ kelal*) versus knowing God in a specific way (*be-'oraḥ perat*). Cf. *Ra'aya Mehemna* in *Zohar* III, 263b.

[196]See Rabbi Moses Cordovero, *Pardes Rimonim* 23:1, s.v. *esh*; and 23:13, s.v. *mayim*.

[197]Cf. *Pinkesei ha-Rayah*, vol. 3, ed. Rabbi Levi Yitsḥaki (Jerusalem, n.d.), 15:40 (pp. 88-89).

[198]Rabbi Ḥayyim Vital, *ʻEts Ḥayyim* 9:1; Rabbi Aharon Halevi Horowitz of Staroselye, *ʻAvodat ha-Levi*, Genesis-Exodus-Leviticus (Lemberg, 1861), *Tetsaveh*, 47b.

[199]See *Raʻaya Mehemna* (cited above note 195). that the individual knowledge (*be-ʼoraḥ perat*) entails knowledge of the six days of the week.

[200]Author Perle Epstein recounts a conversation with her mentor Rav Tsevi Yehudah Hakohen Kook (only son of Rav Avraham Yitsḥak Hakohen Kook). The plan was that Rav Tsevi Yehudah would teach her the basic elements of Kabbalah. However, when Perle arrived at the residence of Rav Tsevi Yehudah, he launched into a discussion of current events in the Land of Israel. Perle chided him: "But let's not waste precious time on politics. Let's talk about Kabbalah, please." Rav Tsevi Yehudah's response was: "*Narele* [Yiddish, foolish child], everything is Kabbalah." Perle Epstein, *Pilgrimage: Adventures of a Wandering Jew* (Boston, 1979), p. 205. Also on p. 209. Rav Kook's name has been changed to "Rav Bloch."

For a discussion of the concepts of *gadlut* (greatness) and *katnut* (smallness) in Lurianic Kabbalah and later in Beshtian Ḥasidism, see Zvi Mark, *Mysticism and Madness in the Work of R. Naḥman of Bratslav* (Hebrew) (Tel Aviv: Am Oved, 2003), chap. 10, pp. 294-329.

The Sea Bird Ziz Sadai

9

Rabbah b[ar] B[ar] Ḥ[annah] said: One time, we were traveling in a ship and we saw a certain bird that was standing with water up to its ankles and its head was **in the sky. And we said** to ourselves that **there is no** deep **water** here, **and we wanted to go down to cool ourselves off. And a Divine Voice emerged and said to us: Do not go down here, as the ax of a carpenter fell here seven years** ago **and** it has still **not reached the bottom. And** this is **not because the water is so vast. Rather,** it is **because the water is turbulent. Rav Ashi said: That** bird **is** called ***ziz sadai*, as it is written:** "I know all the fowl of the mountains; **and the *ziz sadai* is with Me"** (Psalms 50:11).

TALMUD'S TURBULENT WATERS, KABBALAH'S HALCYON SKIES, AND A SEABIRD CALLED "*ZIZ SADAI*"

When it comes to the obligation of apprehending the Torah, the obligation is divided into two parts: to know the commandments and the minutiae of the *Halakhah*;[201] [and to apprehend to the best of one's ability, hidden secrets of the Torah and the mysteries of the world: "The secret (*sod*) of the Lord is revealed to those that fear Him."][202]

Even though the Sages, of blessed memory, said, "'A small thing'—the disputations of Abaye and Rava; 'a great thing'—the Work of the Chariot,"[203] nonetheless, great is the obligation to toil in order to know the laws of the Torah; and to engage in *pilpul* (dialectic) and to create in the revealed wisdom of the Torah. These [exoteric] matters reach to the highest level and convey man to apprehending the hidden "in the pleasantness of the Lord."[204] As the Sages, of blessed memory, said in the Midrash: "'The people walking in darkness'—these are the masters of Talmud—'saw a great light.'"[205] Though it might appear that they are busy with trifling legal matters, nonetheless, their value is exceedingly great. However, this is not the end of man's excellence, for man was created to know the Lord (and to apprehend to the best of one's ability, hidden secrets of the Torah and the mysteries of the world: "The secret [*sod*] of the Lord is revealed to those that fear Him.")[206] But the portion of learning "to know the deed that one must do,"[207] is also a great and very expansive fundamental.

Now it is known that deeds (*'uvdin*) depend on the *sefirah* of *Malkhut* (or the *partsuf* of *Nukva*).[208] All the apprehensions that touch upon deeds, depend on her. "The great man among the giants,"[209] who attains to great realizations through the "wings" of love and fear,[210] mainly devotes his study to great apprehensions that transcend practical affairs. The aspect of his soul that engages in practical wisdom is the lower portion of his wisdom and intellect. Despite that, one must not say that the practical affairs are light and few, and their obligation is not great, so one may be lackadaisical concerning them. Those practical affairs extend very far!

It is known that the seven lower *sefirot* (*Ḥesed*, *Gevurah*, *Tif'eret*, *Netsaḥ*, *Hod*, *Yesod*, *Malkhut*) contain the Written Torah[211] and the Oral Torah,[212] and in *Malkhut* all the aspects depend on deeds (*'uvdin*). But then there is an [even higher] aspect of Torah symbolized by the *sefirah* of *Binah* (Understanding).[213] That is the level of "*pilpul*" (dialectic) in which the Holy One, blessed be He, rejoices.[214] The main part of the joy is situated in [the *sefirah* of] *Binah*.[215] The mystery of "These and those are the words of the Living God"[216] is located in [the *sefirah* of] *Binah*.[217] Thus, the quality of *pilpul* to demonstrate convincingly the opposite sides of an issue—"pure" and "impure"[218]—ascends to [the *sefirah* of] *Binah*, synonymous with the mystery of the Jubilee or fiftieth year, a mystery deeper than that of the Sabbatical or seventh year.[219] And since our entire apprehension is limited to the seven lower *sefirot*, we have no ability to apprehend how it is possible that "These and those are the words of the Living God." For, the *sefirah* of *Binah* "exists only to ask."[220]

Now the **carpenter** does his work in the water, and repairs ships and vessels to "traverse the seaways."[221] These vessels represent the commandments and their laws. Aided by them, we are able to traverse the sea without drowning "when its waves rise up,"[222] as I have written several times concerning the sinking of the ship.[223]

The power to build comes about through truthful dialectic (*pilpul shel emet*),[224] which produces a clarified *Halakhah* (*halakhah berurah*).[225] Sometimes, the matter at hand is so deep that it cannot be resolved by *pilpul*, and there remains doubt. When that happens, what prevents one from reaching a conclusion is that one has touched upon the mystery of "These and those are the words of the Living God (*Elohim Ḥayyim*)."[226] [*Elohim*] *Ḥayyim* is code for the *sefirah* of *Binah*.[227]

Great is the obligation to toil as much as possible until one arrives at a correct understanding of "the word" ("'the word of the Lord'—this is *Halakhah*").[228] Though it would seem that the practical commandments are finite, inasmuch as they do not involve especially lofty matters—in truth, because it is the will of the Lord, blessed be He, to "increase Torah and to strengthen" it,[229] He applied the details of the *halakhot* to all the transitory things and current events of the world, and since the world is constantly in flux, there constantly arise doubts and new studies. Because of the turbulence of events, and the ever-changing studies engendered by them—there arises a great obligation to toil in the practical portion [of Torah] as well. And in turn, this will bring one to an exalted level, to "merit many things,"[230] when that exoteric study is accompanied by the mysteries of the commandments and their secrets.

Now it is known that the *sefirah* of *Malkhut* is referred to as the "apple orchard" (*sdeh ḥakal tapuḥin*)[231] in need of the labor of "gatherers of the field" (*meḥatsdei ḥakla*).[232] This wise man, who together with his theological studies, explores the practical portions [of Torah], works the "field." Yet, *he moves on from the field* (*zaz mi-sadeh*)[233] and arrives in his conception at the heights. In his consciousness, he cleaves to divine subjects, though he makes inquiry into mundane matters.

Rabbah bar Bar Ḥannah related that when they were traveling to study the ways of the Sea of Wisdom, they **saw a certain bird**, a heavenly bird, which is to say a wise soul that through its "wings," its spiritual apprehension, ascends to a lofty place. **Was standing with water up to its ankles.** Only its ankles, its lower extremities were in the lower waters, symbolic of the apprehension of the *halakhot* or laws. **And its head** was **in the sky.** To apprehend lofty secrets and mysteries of the world.[234]

One who observes how that soul's attention is riveted to the lofty apprehensions at the height of the world, supposes that the matters of the *halakhot* are not great and expansive, so it is possible to complete them without tremendous effort. **And we said** to ourselves that **there is no** deep **water** here, i.e. the waters of *Halakhah* are not so multitudinous, **and we wanted to go down to cool ourselves off.** We naively thought that the disputations of Abaye and Rava, and halakhic *pilpul* would be just so much frolicking in the water.

And a Divine Voice emerged. The *"bat kol"* is from the *sefirah* of *Malkhut.*[235] **"Do not go down here!"** It will not be so easy for you to descend to the depth of the *Halakhah*, so in this endeavor too you must greatly exert yourselves.

As the ax (*ḥatsina*) of a carpenter[236] fell here. *Ḥatsina* is the tool of the shipbuilder, as we wrote above. This "shipbuilder" engages in *pilpul* or dialectic. He fell into a very deep *pilpul*.[237] **Seven years** ago. This *pilpul* was so deep that it involved all the chambers of wisdom, of the bottom seven *sefirot* (*Ḥesed, Gevurah, Tif'eret, Netsaḥ, Hod, Yesod* and *Malkhut*), upon which are contingent the deeds and the practical Torah. **And** it has still **not reached the bottom.** The pilpulist could not reach to the bottom of the matter because there is a place in the depth which is the mystery of "These and those are the words of the Living God."[238] This place is symbolized by [the *sefirah* of] *Binah* (Understanding).[239]

And this is **not because the water is so vast**. In truth, these studies [of practical *Halakhah*] are few and facile in comparison with the intellectual studies contained in the mysteries and secrets of the Torah, which in and of themselves are endless and limitless. **Rather,** it is **because the water is turbulent.** The turbulence results from the changes of the wheel of world events which presents numerous doubts in need of a determination based on true Torah law. Therefore there is a great obligation to fulfill the verse "All the labor of man is for his mouth."[240] The "mouth" symbolizes [the *sefirah* of] *Malkhut*, the Oral Torah,[241] upon which deeds (*'uvdin*) depend.[242] "And yet the soul (*nefesh*) is not filled."[243] The surprise is that the [lowest level of soul known as] *"nefesh,"* situated in [the *sefirah* of] *Malkhut*,[244] "is not filled," because the practical wisdom too is very great and profound.

Rav Ashi said: That bird **is** called ***ziz sadai.*** That bird that engages in both these portions of Torah [i.e. the exoteric and the esoteric] is *ziz sadai. Sadai* ("my fields") for it dwells in the field of the apple orchard, and *ziz* because it moves (*zaz*) from there to ascend to the heights of apprehension, **as it is written:** "I know all the fowls of the mountains; **and the *ziz sadai* is with Me."** "With me," with the *sefirah* of *Tif'eret*, symbolized by the heavens.[245] This "bird" ascends heavenward, having united Torah and deeds.

[201]There occurs here in the original this emphatic statement: "This is a great obligation upon man to apprehend and to know."

[202]Psalms 25:14.

This second clause ("and to apprehend to the best of one's ability, hidden secrets of the Torah and the mysteries of the world: 'The secret [*sod*] of the Lord is revealed to those that fear Him'") occurs below in an almost disjointed manner. It has been preserved there in parentheses and relocated here for the sake of continuity.

[203]*b. Sukkah* 28a. The Work of the Chariot (*Ma'aseh Merkavah*) refers to Ezekiel's vision.

[204]Psalms 27:4. The complete phrase reads: "to behold the pleasantness of the Lord, and to visit in His palace."

[205]Isaiah 9:1; *Midrash Tanḥuma, Noaḥ* 3.

[206]See above note 202.

Cf. the remarks of Rav Kook's great uncle, Rabbi Mordechai Gimpel Jaffe in our appendix, "Letter of Rabbi Mordechai Gimpel Jaffe on the Wisdom of Kabbalah."

[207]Adapted from Exodus 18:20: "And you shall let them know … the deed that they must do."

[208]Cf. the "*Likkutim*" incorporated in the commentary to the Passover *Haggadah*: "'*Uvdin* (deeds) are from the side of *Nukva* (the Female)" (*Siddur 'Olat Re'iyah*, vol. 2, p. 273). In his notes to the *Siddur*, RZYH Kook refers the reader to *Zohar* III, 183b.

[209]Joshua 14:15.

[210]See Rabbi Shneur Zalman of Liadi, *Tanya* I, chaps. 16, 40-41. Cf. *Tikkunei Zohar*, *tikkun* 20 (Margaliyot ed., 25b): "Without fear and love, Torah does not fly above."

[211]Synonymous with the *sefirah* of *Tif'eret*.

[212]Synonymous with the *sefirah* of *Malkhut*.

[213]It is obvious that Rav Kook has introjected *Tikkunei Zohar's* reading of this particular *aggadah* (or *haggadah*) of Rabbah bar Bar Ḥannah. The Introduction to *Tikkunei Zohar* explains that the bird whose feet are in the sea and whose head is in the sky is the *Tsaddik* (Righteous), the "pillar" (or *axis mundi*) that extends from earth to heaven. (See *b. Ḥagigah* 12b, quoting Proverbs 10:25.) The sea that covers the bird's ankles symbolizes the "supernal mother" (or *Binah*), comprising fifty gates. In his commentary, the Vilna Gaon clarifies that the Hebrew word for "sea" (*yam*) has the numerical value of 50. See *Tikkunei Zohar* (Vilna, 1867), 3b.

[214]There circulates in later rabbinical literature the saying, "The Holy One, blessed be He, rejoices in *pilpul*." The by now common saying has its source in Rabbi Joseph Karo, *Maggid Meisharim* (Vilna, 1875), *Vayakhel, Mahadura Batra* (27a-b). Rav Kook quotes the saying in his early essay, "*Te'udat Yisrael u-Le'umiyuto*," chapter 6. The essay first appeared in the rabbinic journal *Ha-*

Peless 1 (1901). It was reprinted in Rabbi Moshe Zuriel, *Otserot ha-Rayah* (Tel-Aviv, 1988); see vol. 2, p. 711. See also *Igrot ha-Rayah*, vol. 1 (Jerusalem, 1961), p. 42 (Letter 43).

[215]The prooftext for this statement is the verse in Psalms 113:9: "The mother of the children is joyful" (*'em ha-banim semeḥah*). In Kabbalah, "Mother" is code for the *sefirah* of *Binah*, while her "children" are the seven lower *sefirot* of *Ḥesed* through *Malkhut*. See *Zohar* I, 154a: "'The mother of the children is joyful'—This is Jubilee, for all the freedom and all the joy of all the worlds depend upon it." See further Rabbi Shneur Zalman of Liadi, *Siddur 'im DAḤ* (Brooklyn, 1971), s.v. *'ivdu et Hashem be-simḥah* (45c-d); idem, *Likkutei Torah*, *Derushim le-Sukkot*, s.v. *u-she'avtem mayim be-sasson mi-ma'yenei ha-yeshu'ah* II (79d-80d); idem, *Ma'amrei Admor ha-Zaken: Et-halekh Liozna* (Brooklyn, 2012), s.v. *lehavin 'inyan nissukh ha-mayim ba-ḥag* (p. 49); Rabbi Ya'akov Tsevi Yolles, *Kehillat Ya'akov* (Lemberg, 1870), s.v. *simḥah*.

[216]*b. 'Eruvin* 13b.

[217]See Rabbi Moses Cordovero, *Pardes Rimonim*, Gate 23 (*Sha'ar 'Erkhei ha-Kinuyim*), s.v. *Elohim Ḥayyim*. And ibid. Gate 20 (*Sha'ar ha-Shemot*), end chap. 7.

[218]*b. 'Eruvin* 13b.

[219]Jubilee (Hebrew *Yovel*), the fiftieth year corresponds to *Binah*. See *b. Rosh Hashanah* 21b: "Fifty gates of understanding (*binah*)." *Shemitah*, the seventh year, on the other hand, corresponds to the seven lower *sefirot* (from *Ḥesed* through *Malkhut*).

Rav Kook developed the difference between *Shemitah* and *Yovel* (drawing on their Kabbalistic significance) in the introduction to his Halakhic work, *Shabbat ha-'Arets* (Jerusalem, 1910).

[220]*Zohar* I, 1b, 30a. This saying of the *Zohar* is also quoted by Rav Kook in the *"Likkutim"* incorporated in the commentary to the Passover *Haggadah*; see *Siddur 'Olat Re'iyah*, vol. 2, p. 273.

The *Zohar* conceives the divine name *Elohim* as being composed of two words: *Mi eleh*? (Who are these?) The name *Elohim* is synonymous with the *sefirah* of *Binah*.

See further Rabbi Joseph Gikatilla, *Sha'arei 'Orah*, beginning Eighth Gate. In the words of Gikatilla: "*Mi* [=*Binah*] is given to question (*she'ilta*). Until here, question[ing] (*she'ilta*); beyond, it is like placing a finger in the eye" (*Sha'arei 'Orah*, vol. 2, Ninth Gate [p. 94]).

[221]Hebrew, *"la'avor orḥot yamim."* Cf. Psalms 8:9.

[222]Psalms 89:10. Though the manuscript reads *"be-si galav,"* this is clearly an error. It should read *"be-so galav"* in conformity with the verse in Psalms.

[223]See the first and seventh legends of Rabbah bar Bar Ḥannah.

[224]Cf. *Pinkesei ha-Rayah*, vol. 3 (Jerusalem, n.d.) 16:4 (p. 143).

[225]The term *"halakhah berurah"* comes from the Talmud (*b. Shabbat* 139a). During World War One, while in exile in London, Rav Kook conceived the project of *Halakhah Berurah*. (See

Rabbi Tsevi Yehudah Hakohen Kook, *Li-Sheloshah be-Elul*, vol. 1 [Jerusalem, 1938; reprinted Jerusalem, 1978], par. 66 [p. 29].) The plan called for the printing of the relevant texts of Maimonides' *Mishneh Torah* and Rabbi Joseph Karo's *Shulḥan 'Arukh* alongside the page of the Talmud. Rather than delegating this responsibility to staff, Rav Kook himself did the work of transcription.

At the back of the tractate would appear *"Birur Halakhah,"* synopses of the *sugyah* or Talmudic discussion, designed to streamline study of the development of the *Halakhah* through the ages. At an early stage, Rav Kook's disciple, Rabbi Isaac Arieli, contributed to the project of *Halakhah Berurah*. He wrote that he completed Tractates *Ketubot* and *Makkot* in 1925. (See Rabbi Isaac Arieli, *'Eynayim le-Mishpat, Kiddushin*, Jerusalem, 1936, Introduction, p. 2; and Aharon Ilan, *'Eynei Yitsḥak*, Jerusalem, 2018, pp. 139-140.) Eventually, the work was delegated to the researchers of the Harry Fischel Institute, whose administrator was Rabbi Dov Kook, Rav Kook's younger brother. (In the first years of the Institute, Saul Lieberman was in charge of this research project.) What distinguishes the *Birur Halakhah* is, to use the term of our text, *"pilpul shel emet"* (truthful dialectic), without artifice and without hairsplitting. The *Birur Halakhah* is very useful to scholars for its straightforward approach to study of the Talmud.

Halakhah Berurah is an ongoing project. The Makhon Halakhah Berurah in Jerusalem still exists. Since publication of Tractate *Beitsah* (Jerusalem: Harry Fischel Institute, 1940), several more volumes of the Talmud have appeared in print.

When this writer (BN) met Rabbi Tsevi Yehudah Hakohen Kook for the first time in his home at Reḥov Ovadiah 33 (in the Ge'ulah section of Jerusalem), on the night of 26 Tevet, 5778 (January 4, 1978), Rabbi Tsevi Yehudah confided that the same *"tsav"* ("command") that instructed his father to write *Resh Millin*, commanded him to compose *Halakhah Berurah*. *Resh Millin* is a mystical tract, an original Midrash on the letters of the Hebrew alphabet. It was published in London in 1917. See RZYH Kook, *Li-Sheloshah be-Elul*, vol. 1 (Jerusalem, 1938), p. 29, par. 66; Ḥayyim Avihu Schwarz, *Mi-Tokh ha-Torah ha-Go'elet*, vol. 4 (Jerusalem, 1991), pp. 88-89. According to Rabbi Isidore (Yeḥezkel) Epstein, a disciple of Rav Kook from the London years, Rav Kook wrote *Resh Millin* in three days! See Isidore Epstein, *Avraham Yitzḥak Hacohen Kook: His Life and Works* (n.p. [London], 1951).

[226]Cf. Rabbi Shneur Zalman of Liadi, *Torah 'Or, Vayyeshev*, s.v. *Shir ha-Ma'alot be-shuv … hayinu ke-ḥolemim* (28d), who writes that "These and those are the words of the Living God" is the level of *'Iggulim*, which is undifferentiated.

[227]See Rabbi Moses Cordovero, *Pardes Rimonim*, cited above note 217.

The manuscript states simply "*Ḥayyim*." (And so it was transcribed in *Ma'amrei ha-Rayah*, p. 436.) Perhaps the text should read *"Elohim Ḥayyim."*

[228]Amos 8:12; *b. Shabbat* 138b.

[229]Isaiah 42:21. See *m. Makkot* 3:16.

[230]*m. Avot* 6:1 (*Beraita de-Kinyan Torah*).

[231]The "apple field" (Hebrew, *sdeh tapuḥim*) or the "apple orchard" (Aramaic, *ḥakal tapuhin*) is synonymous in Kabbalah with the *sefirah* of *Malkhut*. Rav Kook has conflated the Hebrew and Aramaic expressions. The trope *"sdeh tapuḥim"* or *"sdeh tapuḥin kaddishin"* or *"ḥakal tapuḥin kaddishin"* ("orchard of holy apples") occurs innumerable times in the *Zohar*. See *Zohar* I, 142b, 143b, 224b; II,12b, 60b, 61b, 84b, 88a; III, 84a, 128b (*Idra Rabba*), 135b (*Idra Rabba*), 288a (*Idra Zuta*) and 292b (*Idra Zuta*).

The term came about in the following manner. In Genesis 27:27, Isaac declares: "See, the aroma of my son is as the aroma of a field which the Lord has blessed." In *b. Ta'anit* 29b (as quoted in Rashi on the verse) this field is identified as an apple orchard (*"sdeh tapuḥim"*). From this source, originated the Kabbalistic term *"ḥakal tapuḥin kaddishin."* See the commentary of Rabbi Judah Leib Ashlag, *Ha-Sulam*, to *Zohar* 142b. And see the Pritzker edition of the *Zohar*, vol. 2, ed. Daniel Matt (Stanford, California, 2004), p. 294, n. 262.

[232]*Zohar* II, 79b, 85b; III, 127b. Rav Kook employs the term *"meḥatsdei ḥakla"* in *Orot* as well; see *Orot ha-Teḥiyah* (Lights of Renascence), chap. 21 and our note 176 thereto. In a Kabbalistic *pensée* on *Megillat Esther*, Rav Kook writes that masters of the esoteric lore (*ba'alei ha-sod*) are called *"meḥatsdei ḥakla"*; *Siddur 'Olat Re'iyah*, vol. 1, p. 437. Cf. *"Likkut me-ha-Gra 'al Reish Idra Rabba Naso* (127b)," published at the beginning of the Vilna Gaon's Commentary to *Tikkunei Zohar* (Vilna, 1867), s.v. *u-meḥatsdei ḥakla*: "masters of mystery (*marei de-raza*)."

Rabbi Reuven Margaliyot suggested that the *Zohar*'s term *"meḥatsdei ḥakla"* should best be appreciated in opposition to the Talmudic term of belittlement, *"katlei kanei be-agma,"* or "cutters of reeds in a marsh" (*b. Sanhedrin* 33a). See Margaliyot's commentary, *Nitsutsei Zohar* to *Zohar* III, 127b, note 6.

[233]See Rashi, Psalms 50:11, s.v. *ve-ziz sadai 'imadi*: "*Ziz* because they move (*zazim*) from place to place, *esmouvement* in Old French." Also Rabbi David Altschuler, *Metsudat Zion* ad loc.

Within the Kabbalistic context, cf. Rabbi Samuel of Kalvaria, *Darkhei No'am*, 62a: "And therefore she is called *Ziz Sadai* because she moves from her supernal place where she is called 'a field which the Lord has blessed' [Genesis 27:27]." (See above n. 231.)

Parenthetically, there is a Kabbalistic commentary to the Legends of Rabbah bar Bar Ḥannah entitled *Ziz Sadai*. Authored by Judah Leib ben Aharon Shmuel of Kremnitz, it was published in Lublin in 1634. (It is only 8 leaves or 16 pages long!)

[234]Cf. Rabbi Samuel Edels, *Ḥiddushei Aggadot Maharasha*. Maharasha writes that the waters below symbolize the exoteric wisdom (*ḥokhmat ha-nigleh*), and the heavens above, the esoteric wisdom (*ḥokhmat ha-nistar*).

[235]*Zohar* I, 137a. See further Rabbi Moses Cordovero, *Pardes Rimonim*, Gate 23 (*Sha'ar 'Erkhei ha-Kinuyim*), s.v. *bat*; Rabbi Ya'akov Tsevi Yolles, *Kehillat Ya'akov*, s.v. *bat kol*. This would be the mouth of *Malkhut*, the Oral Torah, speaking.

[236]Aramaic, *bar nagara*. Maharasha points out that "*bar nagara*" (carpenter) is the Talmudic idiom for a Torah scholar.

[237]Cf. Maharasha.

[238]*b. 'Eruvin* 13b.

[239]See note 227 above.

[240]Ecclesiastes 6:7. The Talmud (*b. Sanhedrin* 99b) derives from this verse that man was created to toil in Torah.

[241]Introduction to *Tikkunei Zohar*, *Pataḥ Eliyahu*: "*Malkhut* is the mouth (*peh*); *Torah she-be-'al peh* (the Oral Torah) we call it."

[242]See above note 208. Cf. the recently unearthed letter of Rav Kook's great-uncle, Rabbi Mordechai Gimpel Jaffe, in which he quotes the *Sifra, Emor*, whereby the actual performance of the *mitsvot* depends upon Mishnah, i.e. the Oral Law. (See Appendix 7.)

[243]Ecclesiastes 6:7.

[244]See the Kabbalistic Chart appended to this volume.

[245]In Kabbalah, the heavens symbolize the *sefirah* of *Tif'eret*. See Rabbi Moses Cordovero, *Pardes Rimonim* 23:21, s.v. *shamayim*.

Elsewhere, Rav Kook understands "the bird of the heavens" ("*tsipor shamayim*") in Psalms 8:9 as a trope for a man whose apprehension extends beyond the rational to the mysteries of Torah. "He is called 'the bird of the heavens' for he flies above the sea and gazes there" (*Metsi'ot Katan*, par. 375, p. 519).

The Fattened Geese

10

And Rabbah bar Bar Ḥannah said: One time, we were traveling in the desert and we saw these geese whose wings were drooping because they were so fat, and streams of oil flowed beneath them. I said to them: Is there from you a portion in the World to Come? One raised a leg, and one raised a wing, signaling an affirmative response. **When I came before Rabbi El'azar, he said to me: In the future, Israel will be held accountable for them** [i.e. for the suffering of the geese].

THE GRIEVANCE OF THE GOOSE: WORLDLY WISDOM WASTED

The goose is a symbol of wisdom, as the Sages, of blessed memory, said: "He who sees a goose in a dream—should look forward to wisdom."[246] But based on the proof-text that the Sages adduce, "Wisdoms call aloud out in the open,"[247] it seems that the Sages intend thereby famous wisdoms that proclaim publicly their usefulness, such as physics, astronomy, etc. This is not the case in regard to our holy Torah, of which it is said, "All glorious is the king's daughter within [the palace]"[248]; and "'The roundings of your thighs are like the links of a chain, [the work of the hands of an artisan]'—Just as the thigh is hidden, so words of Torah are hidden."[249]

Now though not all wisdoms are essential, nevertheless it is worthwhile for Israel, especially the Torah sages, to know them, for thereby the Name of Heaven is sanctified, and Israel will be able to achieve the purpose for which the Holy One, blessed be He, dispersed them throughout the world—namely, to increase converts to Judaism,[250] and to publicize His unity in the world.[251] This is impossible to accomplish unless Israel know the [worldly] wisdoms, for in this way, they will know how "to respond to an Epicurean."[252]

If Israel were to know those [worldly] wisdoms as well and intend by studying them for the sake of heaven, then the Name of Heaven would be sanctified [in two ways]: Through them, they would merit this world, broadening the affairs of this world,[253] which would be a sanctification of the Name among the nations of the world, as the Sages, of blessed memory, said: "From whence do we know that it is incumbent upon man to calculate seasons and constellations? For it says, 'Observe therefore and do them, for this is your wisdom and your understanding to the eyes of the peoples.' Which is a wisdom that is apparent to the eyes of the peoples? This is the calculation of seasons and constellations."[254] Also, by knowing worldly wisdom, it is possible to add knowledge of Torah and fear of the Lord. It is written in the name of the Vilna Gaon, of blessed memory, that whatever a person is lacking in worldly wisdoms, that person is lacking one hundred times over in the study of Torah,[255] for the wisdoms are "perfumers and cooks" for the Torah of the Lord.[256]

Now if Israel would know and understand every wisdom and science, then the wisdoms themselves would be uplifted. Each wisdom would be causative in reaching holiness and an exalted level. Israel would unite them [i.e. those other wisdoms] with the holiness of the Torah, to know more the wisdom of the Lord, blessed be He, through the wisdom discernible in the creations.[257] The result would be the improvement of love and fear [of the Lord],[258] and the other holy attributes, which are the "wings" of the soul, to ascend to the place of the high mountain, the House of the Lord. [There are] also wisdoms whose broadening brings to greater apprehension of theology (*Ḥokhmat Elohut*).

So in reality, when we investigate whether these worldly wisdoms contribute to service of the Lord, we find [that this is so in two respects]: On a purely material plane, by enhancing this-worldly matters, there is increased respect for Israel, and thereby the Name of Heaven is sanctified. And on the spiritual plane, these wisdoms uplift our understanding, as it is written in *Ḥovot ha-Levavot*[259] concerning the obligation to study the creations. "Whoever knows how to calculate seasons and constellations, and refrains from doing so, in regard to such a person Scripture says, 'They do not look at the deed of the Lord, nor do they see the work of His hands.'"[260]

But now that these wisdoms have been handed over to the nations of the world, who are devoid of the knowledge of Torah and fear of the Lord, "the wings have been plucked." By increasing their wisdom, the nations of the world wax arrogant, denying the roots of religion.[261] This comes about because they do not understand the depths of Torah, and the wisdoms that ramify from their wisdoms are secular in nature, even lower than the original wisdoms. [The wisdoms of the nations] do not look up.[262]

One time, we were traveling in the desert, the place of desolation, to investigate worldly wisdoms, as opposed to the wisdoms of the Torah, which is the wisdom mainly responsible for settling the world. **And we saw these geese** that represent the famous wisdoms, **whose wings were drooping because they were so fat.** Fat, or rather oil, alludes to wisdom, as the verse says, "There is desirable treasure and oil in the dwelling of the wise."[263] Because of the increase of their wisdom, they erred on the way of intellect, and their "wings"—that convey man to an exalted end, namely the love and fear of the Lord, and the roots of belief and service that should derive from every wisdom—drooped.

And streams of oil flowed. These are the streams of wisdom that derived from them. **Beneath them.** They bore only lowly wisdoms conducive to the technology of desires. "They do not look at the deed of the Lord,"[264] to know His reality, blessed be He.

I said to them: Is there from you a portion in the World to Come? Is it possible to acquire from you levels of holiness that cause sanctification of the Name?

One raised a leg, symbolizing practical action of which Israel can avail themselves. When these wisdoms return to us,[265] the honor of Israel will be uplifted thereby, and in turn, the honor of the Lord, blessed be He, and the honor of the holy Torah. **And one raised a wing.** This refers to the possibility of extracting from them holy matters that are conducive to a wisdom that would transport Israel to lofty levels of holiness.

When I came before Rabbi El'azar, he said to me: In the future, Israel will be held accountable for them [i.e. for the suffering of the geese]. If Israel would hold fast to the rectitude of the holy Torah, their minds would expand to "merit many things,"[266] and they would sanctify the Name of Heaven through these worldly wisdoms as well. When we prevent the good, we are held accountable.[267] It devolves upon us to be "a light to the nations,"[268] to extend the fear of the Lord and the knowledge of His unity, blessed be He, in the world; and the vessels that are conducive to this are the wisdoms that are visible to the eyes of the peoples, namely, calculating seasons and constellations, and the like. In this way, there will soon approach our final redemption.

[246]*b. Berakhot* 57a.

[247]Proverbs 1:20.

[248]Psalms 45:14.

[249]Song of Songs 7:2; *b. Mo'ed Katan* 16. Rashi explains: "For it is written at the conclusion of the verse, 'the work of the hands of an artisan,' and the Torah is the craftsmanship of the Holy One, blessed be He."

[250]*b. Pesaḥim* 87b.

[251]*Yiḥud Hashem* or the unity of God is the *summum bonum* of the Kabbalah. Cf. Rav Kook's commentary to the first legend (at note 33) and the manuscript of Rabbi Mordechai Gimpel Jaffe appended to this work.

[252]*m. Avot* 2:14.

[253]Rabbi Tsevi Yehudah Hakohen Kook observed that the significance of the name Japheth is "broadening." See Rashi, Genesis 9:27, quoting Targum Onkelos.

> "God shall broaden Japheth and he shall dwell in the tents of Shem" [Genesis 9:27]. In Japheth, which is "breadth" in Aramaic, there are revealed the breadth of the world; the beauty of of a broad compass; human wisdom and song; illustrations and ideas of lofty, exalted matters. But Japheth does not possess the essence of the world, the dimension of the holy. Shem (the Name) is inwardness, the purpose of the world, i.e. the holy.
>
> When the beauty of Japheth resides in the tents of Shem [*b. Megillah* 9b], the secular realm of Japheth bonds to the holy content of Shem. The holy does not oppose the secular; the contrary.
>
> When Japheth disconnects from Shem; when the secular disconnects from the sacred; it loses its value and meaning, and is temporarily subsumed in evil.
>
> (*Pe'amim*: *Siḥot Rabbeinu Tsevi Yehudah Hakohen Kook*, ed. Rabbis Ilan Tor, Shlomo Aviner and Ḥayyim Vidal [Jerusalem, 2007], *Noaḥ*, pp. 33-34)

Rabbi Tsevi Yehudah drew the line between the secular (*ḥol*) and the impure (*tum'ah*). Whereas the secular, personified by Japheth, has the potential of being integrated into the framework of holiness—impurity, personified by Ḥam, is antithetical to holiness. Ibid, p. 34. Cf. Rabbi Shneur Zalman of Liadi, *Tanya* I, 6-7 (p. 11) regarding the difference between *"kelipat nogah"* and *"shalosh kelipot ha-teme'ot."*

[254]Deuteronomy 4:6; *b. Shabbat* 75a.

[255]Quoted by Rabbi Barukh Schick of Shklov in the introduction to his Hebrew translation of Euclides' *Elements*:

> When I was in the glorious community of Vilna, visiting the luminary, the great genius, our teacher and master who lights up the eyes of the Exile, the famous *Ḥasid* Rabbi Elijah, may the Lord protect him, in the month of Tevet, 5538 [1778], I heard from his holy mouth that as much as a man is lacking knowledge of the other wisdoms, in direct proportion to that, he is lacking one hundred times the wisdom of the Torah, for the Torah and Wisdom are intertwined.
>
> He provided a parable of an imprisoned man, whose intellect is confused so that he desires every food. (See *Duties of the Heart*, [the Eighth Gate], the Gate of Self-Reckoning, f. 93, and the wise will understand.)
>
> And he commanded me to translate whatever possible of the wisdoms to our sacred tongue, in order "to bring forth from their mouths that which they swallowed up." (Cf. Jeremiah 51:44)....
>
> Therefore I have taken the initiative to sanctify the Name of Heaven and to fulfill the wish of the righteous, our teacher the *Ḥasid*, may the Lord protect him, to translate whatever possible to our sacred tongue and "to bring forth from their mouths that which they swallowed up." I shall begin with the book of Euclides ....
>
> (Barukh [Schick] of Shklov and Minsk, *Euclides*, The Hague, 1780)

In *'Ikvei ha-Tson*, Rav Kook misquotes the saying ascribed to the Vilna Gaon. There the deficiency is only "ten times" as opposed to "one hundred times" of Rabbi Barukh of Shklov's introduction to *Euclides*. See *'Ikvei ha-Tson* (Jerusalem: Mossad Harav Kook, 1985), p. 129 and note 19 there provided by RZYH Kook.

See further Rabbi Shelomo Zalman Rivlin, *Midrash Shelomo: Derashot* (Jerusalem, 5713/1953), chap. 45, titled "The obligation to know the seven wisdoms according to the command of the Gaon Rabbi Elijah in order to apprehend the wisdom of the Torah and for the sake of sanctifying the name, and bringing the redemption." (The chapter extends for 30 pages, from page 125 through page 155!)

See Eli Eshed, *"Sefer Kol ha-Tor—Aggadah Rivlina'it o Moreshet ha-Gra?"* in *Be-Ḥadrei Ḥaredim, Forum: Sefarim ve-Soferim*, Dec. 11, 2009. Available at the blogspot: bhol.co.il. Eshed speculates that the *eminence grise* behind the works *Midrash Shelomo* and *Kol ha-Tor*, both published by Rabbi Shelomo Zalman Rivlin, was his cousin, the Talmudic genius and Kabbalist, Rabbi Yitsḥak Tsevi Rivlin. More recently, see Isaac Hershkowitz, "Innovative Aspects in the Research of *Kol HaTor*" (Hebrew), *Da'at* 79-80 (2015), pp. 163-182.

In an attempt to portray the Vilna Gaon as an advocate of the Haskalah movement, various *Maskilim* or "Enlightened Jews" tended to exaggerate or overemphasize Rabbi Barukh Schick's testimony. This in turn, provoked the predictable "push back" from traditional Talmudists who minimize Schick's familiarity with the Gaon and even go so far as to impugn his testimony. For a recent discussion from the traditionalist standpoint, see Dov Eliach, *Ha-Gaon* (Jerusalem, 2002), vol. 2, pp. 623-628.

For an appreciation of the *Sitz im Leben* of the sages of Shklov who were adherents of the Vilna Gaon, see David E. Fishman, *Russia's First Modern Jews: The Jews of Shklov* (New York, 1995). Chapter Two of the study is devoted to Rabbi Barukh Schick in particular and scrutinizes his reported conversation with the Vilna Gaon. The book also contains material on members of the Rivlin family. If Vilna was referred to as the "Jerusalem of Lithuania" (*Yerushalayim de-Lita*), Shklov earned the epithet "Yavneh of Belarus" (*Yavneh de-Rassein*).

On the opposite side of the barricades, Rabbi Pinḥas Reizes (son of the Rabbi of Shklov, Rabbi Ḥanokh Henokh Schick) figures prominently in the annals of Ḥabad Ḥasidism. From a staunchly Mitnagdic family, the young Pinḥas defected to become a prime pupil of Rabbi Shneur Zalman (founder of Ḥabad Ḥasidism). In fact, many of the oral discourses of Rabbi Shneur Zalman were preserved thanks to the extremely faithful transcripts of Rabbi Pinḥas Reizes. See Ḥayyim Meir Heilman, *Beit Rabbi*, vol. 1 (Berdichev, 1902), 70b. At his funeral in Lubavitch, the *"Mitteler Rebbe,"* Rabbi Dov Baer (son of Rabbi Shneur Zalman) referred to Rabbi Pinḥas as "the Fieldmarshal of Ḥasidim." Ibid., note 4.

[256]1 Samuel 8:13. See Maimonides' famous response to Rabbi Jonathan Hakohen of Lunel; in *Teshuvot ha-Rambam*, ed. Blau (Jerusalem, 1961), vol. 3, pp. 56-57. In that letter, Maimonides calls the Lord to witness that he engaged in wisdoms other than Torah only that they might serve her as "perfumers, cooks and bakers."

[257]See the commentary of Abraham ibn Ezra to Exodus 20:2: "And from the ways of the Lord, the *maskil* [enlightened] will know the Lord."

[258]See Maimonides, *MT*, *Hil. Yesodei ha-Torah* 2:1 and 4:12.

[259]Baḥya ibn Pakuda, *Ḥovot ha-Levavot* (*Duties of the Heart*), Gate 2 (*Sha'ar ha-Beḥinah*), chap. 2. See *The Book of Direction to the Duties of the Heart* (*Al-Hidaya ila Fara'id al-Qulub*) trans. and ed. Menaḥem Mansoor (Oxford, 1973), Chap. 2 (On the Aspects of Meditation upon Creation), pp. 154-155.

[260]Isaiah 5:12; *b. Shabbat* 75a. Quoted in *Duties of the Heart*, loc. cit.

[261]In an early poem, Rav Kook observed ironically that the Copernican Revolution rather than humbling humanity, had the opposite effect. Mankind's pride swelled:

> After many orbits of
> the speck around the disk,
> the secret is known:
> Man's manor is in motion!

> The discovery is great.
> A mystery has been divulged:
> The entire speck
> revolves around the shining disk.
> The creature is so proud
> of its wonderful discovery.
> As if it created
> worlds for eternity.

See *Otserot ha-Rayah*, ed. Rabbi Moshe Zuriel (Ramat Gan, 2002), vol. 2, pp. 575-577, "*Siḥat Mal'akhei ha-Sharet*" ("The Conversation of the Angels"). Translation by Bezalel Naor, "Rav Kook's Space Odyssey," *Lehrhaus*, August 23, 2018. Also available (with Rav Kook's original Hebrew) at: http://orot.com/rav-kooks-space-odyssey/

[262]In the manuscript, this paragraph precedes the previous one. I have relocated it here for the sake of continuity.

[263]Proverbs 21:20.

[264]Isaiah 5:12.

[265]Hebrew, "*ke-she-yashuvu bi-teshuvah*" ("when they return"). The wording is ambiguous. It may refer to Israel's repentance. I have assumed that the reference is to the wisdoms' return to Israel from the nations of the world. See above (note 255) Rabbi Barukh Schick's quotation of the Vilna Gaon. Cf. Rabbi Ya'akov Moshe Ḥarlap (eminent disciple of Rav Kook), *Leḥem Abirim* (Jerusalem, 1993), chap. 14 (p. 46) on the "enhancements of material existence" that "are waiting to enter into the hands of Israel, who by their material enhancement, reveal their spiritual enhancement."

[266]*m. Avot* 6:1.

[267]Sometime during the Jaffa years (1904-1914), Rav Kook penned this sharp rebuke:

> In the Footsteps of Messiah, the mending of the world (*tikkun ha-'olam*) will not come about other than through the spreading of the wisdoms (*ḥokhmot*) in Israel, through the striving of the righteous. And any *tsaddik* (righteous man) who does not strive for this *tikkun*, in the future will have to give an accounting for this.
>
> (*Pinkas ha-Dapim* 4:9, in *Kevatsim mi-Ketav Yad Kodsho*, vol. 2, ed. Boaz Ofen [Jerusalem, 2008], p. 119)

The language is almost identical with that of the legend of Rabbah bar Bar Ḥannah.

[268]Isaiah 42:6; 49:6.

The Bedouin Divining Water

11

And Rabbah b[ar] B[ar] Ḥ[annah] said: One time, we were traveling in the desert and we were accompanied by a certain Bedouin[269] **who would take dust and smell it, and say: This is the road to such and such a place, and that is the road to such and such a place. We said to him: How far are we from water? And he said to us: Bring me dust. We brought** it **to him, and he said: Eight parasangs.** Later, we said this **a second time, and gave him** dust, and **he said to us that we are at a distance of three parasangs. I switched** this dust with that dust to test him if he was truly an expert, **but I could not** confuse **him.**

DIVINING FOR WATER AND SOULS

The first several stories of Rabbah bar Bar Ḥannah were introduced by saying, "We were traveling by ship." Starting with the previous story, the narrative begins by saying, "We were traveling in the desert." At the root of the difference lies the symbolism of sea and dry land. The sea symbolizes the esoteric Torah; the land, the exoteric Torah.[270] Wisdoms that address exalted, hidden, soulful matters are "marine." Wisdoms that speak of bodily matters (deeds and character traits) are "terrestrial." (However, the source of the Torah is in the desert, which is free for all.)[271]

The Vilna Gaon explained in his commentary on *Tikkunei Zohar*, concerning the passage that the Faithful Shepherd [i.e. Moses] split the sea with his rod and at the End of Days he will split the sea of the Torah[272] with his reed pen,[273] that the esoteric will become exoteric,[274] and the sea will turn to dry land, providing a way that is accessible and apprehensible.[275] [However, the source of the Torah is in the desert, which is free for all.][276]

A certain Bedouin. In the *Zohar*, we find that on several occasions they came across a "*Tay'a*" (Bedouin).[277] The "*Tay'a*" (Bedouin) represents a special level of wisdom. We find in Torah, and students of Torah, two different approaches: [the agriculturalist and the merchant].

The Sages, of blessed memory, said (in regard to a "Sinai," i.e. one who is a living repository of the teachings from Sinai): "All are in need of the master of wheat."[278] By the same token, Rav Yosef said about himself: "Abundant crops come by the strength of the ox."[279] So the interaction of the wise man with the Torah resembles the action of the ox which works to bring crops from the earth, which in turn will provide bread, "the bread of Torah,"[280] to sustain man. And in the *Zohar*, Torah scholars are referred to as *"meḥatsdei ḥakla"* ("gatherers of the field").[281]

In the Bible, there is another metaphor for the apprehension of Torah: Merchandise. "Her merchandise is better than the merchandise of silver."[282] "She is like the merchant ships."[283]

The difference between the one who tills the earth and the merchant is as follows. The farmer dwells in one place, works and produces bread. The merchant moves around,[283*] buying up merchandise; he is constantly wandering from his place.

So too when it comes to wise men. There is the wise man who stays in his place, studying Torah and wisdom; he does not wander about. Then there is another type of wise man that delves into his wisdom with the help of all the things that he sees "under the sun"[284] and all the classes of creations. He also examines many words of Torah from his own soul. He goes from level to level, examining ways and paths of Torah. He also prepares[285] how to actualize the holiness of the Torah; and by which ways one may attain exalted levels, whether it be through the Torah that one creates on one's own, or that which other wise men create. He resembles the merchant who makes the merchandise readily available to the buyers.[286]

Now the ability to teach each individual his or her unique way, how he or she must behave in order to attain wholeness—is great and awesome, for as the Vilna Gaon wrote in his commentary to Proverbs [16:4], each individual has a unique way according to his or her makeup. Just as no two humans have the exact same face,[287] so their ways to attain wholeness are not the same.

And see the words of the Gaon Rabbi Moses Ḥayyim Luzzatto in his commentary to the *Idra Rabba* on the verse, "The way of the righteous is as the light of dawn."[288]

There is a way to analyze the quality of each individual from the angle of the *soul*, whether at the root of its holiness and its essential value, or based on the state of the individual's deeds and affairs.

However, there is a great wisdom that allows one to recognize from a man's *body* all his affairs and the ways of his *tikkun* (spiritual mending). It stands to reason that since the human body was made "in the image of God" ("*be-tselem Elohim*")[289] and by divine compass, just as one may intellectualize from the construction of the body several matters of a theological nature, as it is written, "From my flesh I shall see God,"[290] so *a fortiori* one may analyze the affairs of the soul through the body. [This wisdom of physiognomy] is alluded to in the verse, "This is the book of the generations of Adam."[291] Naḥmanides wrote (*ad locum*), quoting Rav Sherira Gaon, that there is a wisdom whereby one may recognize in the face of a man all his ways and deeds.[292] It is brought in the *Zohar* in the pericope of *Yitro*,[293] and recounted concerning the "Ari" (Rabbi Isaac Luria).[294]

So someone who possesses this wisdom also knows from the construction of the body which way the individual must travel in order to acquire all the possible levels of wholeness and holiness.

Furthermore, there is a wisdom whereby one is able to recognize [an individual's characteristics] simply by smelling. The olfactory sense differs from the other senses. On the one hand, like the other senses, it has a surety about it. However, unlike the other senses, it relates to that which is lofty.

Elsewhere,[295] I have written that the senses are sure but they cannot render judgment in lofty matters. The intellect, [on the other hand,] is sometimes seized with doubts, but it pertains to lofty matters.

The sense of smell is unique in that it is attributed to the soul.[296] Being of the soul, it affords a very lofty benefit which at the same time is sure, because after all, it is sensory.

There follows that the apprehension of this wise man [i.e. "the Bedouin"]—who would investigate the perfection of a man's soul through his body[297]—contained both advantages: Inasmuch as the apprehension was sensory, it was sure. Nonetheless, having transcended the body to the soul, it attained lofty matters of great value.

Now man in his bodily condition is far from any holiness unless he sanctifies his body; by nature the body is far from any excellence, but with preparation it may merit excellence, "grace and glory."[298] However, the excellence of the body consists in meriting to the level of "*ru'aḥ*" (spirit), which is the mainstay of man.[299] Man is situated in the *sefirah* of *Tif'eret*, as it is written, "according to the beauty (*tif'eret*) of man.[300]

The depth of wisdom, the root of the Torah, "comes out of *Binah*" (*'oraita mi-binah nafkat*),[301] which is the eighth *sefirah* (from the bottom up). This is known from the words of the Sages concerning the harp of the Days of Messiah that will be of eight strings.[302] (See *Migdal 'Oz, Hil. Teshuvah*, chap. 8 and Naḥmanides' *Sha'ar ha-Gemul*.)[303]

Thus we find that according to the nature of his body, man is far from the holiness of the root of the Torah a distance of eight levels, for the body is situated in *Malkhut de-'Asiyah*. (See *Zohar*, *Terumah*, on the verse, "All flesh shall come to bow [before Me].")[304] Only if man intends to sanctify himself, will he become "a man in whom resides *ru'aḥ* (spirit)."[305] Then, he will be a distance of [only] three levels from the "supernal waters" of "the Expanses of the River,"[306] the "River issuing from Eden"[307] [i.e. the *sefirah* of *Binah*].[308]

This wise man ("the Bedouin") who recognizes the power of the soul and its level from the body and its faculties, by dint of his great wisdom "sits in the chambers of the heart."[309] Even if a man should outwardly display before him good deeds, if that man's body has not been truly sanctified, the "Bedouin" will discern what is on the inside, as Scripture says: "Their iniquities are upon their bones";[310] "The look on their faces testified against them."[311]

Once we were traveling in the desert, to investigate the lower wisdoms that relate to the body, in order to rise up through them to a higher wisdom that relates to the soul, **and we were accompanied by a certain Bedouin,** a wise man with a worldly bent,[312] wont to correlate to the wisdom of the Torah his sensory findings concerning man and the world. To that end, he explores, searches, and wanders on the roads to see the work of the Lord and His wonders. He knows the characteristics appropriate to each man according to his individual makeup. For the perfection of his wisdom consists in preparing[313] the Torah [in such a way] that it be comprehensible to each man to his satisfaction and benefit. He is like the *merchant* who makes the merchandise readily available to the buyers.

He had a peculiar talent that he **would take dust.** Intellectually, he would contemplate the dust, the human body which is "dust from the earth,"[314] **and smell it,** in order to gain thereby a clear apprehension—as clear as the sense of smell—of the wondrous qualities of the soul and its ways of holiness.

Now he said: **This is the road to such and such a place, and that is the road to such and such a place.** After having recognized from the man's body, his soul and its excellence, he would then counsel the individual which spiritual level would be appropriate to pursue. To each, he would show the way to choose to arrive at wholeness, for no two men travel the same way.

Now, that he could discern [through the body] the practical ways, was not so amazing, because the deeds too depend on the material, but that he was able through the body to discern very lofty subjects—that was truly amazing! **We said to him: How far are we from water?** We were asking him to figure the distance of the soul from the supernal waters, symbolic of the World to Come, the *sefirah* of *Binah*.[315] *Binah* is symbolized by the "River that issues from Eden."[316] (In the *Zohar*, *Terumah*, 175b: "What does 'water' refer to?—This is *Binah*.")[317] **And he said: Eight parasangs.** Originally, before he showed us the way to holiness by which the souls may ascend, we were at the bottom rung, as it is written, "She revealed his feet and she slept,"[318] which is explained in the *Zohar* to mean "that she slept on the ground."[319] And see the *Sefer ha-Gilgulim* (*Book of Reincarnations*).[320]

But afterwards, the "Bedouin" pointed out to us our way of life, how we might assume the [highest] rung possible for man. Afterwards, we said this **a second time (*taninan*), and gave him** dust. The Aramaic word "*taninan*" has a double entendre of "study" (as in the study of *Mishnah*). We *studied* his ways and followed them. And afterwards, we went back to him to inquire as to our [present] status: How far were we [now] from the final perfection of the "World to Come"?

He said to us that we are at a distance of three parasangs. Man merits the level of "*ru'aḥ*" [the intermediate level of the soul] on a permanent basis. The [highest level of] "*neshamah*" only flashes and illuminates man from above. See the book *Nefesh ha-Ḥayyim*.[321]

And the level of *ru'aḥ* is synonymous with the *sefirah* of *Tif'eret*. "The spirit (*ru'aḥ*) of their father Jacob revived."[322]

The *sefirah* of *Tif'eret* is [but] "three parasangs" from the *sefirah* of *Binah*. The order of the levels is *Ḥesed*, *Gevurah*, *Tif'eret*, with *Binah* over them [as a mother] nursing [her] children.[323]

I switched the type of dust to test him. The "switching" consisted of presenting the Bedouin with a man whose exterior is good but whose interior is evil.[324] I thought that since he judges by bodily appearance, he shall surely be confounded.

But I could not confuse **him,** as he was an expert in this matter. "The secret (*sod*) of the Lord is revealed to those that fear Him,"[325] enabling them to recognize by way of the body all its inner content, as it truly is. As it is written, "His counsel is with the upright."[326] The "upright" (*yashar*) refers to one who goes on a straight path of good character traits,[327] and purifies his body, allowing it to become "lodging" (*akhsanya*) for Torah[328] and wisdom. Upon such a person, rest Torah and sanctity, enlightening him with the great light of the Torah of truth. As it is written of David: "My lord is wise, like the wisdom of an angel of God [to know all things that are in the earth]."[329]

[269]I have translated the Aramaic *"tay'a"* as Bedouin. Rashbam translates it "Ishmaelite merchant" (*"soḥer Ishmael"*). So too Rashi, *Pesaḥim* 65b, *Sanhedrin* 110a and *Ḥullin* 7a (*"soḥer 'Aravi"*). See *b. Berakhot* 56b: "He who sees Ishmael in a dream, his prayer is heard. [However,] only [the Biblical personality] Ishmael son of Abraham, but not any *'tay'a.'*" Rav Kook evidently accepted Rashbam's translation for he makes a point of equating the *tay'a* with the merchant. See further RAYH Kook, *Mishpat Kohen,* no. 89 (168a) commenting on Rashi, *Ḥullin* 39b, s.v. *tay'ei.*

[270]See Rabbi Shneur Zalman of Liadi, *Torah 'Or, Beshallaḥ,* 62a: "The sea symbolizes *'alma de-'itkasya* (the concealed world) and the dry land symbolizes *'alma de-'itgalya* (the revealed world).

[271]The sentence in parentheses seems out of place here, so I have relocated it below. See note 276.

[272]In *Canticles Rabbah, parashah* 5 (to Song of Songs 5:14), s.v. *memulla'im ba-tarshish,* the Talmud is likened to the Great Sea (*Yam ha-Gadol*). This is the source of the common expression *"Yam ha-Talmud"* (the Sea of the Talmud).

[273]*Tikkunei Zohar* with *Be'ur ha-Gra* (Vilna, 1867), *tikkun* 21 (43b). Rav Kook has paraphrased. The exact text of *Tikkunei Zohar* reads:

> "And the Children of Israel went on dry land in the midst of the sea" [Exodus 14:29].
> In the first [redemption], in the body of the sea.
> In the last redemption, all in the Sea of the Torah (*Yama de-'Oraita*).
> His [i.e. Moses'] staff with which he splits the sea—this is the reed pen.

Biti Roi explains: "The staff of Moses that split the sea in the first redemption, interchanges with the staff of writing, i.e. the pen of the *Ba'al ha-Tikkunim*, which is destined to bring a new Torah" (Biti Roi, "'And They Were Watering the Torah': The Gaon of Vilna and his Affinity to *Tiqqunei ha-Zohar*" [Hebrew], *Da'at* 79-80 [5775/2015], p. 37). Roi provides the background to this passage. The author of *Tikkunei Zohar* believed that his pen was divinely inspired. This relates to the Kabbalistic notion of the *"Shem ha-Kotev,"* or the divine name invoked to inspire automatic writing. Ibid. pp. 63-64. Cf. Rabbi Moses Ḥayyim Luzzatto, *Takt"u* [515] *Tefillot*, ed. Shalom Ullman (Israel, 1979), *tefillah* 154 (p. 132).

[274]Hebrew, *"she-ha-nistarot yihyu geluyot."*

According to Rabbi David Cohen (the Nazirite), Rav Kook maintained that the esoteric should be revealed. In a tantalizing page from the Nazirite's memoir, *Sefer ha-Zikhronot*, we read:

> In addition, the Rav commended to me the books of Rabbi Naḥman of Breslov and his disciple Rabbi Nathan.
>
> In my heart I rejoiced at this, as it reinforced my opinion concerning the method of Rabbi Naḥman that all should be revealed. And on that account, there arose the opposition of the Shpoler Zeide, of blessed memory.

> And this coincides with the method of our Master [i.e. Rav Kook], may he live, that the esoteric become exoteric (*she-ha-nistar yehi be-nigleh*).

A facsimile of the manuscript is found on page 400 of Rabbi Moshe Tsevi Neriyah's *Bi-Sdeh ha-Rayah* (Tel-Aviv, 1991). Cf. another conversation between Rav Kook and the Nazirite reported in Ḥayyim Lifschitz, *Shivḥei ha-Rayah* (Jerusalem, 1995), p. 160. That conversation took place in 1922 (the year the Nazirite first arrived in Erets Yisrael). See now *Ḥug ha-Rayah: Shi'urei Rabbenu David Cohen, Harav ha-Nazir ... 'al Orot ha-Kodesh,* ed. Rabbi Harel Cohen, vol. 1 (Jerusalem, 2018), p. 101 and facsimile on p. 111.

Postscript: In the final stages of Rav Kook's terminal illness, he was visited by Rabbi Abraham Hakohen Weissbord, accompanied by his nephew, the Nazirite, Rabbi David Cohen. In a tearful voice, Rav Kook expressed to his visitors the thought that his illness was divine punishment for revealing the mysteries of the Torah. See Lifschitz, *Shivḥei ha-Rayah,* pp. 298-299; Hilah Wolberstein, *Ish Ki Yafli*: *Ha-Rav Ha-Nazir* (Israel, 2017), p. 166; and *Ḥug ha-Rayah*, pp. 27-28.

For a comprehensive summation of what Rav Kook considered the parameters of the permitted and forbidden to study in a public forum, see *Igrot ha-Rayah*, vol. 2, pp. 68-70 (Letter 414). The letter was written in defense of the Ashkenazic Kabbalist *yeshivah* in Jerusalem, "Sha'ar ha-Shamayim," founded by Rabbi Shim'on Tsevi Horowitz (a.k.a. Lider). Sha'ar ha-Shamayim's administrators Rabbi Shim'on Horowitz and Rabbi Ḥayyim Leib Auerbach (father of the renowned *posek* or halakhic decisor Rabbi Shelomo Zalman Auerbach) were staunch supporters of Rav Kook.

The letter provides several guidelines, most important being Rav Kook's premise that the Mishnaic prohibition of public study of *Ma'aseh Bereshit* and *Ma'aseh Merkavah* (*m. Ḥagigah* 2:1) is restricted to "practical Kabbalah" (*Kabbalah Ma'asit*), such as creating a hominoid or calf through *Sefer Yetsirah* (à la *b. Sanhedrin* 65b). Interestingly enough, Rav Kook refuses to countenance that the law stated in the Mishnah is subject to change in the pre-Messianic era. This appears to fly in the face of the oral communication from Rabbi Israel Salanter (based on *Zohar* I, 117a) that after the year 5600 [1840 C.E.] the strictures on the study of Kabbalah are no longer in effect. Reported by Rabbi Shelomo Eliashov, *Sefer ha-De'ah* (Piotrków, 1912), Part One, 38c.

As for the mystery of the Shpoler Zeide's antipathy to Rabbi Naḥman of Breslov, this is an ongoing investigation on the part of historians.

[275]The Vilna Gaon writes:

> **And he shall tear the Sea of the Torah**—The tearing consists in the sea becoming as dry land, so that everyone can go there without danger, and they will not have to trouble to row [in a boat]. There will be revealed like dry land the simple sense of the Torah (*peshutah shel Torah*).

> (*Tikkunei Zohar* with *Be'ur ha-Gra* [Vilna, 1867], *tikkun* 21 [43a], s.v. *ve-yikra' Yama de-'Oraita*)

See now Biti Roi, "'And They Were Watering the Torah': The Gaon of Vilna and his Affinity to *Tiqqunei ha-Zohar*" (Hebrew), *Da'at* 79-80 (5775/2015), p. 68.

*

In this regard, there has come down to us a charming anecdote concerning the Vilna Gaon. Once, his disciple Rabbi Ḥayyim of Volozhin visited him accompanied by his son, Itzeleh (endearment for Isaac), yet a lad. The Gaon clearly was in a state of consternation. When aked what was bothering him, the Gaon replied that it had always been his way to find allusions in Scripture for all the sayings of the Rabbis. The Midrash (*Genesis Rabbah* 5:5 and *Exodus Rabbah* 21:6) says that at the time of the Splitting of the Reed Sea, the Sea returned to the condition (*tenai*) that the Holy One, blessed be He, made with it at the time of its creation. Yet the Gaon was unable to find any allusion to that condition in Genesis and for that reason he was much vexed.

Just then, young Itzeleh chimed in: "The verse states, 'Let the waters under the heaven be gathered together unto one place, and let the dry land appear' [Genesis 1:9]. Why does it have to say 'and let the dry land appear'? That is a given. We understand that if all the waters are gathered to one place, then automatically dry land will appear. The words would seem to be superfluous."

Young Itzeleh then proffered an ingenious solution: "The dry land does not refer to the area that has been drained of its waters but rather to the very gathering of the water, to the sea. At some future date, namely the occasion of the Splitting of the Reed Sea, the dry land must appear there. So we have here an allusion to the original condition that God set with the Sea."

Upon hearing this, the Gaon beamed: "I am certain that Itzeleh will one day be a great preacher (*darshan*) in Israel!"

The story is recorded in Dov Eliach's introduction to his edition of Rabbi Isaac of Volozhin's *Peh Kadosh* (Jerusalem, 1995), pp. 15-16.

[276]*Midrash Tanḥuma*, *Bemidbar* 6; and *Mekhilta*, *Yitro* 1.

In Rav Kook's manuscript (and so in *Ma'amrei ha-Rayah*) the bracketed sentence appeared above almost dislocated. See earlier note #269.

[277]A similar comment was made by Rabbi Joseph Ḥayyim of Baghdad in his commentary *Ben Yehoyada'*:

> That Bedouin was a righteous man from the World to Come, whose soul came to this world and assumed the form of a Bedouin. As you will find in the *Tikkunim* and in the *Zohar* in the [section] *Saba de-Mishpatim*, and other places

in the *Zohar*, where holy souls of the righteous come to this world and assume the shape of a donkey-driver (*ta'in ḥamorei*) and the like. Such was the Bedouin who appeared to Rabbah bar Bar Ḥannah.

(*Ben Yehoyada', Bava Batra* 74a, *ta ve-'aḥvei lakh heikha de-nashkei ar'a u-reki'a*)

See also Rabbi Isaac Ḥaver, *Afikei Yam*, *Bava Batra*, 73b, s.v. *ve-'amar Rabbah bar Bar Ḥannah... ve-'itlavei bahadan hahu tay'a* (quoted in our appendix "A Kabbalistic Theory of Personality").

Concerning the mysterious donkey-driver of the *Zohar*, see the *Introduction to the Zohar* 5b-6a; and Daniel Matt's note to the Pritzker Edition of *The Zohar*, vol. 1 (Stanford, California, 2004), p. 31, note 215.

According to Rabbi Ḥayyim Vital (*Sha'ar ha-Nevu'ah* 3:5), "When only the level of *nefesh* of the *tsaddik* (righteous man) is 'dressed' to enter this world, he appears in the form of a donkey-driver (*ta'in hamorei*). So was Rav Yeiva Saba." Quoted in Rabbi Moses Zacuto, *Perush ha-RaMaZ la-Zohar ha-Kadosh*, Exodus (Jerusalem, 2002), *Mishpatim*, p. 200; and Rabbi Ḥayyim Yosef David Azulai (ḤYDA), *Nitsutsei 'Orot* to *Zohar* II, 95a.

[278]*b. Berakhot* 64a; *Horayot* 14a.

[279]Proverbs 14:4; *b. Sanhedrin* 42a. Rav Yosef was the prototypical "Sinai," as opposed to Rabbah, the prototypical "Uprooter of Mountains" (*'oker harim*). See *b. Berakhot* 64a; *Horayot* 14a.

[280]See Proverbs 9:5 and *Midrash Mishlei*, ed. Buber (Vilna, 1893), Proverbs 31:14.

[281]See above note 232.

[282]Proverbs 3:14. See *Be'ur ha-Gra* there.

[283]Proverbs 31:14.

[283*]Hebrew, *ha-soḥer sovev ve-holekh*. The point being made is that etymologically the word for merchant, *soḥer*, connotes circumambulation. Cf. the Talmudic adage: "Nazirite, go around *(seḥor seḥor);* do not approach the vineyard" (*b. Shabbat* 13a). See Rashi, *'Eruvin* 55a, s.v. *saḥranin*.

[284]Ecclesiastes 1:3, 9.

[285]Hebrew, *mekhin*. Syntactically, it is difficult to support this reading (though to be sure, that is exactly what it states in Rav Kook's manuscript.) If we assume that the letter *vav* was inadvertently shortened to *yod*, the word becomes *mekhaven* (directs), which makes perfect sense in context: He *directs* how to actualize the holiness of the Torah.

[286]Rav Kook's portrayal of the peripatetic sage is so vivid that one wonders whether he speaks out of personal experience.

[287]*t. Berakhot*, chap. 7 (Zuckermandel ed., p. 14); *y. Berakhot* 9:1; *b. Berakhot* 58a.

In this famous passage of the Gaon's writings, we read:

> When there were prophets, people would go to the prophets "to seek the Lord" [Genesis 25:22], and the prophet would pronounce, based upon prophetic judgment, the way that one should pursue in accordance with the root of his soul and the nature of his body ... And since the cessation of prophecy (*nevu'ah*), there is divine inspiration (*ru'aḥ ha-kodesh*) in Israel ... And each and every person has divine inspiration.
>
> (*Sefer Mishlei 'im Be'ur ha-Gra*, ed. Moshe Philip [B'nei Berak, 1985], pp. 190-191)

The Vilna Gaon's commentary to the Book of Proverbs was produced by the Gaon's disciple, Rabbi Menaḥem Mendel of Shklov.

[288]Proverbs 4:18. Rabbi Moses Ḥayyim Luzzatto wrote in *'Adir ba-Marom*, his commentary to the *Idra Rabba* section of *Zohar*:

> In the beginning, there is the *kelalut* (generality) of the way ... and [then] there is the *peratiyut* (particularity), that breaks down into six hundred and thirteen ways, corresponding to the six hundred and thirteen roots of the souls, for each root has one way; and after, those very six hundred and thirteen ways break down [further] into—*peratei peratim* (particulars of particulars).
>
> (*'Adir ba-Marom*, ed. Samuel Luria [Warsaw, 1886], 58b; ed. Yosef Spinner [Jerusalem, 1990], p. 207; ed. Mordekhai Chriqui [Jerusalem, 2018], p. 329)

In his famous letter to Ridbaz, Rav Kook quotes the verse from Proverbs but in a different context, based on *Zohar* II, 215a. See *Igrot ha-Rayah*, vol. 2 (Jerusalem, 1961), pp. 196-197 (Letter 555).

[289]Genesis 1:27.

[290]Job 19:26. See Rabbi Shneur Zalman of Liadi, *Tanya* I, beginning chap. 51 (71a); IV, beginning chap. 15 (121a). See also the final stanza of Rabbi Naḥman of Breslov's *Shir Na'im*, in Rabbi Nachman of Breslov, *Shir Na'im/Song of Delight*, ed. Rabbi David Sears (Spring Valley, NY: Orot, 2005), pp. 20-21, and my remarks on pp. 125-126, comparing Rabbi Naḥman's attitude to *Shi'ur Komah* to that of Rav Kook.

[291]Genesis 5:1.

[292]Naḥmanides, Commentary to Genesis 5:2 (Chavel ed., p. 47); idem, "*Torat Hashem Temimah*" in *Kitvei Ramban,* ed. Chavel (Jerusalem, 1968) vol. 1, pp. 161-162. Cf. idem, *Milḥamot Hashem*, end Tractate *Berakhot* (44a in foliation of Rav Alfasi).

See also *Teshuvot ha-Ge'onim*, *Sha'arei Teshuvah*, no. 125; and *Teshuvot ha-Ge'onim* (Lyck), no. 29.

[293]*Zohar* II, 70a-78a.

[294]Besides being adept at physiognomy (*ḥokhmat ha-partsuf*) and chiromancy or palmistry (*ḥokhmat sirtutei ha-yad* or simply *ḥokhmat ha-yad*), the specialty of Rabbi Isaac Luria was his ability to read on the forehead of an individual that person's spiritual history. See Meir Benayahu, *Toledot ha-Ari* (Ramat-Gan, 1967), pp. 156-157; 249-251.

In his perception of the anonymous *Tay'a* as a physiognomist, Rav Kook was preceded by the Kabbalist Samuel of Kalvaria:

> That *Tay'a* alludes to one of the wise men of the generation who was adept in the physiognomy (*ḥokhmat ha-partsufim*) of people.
>
> (Rabbi Samuel of Kalvaria, *Darkhei No'am* [Koenigsberg, 1764], *Derekh ha-Derush*, 69b)

[295]The allusion is to a passage in *Metsi'ot Katan*:

> "And He shall enable him to smell the fear of the Lord." [Isaiah 11:3].
>
> The smell is apprehended by the sense. Nonetheless, it is the extreme of spirituality, as they said: "Something from which the soul derives pleasure" [*b. Berakhot* 43b].
>
> Now the apprehension of the intellect is doubtful, but lofty; while the apprehension of the senses is certain, but lowly.
>
> So the [prophet] said that [the Messiah] would apprehend lofty matters through the sensory.
>
> (Rabbi Abraham Isaac Hakohen Kook, *Metsi'ot Katan* [Israel: Maggid, 2018], par. 128 [p. 208])

See further ibid. par. 271 (p. 425). Cf. *Orot ha-Kodesh*, vol. 1, p. 217 (*Shemonah Kevatsim* 1:641): "Sometimes an important content that is doubtful, is infinitely more valuable than a lowly content that is certain."

[296]*b. Berakhot* 43b. See above adjacent to note 156.

[297]Cf. *Pinkesei ha-Rayah*, vol. 3 (Jerusalem, n.d.), 16:11 (bottom p. 155): "Therefore it is a worthy obligation to engage much in the research of the souls according to the roots of the body and its ways."

[298]Psalms 84:12.

[299]Cf. RAYH Kook, *Metsi'ot Katan* (Israel: Maggid, 2018), par. (8) (p. 13); par. 266 (pp. 415 and 413); and par. 370 (1) (p. 513); and *Pinkesei ha-Rayah*, vol. 3, 15:73 (p. 122) (quoted above note 155) and 16:37 (p. 226).

See *Likkutei ha-Gra* published as an appendix to *Be'ur ha-Gra* to *Sifra di-Tseni'uta*, ed. Samuel Luria (Vilna, 1882), s.v. *yadu'a* (37d):

> For the *ru'aḥ* of man is the man, whereas the *nefesh* is the level below it, and the *neshamah* [the level] above it. The *neshamah* is the level of an angel, as is known. It is the angel assigned to guard him, as it says: "For He shall assign His angels to guard you on all your ways" [Psalms 91:11].

And see ibid., s.v. *'inyan ha-levushim she-na'asim mi-yemei ha-adam* (39c). **(See Appendix 2.)**

The centrality of *ru'aḥ* is stated most clearly in the commentary of the Vilna Gaon to *Sefer Yetsirah*:

> The main vitality of man is the *ru'aḥ*, and that is the man who receives reward and punishment, as is known, and it is that which feels, and it is all of his faculties and senses... The beginning of man is from the *ru'aḥ*, and it is his mainstay. And when the *ru'aḥ* departs from man, he dies... Corresponding to it in the world is the air from which man lives. It is impossible to survive without it for even a single moment. It too is called *"ru'aḥ."*
>
> (Commentary of Gra to *Sefer Yetsirah*, ed. Rabbi Menaḥem Mendel of Shklov [Horadna, 1806], *ofan* 3, s.v. *bi-sheloshim u-shetayim netivot* [3a])

Bibliographic note: Later under Russian rule, Horadna became Grodno.

See further *Siddur 'Olat Re'iyah*, vol. 1, ed. RZYH Kook (Jerusalem, 1939), p. 249, s.v. *ve-'ahavta*; and the *Koren Rav Kook Siddur*, ed. Bezalel Naor (Jerusalem, 2017), p. 157, note 26.

For an expansive treatment of the Vilna Gaon's psychology (and where it differs from the earlier Lurianic psychology), see Yosef Avivi, *Kabbalat ha-Gra* (Jerusalem, 1993), pp. 42-48.

*

In the work of Rabbi Shmuel Shmelke Horowitz of Nikolsburg, a Ḥasidic contemporary of the Vilna Gaon, one finds treatment of the three levels of *nefesh, ru'aḥ* and *neshamah*; and the intermediacy of *ru'aḥ*. See *Divrei Shmuel* (Lemberg, 1862), beginning *Vayyishlaḥ* (11d), and *Vayyeshev—Ḥanukkah* 5536 [1776], s.v. *ner Hashem nishmat Adam* (13b). *Ner* (candle) is designated initials *nefesh ru'aḥ* as well as *neshamah ru'aḥ*. Cf. *Tikkunei Zohar* (Vilna, 1867), *tikkun* 21 (60a).

In his biography of Rabbi Shneur Zalman of Liadi, Heilman transmits that the Vilna Gaon, who was none too fond of the disciples of the Maggid of Mezritch, commented on Rabbi Shmuel of Nikolsburg (quoting Rava in *b. Megillah* 7a): "All of them can be dismissed—except for Shmuel." See Ḥayyim Meir Heilman, *Beit Rabbi*, vol. 1 (Berdichev, 1902), 65b, n. 3.

*

My dear friend Rabbi Dr. Eli DiPoce directed me to a passage in *Sefat Emet* by the Rebbe of Gur (Góra Kalwaria) that echoes this Kabbalistic teaching of the centrality of *ru'aḥ*. The Gerrer Rebbe writes that the three daily prayers of *Shaḥarit, Minḥah* and *'Arvit* correspond to the three levels of the soul from the top down: *neshamah, ru'aḥ* and *nefesh*. He makes a point of saying: "*Minḥah* (the afternoon prayer) is the aspect of *ru'aḥ*...which is the main aspect of man in this world." See Rabbi Judah Aryeh Leib Alter, *Sefat Emet, Vayyetse* 5649, s.v. *vayifga' ba-makom*.

(Inter alia, in later years, Rav Kook was extremely fond of the work *Sefat Emet*, keeping it handy at all times and committing it to memory.)

[300]Isaiah 44:13. See *Masekhet 'Atsilut*, pp. 77-78.

From the bottom up, the three levels of the soul—*nefesh, ru'aḥ* and *neshamah*—correspond respectively to the *sefirot* of *Malkhut, Tif'eret* and *Binah*. For the various correspondences, see the Kabbalistic Chart appended to our work.

[301]*Zohar* II, 85a.

[302]*b. 'Arakhin* 13b.

[303]Shem Tov ben Abraham ibn Gaon, *Migdal 'Oz*, commentary to Maimonides, *MT, Hil. Teshuvah* 8:2, quoting Naḥmanides' *Sha'ar ha-Gemul*, in *Kitvei Ramban*, ed. Chavel (Jerusalem, 1968), vol. 2, *Torat ha-Adam*, pp. 302-303. Naḥmanides writes that the eight-stringed harp represents the eighth *sefirah* (i.e. *Binah*).

[304]Isaiah 66:23; *Zohar* II, 157a. See the commentary of Rabbi ḤYD Azulai, *Nitsutsei 'Orot*, n. 1, that the "*guf*" (body) corresponds to the *sefirah* of *Malkhut*. See also the commentary of the *Sulam* there, par. 558.

[305]Numbers 27:18.

[306]1 Chronicles 1:48. *Reḥovot ha-Nahar* is usually translated into English as "Reḥoboth-on-the-River." *Reḥovot ha-Nahar* is synonymous with the *sefirah* of *Binah*. See Rabbi Joseph Gikatilla, *Sha'arei 'Orah*, ed. Joseph Ben Shlomo (Jerusalem, 1970), vol. 2, Eighth Gate (pp. 52, 59).

[307]Genesis 2:10. Eden is code for the *sefirah* of *Ḥokhmah*. The River that proceeds from Eden symbolizes *Binah*. See Rabbi Joseph Gikatilla, *Sha'arei 'Orah*, vol. 2, Ninth Gate (p. 102).

[308]Whereas the distance from *Malkhut* up to *Binah* is eight levels; the distance from *Tif'eret* up to *Binah* is only three levels. (There intervene *Ḥesed* and *Gevurah*.)

[309]*b. Niddah* 20b. Rashi ad loc. explains the expression to mean one who possesses all manner of wisdom.

[310]Ezekiel 32:27.

[311]Isaiah 3:9.

[312]Hebrew, "*ha-'askan bi-devarim*." So according to the reading of *Ma'amrei ha-Rayah*, vol. 2, p. 441. My own reading of the manuscript is: "*ha-'amkan bi-devarim*" ("who delves deeply into matters").

[313]Hebrew, "*lehakhin*" ("to prepare"). However in *Ma'amrei ha-Rayah* (ibid.), the word is transcribed "*lehavin*" ("to understand").

[314]Genesis 2:7.

[315]See Rabbi Joseph Gikatilla, *Sha'arei 'Orah*, vol. 2, Eighth Gate (p. 65).

[316]Genesis 2:10; *Sha'arei 'Orah*, Eighth Gate (p. 52); Ninth Gate (p. 102); *Zohar* III, 289b, 290b (*Idra Zuta*).

[317]In Rav Kook's manuscript (top 139a), this addition occurs above the line.

[318]Ruth 3:7.

[319]*Zohar Ḥadash, Midrash Ruth*, ed. Reuven Margaliyot, 88a. In the Zoharic rendition, Ruth sleeping on the ground (or in another version, "in the dust") is a trope for *Knesset Yisrael* (*Ecclesia Israel*) who in exile have been reduced to the lowest spiritual level. However, the *Zohar Ḥadash* adduces this from the following verse: "Behold, a woman is sleeping at his feet" (Ruth 3:8). Rav Kook's reading of *"le-'ar'a"* ("on the ground") can be found in Rabbi Meir ibn Gabbai, *'Avodat ha-Kodesh* (Warsaw, 1891; photo offset Jerusalem, 1973), II, 8 (30b).

[320]See Rabbi Ḥayyim Vital, *Sha'ar Ma'amrei Rashbi* (Jerusalem, 1898), *Noah* (14a): "The Rabbis, of blessed memory, said that the soul of the wicked descends to his feet. This is the secret of the verse 'She revealed his feet and she slept,' as mentioned in the *Book of Zohar* and the *Tikkunim*." In his gloss *ad locum*, Rabbi Samuel Vital quotes *Tikkunei Zohar*'s paraphrase of the verse "She revealed his feet and she slept" (Ruth 3:7): "His soul descended to his feet." See *Tikkunei Zohar*, *tikkun* 21 (Margaliyot edition, beginning 50a). Rabbi Samuel Vital has transcribed a *derush* from *Sha'ar ha-Gilgulim* (unaccounted for in our *Sha'ar ha-Gilgulim*). The import of the passage is that when one becomes a *"rasha' gamur"* (a totally wicked person), the soul descends into the midst of the *kelipot*.

Rav Kook interprets the distance of "eight parasangs" symbolically. From the lowest spiritual level of *Malkhut* to the highest spiritual level that man may attain, *"Binah,"* one must ascend eight levels. Reckoned from the bottom up, *"Binah"* is the eighth *sefirah*.

[321]Rabbi Ḥayyim of Volozhin, *Nefesh ha-Ḥayyim* I, 15-16. See above our note 299.

[322]Genesis 45:27. The patriarch Jacob personifies the *sefirah* of *Tif'eret*. In this verse, the level of soul referred to as *"ru'aḥ"* is juxtaposed to Jacob or *Tif'eret*, establishing linkage between the two. See our Kabbalisic Chart.

[323]Having improved themselves spiritually, they were now only "three parasangs" away from the "World to Come" or *"Binah."* To reach *Binah* from *Tif'eret*, one must ascend the three levels of *Tif'eret*, *Gevurah* and *Ḥesed*.

Binah is portrayed in the Kabbalistic literature as the "Supernal Mother" ("*'Imma 'Ila'ah*") nurturing her children, i.e. the *sefirot* below. See e.g. *Nefesh ha-Ḥayyim* I, beginning chap. 16.

Rav Kook's exact phrase *"le'anaka la-banin"* ("to nurse the children") could not be located. However the phrase *"yanka la-banin"* ("nursing the children") occurs in *Zohar* III, 99b. There, the *sefirah* of *Binah* is symbolized by the *"shofar gadol"* (the great ram's horn). (Cf. *Zohar* I, 29b.) See Rabbi Joseph Gikatilla, *Sha'arei 'Orah*, ed. Joseph Ben Shlomo (Jerusalem, 1970), vol. 2, Eighth Gate (p. 68).

[324]Though unstated, this passage was probably influenced by the discussion in *Tikkunei Zohar*. In *tikkun* 60, we learn that an individual whose body is beautiful with regular features, but whose soul on the inside is wicked, is referred to as "a wicked man who has it good" (*"rasha' ve-tov lo"*). Conversely, one whose body is bad on the outside, but whose soul is good on the inside, is called "a righteous man who has it bad" (*"tsaddik ve-ra' lo"*). (The terminology has been appropriated from *b. Berakhot* 7a.) *Tikkunei Zohar* depicts the Messiah as the latter. "Good on the inside and his cloak bad.—This is 'A poor man and riding on a donkey' [Zechariah 9:9]." See the Vilna Gaon's commentary ad loc.

In a famous letter to his adversary, Rabbi Jacob David Wilovsky (Ridbaz), then Rabbi of Safed, Rav Kook extends this characterization of "good on the inside and bad on the outside" to the generation that ushers in the Messiah, writing that they are the "donkey of the Messiah." See *Igrot ha-Rayah*, vol. 2 (Jerusalem, 1961), p. 188 (Letter 555). Rav Kook claims that he is able to sense which individuals fit this description. It is those Jews, outwardly alienated, yet possessing the "inner gift" (*"ha-segulah ha-penimit"*), that he strives to bring close—not those whose wickedness is complete. "The Lord, blessed be He, knows that I do not bring close all sinners, only those that I feel have inside a great gift." When he writes cryptically on the next line, "And there are many ways to know this, which would require volumes to explain" (ibid.), we are reminded of our own *Tay'a*.

Rav Kook firmly believed that "the Lord, blessed be He, who conducts with love each generation, arranges the souls that must appear in the world" in any given time (ibid., p. 186). Cf. *Orot*, *Ha-Milḥamah* (The War), chap. 2: "We understand that the spark of soul is the determining factor: That state of the world that proceeded then [in Biblical times], that necessitated war, caused these souls to appear." See *Orot*, ed. Bezalel Naor (Maggid, 2015), pp. 132-133.

When Warsaw journalist Hillel Zeitlin met Rav Kook in Jerusalem in 1925, he was shown by Rav Kook this same passage in *Tikkunei Zohar*. See Hillel Zeitlin, *Sifran shel Yeḥidim*, ed. Aaron Zeitlin (Jerusalem, 1979), p. 240. (It is interesting that Zeitlin, a student of the *Zohar*, did not notice that Rav Kook had engaged in some original exegesis, extending the *tikkun*'s portrayal of the Messiah—who, the Gaon points out, is David himself—to the entire generation of the Messiah. Rav Kook's disciple, Rabbi Ya'akov Moshe Ḥarlap, followed Rav Kook's lead when he wrote that this entire generation is the soul of King David. See Rabbi Y.M. Ḥarlap, *Mi-M'ayenei ha-Yeshu'ah* [Jerusalem, 1981], chap. 63 [p. 214].)

[325]Psalms 25:14.

[326]Proverbs 3:32.

[327]For *"yashar"* as a *terminus technicus*, see Rabbi Naftali Tsevi Yehudah Berlin's Introduction to the Book of Genesis; in his commentary to the Pentateuch, *Ha'amek Davar* (Vilna: Romm, 1879). Cf. Maimonides, *Guide of the Perplexed* III, 49 (in Michael Schwarz ed., pp. 640-641).

Naftali Tsevi Yehudah Berlin (known by the acronym *Netsiv*) served as Rosh Yeshivah of Volozhin, where he mentored the young soon-to-be-wed Avraham Yitsḥak Hakohen Kook, leaving upon him an indelible imprint. This writer (BN) was told an anecdote by a descendant of Netsiv, Rabbi Aharon Soloveichik of Chicago, whereby Netsiv referred to his disciple Avraham Yitsḥak Hakohen Kook as a *"yashar."* (The context was Netsiv's defense of the young man's practice of wearing *tefillin* all day, behavior viewed by some of his peers as excessive and ostentatious piety.) See the *Koren Rav Kook Siddur*, ed. Bezalel Naor (2017), pp. 17, 270-273.

The *Ra'aya Mehemna* (printed in *Zohar* II, 43a) refers to the hand-phylactery as *"yashar."* See now *Metsi'ot Katan* (Israel: Maggid, 2018), par. 290 (p. 445) and par. 296 (p. 452). There, Rav Kook explains that *"yashar"* (upright) refers to the *middot* or character traits. The hand-phylactery, opposite the heart, corresponds to character; the head-phylactery, opposite the brain, corresponds to intellect.

See also Rav Kook's interpretation of the verse in Psalms 36:11, which Maimonides adopted as the motto of his *Sefer ha-Madda'*. Published as *"Ḥiddushei ha-Rayah le-Yad ha-Ḥazakah le-ha-Rambam,"* in Rabbi Moshe Zuriel, *Otserot ha-Rayah* (Rishon-Lezion, 2002), vol. 3, pp. 15-16.

[328]See *b. Bava Metsi'a* 85a.

[329]2 Samuel 14:20.

The Dead of the Desert

12

And Rabbah bar Bar Ḥannah said: That Bedouin said to me: Come, I will show you the dead of the desert, i.e. the Israelites who left Egypt and died in the wilderness. **I went and saw them; and they had the appearance of those who are intoxicated, and they were lying on their backs. And the knee of one of them was erect, and** he was so enormous that **a Bedouin entered under his knee while riding a camel and with his spear upright, and it did not touch him. I cut one corner of the sky-blue** garment that contains ritual fringes[329*] **of one of them, and we were unable to walk.** The Bedouin **said to me: Perhaps you took something from them? As we learned** by tradition **that one who takes something from them cannot walk. I went** back and **returned it,** i.e. the corner of the garment, **and then we were able to walk.**

When I came before the Rabbis, they said to me: Every Abba is **a donkey, and every bar Bar Ḥannah** is **a fool. For** the purpose of clarifying **what *halakhah* did you do that?** If you wanted **to know whether** the *halakhah* **is in accordance with** the opinion of **Beit Shammai or in accordance with** the opinion of **Beit Hillel,** as to whether there are four or three threads in the ritual fringes, **you should have counted the threads and counted the joints,** before you returned the corner of the garment.

THE GENERATION OF THE DESERT: WHEN GIANTS CANNOT SERVE AS ROLE MODELS

It seems that this sage ("the Bedouin") gave Rabbah bar Bar Ḥannah to understand the exalted level of the generation of the desert. In truth, the generation of the desert were (spiritually) very high. It was a "generation of knowledge" (*dor de'ah*).[330] In the writings of the Ari (Rabbi Isaac Luria), of blessed memory, it is explained that the reason that they chose not to enter the Land was also on account of their level, as it states regarding the verse, "And you who cleave to the Lord your God etc."[331] Their approach was esoteric to the point that the behavior of the Land of Israel—which is exoteric, the Lower World—was not appropriate for them because of their cleaving to a higher place.[332] Their behavior was appropriate for a miraculous existence which is the esoteric way.[333]

Wine is a symbol of the esoteric, as the Sages, of blessed memory, said: "Wine (*yayin*) was given with seventy letters and the secret (*sod*) was given with seventy letters; [when] wine goes in, the secret goes out."[334] This explains why **they had the appearance of those who are intoxicated.** They were full of the secret of the wine.

Now because there had dawned upon them the light of freedom, their having departed Egypt and attained the level of *Binah* (Understanding),[335] **they were lying on their backs.** Lying on one's back symbolizes freedom. Therefore, one may not recite *Shema'* lying on one's back because one's bodily posture must bespeak [acceptance of] the yoke [of the Kingdom of Heaven].[336]

Rabbah bar Bar Ḥannah related that it is impossible to arrive at an understanding of how prodigious their (spiritual) level was. Even the lowest extreme of their spiritual attainment, imaged as the **"knee,"** symbolizing the final *sefirot* of *Netsaḥ* (Eternity), *Hod* (Splendor) and *Yesod* (Foundation),[337] **was erect.** The intention being that even their lowest aspects were of the World of the Male (*'Alma di-Dekhura*), symbolized by standing upright.[338] Their main thing was Torah, the World of the Male (*'Alma di-Dekhura*), as opposed to the World of the Female (*'Alma de-Nukva*), which symbolizes works (*'uvdin*).[339] Truthfully, they had few deeds, for they were lacking several commandments,[340] but they compensated for all with their great stature in Torah.

And the knee of one of them was erect. Only "one of them." It was impossible to assess their collective grandeur. The collective has an enhanced holiness. This is borne out in the importance of the prayer of the many (*tefillatam shel rabbim*).[341] Rabbah bar Bar Ḥannah could only behold the lower levels of the individual.

A Bedouin entered under his knee while riding a camel and with his spear upright, and it did not touch him. In general, the perfection of holiness depends upon three things, as stated in *Zohar*, *Mishpatim* [i.e. *Yitro*] regarding the three advisers to Pharaoh.[342] [The *Zohar* speaks of three negative qualities, but] corresponding to them on the side of holiness are: fear [of the Lord], works and wisdom.

Now the Bedouin is a merchant, which is indicative of his great wisdom, as the verse states: "[Happy is the man that finds wisdom, and the man that obtains understanding.] For the merchandise of it is better than the merchandise of silver...."[343] "She is like the merchant ships."[344]

Also, the Sages, of blessed memory, said that most of the camel-drivers are decent.[345] Because they are exposed to the danger of remote parts, their fear is great. (See Rashi's commentary.)[346] So the camel-driver has the prerequisite fear.

Furthermore, the camel itself is modest, as the Sages, of blessed memory, observed on the verse "Thirty milk camels and their colts (*u-beneihem*)."[347] "This is to be re-vocalized *bana'eihem* (their male consorts). Since [the male camel] is modest when cohabiting, Scripture did not publicize him."[348] Modesty results from the trait of shame, which is synonymous with fear, as it is written, "'In order that His fear be upon your faces'—This refers to shame."[349] So the Bedouin had the prerequisite fear.

And thirdly, the works are alluded to by the "spear." As the Sages, of blessed memory, interpreted the verse, "He took a spear in his hand,"[350] to mean that he recited *Shema'*, which has in it two hundred and forty-eight words,[351] corresponding to the two hundred and forty-eight positive commandments.

Now with all three qualities together (wisdom, fear and works), the Bedouin could not apprehend even "the knee of one of them." Rabbah bar Bar Ḥannah mentioned three qualities corresponding to the three levels of the knees, namely *Netsaḥ* (Eternity), *Hod* (Splendor) and *Yesod* (Foundation).[352]

I cut one corner of the sky-blue garment that contains ritual fringes **of one of them.** Having been able through *ru'aḥ ha-kodesh* (divine inspiration) to apprehend a little of their spiritual level, Rabbah bar Bar Ḥannah then desired to know something of their fear [of the Lord], symbolized by *tekhelet*, the sky-blue hue, as written in the *Zohar*, *Terumah* (that *tekhelet* comes into play when the Heavenly Court judges souls).[353] **And we were unable to walk**, meaning that it is utterly impossible for us to follow their ways, which are much higher than our ways.

The Bedouin **said to me: Perhaps you took something from them?** Seeing that Rabbah bar Bar Ḥannah had adopted for himself a lofty way that he had apprehended from the generation of the desert, and was unable to follow it, the Bedouin explained that it is not possible to adopt their behavior. **As we learned** by tradition **that one who takes something from them cannot walk.** We do not have the ability to follow their way which is very lofty. **I went** back and **returned it,** i.e. the corner of the garment, **and then we were able to walk.** Rabbah bar Bar Ḥannah thereupon decided that such a way was fitting for them but not for us, and resolved to follow the way appropriate for our relatively reduced circumstances. Once he was reconciled to the way befitting us, he was able to go in the way of the Lord and His service worthy of him.

When I came before the Rabbis, and I related to them how mighty was the level [of the generation of the desert], they responded that compared to the generation of the desert, the wise and holy men of our generation are negligible. It is utterly impossible to grasp the affairs [of the generation of the desert], as the Sages said: "[If the early ones were angels, then we are men.] If the early ones were men, then we are as donkeys."[354]

Now the sage possesses two qualities: his own quality which is a matter of work based on choice; and the quality of wisdom, which is one of the things that a father bestows upon his son.[355]

When I informed the Rabbis that the level of the generation of the desert can be apprehended neither in terms of fear [of the Lord] nor of Torah, **they said to me: Every Abba** is **a donkey, and every bar Bar Ḥannah** is **a fool.** ["Donkey" relates to fear; "fool" to wisdom, or lack thereof.] It is known that *yir'at ha-romemut* (awe of the sublime) is not a burden to man; rather it is a crown of glory. One is likened to a donkey, a beast of burden,[356] only when due to one's puny intellect, one reached[356*] to *yir'at ha-'onesh* (fear of punishment).[357] **Every Abba** is **a donkey.** All the great ones of the generation (*gedolei ha-dor*) on the level of Rabbah are considered donkeys who serve out of fear of punishment compared to the sublime awe of the generation of the desert. **And every bar Bar Ḥannah** is **a fool.** And when it comes to wisdom, every son (*bar*) of Bar Ḥannah is reckoned a fool (because wisdom is one of the things that a father bestows upon his son).[358] In comparison with the generation of the desert, we are not reckoned wise men at all.[359]

The Rabbis brought a proof that we are prevented from apprehending the level of the generation of the desert: The main thing that Rabbah bar Bar Ḥannah desired to know of their ways is how to behave in the way[360] of serving the Lord, whether by the way of *gevurot* (rigors) or by the way of *ḥasadim* (love); **in accordance with** the opinion of **Beit Shammai**

or in accordance with the opinion of **Beit Hillel.**[361] Beit Shammai were stringent in their rulings because their souls were of *gevurot*, whereas Beit Hillel were lenient, because their souls were of *ḥasadim*.[362] Having observed the wisdom and the deeds of the generation of the desert, Rabbah bar Bar Ḥannah should have been able to ascertain this.

In the *tsitsit* (ritual fringes) there are strings and joints. The total number of strings is thirty-two, which symbolizes the thirty-two Paths of Wisdom.[363] The knot connotes that the deeds unify the wisdom and give it endurance (*mekayyemim*) in man.[364] So Rabbah bar Bar Ḥannah **should have counted the threads,** to observe their wisdom, **and counted the joints,** to observe their works. Since he did not apprehend from their affairs something practicable, one can (certainly)[365] deduce that all their ways are much higher than we are worthy of, whether it comes to wisdom or service and deeds. In their regard, Scripture says: "Gather My saints (*ḥasidai*) together unto Me; those that have made a covenant (*berit*) with Me by sacrifice."[366] They were special both in piety (*ḥasidut*), which is works; and in wisdom, referred to as the covenant (*berit*), as it is written: "The secret (*sod*) of the Lord is revealed to those that fear Him; and His covenant (*berit*), to make them know it."[367] In the generation of the desert, both qualities [i.e. wisdom and deeds] were of great stature.

[329*]Aramaic, *tekhilta.* In order to avoid confusion, we should clarify that the term may refer to the blue fringes appended to the garment or to the garment itself. In this instance, it is the latter. Thus, Rashi translates *tekhilta* into Hebrew as *tallit.*

[330]*Leviticus Rabbah* 9:1. The Midrash puns on the name "Darda'" (1 Kings 5:11; 1 Chronicles 2:6): "This is the generation (*dor*) of the desert which is knowledge (*de'ah*) throughout."

Rabbi Ḥayyim Vital explains that the generation of the desert were called *"Dor De'ah"* because they were from *"Da'at ha-'Elyon"* (*Da'at* of *Ze'ir Anpin*, etc.). See Rabbi Ḥayyim Vital, *'Ets Ḥayyim, Sha'ar* 32 (*Sha'ar He'arat ha-Moḥin*), chap. 1; idem, *Sha'ar ha-Pesukim* (Jerusalem, 1912), *Shemot*, chap. 1, s.v. *vayyakam melekh ḥadash* (24c); *Shelaḥ*, chap. 13, s.v. *shelaḥ lekha anashim* (34d).

In his commentary to the prayer of Ḥannah, the Vilna Gaon elaborates on the spiritual level of the generation of the desert and why they are referred to as the "generation of knowledge" (*dor de'ah*). See the Gaon's commentary, 1 Samuel 2:6, s.v. *Hashem memit u-meḥayyeh*; in *Likkutei Torah me-ha-Gaon Rabbeinu Eliyahu mi-Vilna*, ed. Yisrael Hayyim Mikhel Levensohn (Warsaw, 1899), 2d-3a. In that regard, the Gaon also speaks of their fear of the Lord (*yir'at Hashem*). This version of the Gaon's commentary to the prayer of Ḥannah is based on a Volozhin manuscript, whose veracity was attested to by Rabbi Naftali Tsevi Yehudah Berlin of Volozhin. (See the Editor's introduction.) It differs significantly from the shorter version included in the standard *Mikra'ot Gedolot* edition.

The incomparable spiritual stature of the generation of the desert also comes up in *b. 'Avodah Zarah* 5a. See Rashi there, s.v. *kemo she-lo ba'nu la-'olam.*

[331]Deuteronomy 4:4.

[332]In Rabbi Ḥayyim Vital, *Sha'ar ha-Pesukim, Shelaḥ*, the difference is drawn between Leah, *'Alma 'Ila'ah* (the Higher World), and her sister Raḥel, *'Alma Tata'ah* (the Lower World). Cf. idem, *Likkutei Torah* (Vilna, 1880), *Shelaḥ*, 84b.

Rabbi Shneur Zalman of Liadi, *Likkutei Torah, Shelaḥ*, s.v. *shelaḥ lekha* (36c-37b) explains that due to their exalted spiritual stature, the generation of the desert did not want to descend to the level of observing the practical commandments that would have been incumbent upon them in the Land of Israel. Further on, Rabbi Shneur Zalman refers to the Lurianic teaching that the souls of the generation of the desert were from Leah, who symbolizes *'Olam ha-Maḥshavah* (the World of Thought), as opposed to her sister Raḥel, symbol of the *'Olam ha-Dibbur* (the World of Speech). Ibid., s.v. *Vayyomru el kol 'adat B'nei Yisrael* (38b).

*

There is a Tannaitic controversy whether the generation of the desert have a portion in the World to Come. Rabbi Akiva was of the opinion that they have no portion (because of the Sin of the Spies, see Numbers 14:35). Rabbi Eliezer (and also Rabbi Shim'on ben Menasya) believed that they have a portion in the World to Come. (See *t. Sanhedrin*, chap. 13; Zuckermandel ed., p. 435.) See *Tosafot*, *Bava Batra* 73b, s.v. *ve-damu ke-man de-mibasmei*; and *Maharasha*, s.v. *ve-'amar 'aḥvei lakh metei midbar.*

In *Talmud Bavli* (*Sanhedrin* 110b), our own Rabbah bar Bar Ḥannah (quoting Rabbi Yoḥanan) makes the bold statement:

> Rabbi Akiva took leave of his piety (*ḥasidut*), for it says, "Go, and call in the ears of Jerusalem, saying: Thus said the Lord: I remembered for you the kindness of your youth, the love of your espousals; your going after Me in the desert, in a land that is not sown" [Jeremiah 2:2].
>
> If others enter [the World to Come] in their merit, then they themselves all the more so!

Rashi explains:

> **Rabbi Akiva took leave of his piety**—for he was accustomed to finding merit in Israel, and now he finds them guilty, by saying, "The generation of the desert have no portion in the World to Come."
>
> **For it says, "Go, and call, etc."**—In other words, Rabbi Akiva could have interpreted that they have a portion in the World to Come, for it is written "Go, and call, etc."

In his ethical work, *Mesillat Yesharim*, Rabbi Moses Ḥayyim Luzzatto concluded that the hallmark of the *"ḥasid"* is precisely this ability to champion Israel by proving their innocence. See Rabbi Moses Ḥayyim Luzzatto, *Mesillat Yesharim*, end chap. 19.

Rav Kook adopted Luzzatto's definition of *"ḥasidut"* as his own. In his abbreviation of Luzzatto's masterpiece, *Kitsur Mesillat Yesharim*, chap. 6, Rav Kook put it rather succinctly: "[The *ḥasid*] will pray for the entire generation to vindicate the guilty as well."

First published as an appendix to Rabbi Tsevi Yehudah Kook's *Li-Sheloshah be-Elul*, vol. 2 (5707/1947), pp. 23-31, Rav Kook's *Kitsur Mesillat Yesharim* has since been reprinted in *Ma'amrei ha-Rayah*, vol. 2 (Jerusalem, 1984), pp. 273-276; and in Rabbi Moshe Zuriel, *Otserot ha-Rayah* (Rishon le-Zion, 2002), vol. 2, pp. 297-300.

According to Rabbi Neriyah, *Kitsur Mesillat Yesharim* was written at the time that Rav Kook studied in the Volozhin Yeshivah. In those days, he would walk around with a copy of *Mesillat Yesharim* in his pocket. See Neriyah, *Tal ha-Rayah*, p. 60.

[333]Cf. the controversy between Rabbi Ishmael and Rabbi Shim'on ben Yoḥai concerning earning a livelihood. Rabbi Ishmael thought it better to combine study of Torah with labor: *"Hanheg bahen minhag derekh erets."* Rabbi Shim'on ben Yoḥai took the more extreme view that one

should engage exclusively in the study of Torah. Abaye observed: "Many did as Rabbi Ishmael and succeeded; [many did] as Rabbi Shim'on ben Yoḥai and did not succeed" (*b. Berakhot* 35b). See the discussion in Rabbi Ḥayyim of Volozhin, *Nefesh ha-Ḥayyim* I, 8-9. (The Generation of the Desert's exclusive preoccupation with study of Torah is discussed in chapter 9.) See also the differing opinions of Rabbeinu Tam and Rabbeinu Elḥanan, whether Torah is the main thing or *Derekh Erets* (earning a livelihood); quoted in *Tosafot Yeshanim*, *Yoma* 85b, s.v. *teshuvah ba'ya Yom ha-Kippurim.*

[334]*b. 'Eruvin* 65a. The Hebrew words *"yayin"* (wine) and *"sod"* (secret) share in common the numerical value of 70. See Rashi ad loc.

[335]This passage was out of sequence in *Ma'amrei ha-Rayah* and belongs here.

There are various ways to justify Rav Kook's statement that the generation of the desert attained the level of *Binah*. For starters, they received the Torah on Mount Sinai fifty days after the Exodus from Egypt. The *sefirah* of *Binah* is equated with the fiftieth year or Jubilee year. See Rabbi Joseph Gikatilla, *Sha'arei 'Orah*, ed. Joseph Ben Shlomo (Jerusalem, 1970), vol. 2, Eighth Gate (pp. 58-59, 68).

In the *Zohar* (II, 46b, 83b, 85b) it states that the freedom of Israel from Egypt came from the *"sitra de-yovela"* ("the side of the Jubilee"). Rabbi Ḥayyim Vital understood that to mean that the souls of the generation of the desert were from the "side of the Jubilee." See *'Ets Ḥayyim* 32:1 and *Sha'ar ha-Pesukim*, *Shemot*. In *Likkutei Torah*, Rabbi Ḥayyim Vital writes:

> I heard from my teacher [i.e. Rabbi Isaac Luria], of blessed memory...that what is stated in *Zohar* that the generation of the desert are "from the side of the Jubilee" (*"mi-sitra de-yovela"*), refers to *Tevunah*, not *Binah* itself ... And I heard from others that what is stated, "from the side of the Jubilee," refers to *Yesod* of *Binah* ....
>
> (Rabbi Ḥayyim Vital, *Likkutei Torah* [Vilna 1880; photo offset Jerusalem 1972], *Devarim* [f. 91])

Furthermore, *Yetsi'at Mitsrayim* (the Exodus from Egypt) is mentioned in the Torah fifty times. See *Zohar* II, 85b; III, 262a. There is a reckoning of the "fifty occurrences" in the *Be'ur ha-Gra* to *Tikkunei Zohar* (Vilna, 1867), *tikkun* 32 (84b).

But all of this derives ultimately from the Talmudic statement, "Fifty gates of understanding were created in the world" (*b. Rosh Hashanah* 21b).

[336]*b. Berakhot* 13b.

[337]See Rabbi Ḥayyim Vital, *"Ma'amar Pesi'otav shel Avraham Avinu,"* in idem, *Sha'ar Ma'amrei Razal*, appended to *Sha'ar Ma'amrei Rashbi* (Jerusalem, 1898; photo-offset Jerusalem, 1988), 9d, commenting on the saying "These knees of the rabbis that are weak—it is from them [i.e.

the demons]" ("*hanei birkhei de-rabbanan de-shalhei—minayhu*") (*b. Berakhot* 6a, and *Saba de-Mishpatim* section of *Zohar* II, 111b and 112b). "*Ma'amar Pesi'otav shel Avraham Avinu*" was also included in *Ketavim Ḥadashim le-Rabbeinu Ḥayyim Vital*, ed. Rabbi Ya'akov Moshe Hillel (Jerusalem, 1988). See there par. 91 (p. 26). Cf. the commentary of the Vilna Gaon to *Sefer Yetsirah*, ed. Samuel Luria (Warsaw, 1884), 5:6 (18d), commenting on *b. Berakhot* 6a.

[338]In Kabbalah, the posture of standing symbolizes the World of the Male (*'Alma di-Dekhura*), whereas seated posture symbolizes the World of the Female (*'Alma de-Nukva*). See *Zohar* (I, 132b; III, 120b) which prescribes donning the hand-phylactery seated and the head-phylactery standing. The *Zohar* assumes that the two *tefillin* represent respectively the feminine and masculine worlds. See Rabbi Nathan Spira, *Matsat Shimmurim*, ed. Rabbi Moshe Zuriel (Jerusalem, 2001), *Sha'ar Tefillin*, p. 309: "Whatever is in the World of the Female (*'Alma de-Nukva*) must be done seated." (See also *'Ets Hayyim* 32:1 where the head-phylactery is equated with Leah and the hand-phylactery with Raḥel.)

[339]See above note 208.

[340]Most notably, they lacked the commandments tied to the Land of Israel (*mitsvot ha-teluyot ba-arets*). See Rabbi Shneur Zalman of Liadi, *Likkutei Torah*, *Shelaḥ*, s.v. *shelaḥ lekha*, 36d.

[341]See *b. Sanhedrin* 39a: "Wherever there are ten, the *Shekhinah* rests." Also *b. Berakhot* 7a: "From whence do we derive that the Holy One, blessed be He, does not detest the prayer of the many (*tefillatan shel rabbim*)? ...."

[342]*Zohar* II, 69a. According to the *Zohar*, of Pharaoh's three advisers, Jethro excelled in astrology; Bil'am excelled in magic; and Job excelled in fear. In Rav Kook's transcription of the *Zohar*, Jethro symbolizes wisdom; Bil'am symbolizes works ("*'uvda*" or in the plural *'uvdin*); and Job symbolizes fear. In the case of fear, the *Zohar* reasons that if fear is required for the *Sitra Aḥera* (the Other Side or the Side of Unholiness), all the more so is fear required for holiness. For the three advisers to Pharaoh, see *b. Sotah* 11a.

[343]Proverbs 3:13-14.

[344]Proverbs 31:14. See above adjacent to notes 254 and 255.

[345]*b. Kiddushin* 82a.

[346]Rashi *ad locum* explains that since the camel-drivers journey to the deserts, a place of wild beasts and brigands, they fear for their lives and subdue their hearts to the Omnipresent.

[347]Genesis 32:16.

[348]*Genesis Rabbah* 76:7, quoted in Rashi on the verse.

[349]Exodus 20:16; *b. Nedarim* 20a.

[350]Numbers 25:7.

[351]The numerical equivalence of the word *"romaḥ"* or spear (248) occurs in many Kabbalistic works. The recitation of the *Shema'*, with its total of two hundred and forty-eight words, is viewed as a "spear" or weapon to dispel the *"mazikin"* or demonic forces. (See e.g. *Zohar* III, 272a and the recently discovered *Hebrew Writings of the Author of Tiqqunei Zohar and Ra'aya Mehemna*, ed. Efraim Gottlieb [Jerusalem, 2003], *ma'amar* 2, lines 233-235 [p. 141].)

It has not been possible to locate an early source for Rav Kook's statement that Pinḥas was reciting *Shema'* at that time. The closest we come to that is the statement of Pseudo-Jonathan that the congregation of the Children of Israel were crying and reciting *Shema'* when Zimri so flagrantly challenged them. See Pseudo-Jonathan to Numbers 25:6.

However, later Kabbalistic works have Pinḥas reciting *Shema'* with its numerical significance of 248 (*"romaḥ"*) at the time that he set out to summarily execute Zimri. See Rabbi Nathan Spira, *Megalleh 'Amukot, Mahadura tinyana 'al ha-Torah*, ed. Rabbi Shalom Weiss (Jerusalem, 1998), *Pinḥas, derush* 5, par. 15 (298b); Rabbi Jacob Isaac Horowitz ("Seer of Lublin"), *Zikhron Zot, Pinḥas.*

[352]In *Yahel 'Or* (commentary of the Vilna Gaon to *Zohar*), ed. Naftali Herz Halevi of Bialystok (Vilna, 1882), it is explained that Pharaoh's three advisers correspond to the three lines of the middle triad of *sefirot* (*Ḥesed-Gevurah-Tif'eret*). In the Gaon's analysis, Job is the left line (*Gevurah* or Fear); Jethro, the right line of *Ḥesed* or Love; and Bil'am *ought* to correspond to the middle line of *Tif'eret* or Beauty (but does not). The Gaon explains that while there is some contiguity between Jethro and Abraham, and between Job and Isaac, there is no contact whatsoever between Bil'am and Jacob (the personification of *Tif'eret*). This perfect equilibrium of Jacob simply does not exist on the Side of Unholiness. (Though unstated, evidently this relates to the concept of the *Mitkala* or Balance expounded at the beginning of the *Sifra di-Tseni'uta*, which is lacking in the *'Olam ha-Tohu* or World of Chaos.)

The Gaon's remarks in *Yahel 'Or* should be juxtaposed to his comment in *Aderet Eliyahu* as to why Bil'am sacrificed a bullock and a ram, corresponding to Abraham and Isaac, but not sheep corresponding to Jacob. See *Aderet Eliyahu* to Numbers 23:2 and the supercommentary of Rabbi Yitsḥak Eizik Ḥaver, *Be'er Yitsḥak* ad locum; in *Aderet Eliyahu*, ed. Samuel Luria (Warsaw, 1887), *Balak* (*Mahadura Kamma*), pp. 221-222. The Gaon's remarks in *Aderet Eliyahu* are best appreciated in light of the interpretation of Rabbi Moses ha-Darshan, as quoted in Rashi, Numbers 28:19. This was pointed out by the Gaon Rabbi Shelomo Fisher *shelit"a*; see his *Beit Yishai: Derashot* (Israel, 2004), chap. 12 (104b).

In Rav Kook's scheme (based on the bottom triad of *Netsaḥ-Hod-Yesod*), fear would correspond to the left *sefirah* of *Hod*; wisdom to the right *sefirah* of *Netsaḥ*; and works to the middle *sefirah* of *Yesod.*

[353]*Zohar* II, 139a, 152. The *Zohar* explains the adage, "All colors are good in a dream except for *tekhelet*" (*b. Berakhot* 57b), in terms of the Seat of Judgment. At the moment one beholds the color blue, one's soul is being judged in the Celestial Court.

[354]*b. Shabbat* 112b.

[355]*m. ʿEduyot* 2:9.

[356]In *Maʾamrei ha-Rayah*, vol. 2, p. 443: *"u-khe-ḥamor le-ʿol ha-massaʾ."* See *b. ʿAvodah Zarah* 5b: *"u-khe-ḥamor la-massa"* ("and as a donkey to the burden"). However, in Rav Kook's manuscript, it appears that the word *"massa"* is missing.

[356*]Hebrew, *hisig*. In *Maʾamrei ha-Rayah* (p. 443) it was transcribed *tsarikh* (needs).

[357]In Rav Kook's manuscript the phrase reads: *yirʾat ha-rom ha-ʿonesh*. In *Maʾamrei ha-Rayah* (p. 443) this was transcribed simply as *yirʾat ha-ʿonesh*. Evidently, the editors assumed that the middle word was a mistake. Rav Kook began to write *yirʾat ha-romemut* but aborted the word *ha-rom* midway and substituted instead *ha-ʿonesh*. However, there is the remote possibility that the word in question should read *ha-rom*[ez]. Then, the phrase translates as: "fear of *that which hints to* punishment." This may be a reference to the *Zohar* 152b (see above note 353) where *tekhelet* is compared to the *neḥash ha-neḥoshet* (copper serpent, see Numbers 21:9), which is to say, that by looking at the fringe of *tekhelet*, a symbolic "strap" *(retsuʿah)*, there is instilled fear, that in turn motivates one to perform the commandments.

In the classic Mussar or ethical literature, the distinction was drawn between two varieties of fear: the higher type brought on as a response to the sublimity of the Lord (*yirʾat ha-romemut*), and the lower type which is bluntly, "fear of punishment" (*yirʾat ha-ʿonesh*).

In Rav Kook's famous response to his critic, Rabbi Jacob David Ridbaz (a.k.a. Wilovsky), Rav Kook goes so far as to say "that it is *forbidden* for Torah scholars involved in the mysteries of the Torah with inner understanding, to magnify it [i.e. external fear]. They should adopt the minimum necessary to chastise the body and its coarse proclivities [expressed] in negative character traits, God forbid" (*Igrot ha-Rayah*, vol. 2, p. 187).

Earlier, Rav Kook wrote to the Jerusalemite Rabbi Yeshʿayah Orenstein that by constant study of *"penimiyut ha-Torah"* ("the inwardness of Torah") one will have minimal need of the *"yirʾah raʿah"* ("the evil fear") of the *"retsuʿah bisha"* ("evil strap"). The latter is a reference to *Zohar* I, 11b. See *Igrot ha-Rayah*, vol. 1 (Jerusalem, 1961), p. 42 (Letter 43).

See further our appendix "Rav Kook's Critique of the Mussar Movement."

[358]Commentators as diverse as Rabbi Joseph Ḥayyim of Baghdad (*"Ben Ish Ḥai"*) and Rabbi Ḥayyim Hirschensohn speculate that the Rabbis were punning on the name *"bar bar,"* imputing to it the sense of "Barbarian" (originally an inhabitant of Barbaria or the Barbary Coast). They cite *b. Yevamot* 63b: "These are the inhabitants of Barbaria and the inhabitants of Mauritania who go about naked in the market place." See further Rabbi Nathan ben Yeḥiel of Rome, *ʿArukh*, s.v. *Barbaria*; and Alexander Kohut, *Aruch Completum*, vol. 1 (Vienna, 1878), pp. 183-184, s.v. *Barbar*.

Perhaps the Rabbis were poking fun at the fact that Rabbah bar Bar Ḥannah was wont to spend prolonged periods of isolation in the desert and had himself taken on the identity of a Berber (or Barbar), denizen of the desert. (In some recensions of the Talmud, the Rabbis omit the name "Ḥannah" and declare *tout court*: "Every *bar bar* is a fool!")

Furthermore, Rabbi Joseph Ḥayyim ventures that the entire vision of the dead of the generation of the desert, as well as the ensuing conversation with the Rabbis, took place in a dream. Puns (such as "Barbar/Berber") are the stuff of dreams. This would explain the undeserved scorn heaped upon Rabbah bar Bar Ḥannah by the Rabbis. It was purely the product of his fertile imagination! See *Ben Yohoyada*ʿ to *Bava Batra* 74a, s.v. *'amrei leh, kol abba ḥamra, ve-khol bar bar sikhsa*; Rabbi Ḥayyim Hirschensohn, *Motsa'ei Mayim* (Budapest, 1924), p. 225.

Mutatis mutandis, in Ḥayyim Naḥman Bialik's retelling of the *aggadah* of Rabbah bar Bar Ḥannah (which Bialik explicitly references before the onset of his poem), Rabbah bar Bar Ḥannah has himself become an Arab! The poem, entitled *"Metei Midbar"* ("The Dead of the Desert") was composed by Bialik in Odessa in 1902. The lines in Bialik's poem read:

ומעשה בערבי שנטל חוט אחד מציצית כנף בגדם—

וייבש כל-גופו מיד עד שהשיב האשם למקומו.

> It once happened that *an Arab* took one string from the fringe on the corner of their garment—
>
> And immediately his entire body froze until he returned the stolen object to its place.

This intriguing passage in Bialik's poem was pointed out by Ḥayah Gilboa in her lecture, "Where Heaven and Earth Kiss" (Hebrew), delivered at the Steinsaltz Center, Jerusalem, on March 29, 2015.

[359]In Rav Kook's explanation of the *aggadah*, the Rabbis were not minimizing Rabbah bar Bar Ḥannah's own greatness, but rather were speaking in generalities how diminished are he and his contemporary sages in comparison to the generation of the desert.

[360]Hebrew, *"be-derekh"* ("in the way"). In *Ma'amrei ha-Rayah*, vol. 2, p. 444, the word has been transcribed *"ve-derekh"* ("and the way").

[361]In *b. Shabbat* 30b, we find the statement of the *beraita*: "Forever let man be humble as Hillel and not strict as Shammai." In his commentary thereto, Rav Kook explains that this statement was not meant to be a disparagement of Shammai, rather it was pointing out that the way of tolerance associated with Hillel can be followed by men of lesser spiritual stature, whereas the way of strictness perfected by Shammai would be exceedingly difficult to emulate if one is not as great as Shammai. See *'Eyn Ayah, Shabbat*, vol. 1, ed. Rabbi Ya'akov Filber (Jerusalem, 1994), chap. 2, par. 112. Cf. Rabbi Israel Salanter, quoted in Rabbi Isaac Blaser, *'Or Yisrael* (Vilna, 1900), chap. 28.

[362]*Ra'aya Mehemna* in *Zohar* III, 245a; Rabbi Ḥayyim Vital, *Sha'ar ha-Gilgulim, hakdamah* 36; Rabbi Shneur Zalman of Liadi, *Tanya* IV, 13 (119a). See also *Tosafot Ḥadashim*, introduction to Tractate *Avot*, quoting the Rabbi of Nikolsburg (i.e. Rabbi Shmuel Shmelke Halevi Horowitz) and Rabbi Levi Isaac of Berdichev. (Evidently, these later accretions to *Tosafot Ḥadashim* stem from the famed Ḥasidic press of Rabbi Israel Jaffe at Kopyst and first appeared in the edition of the Mishnah produced there in 1813. Further research is required.)

[363]*Sefer Yetsirah* 1:1; Rabbi Ezra of Gerona, Commentary to Song of Songs 4:11, in *Kitvei Ramban*, ed. Chavel (Jerusalem, 1968), vol. 2, p. 496; Rabbeinu Baḥya ben Asher, Numbers 15:38 (Chavel ed., p. 101); *Derashot Rabbeinu Yehoshua ibn Shu'aib*, ed. Ze'ev Metzger, vol. 2 (Jerusalem, 1992), end *Shelaḥ*, p. 361.

This reckoning works only for Beit Shammai, who have four strings on each of the four corners. (The four strings are doubled over, so after the knotting there result eight strings. Multiplied by four, this gives a total of thirty-two strings.) However, according to Beit Hillel, who have but three strings on each corner, after doubling them we have a total of twenty-four strings (6 x 4)—not thirty two. As the opinion of Beit Hillel was not adopted by the final *Halakhah*, the numerical symbolism of their *tsitsit* was not addressed in the Kabbalistic literature.

[364]Cf. *m. Avot* 3:9: "Whoever's deeds exceed his wisdom—his wisdom endures (*mitkayyemet*); whoever's wisdom exceeds his deeds—his wisdom does not survive."

[365]Hebrew, *"vadai."* The word is not found in the manuscript, but in the version of *Ma'amrei ha-Rayah*, vol. 2, p. 444.

[366]Psalms 50:5.

[367]Psalms 25:14.

The Scorpions Surrounding Sinai

13

And Rabbah bar Bar Ḥannah said: That Bedouin said to me: Come, I will show you Mount Sinai. I went and saw that scorpions were encircling it, and they were standing as white donkeys. I heard a Divine Voice saying: Woe is Me that I took an oath; and now that I took the oath, who will nullify it for me?

When I came before the Sages, they said to me: Every Abba is **a donkey, and every bar Bar Ḥannah** is **a fool. You should have said: "It is nullified for you."** The Gemara explains: **And Rabbah bar Bar Ḥannah** did not nullify the oath because he **reasoned: Perhaps** God **is referring to the oath of the flood** [i.e. that He will not flood the earth again]**. But the Sages** would argue that **if** that were **so, why** say: "**Woe is Me**"**?** Rather, this must be referring to God's oath of exile upon the Jewish people.[368]

CONVERTING THE SCORPIONS OF SINAI TO WHITE DONKEYS: "THEY SHALL NOT HURT NOR DESTROY IN ALL MY HOLY MOUNTAIN"

Mount Sinai is the source of the giving of the Torah. Through the giving of the Torah to Israel, in the future they will have dominion over the nations of the world and teach them the way of the Lord.[369] But as long as the *tikkun* (mending) is as yet incomplete, all the nations oppose Israel for having accepted the Torah. So for the being, all the nations surround Israel, their accusatory powers poised to sting Israel. However in their interior, they are ready to be yoked to the Torah. Thus [at a future date] they will metamorphose from their judgmental, destructive nature to become *ba'alei ḥesed* ("masters of lovingkindness"), as it is written, "They shall not hurt nor destroy in all My holy mountain."[370]

At the present time, they have two [opposite] qualities ["scorpions" and "white donkeys"]. They are the **scorpions** who wish to destroy the world by destroying Israel, God forbid. Because Israel have not completed the fitting *tikkun*, the world powers have yet to emerge from their impurity. Despite that, inasmuch as Israel grow stronger in holiness, those powers are unable to totally destroy the world. At any rate, they are subdued and appear ready to perform *ḥesed* (lovingkindness). So **they were standing as white donkeys.** "Donkeys" signifies that they are subjugated as beasts of burden.[371] "White" symbolizes that in the end they shall be forced against their will to perform *ḥesed* (lovingkindness).[372]

I heard a Divine Voice saying: Woe is Me that I took an oath...

This [oath] can be interpreted in two ways:

[Either that] based on strict judgment, the world is worthy of destruction and annihilation because of its corruption. This is difficult for the Holy One, blessed be He, as explained at length in the *Zohar, Terumah*, regarding the difficulty of parting the Reed Sea, which required the Holy One, blessed be He, to act in disregard of the judicial process.[373] By the same token, though the world is worthy of destruction and it would be fitting to divest the aspect of the "white donkeys" from the "scorpions" and grant the "scorpions" permission to destroy, God forbid, [the Holy One, blessed be He] has already sworn to be forbearing so as not to destroy the world.

Or, the intention was that it would be fitting to neutralize the power of the "scorpions" and totally subdue them, thus transforming them into "white donkeys" who bear the yoke of lovingkindness (*ḥesed*), but [the Holy One, blessed be He] has sworn that Israel must be in exile in order "to finish sin,"[374] so these [negative] powers are required.

The **nullification** (*hafarah*) of the oath is brought about through the merit of Israel, by their works and wisdom. As the *Zohar* states, through the wisdom of the mysteries of the Torah, "Israel shall go out from exile."[375] For that reason, they complained about the great men of the generation (*hitra'amu 'al gedolei ha-dor*)[376] [that the mysteries of the Torah are not delved into]. But they also mitigated the guilt [by saying] that on account of the heaviness of the exile, the lights of understanding have been closed, so that even the most outstanding individuals are incapable of understanding Torah (and fear of the Lord), which would bestow upon the entire generation a mighty level, until all has reached a state of *tikkun*. (May it be speedily in our days!)

Rabbah bar Bar Ḥannah did not say, "**Your** oath **is nullified.**" He too thought that it is impossible to strive for the redemption; perhaps the time has not arrived and it is forbidden to force the End.[377] But the Rabbis proved from the utterance "**Woe is Me,**" that what was causing pain above, as it were, was the inability to bestow goodness. On the other hand, if the divine litany derived from the inability to comply fully with the demand of the attribute of judgment,[378] then the proper expression would not have been "Woe is Me," but rather "It is difficult for me," as we find in regard to the parting of the Reed Sea.

[368]The anonymous author of *Sefer ha-Ḥinukh* laid down a ground rule that when the Sages speak metaphorically of nullifying a divine oath, they do so only in regard to oaths that are punitive in nature, but never in regard to oaths that would benefit humanity. See *Sefer ha-Ḥinukh, Yitro,* commandment 30 ("Not to swear in vain"). (In Chavel ed., commandment 32; pp. 87-88.) Cf. Maimonides, *MT*, *Hil. Yesodei ha-Torah* 10:4. Our *Gemara* would seem to fly in the face of that rule of the *Ḥinukh.* Rabbah believed that by nullifying the oath, he would be nullifying the oath taken by God not to flood the world once again. This question is raised by Rabbi Abraham Pinso of Sarajevo, Bosnia (c.1740—c.1820), eminent disciple of Rabbi David Pardo, in his work, *Katit la-Ma'or*, ed. Rabbi Ya'akov Moshe Hillel (Jerusalem, 1995), p. 355.

Perhaps this very principle enunciated by the *Ḥinukh* is implicit in the Sages' retort to Rabbah: "If that were so, why say: 'Woe is Me'?" And perhaps Rabbah's ignorance of this very principle is what earned him the sobriquet of "fool."

[369]See Maimonides, *MT*, *Hil. Teshuvah* 9:2; *Hil. Melakhim* 12:4, 5.

[370]Isaiah 11:9.

[371]Hebrew, *"ka-ḥamor le-'ol."* In the printed version of *Ma'amrei ha-Rayah*, vol. 2, p. 444, the phrase reads *"ka-ḥamor le-'ol ha-massa'."* However, the word *ha-massa'* is not found in the manuscript. Cf. above n. 356.

[372]In Kabbalah, white symbolizes *Ḥesed* or the attribute of lovingkindness. See Rabbi Moses Cordovero, *Pardes Rimonim*, Gate 10 (*Sha'ar ha-Gevanim*), chap. 1.

[373]*Zohar* II, 170.

[374]Daniel 9:24. Rav Kook speaks at greater length about this theme, how the Exile puts a finish to sin, in *Pinkas 5* (written 1908-circa 1913). See *Kevatsim mi-Ketav Yad Kodsho*, vol. 3, ed. Boaz Ofen (Jerusalem, 2018), 5:10 (p. 29).

[375]*Zohar* III, 124b (*Ra'aya Mehemna*). Rav Kook quotes this statement *in toto* in his work *Orot*, *Orot ha-Teḥiyah* (*Lights of Renascence*), end chap. 57. (In *Shemonah Kevatsim* 1:869 the quote from *Ra'aya Mehemna* is truncated.)

[376]In the printed version of *Ma'amrei ha-Rayah*, vol. 2, p. 445, the crucial word *"'al"* has been omitted, thus yielding the opposite result: "the great men of the generation complained" (*hitra'amu gedolei ha-dor*)!

[377]See *b. Ketubot* 111a.

[378]In the original, this phrase reads: *"ke-fi tevi'at middat ha-din."* In the printed version of *Ma'amrei ha-Rayah*, vol. 2, p. 445, the order has been reversed: *"ke-fi middat tevi'at ha-din."*

The Swallowed Congregation of Koraḥ

14

And Rabbah bar Bar Ḥannah said: That Bedouin said to me: Come, I will show you those who were swallowed by the earth due to the sin **of Koraḥ. I went and saw two fissures** in the ground **from which was issuing smoke.** The Bedouin **took a shearing of wool, and dipped it in water, and placed it on the head of a spear, and stuck it** in **there. And when he removed** the wool, **it was scorched. He said to me: Listen! What do you hear? And I heard that they were saying: Moses and his Torah are truth, and they,** i.e. we in the earth, **are liars.** The Bedouin further **said to me: Every thirty days Gehinnom returns them to here, like meat in a pot** which is rotated so that it cooks. **And** every time **they say this: Moses and his Torah are truth, and they,** i.e. we in the earth, **are liars.**

KORAḤISM AND THE LOVE BEYOND LOVE

The Bedouin showed him the secret of the controversy stirred up by Koraḥ, and his corruption. Koraḥ's denial extends to both the Written Torah and the Oral Torah. These are the two sources that bestow life to the world. "The Torah was given from [the side of] stern judgment (*gevurah*),"[379] as it is written, "From His right hand [went] a fiery law to them."[380] Yet this fire gives life to all. [The congregation of Koraḥ, on the other hand,] reversed things, so that through these two [i.e. the Written Torah and the Oral Torah] there was brought down upon them a very severe judgment. These are the **two fissures,** which is to say, two corruptions, on whose account they are sentenced to "*'ashan*" (**smoke**). The word *'AShaN* stands for *'akrav* (scorpion), *saraf* (fiery serpent), *naḥash* (snake).[381] It makes sense to say that the "scorpion" alludes to denial of the Written Torah, which certainly kills.[382] And the "snake" alludes to making light of the Oral Torah.[383] Though on occasion a *beit din* (court) has the power to annul the ruling of another *beit din* (court),[384] nonetheless when one denies [the authority of the Oral Torah], one is subject to dying by the snake's bite. And the "fiery serpent" signifies the synthesis, the unity of the Written Torah and the Oral Torah; one who divides them and separates them is burnt by a "consuming fire."

According to the "secret of the Lord" [i.e. Kabbalah], it is written in the book *Beit 'Olamim* on the *Idra* [portion of the *Zohar*] by the Gaon Rabbi Yitsḥak Eizik Ḥaver, that wool symbolizes *"Ḥasadim de-'Atik"* (the Loves of the Ancient of Days).[385] This is above the governance of this world, as written in *KaLaḤ* [*Pithei Ḥokhmah*][386] and in the words of the Vilna Gaon.[387] It is forbidden to amplify the *ḥasadim* (loves) from a place so high that the world cannot support it. It was this which caused the destruction of the *"malkhin kadma'in"* (Primordial Kings): overwhelming light.[388]

The Bedouin **took a shearing of wool, and dipped it in water.** Water alludes to the lower loves (*ḥasadim*) that are drawn into the world.[389] [This symbolic action of the Bedouin] taught that the corruption of the congregation of Koraḥ consisted in their wanting to amplify the power of love (*ḥasadim*) to the level of the "wool" which is beyond the establishment of the world (*tikkun ha-'olam*).[390]

[The Bedouin went on to] demonstrate that even if they should fulfill all two hundred and forty-eight positive commandments—which draw down love (*ḥasadim*)[391]—since they wish to exaggerate overly much, the end result will be the exact opposite: a reinforcement of judgments (*dinim*).[392]

The head of a spear. The Hebrew word for spear, *"romaḥ,"* is code for the 248 (*RMḤ*) positive commandments.

It was scorched. [The scorching symbolizes the preponderance of judgments (*dinim*).]

Rabbah bar Bar Ḥannah then heard the confession of the congregation of Koraḥ which informed of their corruption. They said: **Moses and his Torah are truth.** "His Torah" refers to the Written Torah, while "Moses" refers to the Oral Torah. The Torah which is uniquely Moses' is the *"pilpula de-'Oraita"* (the dialectic of Torah), which is the mainstay of the Oral Torah.[393]

Truth. Despite the fact that they wished to ascend to a higher place, [they were forced to admit that] this way that was transmitted to us by Moses is true and enduring. *Emet* (truth) is code for the middle line: "You will give truth to Jacob."[394]

And they, i.e. we in the earth, **are liars.** By amplifying the love (*ḥasadim*), the world would revert to *Tohu* (Chaos), to the time of the destruction of the [seven][395] Primordial Kings. Then, "*the earth* was nullified,"[396] God forbid. So the *sefirah* of *Malkhut* [which would have suffered most from their bouleversement] exacts revenge from them on account of their great corruption.[397]

The monthly cycle of thirty days relates to the moon, "the little luminary,"[398] the *sefirah* of *Malkhut*. So, **Every thirty days Gehinnom returns them to here.**[399] The judgment of Gehinnom is aroused for their having desired "to push away the feet of the *Shekhinah*."[400]

Like meat in a pot. [Red] meat alludes to the redness of the attribute of judgment. Their desire to amplify the attribute of love (*Ḥesed*) backfired on them, resulting in absolute judgment. Seeing that their vain words (*divrei tohu*)[401] have no permanence, they confess that **Moses and his Torah are truth.** The Torah of our God—a covenant to the People—has permanence.[402]

And they, i.e. we in the earth, **are liars.** This is the punishment of the liar. Even when he tells the truth, no one pays heed to him. What that means in our context is that it is forbidden to follow this way—even to fulfill commandments (whose trope is the "*romaḥ*" or spear). Such a "spear," such performance of commandments, will not save their souls from the flame [of Gehinnom].[403] Though dipped in water, the spear was singed.[404]

[379]*Zohar* II, 81a; *Tikkunei Zohar*, beginning *tikkun* 12 and commentary of the Vilna Gaon *ad loc.*, s.v. *'ityehivat*. See also Rabbi Reuven Margaliyot, *Nitsutsei Zohar* to *Zohar* II, 81a, note 2.

[380]Deuteronomy 33:2. See further *Zohar* II, 84a, 166b; Rabbi Moses Cordovero, *Pardes Rimonim* 23:1, s.v. *'or*.

[381]Cf. Deuteronomy 8:15: *"naḥash saraf ve-'akrav."*

[382]See the commentary of the Vilna Gaon to *Tikkunei Zohar* (Vilna, 1867), beginning *tikkun* 21 (42a), s.v. *lo yafsik*; Rabbi Yitsḥak Eizik Ḥaver, *Pitḥei She'arim* (Tel-Aviv, 1964), *Netiv 'Olam ha-Tikkun*, chap. 3 (65a). The Gaon writes that the word *'akrav* (scorpion) by metathesis becomes *be-'ikar* as in *"kofer be-'ikar"* (one who denies the cornerstone of faith). *Tikkunei Zohar* itself reads *'akrav* as *"'akar bayit"* ("uproots the house"). The passage in *Tikkunei Zohar* references the Talmudic discussion in *m. Berakhot* 5:1 and *b. Berakhot* 33a.

[383]See *b. 'Avodah Zarah* 27b: *"ḥivya de-Rabbanan"* ("a snake of the Rabbis").

[384]*m. 'Eduyot* 1:5; *b. Megillah* 2a.

[385]Rabbi Yitsḥak Eizik Ḥaver, *Beit 'Olamim* (Warsaw, 1889), 42a. A century later, in 1994, there appeared in print Rabbi Eizik Ḥaver's commentary on the *Aggadot* of the Talmud (including the *Aggadot* of Rabbah bar Bar Ḥannah). Predictably, the author explains that the shearings of wool symbolize *"ḥasadim de-ḥotma de-'AK."* See Rabbi Y.E. Ḥaver, *Afikei Yam* (Jerusalem, 5754/1994), vol. 2, p. 391, s.v. *ve-shakli gevava de-'imra.* (*AK* is the initials of *'Atika Kadisha.*)

Rav Kook was especially fond of the work of Rabbi Yitsḥak Eizik Ḥaver. See Rav Kook's letter to his father-in-law Rabbi Elijah David Rabinowitz-Te'omim expressing his gratitude for sending him books of Kabbalah. One assumes from the description of the work that Rav Kook is alluding to Ḥaver's recently published magnum opus, *Pitḥei She'arim* (Warsaw, 1888). See the letter now in *Metsi'ot Katan*, ed. Harel Cohen (Israel, 2018), Introduction, p. 41, and Rav Kook's explicit reference to *Pitḥei She'arim* in par. 192 (bottom p. 309). See also the reference to *Pitḥei She'arim* in *Pinkesei ha-Rayah*, vol. 3, ed. Levi Yitsḥaki (Jerusalem, n.d.), 15:70 (p. 119).

Elchanan Shilo quotes our passage as an example of Rav Kook's intellectual indebtedness to Rabbi Yitsḥak Eizik Ḥaver. (Why Shilo asserts that Rav Kook's conception of Koraḥ as an early egalitarian is beholden to *Mei ha-Shilo'aḥ* of the Izhbitser Rebbe is beyond me. There is no textual evidence for this assertion. Without having read *Mei ha-Shilo'aḥ*, based on Koraḥ's plaint alone, "the entire congregation are holy and in their midst the Lord" [Numbers 16:3], Rav Kook might very well have arrived at the same conclusion. Cf. *Orot*, Israel and Its Renascence, chap. 15, and our discussion below, note 404.) See Elchanan Shilo, "Rabbi Isaac Eisik Ḥaver's Influence on Rav Kook's Interpretation of the Kabbalah" (Hebrew), *Da'at* 79-80 (2015), pp. 98-99; idem, *"Parshanut Harav Kook le-Kabbalat ha-Ari: Hofa'at Neshamot Ḥadashot ve-Tikkun ha-'Olam"* in *'Iyunim bi-Tekumat Yisrael*, vol. 18 (2008), p. 63, n. 42.

[386]*KaLaḤ Pitḥei Ḥokhmah* (138 Entrances of Wisdom) is a primer of Kabbalah attributed to Rabbi Moses Ḥayyim Luzzatto, although of late, the attribution has been called into question. See Rabbi M.Ḥ. Luzzatto, *Da'at Tevunot*, ed. Rabbi Yosef Spinner (Jerusalem, 2012), Introduction, p. 7.

I have been unable to locate an exact reference in the work that fits Rav Kook's description.

[387]See the commentary of the Vilna Gaon to *Sifra di-Tseni'uta*, ed. Samuel Luria (Vilna, 1882), 1c: "Because with *ḥesed* [alone], the world cannot exist, as it says (*b. Ta'anit* 23a): 'If You bestow upon them an [over]abundance of good (*rov tovah*)—they cannot receive.'" (Our edition of the Talmud has "stand" ["*la'amod*"] rather than "receive" ["*lekabbel*"].)

In a letter to Samuel Kook (a younger brother of Rav Kook), dated "8 Tishri, 5671 [1911]," Alexander Ziskind Rabinowitz (known by the acronym AZaR) quotes Rav Kook as saying that according to the line of the Kabbalists, "Evil comes only from the abundance of good [*ribbui ha-tov*] by way of the shattering of the vessels." (Courtesy Moshe Naḥmani)

[388]According to the *Zohar*, the seven Kings of Edom enumerated at the conclusion of the pericope *Vayyishlaḥ* (Genesis 36:31-39), referred to as the Primordial Kings, symbolize the World of Chaos (*'Olam ha-Tohu*) which preceded the World of Establishment (*'Olam ha-Tikkun*). What characterized the World of Chaos and which brought about its destruction, was the preponderance of "light" (*ribbui ha-'or*) and the scarcity of "vessels" (*mi'ut ha-kelim*) to contain the light. This situation was remedied in the following World of Perfection by a diminishing of the light (*mi'ut ha-'or*) and an increase of vessels (*ribbui ha-kelim*). This myth of the Death of the Primordial Kings is presented in the *Idra* section of the *Zohar* (published in *Zohar, Naso*). See also the beginning of the *Sifra di-Tseni'uta* (published in *Zohar, Terumah*).

The Myth of the Death of the Kings is alluded to in the immensely popular Pentateuchal commentary of Rabbeinu Baḥya ben Asher ibn Ḥalawa (1255-1340). Rabbeinu Baḥya juxtaposes the Midrash (*Genesis Rabbah* 3:7, 9:2) that before the Holy One, blessed be He, created this world, "He was constructing worlds and destroying them." See Rabbeinu Baḥya, end *Vayyishlaḥ* (Chavel ed., pp. 301-302).

Rav Kook penned a piece entitled *"Ha-Neshamot shel 'Olam ha-Tohu"* ("The Souls of the World of Chaos"), in which he described most poignantly the tragic shattering of the great idealists who envision a world that exceeds the limits of our circumscribed reality. Subsequently, establishment figures are able to transcribe those ideals in a subdued manner that allows their integration in a well-structured society. See RAYH Kook, *Orot* (Jerusalem, 1950), pp. 121-123.

Rav Kook's "soul brother" and fellow Kabbalist, Rabbi Pinḥas Hakohen Lintop, shared the belief that the "*'Olam ha-Tohu* really exists today too...for today too, there are found these fallen souls" (ms. *Be'er Yisrael*). In his book *Netivot ha-Shalom*, Rabbi Lintop will explain "the different [divine] services according to the roots of the various souls and according to their ascent" (ibid.).

[389]Cf. Rabbi Yitshak Eizik Ḥaver, *Afikei Yam*, vol. 2, p. 391, s.v. *ve-'amshineh be-mayya*.

[390]Rav Kook's opposition of the terms *kilkul* (corruption) and *tikkun* (correction) is highly reminiscent of their usage in *KaLaḤ Pitḥei Ḥokhmah*, *petaḥ* 37, where we are told: "The root of existence of corruption and correction (*kilkul ve-tikkun*) is the matter of the shattering of the vessels and their repair (*shevirat ha-kelim ve-tikkunam*)."

[391]In Kabbalah, the 248 positive commandments are related to love (*ahavah*) and the 365 negative commandments to fear (*yir'ah*). See Naḥmanides, Exodus 20:8 (Chavel ed., p. 399); *Tikkunei Zohar* (Vilna, 1867), Introduction (6a); end *tikkun* 1 (19b).

[392]Rav Kook may be hinting that history has shown time and again that revolutions in the name of love and liberal ideals have a nasty tendency of turning into blood-thirsty, repressive regimes. In modern times, the French, Russian, Chinese and Cuban Revolutions serve as prime examples of unrealistic *ḥasadim* turning to *dinim*. I am indebted to Prof. Shalom Rosenberg for this insight.

[393]*b. Nedarim* 38a.

[394]Micah 7:20. In the Kabbalistic lexicon, the patriarch Jacob is the middle way (*Tif'eret* or *Emet*) that mediates between the two extremes of Abraham's love (*Ḥesed*) and Isaac's fear (*Paḥad* or *Gevurah*). See Rabbi Joseph Gikatilla, *Sha'arei 'Orah*, ed. Joseph Ben Shlomo (Jerusalem, 1970), Fifth Gate (vol. 1, pp. 224-225).

[395]The printed version of *Ma'amrei ha-Rayah*, vol. 2, p. 446, has *"zeman malkin kadma'in"* ("the time of the Primordial Kings"), but it is possible to read the manuscript, *"zayin malkin kadma'in"* ("the seven Primordial Kings"), which is the common Kabbalistic expression. Rather than a *mem*, it is possible that the middle letter in the word is actually a *yod*.

[396]Beginning *Sifra di-Tseni'uta* (printed in *Zohar* II, 176b.) See the commentary of the Vilna Gaon to *Sifra di-Tseni'uta*, ed. Samuel Luria (Vilna, 1882), s.v. *ve-'ara' itbatlat*. The Gaon explains that the catastrophe of the earth's nullification was an event that took place in the *sefirah* of *Malkhut*. See earlier the commentary of Rabbi Isaac Luria to *Sifra di-Tseni'uta*, in *Sefer ha-Derushim*, ed. Rabbi Ya'akov Moshe Hillel (Jerusalem, 1996), p. 238, s.v. *ve-'ara' itbatlat*: "This is *Malkhut*."

In *Pinkas 16*, written in the 1890s (in Zoimel, and after 1895 in Boisk), Rav Kook dwells at length on the portrayal of the *sefirah* of *Malkhut* as "earth" in the beginning of *Sifra di-Tseni'uta*. He juxtaposes the Midrashic derivation of the Hebrew word for earth, *'erets*: "Why was her name called *'erets*? She wanted (*ratsetah*) to do the will of her Creator" (*Genesis Rabbah* 5:8). There follows a discussion of the *ratson ha-mekabbel* (the will of the recipient), i.e. the *sefirah* of *Malkhut*, versus the *ratson ha-mashpi'a* (the will of the bestower), i.e. the *sefirah* of *Keter*. See *Pinkesei ha-Rayah*, vol. 3, ed. Rabbi Levi Yitsḥaki (Jerusalem, n.d. [2011]), 16:29 (pp. 192-193).

*

Rav Kook may be explaining why in the Biblical narrative (Numbers 16:30-34) it was specifically the "mouth of the earth" that swallowed Koraḥ's congregation. For the miraculous nature of this occurrence, see Naḥmanides' commentary, Numbers 16:30, and *m. Avot* 5:6. Naḥmanides (loc. cit.) quotes the Talmud (*b. Sanhedrin* 110a) that the repositioning of the entrance to Gehinnom to match the exact location of the congregation of Koraḥ is deemed supernatural. The story of Rabbah bar Bar Ḥannah's encounter with the congregation of Koraḥ is repeated in *b. Sanhedrin* 110.

397The earth (*'erets*) is represented by the *sefirah* of *Malkhut*; the heavens (*shamayim*) by the *sefirah* of *Tif'eret*. See Rabbi Moses Cordovero, *Pardes Rimonim* 23:1, s.v. *'erets*; and 23:21, s.v. *shamayim*.

398Genesis 1:16. The moon ("the little luminary") is a symbol of the *sefirah* of *Malkhut*; the sun ("the big luminary") a symbol of the *sefirah* of *Tif'eret*. See Rabbi Moses Cordovero, *Pardes Rimonim* 23:13, s.v. *ma'or*.

Rabbi Samuel ben Meir (Rashbam) comments that the thirty-day cycle of judgment recommences every *Rosh Ḥodesh* (New Moon). See Rashbam, *Bava Batra* 74a, s.v. *kol telatin yomin*. Perhaps this is a source for the medieval custom of "*Yom Kippur Katan*," which consists of fasting and saying penitential prayers on *Erev Rosh Ḥodesh* (the Eve of the New Moon).

See Rabbi Naḥman of Breslov, *Likkutei Moharan* I, 10:9:

> Rabbeinu Shmuel [i.e. Rashbam] explained: "Every *Rosh Ḥodesh*."
>
> For everything has a root, and the root of *teshuvah* [return] is *Rosh Ḥodesh*, for on *Rosh Ḥodesh* the Holy One, blessed be He, said: "Bring for me atonement." As our Rabbis, of blessed memory, interpreted [*b. Shavu'ot* 9a; *Ḥullin* 60b]. This is the concept of *teshuvah*, and this [divine] *teshuvah* has a chain reaction in all the creations on *Rosh Ḥodesh*. For this reason, Koraḥ and his congregation too must express remorse on *Rosh Ḥodesh*. But their *teshuvah* does not avail them, for the fundament of *teshuvah* exists only in this world. "He who toiled on the Eve of the Sabbath, will eat on the Sabbath" [*b. 'Avodah Zarah* 3a]. So certainly their admission of remorse does not free them of the punishment of Gehinnom, and that is why "Gehinnom returns them to here," because they are not absolved. Nonetheless, there is no Gehinnom on *Rosh Ḥodesh* [*Zohar* II, 150b]. The Gehinnom of *Rosh Ḥodesh* is only the remorse that they express. This itself is their Gehinnom. This is the precise meaning of "Gehinnom returns them to here," i.e. the very fact that they must repeat their confession, is their Gehinnom.

In his notes to *Zohar*, Rabbi Reuven Margaliyot cites the opinion of the medieval authority Mordechai ben Hillel (end Tractate *Pesaḥim*) that when *Rosh Ḥodesh* falls on Saturday night, one does not recite "*Tsidkatekha*" at the conclusion of the Sabbath afternoon prayer, because it states in the *Pesikta* (*'Aseret ha-Dibrot*) that the fire of Gehinnom rests on the Sabbath and *Rosh Ḥodesh*. See *Nitsutsei Zohar, Zohar* II, 150b.

[399]One might question why the congregation of Koraḥ are judged every thirty days. Generally, sinners are sentenced to Gehinnom for no more than twelve months. See *b. Rosh Hashanah* 17a. The answer lies in the continuation of the *Gemara* there: "But the ... *apikorsim* who denied the Torah ... descend to Gehinnom and are judged in it for generations upon generations ... Gehinnom ends and they do not end." See Rabbi Moshe Shapiro's interpretation of that statement in *"Be'urim ba-Aggadot Rabbah bar Bar Ḥannah,"* in *Yeshurun* 37, p. 509, note 137.

[400]*"Doḥek raglei ha-Shekhinah"* ("pushing away the feet of the *Shekhinah*") is a Talmudic expression for causing the Divine Presence to disappear due to one's misbehavior. See *b. Ḥagigah* 16a and *Kiddushin* 31a. The proof-text is Isaiah 66:1: "The heavens are My throne, and the earth My footstool."

In our context, the *Shekhinah* or Divine Indwelling is yet another synonym for the *sefirah* of *Malkhut* which signifies the telluric aspect of existence. See *Sha'arei 'Orah*, First Gate (vol. 1, p. 65).

[401]Rav Kook puns on the word *Tohu*, which in Kabbalah refers to the *'Olam ha-Tohu* (World of Chaos) that preceded the *'Olam ha-Tikkun* (World of Establishment).

[402]In Hebrew, *"emet"* or truth has the connotation of permanence. Conversely, *"mayim mekhazvin"* (literally "lying waters") are waters that dry up periodically. See Isaiah 58:11; *Sifra, Metsora'*; *m. Parah* 8:9.

[403]In a *pensée* written later in Jaffa, Rav Kook touches on the Lurianic teaching that in the future Koraḥ (and his congregation) will finally achieve *tikkun* and have no less a status than that of a *"tsaddik"* or righteous man. The hint to this is the verse in Psalms 92:13: *"Tsaddi**k** ka-tama**r** yifra**ḥ**"* ("The righteous shall flourish like the palm tree"). The final letters spell the name "Koraḥ." Though in their day they mocked the words of the Sages,

> their flaw is the mystery of the *ma'apilim*, those who desired to ascend to a height of which the world is unworthy. And though they caused much destruction through their struggle, and already received their severe punishment—in the end the spark that rises from the interior of their will not have been in vain, and they will reach their exalted niveau. In their regard, Ḥannah said: "The Lord kills and brings back to life; lowers to She'ol and raises up" [1 Samuel 2:6].
>
> (Rabbi Abraham Isaac Hakohen Kook, *Kevatsim mi-Ketav Yad Kodsho*, vol. 2, ed. Boaz Ofen [Jerusalem, 2008], *Pinkas ha-Dapim* 3:10 [p. 105])

See Rabbi Ḥayyim Vital, *Sha'ar ha-Pesukim* and *Sefer ha-Likkutim* to Psalms 92:13.

Rav Kook revisits the verse from 1 Samuel 2:6 ("lowers to She'ol and raises up") in a later work, *Resh Millin* (London, 1917), *"Tet."*

[404]In the *Aggadah*, Koraḥ is portrayed as an antinomian, who held up to derision Moses' rulings concerning the commandments of *tekhelet* (the blue thread in the *tsitsit* or ritual finges) and *mezuzah*. The *Talmud Yerushalmi* labels Koraḥ an *Apikorus* (Epicurean or heretic). See *y. Sanhedrin* 10:1; *Midrash Rabbah* and *Midrash Tanḥuma*, beginning *Koraḥ*.

Rav Kook's point is much more subtle. Even were Koraḥ and his followers to observe the positive commandments (all 248 of them!), their *mitsvot* would have no validity. The reason for that is that Koraḥ's band of followers wrenched the commandments from their proper matrix (Mosaic authority) and hooked them up to a level (*Ḥesed de-'Atik*) that transcends our normal reality. The *mitsvot* (commandments) have validity only when performed within the context of *Malkhut* or this-worldly reality. Though the term did not exist in his day, it is as if Rav Kook wrote a rejoinder to what has come to be known as "orthopraxy" (as opposed to "orthodoxy").

In this regard, there is a remarkable explanation that Rashi provides for the disagreement of Shammai and Hillel (recorded in *b. Shabbat* 31a) whether to accept an aspiring convert who rejected the Oral Law. In Rashi's understanding, the two great *tanna'im* Shammai and Hillel differ in their interpretation of this *beraita*:

> A gentile who comes to accept the words of the Torah with the exception of one thing—we cannot accept him [into the fold].
>
> Rabbi Yosé be-Rabbi Yehudah says: Even one punctilio of the Rabbis.
>
> (*t. Demai* , chap. 2 [Zuckermandel ed., p. 47]; *b. Bekhorot* 30b)

Shammai understood that the proviso "*ḥuts mi-davar eḥad*" ("except for one thing") extends to belief system; Hillel understood that it is restricted purely to behavior. In Rashi's own words:

> ***Hotsi'o bi-nezifah—***
>
> [Shammai] threw him out, because it states in a *beraita* ... "A convert who comes to convert and accepted upon himself the words of the Torah except for one thing—we cannot accept him [into the fold]." In Tractate *Bekhorot*.
>
> ***Giyyereh—***
>
> [Hillel] converted him and relied on his own wisdom that eventually he would accustom him to accept upon himself, for this [case] does not resemble [the case of] "except for one thing," for the convert did not deny the Oral Law, but rather he did not believe it to be of divine origin; and Hillel was confident that after he taught him, [the convert] would rely upon him.

(For an entirely different approach to Rashi, see Rabbi Isaac Hutner, *Paḥad Yitsḥak: Igrot u-Ketavim* [Brooklyn, NY, 2016], chap. 34 [p. 61-63]. Our own approach coincides with Rabbi Zevin's global perception of Shammai and Hillel, whereby Shammai focused on thought and

Hillel focused on action. See his essay, "*Le-Shitot Beit Shammai u-Veit Hillel*, in Rabbi Shelomo Yosef Zevin, *Le-'Or ha-Halakhah* [Jerusalem, n.d.], p. 302ff.)

But none of this truly does justice to Rav Kook's allusion to the subordination of *mitsvot* to the mysterious "*Ḥesed de-'Atik.*" It is possible that this passage must be read in light of a chapter in Rav Kook's seminal work *Orot* which compares Christianity to Koraḥism. Just as Koraḥ of old adopted the philosophy that "the entire congregation are holy and in their midst the Lord" (Numbers 16:3), so Christianity would level spiritual differences between peoples. (See *Orot*, Israel and Its Renascence, chap. 15.)

We generally associate the corruption of Judaism that occurred in Christianity to the influence of Paul, who nullified the practical commandments, starting with circumcision. Rav Kook's point is that the corruption is pre-Pauline; the corruption (*kilkul*) lies at the very root of Christianity.

Rav Kook may have been aware of the early history of Christianity. In the aftermath of Jesus' death, there arose a congregation of his believers in Jerusalem, led by James (Hebrew *Ya'akov*), who scrupulously observed the commandments of the Torah. When they learned that Paul had preached in the Diaspora the abolition of circumcision, they summoned him to Jerusalem for judgment. In a turnabout of events, the "Judaism" of early Christianity was slated for extinction and Christianity evolved along the lines charted for it by Paul. (Today, scholars question to what degree Paul actually abolished the commandment of circumcision. There are those who would argue that Paul believed it unnecessary for *gentiles* to circumcise, but would have retained it for Jews.)

Rav Kook's critique of Christianity is most radical. Had Christianity retained the commandments, those commandments would have been invalidated! In Rav Kook's imagery, they "will not save their souls from the flame [of Gehinnom]." Inasmuch as the commandments have been subordinated to the "religion of love," a love that is beyond the bounds of this world (call it "*Ḥesed de-'Atik*"), they no longer register as "commandments." In *Li-Nevukhei ha-Dor*, Rav Kook addresses the perception of Jesus as a man who loved doing good for other people. See Rabbi Abraham Isaac Hakohen Kook, *Li-Nevukhei ha-Dor*, ed. Rabbi Shaḥar Raḥmani (Tel-Aviv, 2014), pp. 196-197.

Note that the term "*kilkul*" (corruption) is generally reserved in Rabbinic literature for sectarians. See for example *m. Berakhot* 9:5 ("*mi-she-kilkelu ha-minim*").

This piece with its very incisive indictment of Christianity stands in marked contrast to Rav Kook's commentary to the first legend of Rabbah bar Bar Ḥannah, where the accusation leveled against Christianity is precisely the abolition of the practical commandments.

(See Appendix 10 for an oral testimony whereby Rav Kook, not long for this world, railed against the Vatican.)

Where Heaven and Earth Kiss

15

And Rabbah bar Bar Ḥannah said: That Bedouin said to me: Come, I will show you the place **where earth and heavens touch each other.**[405] **I went and saw that it was made of windows upon windows. I took my basket** [of bread] and **placed it in a window of heaven. After I finished praying, I searched for it but did not find it. I said to him: Are there thieves here? He said to me: This is the heavenly sphere that is turning around. Wait until tomorrow at this time and you will find it.**

A BREADBASKET CIRCLING THE EARTH: THE OVERLAP OF COLLECTIVE AND INDIVIDUAL *TIKKUN*

[The Bedouin] taught Rabbah bar Bar Ḥannah an important lesson concerning the attainment of perfection. The Gaon Rabbi Moses Ḥayyim Luzzatto already explained in the book *'Adir ba-Marom* (on the verse "The way of the righteous" and in regard to the "part of the hair") that there is collective comportment and individual comportment.[406] One must derive from Luzzatto's words that there is a way that a man engages in his work to achieve the perfection of the collective, and by doing so, inasmuch as he is a part of the collective, the blessing to the collective will result in his own blessing as well. He will receive his due share of the abundance in direct relation to what he contributed to the "community chest." [On the other hand,] there is individual comportment whereby one labors for oneself, and "A man's belly shall be filled with the fruit of his mouth."[407]

The Bedouin taught Rabbah bar Bar Ḥannah that these two comportments unite. One must not think that by occupying oneself with the collective perfection one will not receive one's portion to the degree afforded by engaging in individual perfection. This is not so, for those [two perfections] unite. The inner power of the collective perfection works to perfect the individual included [in its midst] to the same degree and even more than if [the individual] engaged in individual perfection. One must not think that these are two [different] things, and that the individual affairs require individual work with thought of self. It is not so. All of one's particulars will be blessed through the collective.

But there is a slight difference. The individual comportment revolves on the axis of man's particular situation; [so] one can see with one's eyes how the turn of events results in his [moral] improvement. Whereas on the scale of collective comportment, it would appear to one that the turn of events benefits others. In reality, those very events contribute equally to one's individual advantage—except that one must be patient, trusting in the Lord, blessed be He. [Eventually,] one will see that the chain of events is for one's individual good. The results return to the central point from which they originally proceeded. There will soon come a precise time when the individual intention will come to light.

The earth alludes to the individual comportment, for the earth is a point [in space] and a point is a particle.[408] **The heavens** surround the earth and include innumerable stars and creations.

The Bedouin taught that these two perfections and their ways match. One need not focus exclusively on one's individual benefit, for one will find one's perfection—in all of its details, whether physical or spiritual—through one's work on behalf of the community.

So this is what Rabbah bar Bar Ḥannah did. **I took my basket** [of bread]**,** i.e. the vessel containing his nourishment, which is another way of saying that he aligned his (spiritual) vessel with the communal affairs, symbolized by the **window of heaven.** The Lord, blessed be He, "supervises from the windows"[409] to bless His people[410] and His inheritance, thereby uniting all of them and all His creations in His blessing. In any case, man is individualistic and must attend a little to his private affairs—but this is not his primary occupation.

The obligation of prayer as well, is founded on individuality. The Torah said: "Do not eat upon the blood."[411] The Rabbis interpreted this to mean: "Do not eat before you have prayed for your blood."[412] And in *Zohar*, *Mishpatim,* it states that one must pray specifically for one's nourishment.[413]

So during prayer (and that which depends upon prayer), Rabbah bar Bar Ḥannah addressed his individuality and wished to observe how his individual perfection too would come about through his communal endeavors, but was unable to see in the short term the fruit of his perfection. A fitting example in the spiritual realm would be the individual who is so occupied with communal affairs that his wisdom decreases.[414] Nevertheless, that person is on a high niveau, just that it is indiscernible at the present time; soon the Lord will return his "captivity"[415] and fill his personal storehouse.

I said to him: Are there thieves here? Is it possible that from the collective perfection for which Rabbah bar Bar Ḥannah worked, others would reap benefit but not he?

He said to me: This is the heavenly sphere that is turning around. The Bedouin replied that it is not so. Rabbah bar Bar Ḥannah too would derive benefit from the perfection, but since the orbit is very great—inasmuch as it orbits the center-point of the collective—one must wait until the orbit on behalf of the collective is complete and will finally deliver to the individual his share.

Wait until tomorrow at this time. That will be the mysterious time in which the deeds double back to their source. **And you will find it.** You will find your individual portion. In this way, the Bedouin transmitted to Rabbah bar Bar Ḥannah a great secret concerning service and perfection. "The way of the righteous is as the light of dawn …."[416]

[405]Rabbeinu Gershom and Rashbam were bothered by the question how it is possible for heaven and earth to touch one another, when the Talmud states elsewhere (*b. Ḥagigah* 13a) that the distance from earth to heaven is 500 years. (See also *y. Berakhot* 9:1.)

However, it is possible that the latter saying should be taken metaphorically. Rabbi Moshe Shapiro heard from his teacher, Rabbi Eliyahu Dessler that the *Gemara Ḥagigah* refers to the astronomic distance between man's heart and his mind. Quoted by Rabbi Alexander Aryeh Mandelbaum at the conclusion of *Kiryat Arba': Torat Talmidei ha-Gra* (Jerusalem, 1995), p. 238. (Rabbi Menaḥem Mendel of Kotsk is reputed to have said: "Just as from heaven to earth there is a distance of five hundred years, so too from the mind to the heart." Quoted by Rabbi Gedalia Schorr, *'Or Gedalyahu*, Leviticus—Deuteronomy [Brooklyn, 1998], Koraḥ [131a].)

Besides the solution offered by Rabbeinu Gershom and Rashbam (of the Franco-German or Ashkenazic tradition), there is found in the Spanish or Sephardic tradition another solution of a rationalist bent, namely that the reference in *Bava Batra* is to an apocryphal "planetarium" constructed in the desert by the King of Alexandria, wherein were depicted the earth and the heavenly bodies. Supposedly, Rabbah bar Bar Ḥannah visited that site. See Rabbeinu Joseph Migash, *Ḥiddushei ha-Ri Migash, Bava Batra*, ed. Politansky and Dahan (2015), *Bava Batra* 74a, quoting his teacher Rabbi Isaac Alfasi (Rif), and the earlier responsum of Rif himself (*She'elot u-Teshuvot Rabbeinu Yitsḥak Alfasi*, Livorno 1781, no. 314); and Ritba, *Bava Batra*, referencing an epistle of Maimonides.

The text of Ritba reads as follows:

> It is written in the *sefarim ḥitsonim* (general works) that King Hermes made a replica of the heavenly bodies to demonstrate to the world their orbits. This is the place that [the *tay'a*] showed him [i.e. Rabbah bar Bar Ḥannah].
>
> And so wrote Maimonides, of blessed memory, in an epistle.
>
> (Rabbeinu Yom Tov ben Abraham Asevilli, *Ḥiddushei ha-Ritba, Bava Batra*, ed. Rabbi Moshe Yehudah Hakohen Blau [New York, 1977], 147a)

"King Hermes" is probably a reference to Hermes Trismegistus.

[406]Rabbi Moses Ḥayyim Luzzatto, *'Adir ba-Marom*, ed. Rabbi Joseph Spinner (Jerusalem, 1990), 185ff.

Luzzatto juxtaposes to the passage in the *Idra*, "In the part of the hair, goes one way" (*Zohar* III, 129a), the verse "The way of the righteous is as the light of dawn, that shines more and more until the perfect day" (Proverbs 4:18). In the discussion that follows, Luzzatto writes: "The way of the righteous, which consists in an individual way (*oraḥ perati*) of each righteous man, and a collective way (*oraḥ kelali*) perfected by all the righteous [together]" (*'Adir ba-Marom*, p. 186). (In the older edition of Samuel Luria, Warsaw 1886, the quote is found on f.52r.; in the recent edition of Rabbi Mordekhai Chriqui, Jerusalem, 2018, on p. 300.)

See above note 288.

Concerning *'Adir ba-Marom* and *KaLaḤ Pithei Ḥokhmah*, see our appendix.

[407]Proverbs 18:20.

[408]Rav Kook composed a poem concerning the planet Earth's revolution around the Sun. See *Otserot ha-Rayah*, ed. Rabbi Moshe Zuriel (Ramat Gan, 2002), vol. 2, pp. 575-577, *"Siḥat Mal'akhei ha-Sharet"* ("The Conversation of the Angels"). The poem traces the successive stages in the evolving consciousness of Earth's inhabitants: from primitive man who engages in worship of the sun; to the Copernican Revolution whereby man discovers that rather than stationary, the Earth revolves around the Sun; to the gradual, inexorable development of a global consciousness; and finally, to future man who will venture beyond the Earth to outer space. Man's development over eons of time is viewed frm the celestial vantage point of the "Ministering Angels."

The first stanza reads:

> A speck of dust
> orbits a shining disk.
> Some fragile creatures call it "Earth."
> The disk they revere as "Sun."

See Bezalel Naor, "Rav Kook's Space Odyssey," *Lehrhaus*, August 23, 2018. Also available (with Rav Kook's original Hebrew) at: http://orot.com/rav-kooks-space-odyssey/

Rav Kook's disciple, Dr. Moshe Seidel, reported that when Rav Kook served as Rabbi of Boisk, Latvia, he once predicted: "I am certain that one day humans will fly from one planet to another, for this is good and beautiful, and everything that is good and beautiful—will be!" (Ḥayyim Lifschitz, *Shivḥei ha-Rayah* [Jerusalem, 1995], p. 70)

[409]Song of Songs 2:9.

[410]Hebrew, *"levarekh 'et 'ammo."* These words are taken from the benediction that the *kohen* or priest recites before actually blessing the people (*"asher kiddeshanu bi-kedushato shel Aharon ve-tsivanu* levarekh 'et 'ammo *Yisrael be-'ahavah"*). See *Shulḥan 'Arukh, Oraḥ Ḥayyim* 128:11.

Midrash Tanḥuma (*Nasso* 8) has a dialogue between *Knesset Yisrael* (Ecclesia Israel) and the Holy One, blessed be He, in which the Jewish People express their wish to be blessed directly by God rather than by the priests, and God reassures them that He stands behind the priests and blesses the people through them. The verse adduced is from Song of Songs 2:9: "Behold, he stands behind our wall, he supervises from the windows (*mashgi'aḥ min ha-ḥalonot*), he peers from the lattices."

From this Midrash derives the practice of the priests holding their fingers apart to form "lattices" (*ḥarakim)* while extending their hands in blessing. See Rabbi Jacob ben Asher, *Arba'ah Turim*, *Oraḥ Ḥayyim*, chap. 128; and Rabbi Israel Meir Kagan, *Mishnah Berurah* to *Shulḥan 'Arukh*, *Oraḥ Ḥayyim* 128:12.

[411]Leviticus 19:26.

[412]*b. Berakhot* 10b.

[413]It seems that Rav Kook's prodigious memory deceived him. *Zohar*, *Mishpatim* (vol. 2, 122a) does quote the verse in Lev. 19:26, but in another regard. The *Zohar* discusses the need to pray for nourishment in *Pinḥas* (*Zohar* III, 126).

[414]See *Exodus Rabbah* 6:2.

[415]Cf. Psalms 14:7; 53:7.

[416]Proverbs 4:18.

Conclusion

I bless the Lord who has counseled me and helped me thus far to commence and to conclude my thoughts concerning the words of the Living God; to find enlightenment in the words of the wise and their riddles; and to delve—as much as my limited intellect allows—into the mysteries of the great adventurer Rabbah bar Bar Ḥannah, who included in his tales fifteen lessons, to draw wisdom from the depths; corresponding to the fifteen Songs of Ascent in the Psalms composed by King David,[417] peace be unto him, to raise up waters from the deep, to moisten the world (as stated by the Sages, of blessed memory, in *Perek he-Ḥalil*).[418] By the same token, Rabbah bar Bar Ḥannah taught fifteen great lessons that raise wisdom from the depths,[419] as it is written, "Counsel in the heart of man is like deep water; and a man of understanding will draw it out."[420]

May the Lord enlighten our eyes with His Torah, and may He grant us from His mouth "knowledge and understanding."[421]

[417]See our Appendix "A Kookian Midrash on the Name 'David.'"

[418]*b. Sukkah* 53. This Talmudic legend is of great symbolic significance. The Mishnah, *Sukkah* 5:4, relates that during the ceremony of *Simḥat Beit ha-Sho'evah*, the Rejoicing of the Water-Drawing (for the water libation upon the Altar), the Levites were stationed on the fifteen levels descending from the Court of the Israelites to the Court of the Women. The Levites sang as they played their musical instruments. The Mishnah makes the point that those fifteen levels correspond to the fifteen Songs of Ascent in the Book of Psalms (Psalms 120-134).

In that connection, the Gemara elaborates:

> Said Rav Ḥisda to a rabbi who was arranging *aggadeta* before him: Did you perhaps hear what correspondence David had in mind when he uttered these fifteen Songs of Ascent?
>
> He answered him: So said Rabbi Yoḥanan: At the time that David dug the foundations [of the Temple], the [waters of] the Deep surged up and threatened to flood the world. David uttered fifteen Songs of Ascent and lowered them.
>
> If so, they should be labeled fifteen Songs of (Ascents) Descents?
>
> Said Rav Ḥisda to him: Since you reminded me, actually this is the way it was said:
>
> When David dug the foundations [of the Temple], the [waters of] the Deep surged up and threatened to flood the world.
>
> David asked: Is there anyone who knows whether it is permissible to write the Name on clay and throw it into the Deep that it may plug the hole of the Deep?
>
> No one responded.
>
> David threatened: Whoever knows and does not speak up, his neck shall be wrung!
>
> Aḥitophel reasoned *a fortiori*: If to make peace between husband and wife, the Torah prescribes that the Name be erased into the water [Numbers 5:23], then to secure the peace of the entire world, all the more so! He said to David: "It is permitted."
>
> David wrote the Name on clay and threw it into the Deep. The Deep subsided sixteen thousand *garmidi*. When David saw that the Deep had subsided so much, he said that if the Deep should rise up close to ground level, it would moisten the soil (which would then bear its fruits). He uttered fifteen Songs of Ascent and raised the level of the Deep by fifteen thousand *garmidi*, stabilizing it at a thousand *garmidi* (below the surface of the earth).

Rav Kook may well be hinting that the subterranean waters of the Deep, the primordial *Tehom*, symbolize psychic energies lying below the surface of consciousness. If unchecked, these primal instincts threaten to overwhelm civilization. After initially subduing them by sheer power of the divine Name, David was able to gradually bring these basal waters back up. Rather than forever banishing them to the netherworld, David—with his sweet singing—coaxed them into the service of humanity. He realized that there were benefits to be reaped by allowing the "lower waters" to remain slightly below the surface. They provide *"retivut"* (moisture) and fecundity to an otherwise arid mindscape. Humanity's creative processes are fertilized by the unconscious.

(In the parallel *sugya* of the *Talmud Yerushalmi*, David excavated to a depth of fifteen hundred cubits before reaching the Deep, which then threatened to flood the world. Aḥitophel said some incantation to subdue the waters. Overjoyed, David recited Psalms as the waters subsided. For every hundred cubits that the waters subsided, David recited another Song of Ascent [*Shir ha-Ma'alot*]. The *Yerushalmi* plays on the word *Ma'alot* [Ascents]: *Me'ah 'olot* [one hundred levels]. See *y. Sanhedrin* 10:2.)

Rabbi Samuel Bornstein of Sokhatchov writes that the fifteen Songs of Ascent symbolize the ascents of the souls from the Lower Garden of Eden to the Higher Garden of Eden. His source is the *Silluk* composed by Rabbi El'azar ha-Kalir for the second day of *Sukkot*. See Rashi, Psalms 121:1 and *Shem mi-Shmuel* (Jerusalem, 1974), *Sukkot* 5677, Second Night, s.v. *t"u ha-ma'alot ha-yoredot* (160a). In a later piece, the author adds that this symbolism may be extended to the ascent of souls from the midst of Gehinnom. Ibid., *Sukkot* 5679, s.v. *'inyan shnei ha-nissukhin* (174b).

*

Inter alia, the son and successor of Rabbi Samuel Bornstein (author of *Shem mi-Shmuel*), Rabbi David Bornstein of Sokhatchov, was a great admirer of Rav Kook, whom he visited in Jerusalem in 1925. The letter of consolation that the Rebbe of Sokhatchov wrote to Rabbi Tsevi Yehudah after his father, Rav Kook's passing, is a very moving tribute to the deceased. See Yehoshua 'Uziel Zilberberg, *Malkhut Beit David* (B'nei Berak, 1991), pp. 350-351 (and earlier, p. 251). Evidently the recipient, Rabbi Tsevi Yehudah Kook, was very touched by this tribute, for he quoted a line from it at the conclusion of his introduction to the collected letters of his father, entitled *"Al kol divrei ha-'iggeret."* See *'Igrot ha-Rayah*, vol. 1 (Jerusalem, 1961), Introduction, p. 11. The version of Rabbi David Bornstein's letter that appears in *Malkhut Beit David* differs significantly from that of *'Igrot la-Rayah*, ed. Rabbi Ben Zion Shapira [Jerusalem, 1990], pp. 575-576 (Letter 38). The conclusions to the two letters are totally different! In an address delivered on the *Yahrzeit* of Rav Kook in the year 5738 [1978], Rabbi Tsevi Yehudah ad-libbed the contents of the letter from Rabbi David Bornstein of Sokhatchov; see Ḥayyim Avihu Schwarz, *Mi-Tokh ha-Torah ha-Go'elet*, vol. 1 (Jerusalem, 1989), p. 157.

After referring to Rav Kook as "Master of the Land of Israel" (*Mara de-'Ara' de-Yisrael*), the Sokhatchover writes: "Woe to a ship that has lost its captain, for unfortunately the Land of

Israel is like a ship tossed about in the sea of differing opinions, and he, of blessed memory, was the singular captain whose spirit was capable of 'meeting the spirit of each and every one' (*'la-halokh ke-neged ruḥo shel kol 'eḥad ve-'eḥad'*) [Rashi, Numbers 27:18]. Truly, the Land has lost her leader."

In the last year of his life, Rav Kook wrote a glowing tribute to the original halakhic methodology of Rabbi Abraham Bornstein, author Responsa *Avnei Nezer* (founder of the Sokhatchov dynasty and father of the *Shem mi-Shmuel*). See *Ma'amrei ha-Rayah*, vol. 1 [Jerusalem, 1980], pp. 203-204.

I was dismayed to discover that an anecdote concerning Rav Kook and Rabbi Michael Forshlager (a disciple of the *Avnei Nezer*) that took place in Baltimore in 1924, was camouflaged. In this sanitized version, Rav Kook is referred to obliquely as "one of the famous *ge'onim* of the generation from the Holy Land, of blessed memory." See *Mikha'el be-'Aḥat*, ed. Ben Zion Bergman (Ashdod, 5774/2013), p. 58.

*

At the conclusion of the third legend (Hurmin bar Lilitha), there was invoked the verse in Psalms 107:26: "They mounted up to the heavens, they went down to the depths." In that regard, the great Baghdadi Kabbalist, Rabbi Yosef Ḥayyim (*"Ben Ish Ḥai"*), wrote in his commentary *Ben Yehoyada'*:

> The sparks of holiness that are the portion of heaven shall rise from below; and the lights that are called "masculine waters" (*mayyin dukhrin*) shall descend to the *Yesod* of *Malkhut*, which is called "the Deep" (*Tehom*) ….

*

There is much Ḥasidic literature on the symbolism of the *Tehom* (Deep), the *mayim taḥtonim* (lower waters), and the *Simḥat Beit ha-Sho'evah* (Rejoicing of the Water-Drawing). Rabbi Aharon Halevi Horowitz of Staroselye expounds upon the two *Tehomot*, the upper *Tehom*, symbolizing *Binah*, and the lower *Tehom*, symbolic of *Malkhut*. See *'Avodat ha-Levi*, Deuteronomy (Warsaw, 1866), *Derushim le-Simḥat Beit ha-Sho'evah* (13d-14a and 15a). Rabbi Tsevi Elimelekh Spira of Dynów writes that the intention of the *Simḥat Beit ha-Sho'evah* is to uplift the "fallen loves" from the World of Chaos *('Olam ha-Tohu)* to the World of Restoration (*'Olam ha-Tikkun*). See *B'nei Yissakhar, Ma'amrei Ḥodesh Tishri* 10:30-32. Rabbi Gershon Ḥanokh Leiner of Radzyn preserved a teaching of his grandfather Rabbi Mordechai Joseph Leiner of Izbica concerning the symbolism of David digging the foundation; see *Sod Yesharim, Sukkot* (Warsaw, 1903), *Leil Sheini de-Sukkot*, par. 59 (30d-31a); par. 63 (32d-33b); par. 74 (38a-b); par. 77 (39a-b). Rabbi Jacob Perlow of Novominsk taught that the upper waters (*Ḥokhmah*) and the lower waters (*Malkhut*) shall combine; see *Shufra de-Ya'akov*, ed. Rabbi Yosef Perlow (Jerusalem, 2016), *Balak*, 449b-450b. See also Rabbi Isaac Hutner, *Paḥad Yitsḥak—Yom ha-Kippurim* (New York, 2004),

Ma'amar 10 (pp. 113-117); and Bezalel Naor, *Be-Mayim 'Azim Netivah* (n.p., 1988), *"Simḥat Beit ha-Sho'evah,"* pp. 133-136.

In the older Rabbinic sources, the "upper waters" (*mayim 'elyonim*) are masculine, and the "lower waters" (*mayim taḥtonim*) are feminine; see *y. Berakhot* 9:2; and *t. Ta'anit*, chap. 1 (Zuckermandel ed., p. 215).

[419]One is intrigued why Rav Kook juxtaposed the fifteen legends of Rabbah bar Bar Ḥannah to the fifteen Songs of Ascent of King David. Is it merely the numerical coincidence? I believe that the answer lies in the following fact. In regard to the *shitin* or foundations of the Temple—hollows that extend down to the *Tehom* or Deep—we have this statement of Rabbah bar Bar Ḥannah:

> Rabbah bar Bar Ḥannah said in the name of Rabbi Yoḥanan: The *shitin* were created from the six days of Creation…
>
> (*b. Sukkah* 49a)

Now this statement attributed to Rabbah bar Bar Ḥannah's teacher, Rabbi Yoḥanan, is problematic because further in Tractate *Sukkah* (53a) we have a seemingly contradictory statement of Rabbi Yoḥanan: "At the time that David dug the *shitin* … " Either the *shitin* are the handiwork of the Creator or of King David. Which is it? *Tosafot* (*Sukkah* 49a, s.v. *'al tikrei bereshit 'ela bara shit*) wriggle out of the dilemma by assuming that two *amoraim* transmitted conflicting sayings in the name of Rabbi Yoḥanan. Rashi (*Sukkah* 53a, s.v. *be-sha'ah she-karah David shitin*) and Ritba (*Sukkah* 49a, s.v. *amar Rabbah bar Bar Ḥannah*) offer the ingenious solution that the *shitin* dating back to Creation had filled in with soil or rocks, and therefore David had to excavate them once again.

The famed Rogatchover Gaon, Rabbi Joseph Rosen, understood the clogging with soil and rocks as symbolic of the spiritual blocking of the heart due to sins. By the same token, David's subsequent excavation symbolizes *teshuvah* or spiritual return. See *She'elot u-Teshuvot Tsafnat Pa'ane'aḥ ha-Ḥadashot*, vol. 1 (Modi'in 'Ilit, 2010), Letter 11 (p. 359); vol. 2 (Modi'in 'Ilit, 2012), Letter 11 (p. 442).

Recently, Rabbi Shlomo Zuckier published an article in which he takes up Rashi and Ritba's suggestion that this incursion into the Netherworld represents an interaction or synergy of the divine and the human. See Shlomo Zuckier, "Of Divine Nostrils and the Primordial Altar," *Lehrhaus*, March 8, 2018.

[420]Proverbs 20:5. In *b. Pesaḥim* 53b-54a, the end of this verse was applied to Rabbah bar Bar Ḥannah:

> Rav Yosef invoked [the verse] "Counsel in the heart of man is like deep water; and a man of understanding will draw it out."

"Counsel in the heart of man is like deep water"—This is 'Ulla.

"And a man of understanding will draw it out"—This is Rabbah bar Bar Ḥannah.

Rashi explains:

> **This is 'Ulla**—who understood from the words of Rabbi Abba that the error [in transmission of a halakhic position of Rabbi Yoḥanan] had arisen with Rabbah bar Bar Ḥannah, and [therefore] 'Ulla looked at him askance, but contained himself and did not say anything to him. This is the meaning of "counsel in the heart of man." He kept it in his heart and did not say to Rabbah bar Bar Ḥannah: "Why did you say so?"
>
> **"And a man of understanding will draw it out"**—[Rabbah bar Bar Ḥannah] understood what was going on in the heart of 'Ulla that caused him to look askance at him.

[421]Cf. Proverbs 2:6.

Appendix 1

"*Barukh ha-Ba, Señor*"
Rav Kook and the *Dybbuk* in Jaffa

Over the ages there were reported numerous cases in which the great men of Israel were called upon to exorcise a disembodied spirit—usually of a malevolent nature—that inhabited a living person. Such a possessing spirit is referred to in the literature as a "*dybbuk*" (literally "cling-on"). In recent times, the saintly sage of Radin, Rabbi Israel Meir Kagan (1838-1933), known by the title of his book as the "*Ḥafets Ḥayyim,*" performed such an exorcism. His devoted disciple, Rabbi Elḥanan Wasserman, who participated in the ritual, would retell the story to his *yeshivah* students in Baranovich every year on Purim.[422]

A.S. Ansky immortalized the theme in his Yiddish play by that name, *Der Dibuk* (1920). For an academic treatment of the subject, see J.H. Chajes, *Between Worlds: Dybbuks, Exorcists, and Early Modern Judaism* (Philadelphia: University of Pennsylvania Press, 2003).

The following report comes from a personal letter written by Rav Kook's son, Tsevi Yehudah, to his friend, Rabbi Ya'akov Moshe Ḥarlap of Jerusalem. (Rabbi Ḥarlap was the eminent disciple of Rav Kook.) The letter was composed in Jaffa in the year 1912. It was published in the collected letters of Rabbi Tsevi Yehudah Hakohen Kook, *Tsemaḥ Tsevi*, vol. 1 (Jerusalem, 1991), no. 13 (pp. 40-41).

> ...
>
> While I am the process of writing, I will tell you an incident that took place here, of which you are certainly yet unaware, though other such incidents are given much publicity by the masses.
>
> Three weeks ago—as I recall, on Saturday night of *Parashat Terumah*—two Sephardim, one old, the other young, came before my father [i.e. Rav Kook], imploring on behalf of the son (of the old man) and the brother (of the young man). There had entered him a disincarnate spirit. For about a year he suffered intermittently from month to month. He consulted gentile physicians and also employed medicines prescribed by gentile women.[423]
>
> Now [the sick man] says that he will not receive any physician or medicine in the world. He insists that *Ḥakham* Abraham Kohen Kook come to him,

whereupon he (or the possessing spirit) will confide something to my father [i.e. Rav Kook], and will obey him if and when he commands him to exit from the sick man's body, allowing him to live.

Rav Kook commanded them to transmit to him that this night he should be at rest and not afflict the sick man, and tomorrow the Rav will come to him. Following this order, the sick man was left alone [by the spirit] until the next day.

Sunday afternoon, the Rav went to visit him. On the way, the Rav asked the brother of the sick man in which language he should speak to him, and whether he knows the Holy Tongue [i.e. Hebrew]. The brother answered in the negative, saying that he would translate for him to Arabic. He also said that no one had ever mentioned Rav Kook to his brother as someone capable of healing him. He did not know Rav Kook before.

When the Rav arrived at the house, the sick man raised himself a bit from his bed, saying: "*Barukh ha-ba, Señor*" (Welcome, Sir).[424] The Rav asked him a question in the Holy Tongue, and he answered in the Holy Tongue. And thus their entire conversation was conducted in the Holy Tongue. (On their way back, the sick man's brother testified once again that his brother never knew how to speak in the Holy Tongue.)[425]

When the Rav commanded the spirit to depart from the sick man's midst and to leave him alone, the sick man thanked him profusely, saying that he now feels relieved.

A few days later, the members of the family came once again. They brought with them the *Ḥakham Bashi* (the Chief Sephardic Rabbi)[426] and additional local Sephardic *ḥakhamim*, entreating [Rav Kook] to pay a second visit. For after feeling some relief, the sick man was grievously afflicted once again.

The Rav set out a second time, accompanied by several men. This time too, they spoke in the Holy Tongue. This time, the Rav yelled at the spirit loudly, invoking severe oaths, that he must exit the sick man immediately through the left toe.[427]

After several refusals, the spirit finally agreed to exit but only through the sick man's eye or head. He screamed: "Through his eye! Through his head!"

But the Rav continued to shout at him in a loud, frightening voice that he must exit only from the toe, and in so doing, not injure the sick man.

After several refusals, the sick man's body began to jerk wildly for a short while, and he shouted: "*Oy*, my foot, my foot!" And then he was relieved.

A day later, the family members came once again saying that the sick man complains about the pain in his foot. The Rav told them that it would subside in a few days ....

Last week, the Rav responded to a famous rabbi in Romania in regard to the new techniques of conversing with spirits of the deceased, which have gained currency as of late. The questioner wrote that this will strengthen belief.[428] In his response, the Rav was inclined to forbid [this practice]. "Anyway, not through such means will we strengthen faith."[429]

Likewise, the Rav belittles the value of stories such as the above [of the exorcism], for "Let not the wise man glory in his wisdom ... but let him that glories, glory in this, that he understands, and knows Me, that I am the Lord who exercises mercy, justice, and righteousness, in the earth; for in these things I delight, says the Lord" (Jeremiah 9:22-23).

[422]Rabbi Ya'akov Kanievsky, *Ḥayyei 'Olam* (Tel-Aviv, 1967), chap. 12 (p. 20). In order to perform the exorcism, the *Ḥafets Ḥayyim* assembled a *minyan* (quorum) of ten men. One of the ten was his disciple Rabbi Elḥanan Wasserman.

Inter alia, in *Ḥayyei 'Olam*, Rabbi Kanievsky (known as the Steipeler Ga'on after his birthplace of Hornosteipel, Ukraine) relied heavily on Rabbi Menasseh ben Israel's earlier work *Nishmat Ḥayyim*, referring to the author as "the *Ga'on* Menashe ben Yisrael" (*Ḥayyei 'Olam*, beginning chap. 7 [p. 13]). Regarding *Nishmat Ḥayyim*, see below note 428.

A letter from Rabbi Kanievsky's brother-in-law, the renowned *posek* (halakhic decisor) Rabbi Abraham Isaiah Karelitz (author of *Ḥazon Ish*) seems to frown upon the practice of exorcism. To Rabbi [Yeshayah] Asher Zelig Margaliyot, a Kabbalist of Jerusalem, Rabbi Karelitz wrote:

> We have no permission to excommunicate "the external powers" (*ha-koḥot ha-ḥitsoniyot*), for they are the creations of the *Ein Sof*, blessed be He, and perform His will. Only the supernal holy men such as Rabbi Shim'on ben Yoḥai and his companions, who stand in the counsel [of the Lord] rule over the external [powers] and they must hearken to them. And when they have been obligated to vacate their residence by virtue of the recitation of the divine name, and they do not vacate, then they are permitted to excommunicate them as is the law regarding one who disobeys the [court of] law (*lo tsayyit dina*). And even this is in accordance with a mystery that is incomprehensible to us, for according to that which is revealed, they [i.e. the external powers] have no free will.
>
> But we retain nothing of this, and God forbid that we make use of this. The *Tanna'im* and *Amora'im* made use of doctors and medicines, and did not make use of this. As for us, our power is in our mouth, in prayer and supplications before the Omnipresent, blessed be He, that he send His word and heal [...] speedily.
>
> (Benjamin Brown, *The Ḥazon Ish: Halakhist, Believer and Leader of the Ḥaredi Revolution* [Hebrew] [Jerusalem, 2011], p. 175)

Brown speculates that in the original of the letter, the ellipsis indicated the name of the sick person whom Rabbi Margaliyot thought might benefit from the ritual of exorcism or "excommunication of the external powers" (*niddui ha-koḥot ha-ḥitsoniyot*).

For earlier *dybbukim* recorded in the Lithuanian Kabbalistic tradition of the Vilna Gaon and his disciple Rabbi Ḥayyim of Volozhin, see Dov Eliach, *Ha-Gaon*, vol. 2 (Jerusalem, 2002), pp. 499-502; idem, *Avi ha-Yeshivot* (Jerusalem, 2011), pp. 245-246.

For a recent interpretation of the phenomenon of *dybbukim* by a representative of the Lithuanian tradition, see Rabbi Moshe Shapiro, *"Be'urim ba-Aggadot Rabbah bar Bar Ḥannah,"* in *Yeshurun* 37, p. 509, note 137.

[423]When it came to spirit possession, Jews were remarkably open to consulting non-Jewish healers. Generally, pragmatism was the ruling principle. See J.H. Chajes, *Between Worlds: Dybbuks, Exorcists, and Early Modern Judaism* (Philadelphia: University of Pennsylvania Press, 2003), pp. 51, 93-95.

[424]Cf. the anecdote reported in *Toledot ha-Ari*, where the spirit greets Rabbi Joseph Ashkenazi, the *"tanna"* of Safed, with the identical greeting of *"Barukh ha-ba!"* See Meir Benayahu, *Toledot ha-Ari* (Ramat-Gan, 1967), p. 192. Later, in 1609, in Damascus, Rabbi Ḥayyim Vital performed an exorcism on the daughter of Raphael Anav. In that case too, no sooner did the Rabbi arrive at the entrance than he was greeted thrice by the demon, *"Barukh ha-ba!"* See Rabbi Ḥayyim Vital, *Sefer ha-Ḥezyonot*, ed. Netanel Moshe Mansour (Jerusalem, 2002), chap. 22 (p. 66). An English translation of the episode is provided in Chajes, p. 166: "When I entered the doorway, he said to me three times, 'Blessed is he who comes!'"

[425]In the classic cases of exorcism practiced in sixteenth-century Safed, xenoglossia or knowledge of foreign languages would convince the exorcist that this was indeed an instance of spirit possession. See Raphael Patai, "Exorcism and Xenoglossia Among the Safed Kabbalists," *Journal of American Folklore* 91 (1978), pp. 823-835; Chajes, pp. 41, 90.

[426]The reference is to the *Ḥakham Bashi* of Jaffa, Rabbi Ben-Zion Meir Ḥai Uziel (1880-1953).

[427]This is standard procedure when exorcising a *dybbuk*. In this manner, the "exit wound" causes the least possible damage to the afflicted. See Meir Benayahu, *Toledot ha-Ari* (Ramat-Gan, 1967), pp. 196, 300, 304, 305.

[428]In this respect, the Romanian rabbi was following in the footsteps of Rabbi Menasseh ben Israel, who wrote *Nishmat Ḥayyim*, a rich repository of demonology, in an attempt to combat the "Sadducees" of his day in the Marrano community of Amsterdam. See Chajes, chap. 5 (pp. 119-138).

[429]Rav Kook's lengthy responsum concerning "spiritism" or spiritualism (conversing with spirits) was published in his halakhic work *Da'at Kohen*, no. 69. See there page 167 (column a): "In my humble opinion, it is not worthwhile to strengthen faith through such techniques." Quoted in H.J. Zimmels, *Magicians, Theologians, and Doctors* (Northvale, NJ, 1997), p. 219, note 53.

Appendix 2

Man and Time: The Vilna Gaon on the Three Levels of the Soul

In this pithy piece, printed as an appendix to the Gaon's commentary to *Sifra de-Tseni'uta* (Vilna, 1882),[430] parallels are established between man and time. According to this remarkable analysis, the three tenses of past, present and future, correspond anatomically to the head, the chest and the belly, and spiritually to the three levels of soul: *neshamah*, *ru'aḥ* and *nefesh*.[431] What comes out of the discussion is the supreme importance of the present (over and against past and future) and the centrality of the intermediate level of *ru'aḥ*—a teaching of great significance for Rav Kook.

THE GARMENTS (*LEVUSHIM*) MADE FROM THE DAYS OF MAN[432]

Man and time are male and female. The sum total of humanity—all the souls that comprise a single body[433]—is a male. And the sum total of the years of the world is a female. (See what I have written in the *Tikkunim*, at the beginning of *tikkun* 69 [103a], that they [i.e. time and man] are *nefesh* and *ru'aḥ*.)[434] *Nefesh* is partner to the body (*shittufa de-gufa*),[435] so from the days and years is made a body for the *ru'aḥ*. This is the mystery of "A female shall surround a man."[436] (And as I have written in *tikkun* 22, the female is the body to the male.) For this reason, the 248 limbs correspond to man,[437] and the 365 negative commandments correspond to the days of the [solar] year.[438]

The wise men did well when they said that time is man's friend and his beloved.[439] They divided time in three parts: past, future and present, corresponding to the *nefesh*, *ru'aḥ* and *neshamah* of man,[440] [located] in the head, the belly and the chest.[441]

And just as the head is respected and diminishes in size,[442] so too time. "Do not say…that the former days were better than these,"[443] for so must it be, just as in the body of man.

And just as the heart is the mainstay of man, so the *ru'aḥ*. The *neshamah* merely imparts to man intellect that he might conduct himself. So the entire purpose of time is but the present, whereas the past has already gone away. The past is [but][444] a helpful instructor.

The future—"Do not fret over tomorrow's trouble!"[445] A man should not think about it because it is not his, as it is written, "What results is that he is worrying about a world that is not his."[446] So when it comes to the *nefesh*, one should not think about it. It is partner to the body (*shittufa de-gufa*). "When your soul (*nefesh*) will crave to eat meat."[447] [It is] a world that is not his. Tomorrow is not. For it is an inn ....[448]

They [i.e. man and time] are bound together through Torah, as the Epigrammatist wrote.[449] By bonding to time, the Torah is learned, for it is impossible to learn it other than through time.

The ten *sefirot* are included in *nefesh*, *ru'aḥ*, *neshamah*;[450] and in *'Olam* (Space), *Shanah* (Time), *Nefesh* (Soul).[451] *'Olam* is the Torah, as it is written: "'In the beginning (*be-reshit*) God created' [Genesis 1:1]—There is no beginning (*reshit*) other than Torah."[452] "Then I was by Him, as a nursling."[453] And so in *'Olam*, man and time bond together ... And that is the Torah through which all was created ... Man and time are bound together through *'Olam*; *'Olam* is the mother who bears both of them, male and female.

(*Likkutei ha-Gra,* appended to *Be'ur ha-Gra* to *Sifra de-Tseni'uta*, ed. Samuel Luria [Vilna, 1882], 39c-d)

In order to better understand the selection from *Likkutei ha-Gra*, I have provided below the passage from the Gaon's commentary to *Tikkunei Zohar* that was referenced:

Man and time correspond to male and female, *ru'aḥ* and *nefesh*.

Now all the spirits (*ruḥot*) [of man] emanate from the six days of creation; they are all the souls in the body [of the King] according to the limbs. "Some are connected to the head [of the King]; some to the hairs [of the head]," as it is written above *tikkun* 18, and there it is explained.[454]

The *nefashot* [on the other hand] are connected to time; all the time of the six millennia constitutes one body of all the *nefashot*. For every year is divided into 365 days; and every day is divided into minutes.

Now the limbs of the body of the *ruḥot* (spirits) line up opposite the limbs of the body of time. They are [in that sense] male and female.

This is what is written in *Sefer Yetsirah* that [existence] divides into three [dimensions]: *'Olam* (Space), *Shanah* (Time), *Nefesh* (Soul). *Shanah* (Time) and *Nefesh* (Soul) [or rather *Nefesh* and *Shanah*] are the male and female mentioned above; and *'Olam* (Space) includes male and female, *ru'aḥ* and *nefesh*, for it emanates from the two of them.[455]

If a man merits that the *ru'aḥ* emerges at precisely the hour corresponding to it, this is when one merits to his [soul] mate, for the *nefesh* [which is "female"] emerges only at its proper hour, and therefore it is not subject to reincarnation, for it is impossible for it to emerge other than at its proper time. The emergence of the *ru'aḥ* [on the other hand] does not depend on the hour, but rather on the place, *'Olam*. For the entire world is one body, as mentioned above. But by reincarnation one cannot merit one's mate, if the first [wife] was not his [soul] mate; neither [can one merit one's mate] in the second or third reincarnation.

And this is what is meant by "*ve-'ihi sha'ata de-kayma leh*" ("And she is the hour that exists for him").

(Commentary of Vilna Gaon to *Tikkunei Zohar, tikkun* 69 [old edition, 103a; edition of Vilna 1867, 115b], s.v. *ve-'ihi sha'ata*)

[430]Questions have been raised as to the provenance of the *Likkutim* or Collectanea appended to Rabbi Samuel Luria's Vilna 1882 edition of *Be'ur ha-Gra* to *Sifra di-Tseni'uta*. In particular, the *Likkut* concerning *Tsimtsum* (38b-39b) was impugned by Rabbi Shelomo Eliashov, *Leshem Shevo ve-Aḥlamah: Ḥelek ha-Be'urim* (Jerusalem, 1935), 5b. However, Yosef Avivi has pointed out that that *Likkut* was attested to by Rabbi Yitsḥak Eizik Ḥaver in his work *Magen ve-Tsinah* (Koenigsberg, 1855). See Yosef Avivi's introduction to *Kabbalat ha-Gra* (Jerusalem, 1993), p. 27. Rabbi Eliashov (loc. cit.) lent more credence to the preceding *Likkutim* that appeared in the earlier 1820 edition of *Be'ur ha-Gra* to *Sifra di-Tseni'uta* published in Vilna by the author's grandson, Rabbi Jacob Moses of Slonim (son of the Gaon's son, Rabbi Abraham). Though our piece did not appear in that earlier collection, it is safe to assume that it too issued from the Gaon's pen, as it parallels a passage in the Gaon's commentary to *Tikkunei Zohar*, provided below for the sake of comparison. For what it is worth, Rabbi Joshua Heschel Levin quotes our piece from the *Likkutim* in his biography of the Vilna Gaon, referring to it as "truly the handwriting" of the Vilna Gaon. See J.H. Levin, *'Aliyot Eliyahu* (Vilna, 1856), f. 25, n. 22.

There is also overlap between our piece and a commentary of the Vilna Gaon to *Sefer Yetsirah* that was edited by the Gaon's disciple Rabbi Menaḥem Mendel of Shklov.

In the *Likkutim* we read:

> And just as the heart is the mainstay of man, so the *ru'aḥ*. The *neshamah* merely imparts to man intellect that he might conduct himself.

In the commentary to *Sefer Yetsirah* there occurs an almost identical statement:

> The main vitality of man is the *ru'aḥ*, and that is the man who receives reward and punishment, as is known, and it is that which feels, and it is all of his faculties and senses; and the *neshamah* is the intellect that imparts to man knowledge, and it is the *mazal* (luck) of man and his *mal'akh* (angel), as is known. And it [i.e. the *neshamah*] is in heaven; only sparks shine down from it upon man to conduct him and enlighten him.
>
> (Commentary of Gra to *Sefer Yetsirah*, ed. Rabbi Menaḥem Mendel of Shklov [Horadna, 1806], *ofan* 3, s.v. *bi-sheloshim u-shetayim netivot* [3a])

[431]Without going into a tremendous amount of detail, we might reduce *nefesh* to the hematologic, *ru'aḥ* to the pneumatic, and *neshamah* to the cerebral realms. A convenient way to conceive of them is in terms of *maḥshavah*, *dibbur* and *ma'aseh*. In this schemata, *neshamah* corresponds to thought (*maḥshavah*); *ru'aḥ* to speech (*dibbur*); and *nefesh* to action (*ma'aseh*).

For an encyclopedic array of the levels of the soul in the Zoharic literature, see Rabbi Reuven Margaliyot, *Kuntres NaRaN*, in his *Sha'arei Zohar*, 129b-135b. For some speculations of Rav

Kook concerning the three levels of *nefesh*, *ru'aḥ* and *neshamah*, see *Pinkesei ha-Rayah*, vol. 3, ed. Rabbi Levi Yitsḥaki (Jerusalem, n.d.), 16:37 (pp. 224-226).

Concerning the five names for the soul, see Rabbi Reuven Margaliyot, *Nitsutsei Zohar* to *Zohar* I, 81a. For speculations of Rav Kook concerning the five levels of *nefesh*, *ru'aḥ*, *neshamah*, *ḥayah*, *yeḥidah*, see *Pinkesei ha-Rayah*, vol. 3, 15:46 (p. 94).

[432]Cf. *Zohar* I, 129a: "'And Abraham was old, come with days' [Genesis 24:1]—with those supernal days."

[433]The notion of a body that comprises all the souls throughout time, originates with the saying in *b. Yevamot* 62a: "The [Messiah] son of David cannot come until all the souls in the body (*guf*) have been exhausted." Rashi (ad loc.) explains that the souls are stored in a treasury (*'otsar*) whose name is "*Guf*." This saying occurs also in *b. 'Avodah Zarah* 5a. See Rabbi Reuven Margaliyot, *Nitsutsei 'Or* ad loc.

In the Midrash, the body of Adam contains the righteous of future generations:

> While the body of Adam was yet a *golem* (raw material), the Holy One, blessed be He, showed him each and every *tsaddik* (righteous man) who would come out of him. There is one who depends upon the head of Adam; one who depends upon his hair; one who depends upon his forehead; one upon his eyes; one upon his nose; one upon his mouth; one upon his ear; and one upon his earlobe. [Rabbi David Luria emends this last organ to read "his penis."]
>
> (*Exodus Rabbah* 40:3)

See also *Midrash Tanḥuma*, *Ki Tissa* 12.

This theme is expanded upon in Lurianic Kabbalah (where it is no longer restricted to the righteous): "All the souls were included in Adam at the time that he was created. There is a soul that was connected to Adam's head; some to his eyes; some to his orifices; and so all of his limbs" (Rabbi Ḥayyim Vital, *Sefer ha-Gilgulim*, Frankfurt am Main, 1684, chap. 1). In the course of the six millennia of history, the souls appear in descending order, until finally, there appear the souls of the generation preceding the coming of Messiah, once located in the soles of Adam's feet. For that reason, the Sages referred to the pre-Messianic era as "the heels of Messiah" ("*'Ikvot Meshiḥa*"): "In the heels of Messiah, *ḥutspah* (impudence) will increase" (*m. Sotah* 9:15; *b. Sotah* 49b). "Since the heels are very coarse, therefore the souls that are connected to them are very coarse, and therefore—'*ḥutspah* will increase'" (*Sefer ha-Gilgulim*, end chap. 1). Thus, in the Lurianic understanding of the saying, "The [Messiah] son of David cannot come until all the souls in the body (*guf*) have been exhausted," the *guf* or body refers to that of Adam, which served as the repository of all future souls of mankind. Ibid. See Rabbi Shneur Zalman of Liadi, *Tanya* I, 2 (6b). And see now Elchanan Shilo, "*Parshanut Harav Kook le-Kabbalat ha-Ari: Hofa'at Neshamot Ḥadashot ve-Tikkun ha-'Olam*" in *'Iyunim bi-Tekumat Yisrael*, vol. 18 (2008), pp. 61-63, 73-76.

[434]Excerpted below.

[435]The Kabbalistic notion of the *nefesh* as being the "partner of the body" may have earlier precedent in Rashi, *Ḥagigah* 12b. Commenting on the phrase of the Talmud "*ruḥot u-neshamot,*" Rashi writes:

> It is one.
>
> *And some interpret that ru'aḥ is the neshamah made in the shape of the body.* [Italics—BN.]
>
> *Neshamah—neshimah, haleine* (breath) in French.

For recent discussions of *Doppelgänger*, astral body and autoscopy in Jewish mysticism, see Gershom Scholem, "*Tselem*: The Concept of the Astral Body," in idem, *On the Mystical Shape of the Godhead* (New York: Schocken, 1991), chap. 6; and Shaḥar Arzy and Moshe Idel, *Kabbalah: A Neurocognitive Approach to Mystical Experiences* (New Haven: Yale University, 2015).

[436]Jeremiah 31:21.

[437]A scribal error. The text should read: "The 248 positive commandments correspond to the limbs of man."

[438]*b. Makkot* 23b.

[439]I have not succeeded in finding the source of this maxim.

[440]The Gaon will clarify in the continuation that the past corresponds to the *neshamah*; the present to the *ru'aḥ*; and the future to the *nefesh*.

[441]The abbreviation *rbg* in the text signifies: *rosh*, *beten*, *geviyah* or head, belly, chest. See *Sefer Yetzirah*, ed. Rabbi Aryeh Kaplan (York Beach, Maine: Samuel Weiser, 1997), 3:6 (pp. 150-152). It should be clarified that the three levels of the soul *nefesh*, *ru'aḥ* and *neshamah* correspond to belly, chest and head, respectively.

[442]The neck is smaller in circumference than the head.

[443]Ecclesiastes 7:10.

[444]In Levin's version (see above note 430): *rak* (only). In Luria's version: *rav* (teacher).

[445]Ben Sira, quoted in *b. Sanhedrin* 100b.

[446]Ibid. Rashi explains that one may not live to see that future day, so one's worrying is in vain.

[447]Deuteronomy 12:20.

[448]The exact reference is unclear, though the gist is that the body is but an inn for the soul of man.

[449]The *Melits* or Epigrammatist is Rabbi Yedayah Bedersi (or Rabbi Yedayah ha-Penini). See his *Beḥinat 'Olam* 16:1: "Torah and man bound together—this is the candle of God on earth." Rav Kook was fond of that saying. See Bezalel Naor, *The Limit of Intellectual Freedom: The Letters of Rav Kook* (Spring Valley, NY, 2011), p. 227, n. 211.

[450]See the Kabbalistic Chart appended to this volume. *Nefesh* corresponds to *Malkhut*; *ru'aḥ* to *Vav Ketsavot*; and *neshamah* to *Binah*.

[451]These are the three dimensions of *Sefer Yetsirah*. The terminology can be a bit confusing. We should clarify that in the Gaon's scheme, *Sefer Yetsirah*'s *'Olam* (Space) corresponds to the level of soul designated as *"neshamah"*; *Sefer Yetsirah*'s *Shanah* (Time) corresponds to the level of *"nefesh"*; and *Sefer Yetsirah*'s *Nefesh* (Soul) corresponds to the level of *ru'aḥ*. (See our Kabbalistic Chart at the conclusion of this volume.) Furthermore, the Gaon will equate *'Olam* with Torah. Torah is that which binds man and time together; it is the "mother" who bears children male (man) and female (time).

[452]*Genesis Rabbah* 1:1.

[453]Proverbs 8:30; quoted in *Genesis Rabbah* there.

[454]*Tikkunei Zohar*, *tikkun* 18, explains that each prophet availed himself of the sensory organ (in the Godhead, as it were) from which his soul emanated. Thus Isaiah drew on the sense of sight, for his soul emanated from the eyes; while Ḥabakkuk drew on the sense of sound, for his soul emanated from the ears, etc. Only Moses had access to the full panoply of organs: "In *all* My house he is trusted" (Numbers 12:7). See *Be'ur ha-Gra* there (in Vilna 1867 edition, 32b), s.v. *minehon ba-reisha*.

[455]The original reads: "*'Olam* (Space) and *Shanah* (Time) are the male and female mentioned above; and *Nefesh* (Soul) includes male and female, *ru'aḥ* and *nefesh*, for it emanates from the two of them."

The wording, as it stood, was incomprehensible to the writer (BN). I have taken the liberty of emending the wording slightly to conform to that in the passage in the *Likkutim* above. If I have erred, may the good Lord forgive me.

Appendix 3

Rabbi Ḥayyim Hirschensohn's *Motsa'ei Mayim* and Rav Kook

In 1924, the brilliant if controversial Rabbi of Hoboken, New Jersey, Ḥayyim Hirschensohn, published his own interpretation of the Legends of Rabbah bar Bar Ḥannah, entitled *Motsa'ei Mayim* or *Watersprings*, a phrase taken from Psalms.[456] The subtitle of the book reads: "A Scientific Commentary According to the Method of the *Peshat* (Plain Meaning) and the *Remez* (Allegory)." The title-page goes on to clarify what is meant by *Peshat* as opposed to *Remez* or Allegory. *Peshat* refers to the *variae lectiones* and the derivation of obscure words. As for the allegorical portion of the work, Hirschensohn, writing in the wake of the recent Balfour Declaration (1917) and its confirmation by the Allies at the San Remo Conference (1920),[457] reads the various legends as a sort of prototypical Zionist treatise in which various Amoraic contemporaries of Rabbah bar Bar Ḥannah state their differing opinions regarding the proposed Return to Zion. Once again, the author lays his cards out on the title-page: "About … the arousal to return to Zion, which took place in the days of Rabbi Shim'on ben Lakish and Rabbah bar Bar Ḥannah, who worked enthusiastically in that movement, and their relation to the Arabs; and about the moderates in the movement such as Rabbi Yoḥanan; and those opposed to it such as Rav Yehudah."

In two passages of *Motsa'ei Mayim*, Rabbi Hirschensohn comments on the contemporary scene in Erets Yisrael and the controversy surrounding Chief Rabbi Kook's sensational work *Orot* (1920):

> If we…adopt the lyrical philosophy of the High Priest of the Land of Israel, the Gaon, our teacher Rabbi Abraham Hakohen Kook, may his light shine, in his book *Orot*…the precious must come out from the dross,[458] and the strong is necessary to produce the sweet,[459] and the shattering of the vessels is necessary for fixing the lights—and even the whole lights that haven't fallen yet to the depth of the pit will not afford us their light without this descent—and for the true revelation of the light of Torah, that will fill the earth with the knowledge of the Lord,[460] there is required first the latest literature built on the foundation of the power of imagination (the aphorists, the raconteurs, the dramatists and all those involved in *les beaux-arts*, who predominate in our contemporary culture). And though true wisdom suffers on this account and melts away, and "impudence increases … and

the wisdom of sages rots"[461]—all of this is a far-reaching plan, the Lord's plan to perfect the power of imagination, for imagination is the healthy basis for the supernal spirit that will manifest thereon. Therefore, now the power of imagination is being firmly established. When it is completely finished, the seat will be ready and perfect for the supernal spirit of the Lord, and fit to receive a new light,[462] which is the spirit of the Lord, a spirit of wisdom and understanding, a spirit of counsel and strength, a spirit of knowledge and awe of the Lord." (This is the gist of his words in *Orot me-Ofel* [Lights from Darkness], chapter 17.)

Rav Kook's words in this chapter are short, allowing the overly pious to oppress him, saying that he sanctifies the new literature with all of its atheism and amorality. However, one who reads his entire book in depth, and is not blinded by the intensity of its light, will understand his meaning: The power of imagination—which is also one of the powers necessary for the wholeness of the soul—melted away. The melting of the power of imagination [in turn] weakened the standing of *ru'aḥ ha-kodesh* (divine inspiration). The divine plan is that the power of imagination will be fortified so that it will serve—upon completion—as the basis for the supernal spirit to manifest thereupon. Though this entails that there also arise in the rose-bed of literature weeds (amorality, atheism, and rebellion against all that is sacred), in the end, the ugly paganism in literature will totally disappear, and there will remain but a garden of delights, a plantation of the Lord to be proud of....

And as he said in *Orot ha-Teḥiyah*, chapter 36: "It is impossible for Israelite literature to succeed without the sanctification of the souls of the writers. Any writer who does not labor to purify his character, to crystallize his deeds and thoughts, until his internal world is itself full of light and internal wholeness perceptible within him, together with concern to make up for lackings; to be filled with humility mixed with strength, and tranquility of spirit coupled with an intense intellectual and emotional arousal to improve and comprehend himself, and an exalted desire to reach the pinnacle of purity and holiness—as long as one does not stand on such a niveau, he cannot rightfully be called a writer." Clearly, a writer who has achieved such a state—his esthetic literature too is holy and pure, and a basis for divine inspiration, such as the poetry of Rabbi Solomon ibn Gabirol, Rabbi Judah

Halevi, Rabbi Abraham ibn Ezra, Rabbi Israel Najara, et al.[463]

Later, Rabbi Hirschensohn revisits some of those themes from Rav Kook's masterpiece *Orot*, while addressing the *ad hominem* attacks on the Chief Rabbi:

> One who looks with an open eye at the situation in Erets Israel now and thinks into the consternation of the mighty Gaon, *Mara de-'Ara' de-Yisrael* (Master of the Land of Israel), our teacher Rabbi Abraham Isaac Kook, may he live, and how much mental anguish he suffered from the time that he settled in Erets Yisrael on account of the "arrows shot at him"[464]—just because of the beauty of his soul to give every man the benefit of the doubt and to find the good in the evil; and because of his optimistic historical philosophy, that extracts the precious from the dross,[465] and that believes that out of the strong too must come the sweet,[466] and [that] the shattering of the vessels is a building for holiness that thirsts for the "*nitsotsim*" (sparks) that it shall suck from the marrow of their bones—so as not to destroy the heir and not to extinguish the coal. "God shall not destroy the soul, but rather think thoughts, that he that is banished be not an outcast from Him" [2 Samuel 14:14].[467] And [believes] that all these are necessary for the building of the nation.[468]

Rabbi Hirschensohn continues in an esoteric vein, referencing the mystery of levirate marriage (*sod ha-yibbum*) in Naḥmanides' commentary to the Book of Job;[469] the verse in Ruth 3:13,[470] the passage in the Talmud regarding Rabbi Meir's relation to his heretical master Elisha ben Abuyah;[471] and trails off cryptically: "And the understanding shall understand, but 'the people who do not understand are distraught.'"[472]

Returning to current events, Rabbi Hirschensohn writes:

> Not only did they set out to provoke him [i.e. Rav Kook], but they also attempted to pain his parents and his brothers' families, as explained in *'Igrot Rayah* (*Letters of Rav Kook*).[473] Evidently the name [i.e. *Rayah*] is not merely initials [of Rav Avraham Yitsḥak Hakohen] but rather a "proof" [Hebrew, *re'ayah*] of the fact. How humiliating that a great man such as this should have to publish his letters as a proof! One who considers well the situation will see that all this came to him from these "scorpions" who sting time and time again,[474] in every generation...The chilling of the soul in regard to the building of our land, comes from the scorpion's bite.[475]

[456]Psalms 107:33, 35. An earlier verse in that Psalm shows up in the third legend of Rabbah bar Bar Ḥannah: "They mounted up to the heavens, they went down to the depths; [their soul melted away because of trouble]" (Psalms 107:26). Truthfully, it is not readily comprehensible how that verse fits into the context of the story. Rabbeinu Gershom understood the connection in the following manner:

> **That day**—there was a great storm wind which caused the mariners in their boats to ascend to the heart of heaven and descend to the depths, and despite that, not a drop [of water] fell to the earth.
>
> (Rabbeinu Gershom, *Bava Batra* 73b)

So too Rashbam (who copied Rabbeinu Gershom's words verbatim).

Recently, Reuven Kiperwasser has asserted that the cycle of legends of Rabbah bar Bar Ḥannah pivots on Psalm 107. See Reuven Kiperwasser, "Rabba bar bar Ḥana's Voyages" (Hebrew), *Jerusalem Studies in Hebrew Literature* 22 (2008), pp. 231-233. And see earlier Yonah Frankel, *Darkhei ha-'Aggadah ve-ha-Midrash*, vol. 1 (Giv'atayim, 1991), p. 259. This observation was made already by none other than the Vilna Gaon. See Rabbi Elijah of Vilna, *Peirush 'al Kamah Aggadot* (Vilna, 1800), 1a.

As Kiperwasser points out, in the Talmud, the verses of that Psalm serve as the basis for the "four [who] must offer thanks" (*b. Berakhot* 54b).

In the Beshtian Ḥasidic tradition, the Psalm is construed as alluding to raising up sparks (*ha'ala'at nitsotsot*) of fallen souls, and is recited at the Afternoon Service preceding the Sabbath. In the various Ḥasidic *siddurim* (prayer books), it appears at that station. In recent scholarship there is discussion whether the commentary to Psalm 107 attributed to the Ba'al Shem Tov is truly his, or has been misattributed. See Rivka Schatz-Uffenheimer, *"Peirusho shel ha-Besht le-Mizmor 107," Tarbiz* 42 (1973):154-184; Moshe Rosman, *Founder of Ḥasidism: A Quest for the Historical Ba'al Shem Tov* (Berkeley: University of California Press, 1996), pp. 122-123.

Motsa'ei Mayim was printed by the brothers Meshulam Zalman and Menaḥem Hakohen Katzburg in Budapest in 1924.

[457]*Motsa'ei Mayim*, p. 187.

[458]Cf. Jeremiah 15:19.

[459]Cf. Judges 14:14.

[460]Cf. Isaiah 11:9.

[461]*m. Sotah* 9:15.

[462]Rav Kook wrote "the light of the divine spirit" (*'or ru'aḥ ha-kodesh*). Rabbi Hirschensohn substituted: "a new light" (*'or ḥadash*).

[463]*Motsa'ei Mayim*, pp. 123-124. The passages that Rabbi Hirschensohn quotes may be found in Rabbi Abraham Isaac Hakohen Kook, *Orot*, ed. and transl. Bezalel Naor (Maggid, 2015), pp. 202-205, 358-359. In my introduction to *Orot*, I dwelt at length on Rabbi Hirschensohn's defense of Rav Kook at the time of the *Orot* imbroglio in the early 1920s. There, I quoted pertinent passages from Rabbi Hirschensohn's magnum opus, *Malki ba-Kodesh*. See *Orot*, pp. 45-46, 80-82, 434-436.

[464]Cf. Genesis 49:23.

[465]Cf. Jeremiah 15:19.

[466]Cf. Judges 14:14.

[467]My English translation is based on Malbim's interpretation, which seems most conducive for what Rabbi Hirschensohn wishes to convey.

[468]*Motsa'ei Mayim*, p. 206.

[469]Naḥmanides included in his commentary to Job chapter 33 a few lines of rhymed poetry that allude to the mystery of levirate marriage (which for Naḥmanides, revolves around the theory of reincarnation) and the final Messianic redemption. The poem concludes with the words "*ve-ha-gizrah ve-ha-binyah*." It is those two words (from Ezekiel 41:13) that Rabbi Hirschensohn quotes. In the context of Ezekiel's prophecy, they refer to "the courtyard and the building" of the Third Temple. Although they retain that original meaning in Naḥmanides' poem (as Rabbi Chavel points out in his footnote), it is apparent that Naḥmanides has endowed them with philosophic significance. Thus, they should be translated in this new context as: "[divine] decree and reproduction." *Gizrah* should be re-vocalized *gezerah* (decree) and *"binyah"* related to *"ben"* (son). See Naḥmanides' commentary to Job, in *Kitvei Ramban*, ed. C.B. Chavel, vol. 1 (Jerusalem, 1968), p. 101.

[470]This too was an instance of the next of kin of the deceased marrying the deceased's widow. The *Zohar Ḥadash*, Ruth discusses at great length the *sod ha-yibbum*.

[471]*b. Ḥagigah* 15b: "When Rabbi Meir died, there arose smoke from the grave of Aḥer."

[472]Hosea 4:14. *Motsa'ei Mayim*, pp. 206-207. Rabbi Hirschenson would appear to be crediting

Rav Kook with a mystical appreciation of the redemptive process and its complexity that is beyond the understanding of his ideological opponents. Rav Kook's insight into souls and their past lives, and how they contribute to the building of the Land, grants him perspective that others lack.

[473]*'Igrot ha-Rayah*, a collection of Rav Kook's letters spanning the years 1908-1920, appeared in Jerusalem in 1923.

[474]*y. Berakhot* 5:1.

[475]*Motsa'ei Mayim*, p. 207. Earlier (p. 205), Rabbi Hirschensohn relates that when he was about nine years old, on Lag ba-'Omer, he sat out in the field adjacent to the tomb of Shim'on ha-Tsaddik (on the outskirts of Jerusalem), and was bitten by a scorpion. He describes the chill that he subsequently felt throughout his body. To cure him of the scorpion bite, they caught the scorpion and fried it in oil, and produced from it a salve, which they then rubbed on the red spot marking the bite. Two days later, young Hirschensohn was fully recovered. (He does express some skepticism whether it was the salve that brought about his cure or the fact that the scorpion had bitten him through his shoe.)

There is a third passage in *Motsa'ei Mayim* where Rabbi Hirschensohn quotes Rav Kook's *Orot* (*Orot me-Ofel*, chap. 6). The context is the blessing in disguise that came out of World War One. Out of the phenomenon of nationalism that reared its ugly head in World War One, came Israel's rebirth. See *Motsa'ei Mayim*, p. 133.

Appendix 4

A Kabbalistic Theory of Personality

Rav Kook's opening lines to his commentary to the Legends of Rabbah bar Bar Ḥannah read:

> The voyagers on the Sea of Divine Wisdom are referred to as "seafarers." Essentially, it appears to me that they are the souls that would appear to Rabbah bar Bar Ḥannah to teach him novel thoughts and mysteries of the Torah regarding the divine governance. Alternatively, the ministering angels are the voyagers on that sea.

One would have expected that the "*Tay'a*" too—the Ishmaelite merchant (or as we have rendered the term, the Bedouin) who serves as Rabbah bar Bar Ḥannah's guide through the desert (ostensibly the Sinai Desert)—be interpreted by Rav Kook as some sort of celestial teacher. And while Rav Kook does refer us to the mysterious "*Tay'a*" of the *Zohar*, he leaves it at that. Rather than being subjected to spiritualization, the *Tay'a* remains a roaming merchant, uncannily wise, but a mortal man.

When confronted in Kabbalistic literature with some astral guide, one must always question whether this is truly a distinct entity or rather but another aspect of the Kabbalist's own personality, which as it were, has broken loose and taken on a life of its own.

No one would have known that better than Rav Kook himself. While yet a very young man, he was asked point-blank by the renowned Lithuanian Kabbalist and miracle-worker Rabbi Mordechai Veitzel Rosenblatt of Ashmina (and Slonim), whether he was privy to "*Gillui Eliyahu*" (Revelation of Elijah the Prophet). Young Rav Kook responded by saying that there is the revelation of Elijah that comes by way of the intellect (*be-'oraḥ sekhel*).[476]

Rav Kook was merely quoting from the opening of *Tikkunei Zohar*, a remarkable passage in its own right:

> It is written, "And they that are wise (*ve-ha-maskilim*) shall shine as the brightness of the firmament" [Daniel 12:3]. "And they that are wise"—These are Rabbi Shim'on and company. "Shall shine"—When they assemble to make this composition, permission is granted to them and to Elijah with them and to all the souls of the *Metivta* (Celestial Academy) to descend among them, and to all the angels, in a concealed manner (*be-'itkasya*) and by way of intellect (*be-'oraḥ sekhel*).

On those last words, "in a concealed manner and by way of intellect," the Gaon Rabbi Elijah of Vilna comments:

> It wishes to say that they did not see them with their sense[s] but rather with their [mental] apprehension.

A more comprehensive statement is the following:

> "Arise, Elijah, to praise the Cause of All Causes, for you shall precede all the prophets in the generation of Messiah, for there is one to whom you will be revealed from the side of his soul, in his intellect (*be-sekhel dileh*); and there is one to whom you will be revealed in his wisdom; and there is one to whom you will be revealed face to face, from the side of his body."
>
> (*Tikkunim mi-Zohar Ḥadash*, in *Tikkunei Zohar* with Commentary of Vilna Gaon [Vilna, 1867], 15c)

It has been pointed out that this idea of non-sensory contact with Elijah the Prophet surfaces later in the writings of Rabbi Judah Löw (Maharal) of Prague:

> There is no difference whether he [i.e. Elijah] was revealed to him in a vision or was revealed to him without a vision, for many times Elijah would tell things to someone and the man would not know where these things came from. It would seem to him as if the things were from himself when they were none other than the words of Elijah who told him the things.
>
> (Rabbi Judah Löw, *Netsaḥ Yisrael* [London, 1957], chap. 28 [pp. 136-137])

We come now to the *maggidim*. It is reported that various Kabbalists throughout the ages enjoyed the tutelage of a *maggid*, a celestial guide.[477] The most famous of these *maggidim* was that of Rabbi Joseph Karo (1488-1575).[478] The communications of that particular *maggid* were preserved for posterity in the work *Maggid Meisharim*.[479] The *Maggid* first manifested at a *Shavu'ot* night vigil (*Tikkun Leil Shavu'ot*) in Adrianople (today Edirne, Turkey),[480] and persisted long after Rabbi Joseph Karo ascended to Tsefat in the Upper Galilee. The catalyst for contact with the *Maggid* was the study of Mishnah. In fact, the *Maggid* introduced herself as the genius of the Mishnah![481] Appropriately enough, the *Maggid* would signal its presence with these words: "I am the Mishnah speaking through your mouth."

Despite the audibility of the *Maggid*, we have on the sound authority of the sage of B'nei Berak, Rabbi Abraham Isaiah Karelitz (author of *Ḥazon Ish*): "The *Maggid* too is Rabbi

Joseph Karo."[482] Not that the great halakhist of the modern era was implying any deceit on the part of Rabbi Joseph Karo. Heaven forfend! Rather, Rabbi Abraham Isaiah's insight into the labyrinth of the human soul told him that the *Maggid* was a spin-off of Rabbi Joseph Karo's own psyche.[483]

Fast forward a century and a half to Padua, Italy. The second most famous *maggid* in Jewish history is that of Rabbi Moses Ḥayyim Luzzatto. We even have the *Maggid*'s name: Shmu'iel. While inaudible (at least to others), the *Maggid*'s influence was clearly evidenced in young Luzzatto's automatic writing. (Luzzatto was twenty when first contacted by the *Maggid*.) The writing poured out of him at an unbroken frenetic pace that filled quires within no time. When word of the young Kabbalist's psychopomp leaked out (thanks to the unwanted publicity drawn by the letter written by Luzzatto's disciple, Yekutiel Gordon, to Rabbi Mordechai Jaffe of Vienna),[484] Luzzatto came under the scrutiny of the vigilantes Rabbis Moses Ḥagiz and Jacob Emden, who suspected him of Sabbatian leanings. There followed unspeakable persecution, which ended in the destruction of Luzzatto's Kabbalistic writings. (Fortunately, unbeknown to the rabbinic tribunal of Venice, students—such as Yekutiel Gordon and others—made backup copies.)

How would one define the nature of Luzzatto's *Maggid*? In this case, we have the opinion of Rav Kook's disciple, the Nazirite:

> … the principles came to him *verbatim* in a revelation from above, and that was the *Maggid*, as is known, i.e. the revelation of verbal thoughts heard *as if* from the mouth of the *Maggid*. (Italics—BN) [485]

Let us return to the mysterious *Tay'a* who acts as Rabbah bar Bar Ḥannah's guide in the Sinai Desert. The Talmudic exegete (with occasional Kabbalistic leanings) Rabbi Samuel Edels noticed that the anonymous Bedouin's favorable portrayal of the generation of the desert coincides with that of Rabbah bar Bar Ḥannah's own teacher Rabbi Yoḥanan (*b. Sanhedrin* 110b).

> It is possible that that *Tay'a* is a parable for Rabbi Yoḥanan his teacher, and in conformity with his line of thinking [he] said: "I will show you the dead of the desert." [486]

While perhaps not quite as bold as our own suggestion that the *Tay'a* is an alter ego of Rabbah bar Bar Ḥannah himself, Rabbah Samuel Edel's proposal is intriguing none the less.[487]

I see now that I have been preceded by the great Lithuanian Kabbalist, Rabbi Eizik Ḥaver.[488] Commenting on the eleventh legend of Rabbah bar Bar Ḥannah, he writes:

> **We were accompanied by a certain Bedouin**—There combined with them the soul of a *tsaddik* (righteous man) who came to them through the mystery of *'Ibbur* (impregnation of the soul)[489] as a donkey-driver (*ta'in ḥamara*), as it is written in the Introduction of the *Zohar* [5b] and in the *Tikkunim* in several places.[490]

[476]Rabbi Moshe Tsevi Neriyah, *Siḥot ha-Rayah* (Tel-Aviv, 1979), footnote to p. 191. Cf. RZYH Kook, *Li-Sheloshah be-Elul*, vol. 1 (Jerusalem, 1938), par. 1 (p. 6).

In a letter to Rabbi Naḥman Greenspan of England, Rav Kook explained that

> according to *Zohar*, the content of *Gillui Eliyahu* (Revelation of Elijah) assumes many hues: by way of vision, and also by way of intellect (*be-derekh sekhel*).
>
> (*Ginzei Rayah*, vol. 3 [n.p., n.d.], p. 10, "The Revelation of Elijah and the Clarification of Doubts before the Arrival of the Messiah" [Hebrew])

In a *pensée* entitled by the Nazirite, *"Middat Gillui Eliyahu"* ("The Quality of the Revelation of Elijah"), Rav Kook writes:

> Whoever belongs to the yearning for the mysteries of Torah, which is the quality of the Revelation of Elijah, to some degree, even if it is only by way of imagination, or feeling, or rational apprehension (*hassagat ha-sekhel ha-'enoshi*), and all the more so if one has ascended—by a supernal love—to higher levels ....
>
> (*Orot ha-Kodesh*, vol. 1, p. 136 = *Shemonah Kevatsim* 6:120)

In yet another *pensée*, Rav Kook uses the exact terminology of *Tikkunei Zohar*: *"Gillui Eliyahu be-'oraḥ sekhel"* ("Revelation of Elijah by way of intellect"). See *Orot ha-Kodesh*, vol. 3, p. 362 = *Shemonah Kevatsim* 6:139. Appropriately, the Nazirite gave the piece that very title.

In the recently published *Pinkas 5*, Rav Kook quotes *Tikkunei Zohar* as saying: "Elijah will be revealed in the future by way of intellect" (*be-'oraḥ sekhel*). See *Kevatsim mi-Ketav Yad Kodsho*, vol. 3, ed. Boaz Ofen (Jerusalem, 2018) 5:9 (p. 28). So too in the just released *Pinkesei ha-Rayah*, vol. 4, ed. Z.M. Levin and B.Z. Kahana-Shapira (Jerusalem, 2017), *Nispaḥot*, p. 485.

*

Rabbi Neriyah sources this motif of the revelation of Elijah within the brain of the individual, in the work by the Ḥasidic master, Rabbi Menaḥem Naḥum of Chernobyl, *Me'or 'Eynayim* (Slavuta, 1798), *Vayyetse*, 78a-78c, s.v. *vayyisa Ya'akov raglav* [Genesis 29:1]. See Neriyah, loc. cit.

This reference to *Me'or 'Eynayim* is of particular interest because evidently Rav Kook's distant ancestor was a kinsman of Rabbi Menaḥem Naḥum of Chernobyl!

Rav Kook's great-uncle, Rabbi Mordechai Gimpel Jaffe of Rozhinoy (brother to Rav Kook's paternal grandmother Freida Batyah née Jaffe, married to Naḥum Hakohen Kook) raised this familial relation in a letter to the Trisker Maggid, Rabbi Abraham Twersky (son of Rabbi

Mordechai Twersky, son of Rabbi Menaḥem Naḥum Twersky, Maggid of Chernobyl). See Rabbi Moshe Nathan Halevi Rubinstein, *Kelilat ha-Menorah* (Berdichev, 1892), 52d (*Hesped* or Eulogy for Rabbi Mordechai Gimpel Jaffe of Rozhinoy).

In the letter to the Trisker Maggid (dated Thursday, 18 Menaḥem-Av 5646/1886), Rabbi Mordechai Gimpel Jaffe introduces his son Dov Baer Jaffe, manufacturer of a liquor that is kosher for Passover. As Dov Baer seeks to market his wares in Volhynia (the vicinity of the Trisker Maggid), Rabbi Mordechai Gimpel appeals to the Maggid to vouch for the *kashrut* of the product. In this connection, Rabbi Mordechai Gimpel brings up to the Maggid that their grandfathers—[Menaḥem] Naḥum of Chernobyl, grandfather of the Trisker Maggid, and Rabbi Mordechai Gimpel's own grandfather, the *Mekubbal* (Kabbalist), Rabbi Mordechai Jaffe of Karelitz, Lithuania—were kinsmen ("*'anashim 'aḥim*"). Beyond this rather recent relation, Rabbi Mordechai Gimpel reminds the Trisker Maggid of their common ancestor, Rabbi Mordechai Jaffe of Prague, the "*Levush.*"

Quoting from memory, Rubinstein mistakenly substituted Rabbi Mordechai Gimpel Jaffe's paternal grandfather, Rabbi Ya'akov Jaffe of Karelitz (father of Rabbi Dov Baer Jaffe of Utian) for his great-grandfather Rabbi Mordechai Jaffe of Karelitz. The Kabbalist Rabbi Mordechai Jaffe of Karelitz was in fact the father-in-law of Rabbi Ya'akov Jaffe. See the clarification by the genealogist Naftali Aharon Vekshtein in his column "*Vayityaldu*" in the Torah supplement to *Hamodi'a*, *Mishpatim*, 23 Shevat, 5771 (2011). (On the other hand, Vekshtein tends to accept Rubinstein's testimony that the expression "*'anashim 'aḥim*" ["kinsmen"] should not be construed literally as "brothers." It may have the sense of "brothers-in-law.")

Today, the letter from Rabbi Mordechai Gimpel Jaffe to the Trisker Maggid is in the possession of Rabbi Meyer Yechiel Knobloch of New Square, New York, and should appear shortly in the volume *'Igrot Kodesh le-Beit Chernobyl*, edited by Rabbi Shmuel Gruber of New Square (Yiddish, Skver).

*

Rav Kook and Rabbi Ze'ev Twersky, son of Rabbi Yoḥanan Twersky of Rachmistrivka (youngest son of Rabbi Mordechai Twersky of Chernobyl) were steadfast friends, but I don't know whether their familial relation ever came up in conversation. Concerning Rabbi Ze'ev Twersky of Rachmistrivka (1850-1937), see Neriyah, *Siḥot ha-Rayah*, pp. 139-140; footnote of RZYH Kook to *'Ittur Soferim*, vol. 1 (Vilna, 1888; photo offset Jerusalem, 1974), 9d; *'Igrot la-Rayah*, ed. B.Z. Shapira (Jerusalem, 1990), pp. 378 (Letter 260), 477 (Letter 337); *Admorei Malkhut Beit Chernobyl/Grand Rabbis of the Chernobyl Dynasty* [bilingual edition], ed. Y.M. Twersky and Zisha Novoseller (New York, 2003), pp. 230-231.

[477]A brief survey of recorded *Maggidim* is contained in the work of the "Nazirite," Rabbi David Cohen, *Kol ha-Nevu'ah* (Jerusalem, 1979), pp. 310-314.

[478]See R.J. Zwi Werblowsky, *Joseph Karo: Lawyer and Mystic* (Oxford, 1962).

A rather curious work is that of New York psychiatrist Hirsch Loeb Gordon, *The Maggid of Caro* (New York, 1949). Gordon coined the term "Maggidism" for this form of possession. The author writes that he is a direct descendant of Yekutiel Gordon (disciple of Rabbi Moses Ḥayyim Luzzatto) and that like his famous ancestor, he was born in Vilna and studied medicine at the University of Padua.

[479]First edition Lublin 1646. For a survey and analysis of the manuscripts, see Meir Benayahu, *Yosef Beḥiri* (Jerusalem, 1991), pp. 391-412. Selections from *Maggid Meisharim* were translated into English by Louis Jacobs. See L. Jacobs, *The Jewish Mystics* (Reading, England, 1990), pp. 98-122.

[480]One may read Rabbi Shelomo Halevi Alkabets' report of the Maggid's first visitation in Rabbi Isaiah Halevi Horowitz, *Shnei Luḥot ha-Berit, Masekhet Shavu'ot.*

[481]In Alkabets' transcript of the Maggid's transmissions on both nights of *Shavu'ot*, the Hebrew grammar consistently reflects a feminine persona.

[482]Cf. *Yahel 'Or* (Commentary of Vilna Gaon to *Zohar*), ed. Naftali Herz Halevi of Bialystok (Vilna, 1882), Part One, *Hashmatot Ra'aya Mehemna*, 30d, s.v. *Ra'aya Mehemna:* "Also the phenomenon of the *maggid* that comes to man—*it is his soul, himself* [italics—BN], except that it is the way to speak to his soul mouth to mouth, as it is clothed in the *mitsvot* that he performed."

[483]We have this "psychoanalysis" of the phenomenon of Maggidism from the pen of the Ḥasidic master, Rabbi Zadok Hakohen (Rabinowitz) of Lublin:

> [Rabbi Isaac Luria] did not explain the difference between *nevu'ah* (prophecy) and *maggidim* (such as occurred to the *Beit Yosef* [i.e. Rabbi Joseph Karo]), which is a level lower even that of *ru'aḥ ha-kodesh* (divine inspiration)...The phenomenon of *maggidim* resembles that of *dybbukim* which are "naked souls" (*nafshin de-'azlin 'artila'in*). So the *maggidim* are *mal'akhim* (angels) produced from [observance of] *mitsvot* or commandments (specifically the person's own commandments). The angel speaks from the individual's throat, and it is well known and felt by all that it is not the individual speaking, rather another power speaking from his throat. For the angel does not have within its power to become truly the essence of the man, and therefore his communications are not clarified (as Rabbi Isaac Luria stated).

> This is not so in the case of the prophet who speaks—assuming that he is not a false prophet. He speaks in the name of the Lord. In that case, there is no room for falsehood, for the essence of the Lord, blessed be He, is garbed in him and speaks from his throat. And the Lord, blessed be He, who is the source of all and the source of the soul as well, is integrated in the soul, to the effect that the prophet speaks just like any man…In truth, it is the prophet's own voice, except that he realizes and knows that it is the voice of the Lord speaking from his midst.
>
> (Rabbi Zadok Hakohen of Lublin, *Dover Zedek* [Piotrków, 1911], 81a)

According to Rabbi Zadok, it is the foreignness or alienness of the voice that gives it away as being from a level lower than authentic prophecy. The phenomenon of "possession" by an alien force is common to both the malevolent *dybbukim* and the more benevolent *maggidim*. In neither case, is there the kind of true integration into the personality that is reserved for classical Biblical prophecy.

What will probably strike the reader as simply astounding is the tradition that Rabbi Zadok received from his teacher, the Rebbe of Izbica, Rabbi Mordechai Joseph Leiner:

> I heard in regard to the voice of the Giving of the Torah and the first [two] commandments which were from the "mouth of the Strength," that [what occurred was that] the mouths of all Israel were opened and they spoke these commandments.
>
> (Ibid.)

In truth, medieval thinkers grappled with the nature of the "speech" divinely communicated at Mount Sinai. In his famous thirteen fundamentals of faith, Maimonides wrote:

> The eighth fundamental is Torah from Heaven (*Torah min ha-shamayim*). And that is, that we believe that this entire Torah…was given to Moses, and that it is all from the mouth of the Power, which is to say that it all reached Moses from the Lord by a communication that we call figuratively "speech," and none knows the quality of that communication but the one whom it reached, peace unto him.
>
> (Maimonides, *Commentary to the Mishnah*, Introduction to *Sanhedrin*, chapter 10; Kafaḥ ed., p. 143)

This abstract understanding of Maimonides is in marked contradistinction to the earlier attempt of Rabbi Judah Halevi to explain the miracle by which physical speech was created at the time of the Sinai revelation. See *Kuzari* I, 87-91.

For Rabbi Shneur Zalman of Liadi's understanding of Rabbi Joseph Karo's *maggid,* see *Ma'amrei Admor Hazaken: Et-halekh Liozna* (Brooklyn, 2002), s.v. *Le-'Olam ya'asok adam* (pp. 2-3). See also Rabbi Pinḥas Elijah Hurwitz of Vilna, *Sefer ha-Berit,* Pt. II (Brünn, 1797) 11:4 (32b), citing *Sefer ha-Gilgulim.*

[484]Gordon's letter was published by Simon Ginzburg, *Rabbi Moshe Ḥayyim Luzzatto u-V'nei Doro* (Tel-Aviv, 1937), pp. 18-20. An English translation is available in Louis Jacobs, *The Jewish Mystics*, pp. 137-139.

[485]Rabbi David Cohen, Overture to *Mangeinot ha-Tikkunim*, commentary to *Tikkunei Zohar*; excerpted in *KaLaḤ Pitḥei Ḥokhmah* with commentary *Pitḥei ha-Pardes* by Rabbi David Cohen (Jerusalem 2009), p. 20, n. 79.

A photocopy of that portion of the Nazirite's manuscript (3 pages) is available in the Gershom Scholem Collection at the National Library of Israel. A note in Scholem's handwriting records that the photocopy was delivered to him by Rivka Schatz. Evidently, the document was deemed important by Scholem because it records Rav Kook's thoughts on the "antiquity" of the *Zohar,* as transmitted to the Nazirite in oral conversation.

My thanks to my dear friend, Rabbi Dr. Zvi Leshem, Director of the Gershom Scholem Collection, for sharing this information with me. The catalogue number is: RS 1490.52.

[486]Maharasha, *Ḥiddushei Aggadot, Bava Batra* 73b, s.v. *ve-'amar leh 'aḥvei lakh metei midbar.*

[487]An insight that took me totally by surprise is that of Rabbi Tsevi Yehudah Kook concerning the "man" created by Rava. The Talmudic anecdote goes as follows:

> Rava (or Rabbah) created a man. He sent him before Rabbi Zeira. [Rabbi Zeira] conversed with him but he did not respond to him. [Rabbi Zeira] said to him: "You are from the companions (*min ḥavraya*). Return to your dust!"
>
> (*b. Sanhedrin* 65b)

Rashi clues us in that this humanoid was created by way of *Sefer Yetsirah*, the *Book of Creation*, and permutation of the letters of the Name. Though by outer appearances it resembled a man, it lacked the power of speech. Rabbi Zeira gathered that this "man" was created by the sages (referred to as *"ḥaverim").*

Rabbi Tsevi Yehudah seizes the word *"min"* (from). Unlike Rashi, who interprets the word loosely (paraphrasing *"'al yedei"* or "by"), Rabbi Tsevi Yehudah understands it literally. Rabbi Zeira was not saying, "You were created *by* the sages." Rather, he was saying, "You were created *from* the sages." "As if to say, the 'man' is the continuation of the personality of Rava." *Pe'amim:*

Siḥot Rabbeinu Tsevi Yehudah Hakohen Kook, ed. Rabbis Ilan Tor, Shlomo Aviner and Ḥayyim Vidal (Jerusalem, 2007), p. 259.

In a personal memoir, author Perle Epstein records a similar if not identical teaching of Rav Tsevi Yehudah Kook (whose name has been changed to "Rav Bloch"):

> The difference between mysticism and magic ... Yes, let's talk about that. Did you know that there were esoteric societies during the Babylonian period that interpreted metaphysics as the scientific study of the faculty beyond the intellect, what I referred to the other day as "supernatural" power? In these societies, long before the sixteenth-century Maharal of Prague, the rabbis were creating "golems" through the force of concentrated thought. Telepathic phenomena represent the point where science borders on parapsychology and metaphysics.
>
> (Perle Epstein, *Pilgrimage: Adventures of a Wandering Jew* [Boston, 1979], p. 103)

*

Another famous exchange between Rabbah and Rabbi Zeira (assuming Emden's gloss of "Rabbah" in *b. Sanhedrin* 65b is correct) took place on the day of Purim. The two men feasted together and became intoxicated from the wine they imbibed. Rabbah got up and slaughtered Rabbi Zeira. On the morrow, Rabbah prayed and revived him. The next year, Rabbah said to Rabbi Zeira: "Let us make the Purim feast together." Rabbi Zeira answered him: "Not every day does a miracle occur." See *b. Megillah* 7b.

A slew of commentators understands this story in a non-literal manner. Rabbi Samuel Edels assumes that "slaughtering" in this context refers to one man prevailing upon another man to drink beyond his capacity. Rabbi Jacob Emden chalks the "slaughtering" up to a feat of magic or sleight of hand (*"aḥizat 'eynayim"*). Rabbi Joseph Ḥayyim of Baghdad (*Ben Yehoyada'*), quoting the Kabbalists, posits that as a result of the two men's study of Torah, Rabbi Zeira underwent some ecstatic experience whereby his soul departed from his body.

Thus, the "slaughtering" did not actually happen but was seen in a hallucinatory vision or altered state of consciousness. Though it did not occur on the material but rather spiritual plane, nevertheless, its impact on Rabbi Zeira was so traumatic, that a year later he was unwilling to feast again with Rabbah. Perhaps the story of the "man" that Rabbah sent to Rabbi Zeira should also be understood in a non-literal manner. It is likely that it too represents a foray into another dimension of consciousness.

*

Today, we refer to such a humanoid as a "Golem." For academic studies on the Golem, see Gershom G. Scholem, "The Idea of the Golem" in idem, *On the Kabbalah and Its Symbolism* (New York, 1970), pp. 158-204; and Moshe Idel, *Golem: Jewish Magical and Mystical Traditions on the Artificial Anthropoid* (Albany, 1990).

Shnayer Z. Leiman has written several articles to disprove that Maharal of Prague or one of his disciples ever created a Golem. See Shnayer Z. Leiman, "The Adventure of the Maharal of Prague in London: R. Yudl Rosenberg and the Golem of Prague," *Tradition* 36:1 (2002), 26-58; idem, "Did a Disciple of the Maharal Create a Golem?" *the Seforim blog*, Thursday, February 8, 2007; idem, "The Letter of the Maharal on the Creation of the Golem: A Modern Forgery," *the Seforim blog*, Sunday, January 3, 2010.

(A point of interest in the last regard: As recorded by Prof. Leiman, the Rebbe of Munkatsh [Mukačevo], Rabbi Ḥayyim El'azar Spira, exposed the letter of Maharal as a forgery when consulted by the Rebbe of Spinka, Rabbi Yitsḥak Eizik Weiss. On the other hand, it may be of interest that the Munkatsher's ancestor, Rabbi Tsevi Elimelekh Spira of Dynów, subscribed to the notion that Maharal had once created a Golem. See *B'nei Yissakhar*, Part 2 [Zolkiew or Lvov, 1850], *Ma'amrei Ḥodesh Kislev-Tevet* 2:21; and Bezalel Naor, *Maḥol la-Tsadikim* [Monsey, NY and Jerusalem, 2015], pp. 121-122, n. 16.)

[488]Rabbi Yitsḥak Eizik Ḥaver (Wildman) studied under Rabbi Menaḥem Mendel of Shklov, who in turn, was a disciple of the Vilna Gaon. For this reason, Rabbi Yitsḥak Ḥaver is referred to as *"peh shelishi la-Gra"* ("the third mouth to the Vilna Gaon"). He served as rabbi in the communities of Rozhinoy, Volkovysk, Tiktin, and Suvalk.

[489]According to the theory of *'Ibbur*, the soul of a departed saint may "impregnate" the soul of the living.

For example, in *Tanya*, the classic text of Ḥabad Ḥasidism, hope is held out to the *"beinoni"* (spiritual middle-class Jew) that he may yet attain the level of a *tsaddik* (righteous man): "With all this, perhaps there will descend upon him a spirit from above, and he will merit to the level of *ru'aḥ* from the root of some *tsaddik* that will be 'impregnated' [*tit'abber*] in him" (*Tanya* I, end chap. 14 [20b]).

[490]Rabbi Isaac Ḥaver, *Afikei Yam* (Jerusalem, 1994), vol. 2, *Bava Batra* 73b, s.v. *ve-'amar Rabbah bar Bar Ḥannah…ve-'itlavei bahadan hahu tay'a* (pp. 383-384).

Appendix 5

Luzzatto's *'Adir ba-Marom* and *KaLaḤ Pitḥei Ḥokhmah*

'ADIR BA-MAROM

Even before its appearance in print, *'Adir ba-Marom* circulated in manuscript in Lithuania, evidently having been brought there by Rabbi Moshe Ḥayyim Luzzatto's disciple, Yekutiel Gordon, a native of Vilna. As pointed out by David E. Fishman, Rabbi Barukh Schick quoted from *'Adir ba-Marom* in the introduction to his work of anatomy, *Tif'eret Adam*. Fishman surmises that Gordon, who resided in Shklov for a time, shared the manuscript with Schick, a native of Shklov.[491]

A copy of *'Adir ba-Marom* was in the possession of the Vilna Gaon's *meḥutan* or relation by marriage, R. Noah Mindes. (Mindes' daughter Sarah married the Gaon's son Abraham.) It was this copy that Rabbi Pinḥas Hakohen Lintop (Rabbi of Vabolnik and later Birzh) sought to publish. Eventually, the work was published in Warsaw in 1886 by Rabbi Samuel Luria.[492]

Rabbi Lintop and Rabbi Shelomo Eliashov of Shavel (author of *Leshem Shevo ve-'Aḥlamah*) were mutually antagonistic. (Despite this, Rav Kook was able to maintain cordial relations with both men.)[493] It seems that one of the ideological differences between Rabbis Lintop and Eliashov concerned their reception of Luzzatto's Kabbalistic writings. Whereas Rabbi Eliashov looked at them with a jaundiced eye, Rabbi Lintop held Luzatto in the highest regard. According to oral tradition, at various times Rav Kook attempted to soften Rabbi Eliashov's stance on the Kabbalah of Luzzatto.[494]

*

On *Rosh Ḥodesh* Elul, 5685 (1925 C.E.), Rav Kook's disciple, the Nazirite, Rabbi David Cohen, recorded the gist of a conversation that he had with Rav Kook concerning different levels of mystical inspiration. Among other authors, the discussion touched on the writings of Rabbi Moshe Ḥayyim Luzzatto. That paragraph reads:

> And so we should vindicate the holy words of Rabbi Moshe Ḥayyim Luzzatto in the beginning of *KaLaḤ Pitḥei Ḥokhmah*, that he found them in an ancient book, which is to say, that the principles came to him *verbatim*

> in a revelation from above, and that was the *Maggid*, as is known, i.e. the revelation of verbal thoughts heard as if from the mouth of the *Maggid*. Afterward, when the flow of the revelation stopped, Rabbi Moshe Ḥayyim Luzzatto made a commentary to it, which in a sense, is a commentary to his own words, except that in the beginning it was in a revelation, and after in rational explanation and examination, arranged, as in his commentary to *Idra Rabba—'Adir ba-Marom*—where one feels ascents and descents such as these.[495]

The Nazir concluded the entry in his diary with these words:

> The foundation of the things I received from the mouth of our Master [i.e. Rav Kook], may he live long.[496]

This perspective on the writings of Luzatto (*'Adir ba-Marom* in particular), tallies with what was reported in Rav Kook's name by another close disciple, Rabbi Dr. Moshe Seidel:

> In the words of Rabbi Moshe Ḥayyim Luzzatto it is possible to distinguish between those that are rational matters and those that are revelations from above.[497]

*

KALAḤ PITḤEI ḤOKHMAH (138 ENTRANCES TO WISDOM)

It seems that the preamble to *KaLaḤ Pitḥei Ḥokhmah*, with its vexatious statement, "I found in an ancient script *KaLaḤ [138] Pitḥei Ḥokhmah*," exercised the Nazirite on more than one occasion. In his magnum opus, *Kol ha-Nevu'ah* (*The Voice of Prophecy*), he once again grapples with the meaning of those mysterious words:

> Truly, the *138 Entrances* are the words of Rabbi Moshe Ḥayyim Luzzatto. As for what he says, "I found in an ancient script," the [author's] intention should be explained by the difference between *maḥshavah* (disembodied thought) and *hirhur* (embodied thought).
>
> *Hirhur* refers to thinking in words; words spoken in internal thought; inner speech, such as the recitation of *Shema'* by *hirhur*, when one thinks the actual words of the passage of *Shema'*. "*Hirhur* is as speech" (*b. Berakhot* 20b).
>
> Thought poured into inner speech is concise.

> And so the *KaLaḤ Pitḥei Ḥokhmah* (*138 Entrances to Wisdom*) are principles exact in their language, molded in inner speech, and written upon the the tablet of the heart, as if they are found in an ancient script … And after comes the commentary, the expanded explanation; free, unlimited in its language.[498]

There are a couple of problems with the Nazirite's cryptology. First, he was laboring under the mistaken impression that it was Luzzatto himself who wrote the words, "I found in an ancient script *KaLaḤ [138] Pitḥei Ḥokhmah*." As the Nazirite later discovered (one would imagine, to his chagrin) the Introduction to the first edition of *KaLaḤ Pitḥei Ḥokhmah* (Koretz, 1785) was not written by Luzzatto, but by another man. (Meir Benayahu speculated that the vast majority of the Introduction, entitled *Derekh 'Ets Ḥayyim*, was the work of Yekutiel Gordon, while the last few lines—including, "I found in an ancient script *KaLaḤ [138] Pitḥei Ḥokhmah*" (f.8v.)—were the finishing touch of the editor Rabbi Elijah of Brisk, Gordon's disciple. *Derekh 'Ets Ḥayyi*m first appeared in print as an addendum to the Zolkiew 1766 edition of *Mesillat Yesharim*.)[499]

(The second problem is of a halakhic nature. The Nazirite posited that the technical term "*hirhur*" refers to thinking in words, or to express it differently, words that are thought. This flies in the face of what the great Catalan commentator Rabbi Solomon ben Abraham ibn Adret [Rashba] wrote in his novellae to the Talmud: "In *hirhur*, language does not apply."[500] Rashba's point is that *hirhur* is pre-verbal thought, undifferentiated linguistically.)

Today, there are those who call into question Luzzatto's authorship altogether. Rabbi Yosef Spinner is convinced that *KaLaḤ Pitḥei Ḥokhmah* was written by one of Luzzatto's greatest disciples.[501] Rabbi Mordekhai Chriqui shared with this writer (BN) in private conversation that he believes (based on linguistic analysis) that Luzzatto wrote the short principles himself, while the expansive commentary may be the work of a disciple whose syntax is decidedly Ashkenazic. (Benayahu assumed that these corruptions originated with Ashkenazic copyists, whereas in the single Italian manuscript containing the commentary—Oxford 1902—many of the corruptions do not occur.)[502]

So enamored was the Nazirite of the work *KaLaḤ [138] Pitḥei Ḥokhmah* that he organized his master's *Orot ha-Kodesh* (or at least the first Gate thereof, *Ḥokhmat ha-Kodesh*) into 138 chapters, the last, crowning chapter deliberately left untitled. Not only does a title not adorn this chapter, it begins with a most puzzling ellipsis. We now know the reason for the mystery surrounding this chapter. Chapter 138 is an excised entry from one of Rav Kook's journals. Clearly writing under the impact of a prophetic experience, Rav Kook expresses his subsequent trepidation lest he be accused of being a false prophet. The unexpurgated text is now available in *Shemonah Kevatsim* 4:17.

*

A little known fact is that roughly in the year 1717, a Kabbalist living in Fez, Morocco, by the name of Rabbi Moshe ibn Tsur (of Castilian descent), composed a poem divided into 138 stanzas that serves as a summary of the Kabbalistic principles set down earlier in Rabbi Ḥayyim Vital's *'Otserot Ḥayyim*.[503] The text of the poem is accompanied by two commentaries: *"Divrei Kabbalah"* (a summary of *'Otserot Ḥayyim*) and *"Halakhah le-Moshe."* The work in its entirety is entitled *Me'arat Sdeh ha-Makhpelah*. Based on the number of manuscripts available, it would seem to have enjoyed some popularity in Kabbalist circles. The library of the Jewish Theological Seminary possesses a copy that once belonged to "Shalom Mizraḥi Shar'abi" (a.k.a. Shemesh or Rashash), famous for his *kavvanot* or Kabbalistic meditations on the prayer book (*Siddur Rashash*). Rabbi Shar'abi's student, Rabbi Ḥayyim Yosef David Azulai (ḤYDA) catalogued *Me'arat Sdeh ha-Makhpelah* in his bibliography *Shem ha-Gedolim*.

Me'arat Sdeh ha-Makhpelah was finally published in Jerusalem at the press of Samuel Zuckerman in the year 1910, the manuscript having been brought from Morocco by Rabbi Isaac Souissia. One wonders aloud. Is it sheer coincidence that in the eighteenth century there circulated two works, both intended as summaries of Lurianic kabbalah; both containing 138 units; and both accompanied by commentary to the text (by the same author)? This is something that enterprising researchers should look into. And what, pray tell, is the significance of the number 138?

[491]See Rabbi Barukh Schick, *Tif'eret Adam* (Berlin, 1777), 2a; David E. Fishman, *Russia's First Modern Jews: The Jews of Shklov* (New York, 1995), pp. 27, 29-30.

[492]For the history of Rabbi Lintop's involvement with the manuscript of *'Adir ba-Marom*, see Bezalel Naor, *"Gilgulei Ketav-Yad 'Adir ba-Marom' le-Ramḥal," Sinai, Tishrei-Ḥeshvan* 5759 (1999), pp. 53-62; and idem, *Kana'uteh de-Pinḥas* (Spring Valley, NY, 2013), pp. (7-8); 97; 104, n. 7-8.

[493]See RZYH Kook, *Li-Sheloshah be-Elul*, vol. 1 (Jerusalem, 1938), par. 1 (pp. 5-6).

[494]See *Kana'uteh de-Pinḥas*, pp. 127-130, n. 106.

[495]Rabbi David Cohen, Overture to *Mangeinot ha-Tikkunim*, commentary to *Tikkunei Zohar.* See above note 485.

[496]Ibid.

[497]Rabbi Tsevi Yehudah Hakohen Kook, *Li-Sheloshah be-Elul*, vol. 2 (Jerusalem, 1947), par. 35-1 (p. 17). This remark concerning the different levels of consciousness in the writings of Luzzatto, was heard from Rav Kook by Meir Medan as well; see Rabbi Neriyah, *Tal ha-Rayah*, p. 278.

[498]Rabbi David Cohen, *Kol ha-Nevu'ah* (Jerusalem, 1979), p. 283.

[499]*KaLaḤ Pitḥei Ḥokhmah* with commentary *Pitḥei ha-Pardes* by Rabbi David Cohen (Jerusalem 2009), p. 20, n. 78; Meir Benayahu, *Kabbalistic Writings of R. Moshe Ḥayyim Luzzatto* (Hebrew) (Jerusalem, 1979), pp. 133-139.

[500]*Ḥiddushei ha-Rashba, Berakhot* 15a, s.v. *ve-Rabbi Yosé 'amar lakh* (based upon Rashi's comment there).

[501]See Spinner's overture to his new edition of Luzzatto's *Da'at Tevunot* (Jerusalem, 2012), p. 7.

[502]Benayahu, op. cit., p. 135.

[503]See Rabbi Joseph Ben Naïm, *Malkei Rabbanan* (Jerusalem, 1931), 91c-92b, s.v. *Moshe ibn Tsur.*

Recently, Rabbi Moshe Hillel discovered that a copyist, Rabbi Isaac Copio (no pun intended) tried to pass off *Me'arat Sdeh ha-Makhpelah* as his own creation, rather than that of Rabbi Moshe ibn Tsur. (Rabbi Hillel credits this same Copio with cobbling together the spurious work *'Arba' Me'ot Shekel Kesef* from bits and pieces of authentic Lurianic tradition, as well as some elements of questionable legitimacy.) See Rabbi Moshe Hillel, *'Over la-Soḥer: R. Yitsḥak ben R. Michael Copio: Bein Me'arat Sdeh ha-Makhpelah le-'Arba Me'ot Shekel Kesef* (Jerusalem, 2016).

Appendix 6

Rav Kook's Critique of the Mussar Movement

When young Avraham Yitsḥak Hakohen Kook, then an eighteen-year-old Talmudic student in Smargon (today Smarhon, Belarus) heard of the passing of Rabbi Israel Salanter,[504] founder of the Lithuanian Mussar movement, he rent his garment, removed his shoes and sat on the ground in ritual mourning.[505] And when the premier disciple of Rabbi Salanter, Rabbi Isaac Blaser (known as "Reb Itzeleh Peterburger" after his rabbinate in the Russian imperial capital),[506] was hospitalized in Jaffa, Rav Kook walked to Sha'arei Zion hospital, rather than ride in a wagon. Rav Kook explained that to pay a visit to someone of Reb Itzeleh's spiritual stature, it is fitting to set out on foot as a pilgrim.[507] And despite the obvious awe in which Rav Kook held the founders of the Mussar movement,[508] he voiced some severe criticisms of what he viewed as the movement's shortcomings—a theme that he would revisit on several occasions in the course of a literary lifetime.[509]

The indefatigable researcher Rabbi Moshe Zuriel of B'nei Berak has assembled some of the basic texts in his monumental compendium *'Otserot ha-Rayah*, and the reader would do well to consult them.[510]

Before we launch into an analysis of Rav Kook's critique of the Mussar movement then making inroads into the Lithuanian *yeshivot*, it is imperative to explain how Rav Kook's perception was formulated as a student of the Volozhin Yeshivah, "Mother of the Yeshivot."[511] In many ways, Rav Kook's critique is typical of a product of Volozhin; in other ways, it is uniquely his own.

The Mussar movement met with some stiff opposition from some members of the Russian rabbinate. Of particular interest to us is the response of Rabbi Ḥayyim Soloveichik, the junior Rosh Yeshivah of Volozhin.[512] When Rabbi Isaac Blaser traveled to Volozhin to attempt to persuade its heads to introduce the formal study of Mussar (Ethics) into the official curriculum of the Yeshivah, Rabbi Ḥayyim countered his proposal with a passage from the Talmud:

> Said Rabbi Levi bar Ḥama in the name of Rabbi Shim'on ben Lakish:
> Man should always incite the good inclination against the evil inclination…
> If he triumphs over it [i.e. the evil inclination], good. If not, he should study Torah…

If he triumphs over it, good. If not, he should recite *Shema'*.
If he triumphs over it, good. If not, he should remember the day of death.[513]

Rabbi Ḥayyim reasoned with Reb Itzeleh that the approach of the Mussar movement is too severe. Remembering the day of death is a last resort, reserved for the severely ill. That is the last line of defense. The healthy students of Volozhin do not require such radical shock therapy. They are able to overcome the evil inclination by their total immersion in Torah, the earlier line of defense.[514]

In piece after piece, Rav Kook states his objections to the Mussar movement. One of Rabbi Salanter's innovations was that the classic texts of Mussar be read aloud with "burning lips" (*"sefatayim dolekim"*),[515] thus engaging the emotion. Students were encouraged to recite the texts in a mournful tune.[516] Rav Kook believed that this emotional overload was counterproductive and potentially hazardous. It was conducive to depression (*'atsvut*), whereas the study of Torah should be pursued with a cheerful outlook and in a state of equanimity.

As for long-term results, Rav Kook observed that the spiritual development of the adherent to the Mussar movement would be arrested at the stage of *"yir'at ha-'onesh"* (fear of punishment) and that the individual would never graduate to the higher levels of *"yir'at ha-romemut"* (awe of the sublime), and *"ahavah"* (love), to employ the classic medieval hierarchy.[517] While there are certain coarse types who must have recourse to *yir'at ha-'onesh* and be bludgeoned into submission by the fear factor, in sensitive individuals this would result in severe depression. Rav Kook ruled out categorically founding an entire yeshivah on this philosophy. Even more absurd would be subjecting the entire Jewish People to this outlook.

Rather, Rav Kook advocated for what has come to be know as *Maḥshevet Yisrael* (Jewish Thought) or simply *"Maḥshavah."* He would go on to found *yeshivot* (first in Jaffa and later in Jerusalem) where the cerebral study of the classic works of Jewish Philosophy would be an integral part of the curriculum and a staple of the student's spiritual diet.[518]

In this respect—the new emphasis on works of Jewish thought—Rav Kook parted ways with the Volozhiner model, where Talmud was emphasized to the exclusion of other studies.[519] At least some of the motivation for delving into the more thoughtful and soulful portions of Torah was Kabbalistic and ultimately Messianic. On more than one occasion, Rav Kook would quote the byword of Rabbi Ḥayyim Vital in his introduction to *'Ets Ḥayyim*: *"Vay lon ... de-'avdin la-'Oraita yeveshah."* "Woe to those who make the Torah dry.'"[520] "All the debasement and length of the exile is only because 'they make the Torah dry.'"[521] "With one mouth, all the great Kabbalists 'scream as a crane' that as long as we remove from the Torah its mysteries and do not delve into its secrets, we destroy the world. 'The waters are gone from the sea and the river is drained dry' [Job 14:11]. 'Those who remove the mystery and wisdom from the Torah and make the Torah dry.' That is a famous saying in *Tikkunei Zohar*."[522]

(Along such lines, one often hears the refrain in Ḥabad circles that the study of Ḥasidism provides *"laḥluḥit"* ["moisture"] where it is otherwise sorely lacking.[523])

Overall, the truth is that with the passage of time, as the Mussar movement developed, some of these concerns voiced by Rav Kook were addressed. Mussar subdivided into many different schools and took on new forms including some more sanguine. In Slabodka, Rabbi Nathan Tsevi Finkel (revered as *"Der Alter fun Slabodka"*) placed the emphasis on *"gadlut ha-adam"* ("the greatness of man").[524] In Kelm, under Rabbi Salanter's disciple, Rabbi Simḥah Zissel Ziv (*"Der Alter fun Kelm"*), Mussar became more *"lomdish,"* acquiring an academic nature. Appropriately enough, the title of Rabbi Simḥah Zissel's work is *Ḥokhmah u-Mussar* (*Wisdom and Ethics*). This intellectual variety of Mussar reached its crescendo in the oral teaching and written record of Rabbi Simḥah Zissel's disciple, Rabbi Yeruḥam Levovitz, *Mashgi'aḥ* of the Mirrer Yeshiva in Poland. (The collection of his teachings is entitled appropriately *Da'at Ḥokhmah u-Mussar*.)[525]

[504]The surname is Lipkin. He was called "Salanter" after his birthplace of Salant, Lithuania.

[505]RZYH Kook, *Li-Sheloshah be-Elul*, vol. 2 (Jerusalem, 1947; photo offset Jerusalem 1978), par. 3 (p. 7); Rabbi Moshe Tsevi Neriyah, *Siḥot ha-Rayah* (Tel-Aviv, 1979), p. 85 (quoting Rabbi Ya'akov Moshe Ḥarlap). Thus, one may disregard the contrary report of Hillel Goldberg, "Rabbi Isaac Hutner: A Synoptic Interpretive Biography," *Tradition* 22 (4), Winter 1987, pp. 41-42, note 14.

[506]One of the *Maskilim* or Enlightened Jews of the day referred to him derisively as "Rabbi Yitsḥak Napaḥa" (Rabbi Isaac the Blacksmith) after the famous Talmudic sage. *"Blaser"* in Yiddish is a "blower" or blacksmith.

[507]RZYH Kook, *Li-Sheloshah be-Elul*, vol. 2, p. 12, par. 17 (quoting Rabbi Benzion Yadler); Neriyah, *Siḥot ha-Rayah*, p. 94.

[508]In some sense, the favor was returned. One of the great exponents of Mussar, Rabbi Nathan Tsevi Finkel (*"Der Alter fun Slabodka"*) once confided to his student Rabbi Isaac Hutner concerning Rav Kook: "Though he did not study in a Mussar Yeshivah, he is the embodiment of Mussar!" (In Yiddish: *"Er iz der tsurah fun Mussar!"*) Quoted in Rabbi Moshe Tsevi Neriyah, *Bi-Sdeh ha-Rayah* (Tel-Aviv, 1991), p. 427.

A letter from Rabbi Finkel to Rav Kook was published in *Igrot la-Rayah*, ed. Ben Zion Shapira (Jerusalem, 1990), Letter 202 (p. 310). A facsimile of the first portion of the letter wherein Rabbi Finkel sings the praise of Rav Kook is found in *Bi-Sdeh ha-Rayah*, p. 251.

[509]In the Introduction (*"'Al kol divrei ha-'iggeret"*) to the collected letters of Rav Kook, the editor, Rabbi Tsevi Yehudah Kook, bemoans the loss of the letters to Rabbi Isaac Blaser concerning the study of Mussar in general, and in particular in regard to the appearance of the work *'Or Yisrael*, containing the teachings of Rabbi Israel Salanter. See *'Igrot ha-Rayah*, vol. 1 (Jerusalem, 1961), p. 9, par. 3.

[510]See Rabbi Moshe Zuriel, *'Otserot ha-Rayah*, vol. 2 (Tel-Aviv, 1988), pp. 311-312, 314, 329-330.

[511]Volozhin was the oldest of the Lithuanian *yeshivot*, founded in 1803 by Rabbi Ḥayyim Volozhiner, disciple of the Vilna Gaon, with the Gaon's express approval. Later, there sprang up other *yeshivot* in Mir and Telz (Telšiai), but Volozhin always retained about it an aura of antiquity and authority. Needless to say, it attracted some of the finest minds among Russian Jewry.

[512]The senior Rosh Yeshivah was Rabbi Ḥayyim's grandfather by marriage, Rabbi Naftali Tsevi Yehudah Berlin (Netsiv). Rav Kook developed a strong connection with Netsiv, whom he viewed as his mentor.

[513]*b. Berakhot* 5a.

[514]Heard from Rabbi Ḥayyim's grandson Rabbi Joseph Baer Soloveitchik of Boston.

Rabbi Blaser attempted to provide his master Rabbi Israel Salanter's innovative Mussar movement with a Volozhiner pedigree. Rabbi Israel Salanter was inspired to study ethical works by his teacher Rabbi Joseph Zundel of Salant, who in turn was a prime disciple of the founder of the Volozhin Yeshivah, Rabbi Ḥayyim. "And without doubt he [i.e. Rabbi Zundel Salanter] received the method of study of Mussar from his teacher Rabbi Ḥayyim of Volozhin" (*Sha'arei 'Or*, chap. 7; in Rabbi Isaac Blaser, *'Or Yisrael* [Vilna, 1900], 16a).

[515]A quote from Proverbs 26:23. The term was meant by Rabbi Blaser to convey a hot, passionate recitation of the Mussar text rather than a cold, dispassionate singsong (such as that in vogue when reading Talmudic texts).

[516]Rabbi Isaac Blaser, *Sha'arei 'Or*, chap. 9; in Blaser, *'Or Yisrael*, 16d-17c.

[517]A glaring example of Rabbi Isaac Blaser's stress on *yir'at ha-'onesh* (fear of punishment) is the passage in *Sha'arei 'Or*, chap. 6; anthologized in Blaser, *'Or Yisrael*, 14c: "The foundation of it [i.e. the study of Mussar] is taking stock of the soul out of *fear of punishment*."

Further, we read: "Our master, teacher and Rabbi, the Gaon, the Ḥasid, of blessed memory [i.e. Rabbi Israel Salanter], in his method of Mussar did not overreach and did not preach about lofty levels of *yir'at ha-romemut* (awe of the sublime) and *'ahavat Hashem* (love of God), but only of *yir'at ha-'onesh* (fear of punishment), for that is the beginning of knowledge and the first step toward His worship, blessed be His name" (*Sha'arei 'Or*, beginning chap. 10 [17c]).

[518]It is interesting that what stood out most in the minds of Rav Kook's students and his contemporaries (including those opposed to his educational methods) was the study of *Kuzari* by Rabbi Judah Halevi. See RZYH Kook, *Li-Sheloshah be-Elul*, vol. 1 (Jerusalem, 1938), p. 16, par. 31; Ḥayyim Avihu Schwarz, *Mi-Tokh ha-Torah ha-Go'elet*, vol. 1 (Jerusalem, 1989), p. 5; Rabbi Moshe Blau, *'Al Ḥomotayikh Yerushalayim* (Tel-Aviv, 1946), p. 50; Rabbi Abraham Isaac Hakohen Kook, *Orot*, ed. Bezalel Naor (2015), p. 454, n. 174. Lectures (*Shi'urim*) in *Kuzari* delivered by Rav Kook in Jerusalem in 1921 were preserved in *Ma'amrei ha-Rayah*, vol. 2, ed. Elisha Aviner-Langenauer (Jerusalem, 1984), pp. 485-495.

Kuzari was typified by Rav Kook's son, Rabbi Tsevi Yehudah Hakohen Kook, as the "philosophy of anti-philosophy." See RZYH Kook, *Li-Netivot Yisrael*, vol. 2 (Jerusalem, 1979), p. 215.

Into the next generation, Rabbi Tsevi Yehudah Kook adopted at Yeshivat Mercaz Harav in Jerusalem, a syllabus that consisted of *Kuzari*; works of Maharal of Prague; *Nefesh ha-Ḥayyim* by Rabbi Ḥayyim of Volozhin; and *Tanya* by Rabbi Shneur Zalman of Liadi. Rabbi Tsevi Yehudah eschewed the term *"Maḥshavah"* (Thought), preferring instead to typecast the specialty of Mercaz Harav as the study of *"Emunah"* (Faith). See Ḥagay Shtamler, *Eye to Eye: The Thought of Rav Zvi Yehuda Kook* (Hebrew) (Jerusalem, 2016), pp. 204-205; Ḥayyim Avihu Schwarz, *Mi-Tokh ha-Torah ha-Go'elet*, vol. 1 (Jerusalem, 1989), pp. 6-7; vol. 4 (Jerusalem 1991), pp. 89-90.

[519]The one notable exception was the matinal study of the Pentateuchal portion of the week taught by Netsiv. See *"Kidmat ha-'Emek,"* the Introduction to Netsiv's commentary to the Pentateuch, p. III, par. 5.

Netsiv continued the tradition started by his father-in-law, Rabbi Isaac ("Itzeleh") of Volozhin. A German visitor to Volozhin by the name of Max Lilienthal quotes his host as saying:

> "We have prayers in the morning as early as possible; all the students have to be present during the service. After the service I explain to them some chapters of the Sidrah of the week, and the Haphtarah with the commentary of Rashi, adding some free explanations of my own, into which I interweave some remarks from the commentary of Moshe Dessau (Mendelssohn)."
>
> (David Philipson, *Max Lilienthal American Rabbi: Life and Writings* [New York, 1915], "My Travels in Russia," p. 348]

The last remark attributed to "Rabbi Itzeleh" by the German rabbi (concerning Mendelssohn's *Be'ur*) should probably be taken *cum grano salis*. The original comments of Rabbi Isaac of Volozhin on the Pentateuch, printed under the title *Peh Kadosh*, do excel in the method of *Peshat*, but I am unaware of Mendelssohnian traces.

Rabbi Yeḥiel Ya'akov Weinberg writes that this custom of the Rosh Yeshivah teaching the weekly *Parashah* of Pentateuch was innovated by the founder of the Volozhin Yeshivah, Rabbi Ḥayyim (father of Rabbi Isaac). See *Collected Writings of Rabbi Yeḥiel Yaakov Weinberg* (Hebrew), ed. Marc B. Shapiro, vol. 2 (Scranton, PA, 2003), *"Ha-Yeshivot Be-Russia,"* p. 217.

[520]Rabbi Ḥayyim Vital is quoting *Tikkunei Zohar*, *tikkun* 30, *netiv tinyana*. In its entirety, the sentence reads: "Woe to those who make the Torah dry and do not wish to strive in the wisdom of Kabbalah."

[521]*'Igrot ha-Rayah*, vol. 1, p. 110 (Letter 95).

[522]*'Igrot ha-Rayah*, vol. 2, p. 231 (Letter 602). In the footnote (#1), the editor Rabbi Tsevi Yehudah Hakohen Kook refers to the Introduction to *Tikkunei Zohar*, s.v. *'ilein marei mikra* (Vilna 1867 ed., bottom 15a). However, the verse quoted there is not that from Job but rather that from Isaiah 19:5. The verse from Job 14:11 is quoted in *Zohar* III, 150b (cited by Rabbi Tsevi Yehudah) but in a different context.

[523]One would have imagined that in the study of Ḥabad Ḥasidism, Rav Kook would have found the exact recipe that he was looking for. As its very name indicates, ḤaBaD (acronym of *Ḥokhmah*, *Binah*, *Da'at* or Wisdom, Understanding, Knowledge) is an intellectual variety of Ḥasidism geared to a Lithuanian audience. *Lita* was renowned as a bastion of Jewish learning and rigorous scholarship. Besides its intellectual component, in terms of long-term goals, Ḥabad sought to achieve *yir'at ha-romemut* (awe) and *'ahavah* (love), as opposed to the negative affect of *yirat ha-'onesh* (fear of punishment). Thus, one may be surprised to learn that despite all that, in Rav Kook's assessment, Ḥabad—at least as studied in the Ḥasidic *yeshivot*—comes up short:

> Among some of the Ḥasidim there are also found those who set aside time for the study of the portion of ethics, by way of [studying] Ḥabad, but since it is but a specific style and specific way, while other ways are closed to them (or at least not opened sufficiently), they cannot arrive at an exalted, universal level; to a whole, all-emcompassing knowledge ....
>
> (*Kevatsim mi-Ketav Yad Kodsho*, vol. 3, ed. Boaz Ofen [Jerusalem, 2018], *Pinkas* 5:9 [p. 24])

This same criticism of the insularity of Ḥabad is voiced in a letter to the Ḥabad Rabbi of Jaffa, Rabbi Shneur Zalman Slonim:

> Truly great and exalted is the study of the subject of Ḥabad, the subject that enlightens most the teaching of the holy man of Israel, Ba'al Shem Tov, his soul [rests in] Eden. Certainly, it was prepared for Redemption. However, I customarily arouse the great ones of our nation not to be satisfied with but a single subject in the spiritual portion of Torah, just as in the practical portion of Torah we are not satisfied with one way or one method. Our Halakhic studies are composed of all the schools of our rabbis, *Rishonim* (Early) and *Aḥaronim* (Late). Exactly so must it be in regard to spiritual subjects. Together with the subject of Ḥabad it is necessary to study the wisdom of the early ones, the Godly philosophers, continuing through later generations; and all the schools of the Kabbalists, and all the revelations of mysteries of the Vilna Gaon and his disciples. And from the synthesis of thought and its expansion, there will emerge a great light ... in the entirety of the nation; and from all the directions together, there will shine the light of Messiah.
>
> (*'Igrot ha-Rayah*, vol. 4: 1920-1921 [Jerusalem, 2018], p. 187 [Letter 148])

In a letter to his fellow Kabbalist, Rabbi Pinḥas Hakohen Lintop of Birzh, Rav Kook wrote:

> Serenity in the world and in Judaism comes about only as a result of the multiplicity of light sources shining and streaming at once. The old way of choosing one of the ways [and] treading upon it gradually—"shall not stand, neither shall it come to pass" [Isaiah 7:7]. We have grown and evolved so much beyond this. To grasp the *gestalt* of all the ways, and to bind them in a state of serenity, whole and confident—this is the start of the way of converting the *'ayin* of *'or* (skin) to the *'aleph* of *'or* (light)...
>
> (*'Igrot ha-Rayah*, vol. 1, p. 142 [Letter 112])

[524]Rabbi Finkel was a disciple of Rabbi Simḥah Zissel of Kelm.

[525]Rabbi Neriyah discusses the transformation that took place within the Mussar movement. Whereas Rabbi Israel Salanter, founder of the movement, was adverse to the study of Kabbalah, some of his disciples took to the study of Luzzatto's Kabbalistic works. Neriyah highlights the attraction to Luzzatto's *Da'at Tevunot* on the part of Rabbi Simḥah Zissel Ziv, "the Elder of Kelm," and subsequently Rabbi Joseph Leib Bloch (*Rosh Yeshivah* of Telz) and Rabbi Eliyahu Dessler (*Mashgi'aḥ* of Gateshead Yeshivah, England, and Ponevezh Yeshivah, B'nei Berak), both students of the *Beit ha-Talmud* of Kelm in their youth. See Neriyah, *Tal ha-Rayah* (Tel-Aviv, 1993), pp. 270-278; and Rabbi Ḥayyim Friedlander's introduction to *Da'at Tevunot* (B'nei Berak, 1975), p. 12. The title of Rabbi Bloch's work, *Shi'urei Da'at*, also bespeaks the new emphasis on the cognitive rather than the emotional.

Rabbi David Kronglass (or "Dovid Kobriner," as he was known in the Mirrer Yeshivah in Poland, after his city of origin), who served after World War Two as *Mashgi'aḥ* of Yeshivat Ner Yisrael in Baltimore, once taught the primer of Kabbalah, *Sha'arei 'Orah* by Rabbi Joseph Gikatilla, to a select group of married students. One supposes that this relatively positive attitude to the study of Kabbalah (albeit within an elite circle) was a carry-over from the intellectual climate created by Rabbi Yeruḥam Levovitz in Mir.

Appendix 7

Letter of Rabbi Mordechai Gimpel Jaffe on the Wisdom of Kabbalah

Recently, there was unearthed a manuscript of Rabbi Mordechai Gimpel Jaffe (1820-1891), who served as Rabbi of Rozhinoy (today Ruzhany, Belarus), and after his *'aliyah* to Erets Yisrael, of the newly established settlement of Yahud, near Petaḥ Tikvah.[526] He is most famous for his important super-commentary on Naḥmanides, *Tekhelet Mordekhai*. Rabbi Jaffe was a second-generation student of the Volozhin Yeshivah. His father, Rabbi Dov Baer of Turetz (d. 1829), later Rabbi of Utian, had been one of the first ten students of Rabbi Ḥ ayyim Volozhiner, who founded the Yeshiva.[527] Rabbi Mordechai Gimpel was a disciple of Rabbi Isaac, who succeeded his father Rabbi Ḥayyim as Rosh Yeshivah.[528]

In this letter, Rabbi Mordechai Gimpel introduces *Ḥokhmat ha-Kabbalah*, the Wisdom of Kabbalah, and its utter necessity for arriving at man's goal of knowledge of the Lord. He refers to Kabbalah as *"Nishmat ha-Torah,"* "the soul of the Torah." I have included the letter in our collection as it may shed some new light upon the ideology of Rabbi Mordechai Gimpel Jaffe's great-nephew, Rabbi Abraham Isaac Hakohen Kook.[529]

I have provided minimal punctuation. There follows an English translation.

ההצלחה והאושר האמתיים אשר הם פרי כל הבריאה וכל חפץ וכל ישע, הם ידיעת היחוד, כי הוא הדעת את ד'. וכל מה שיוסיף המיחד ידיעה והשגה ביחוד, הנה הוא מוסיף דעת. והתורה ומצותיה סובבות על זה, והם הדרך לידיעה זו, שהוא היחוד. וזולתם, אין שם יחוד ולא דעת את ד'. ואי-אפשר להשיג זה הדעת כי-אם בעסק התורה ומצותיה, ומהם נשכיל אופן העשיה, שהוא תיקון הכבוד, והוא היחוד.

וזה רמזו אדון הנביאים, עליו השלום, באמרו "ושמרתם את (כל) דברי הברית [הזאת ועשיתם אותם] למען תשכילו את כל אשר תעשון" [דברים כט, ח]. והכונה, כי השמירה שהוא העסק בתורה שבעל-פה, כמאמרם ז"ל, "ושמרתם—זו משנה", ועשיתם, שהוא קיום המצות בפועל—מתוך שניהם, נשכיל את אשר נעשה, שהוא הפרי היוצא משנים אלה. וזאת העשיה לשון תיקון הוא, והוא תיקון הכבוד.

ואי-אפשר שיעלה תיקון זה, ידיעת זה התיקון ואופן עשיתו, אם לא יהיה מתוקן ממילא בנשמת התורה, והיא חכמת הקבלה, העוסקת בהישרת הדעת את ד', שהוא יחודו, כידוע למהלכים בה. כי אי-אפשר לראות אור היחוד, שהוא הדעת האמיתי, כי-אם באורה, לפי שחכמת האמת אין עסקה כי-אם להיישיר אל זה השלימות. ולזה היתה החכמה הזאת הפתח לדעת את השם הנכבד והנורא.

Translation

True success and fortune, which are the fruit of the entire creation, and all desire and salvation—are the knowledge of the Unity, for it is the knowledge of the Lord. And the more the unifier adds knowledge and apprehension of the Unity, the more his knowledge increases. And it is impossible to apprehend this knowledge other than by engaging in Torah and her commandments. From them, we shall be enlightened as to the method of acting, which is the *tikkun* (perfection) of the *Kavod* (Glory),[530] and that is the Unity.

And this was alluded to by the Master of Prophets [i.e. Moses], peace be unto him, when he said: "Observe the words of this covenant, and do them, so that you may be enlightened as to all that you shall do" [Deuteronomy 29:8]. The intention is that [from] the "observance," which is the study of the Oral Law (as the Sages, of blessed memory, said: "'Observe'—This is Mishnah"),[531] and their performance, which is the actual fulfillment of the commandments—from both of them, we shall be enlightened as to what we shall do, which is the fruit produced from these two. And this "doing" (*'asiyah*) is an expression for "perfecting" (*tikkun*),[532] and it is the *tikkun* (perfection) of the *Kavod* (Glory).

And it is impossible that this *tikkun*—the knowledge of this *tikkun* and the method of effecting it—succeed, if it is not perfected *ipso facto* by the soul of the Torah (*nishmat ha-Torah*), and that is the Wisdom of Kabbalah (*Ḥokhmat ha-Kabbalah*) that busies itself with straightening knowledge of the Lord, i.e. His unity, as is known to those who are conversant with it. For it is impossible to behold the light of the Unity, which is the true knowledge, other than through her light [i.e. the light of the Torah]. For the Wisdom of Truth (*Ḥokhmat ha-Emet*)[533] is occupied solely with directing to this wholeness. And for this reason, this wisdom was the the entrance to know "the glorious and awful Name" [Deuteronomy 28:58].

[526]The manuscript was sold at a Winner's Auction, Winner's Unlimited No. 105 (Wednesday, February 21, 2018). Lot 516 was titled, "Kabbalistic Ideas Written by Rabbi Mordechai Gimpel Jaffe." A facsimile was circulated online.

[527]Rabbi Ḥayyim of Volozhin said of Rabbi Dov Baer: "In his *pilpulim*, he strides straight as one of the early ones, the Rashba and the Ran." Quoted in *Tsemaḥ David he-Ḥadash*, Part III (Warsaw, 1871), p. 144, s.v. *Rabbi Dov Baer Karelitsher, Rav be-K.K. Utian.*" See Dov Eliach, *Avi ha-Yeshivot* [Biography of Rabbi Ḥayyim of Volozhin] (Jerusalem, 2011), p. 465.

Rabbi Dov Baer's prayers were inordinately long. An evening prayer might go on all night. Rabbi Ḥayyim of Volozhin said that he had taught Rabbi Dov Baer to pray. See Rabbi Neriyah, *Siḥot ha-Rayah* (Tel-Aviv, 1979), p. 31; Ḥayyim Lifschitz, *Shivḥei ha-Rayah* (Jerusalem, 1995), pp. 24-26; and Rabbi Ya'ir Uriel, *Be-Shipulei ha-Gelimah* [Biography of Rabbi Tsevi Yehudah Hakohen Kook] (Israel, 2012), p. 55.

Further details concerning Rabbi Dov Baer may be found in *Siḥot ha-Rayah*, p. 136 (footnote).

[528]Rabbi Reuven Halevi of Dinaburg (Dvinsk) would send young men whom he ordained to Rozhinoy. He justified this by saying: "*Shulḥan 'Arukh* you know, but now you must go to Rozhinoy to Rabbi Mordechai Gimpel. From him you will learn the laws of leadership. He learned them from Rabbi Itzeleh of Volozhin." Neriyah, *Tal ha-Rayah*, p. 46, note 1.

[529]See letters of Rabbi Mordechai Gimpel Jaffe to his great-nephew Rav Kook in *'Igrot la-Rayah*, ed. Ben Zion Shapira (Jerusalem, 1990), nos. 5 (pp. 16-18) and 6 (pp. 18-19); and additional nos. 12 (p. 543) and 14 (pp. 545-546).

Letters 5 and 6, which concern the publication of *'Ittur Soferim*, the rabbinical journal edited by Rav Kook, are transcribed as well in Rabbi Moshe Tsevi Neriyah, *Tal ha-Rayah* (Tel-Aviv, 1993), pp. 78-80. (The transcriptions differ somewhat.) A facsimile of the second letter, datelined "Monday, 26 Tammuz, 5647 [1887], Rozhinoy," is found there on page 77.

A letter from Rabbi Mordechai Gimpel to an adolescent Avraham Yitsḥak Hakohen (dated *Erev Rosh Ḥodesh Menaḥem-Av* 5641 [1881]) may be found in Neriyah, *Tal ha-Rayah*, p. 47. Then aged sixteen, the recipient was studying with Rabbi Mordechai Gimpel's son, Rabbi Jacob Rabinowitz, in Lutzin.

Finally, in *Tal ha-Rayah*, pp. 96-99, there is a facsimile and transcription of Rabbi Mordechai Gimpel's letter of congratulation to his great-nephew upon his assuming the rabbinate of Zoimel.

[530]The term *Kavod* (roughly synonymous with the *Shekhinah* or immanence of God) figures prominently in the writings of Rabbi El'azar Roke'aḥ of Worms, a member of the medieval school of *Ḥasidei Ashkenaz*. Lately, Isaac Lifshitz has devoted a study to the relation of Rabbi

Ḥayyim Volozhiner's theology in *Nefesh ha-Ḥayyim* to that of the *Roke'aḥ*. The editor of *Nefesh ha-Ḥayyim* (a posthumous book) was none other than the author's son, Rabbi Isaac of Volozhin. (Rabbi Isaac also contributed a major *Hagahah* or Gloss to his father's manuscript, in which he manifests his own vast knowledge of Kabbalah.) Thus, it is no wonder that Rabbi Mordechai Gimpel Jaffe, a major disciple of Rabbi Isaac (Itzeleh) of Volozhin, employs vocabulary distinctly that of the *Roke'aḥ*. See Joseph Isaac Lifshitz, "*Nefesh HaḤayyim* and its Sources in Ḥasidei Ashkenaz" (Hebrew), *Da'at* 79-80 (5775/2015), pp. 77-93.

[531] *Sifra*, *'Emor* 9 (to Leviticus 22:31): "'Observe'—This is Mishnah; 'and do'—This is the action."

[532] See Ibn Ezra, Deuteronomy 21:12, s.v. *ve-'asetah*; Pseudo-Rashi, *Genesis Rabbah* 11:6, s.v. *'afilu 'adam tsarikh tikkun.*

[533] A synonym for the Wisdom of Kabbalah.

Appendix 8

Rabbi Samuel of Kalvaria's *Darkhei No'am*

In his work *Darkhei No'am* (Koenigsberg, 1764), the Kabbalist, Rabbi Samuel ben Eliezer of Kalvaria, interpreted the Legends of Rabbah bar Bar Ḥannah according to the fourfold method of *"Pardes."* Each legend is interpreted first according to the *Peshat*, second according to the *Remez*, third according to the *Derush*, and fourth according to the *Sod*. The book has the distinction of being perhaps the only book to receive the *Haskamah* or formal approbation of the Vilna Gaon.[534]

Rabbi Samuel's balanced view is refreshing. Despite his obvious proficiency in the intricacies of Lurianic Kabbalah, he displays a surprising tolerance of the rationalist mindset of Maimonides and Gersonides, and their naturalistic downplaying of miracles:

> There are [differing] opinions among the philosophers. Some say that the natural is superior to the supernatural. For this reason, it was the opinion of Maimonides and Gersonides to reconcile with nature all the miracles performed under the sun. Though we are believers, sons of believers, that He, blessed be He, is the master of will (*ba'al ha-ratson*) and master of ability (*ba'al yekholet*)—nonetheless, that which is natural is superior for the likes of us humans who are creatures of nature (*mutba'im*). As they, of blessed memory, said: "It is best to reduce the number of miracles."[535]
>
> And some say the opposite, that the suprernatural is superior, for it is wondrous.
>
> And each provides a rationale for his words.[536]

Though earnestly, there is no evidence that Rav Kook ever read *Darkhei No'am*, I believe that the reader will certainly benefit from the following translation of the Second Introduction to the book. It may shed light on the Kabbalistic perception of the Legends of Rabbah bar Bar Ḥannah. (Unrelated to the Kabbalistic discussion, much of Rabbi Samuel's commentary is taken up by sociological observations on the tense relations that prevail between rabbis and their communities.)

Second Introduction

"SHIP", "SEA" AND "WAVES OF THE SEA"

We found in the Midrash of Rabbi Shim'on ben Yoḥai,[537] peace be unto him, and the *Tikkunim*, that the body of man is called a "ship" by way of parable. Thus, they interpreted the entire story of the ship of Jonah the Prophet in regard to the body of man. It is a trope for all the bodies of mankind.

However, essentially this trope relates exclusively to the Torah scholar. He is referred to as a "ship" because of his Torah, of which it is said, "She is like the merchant ships."[538] As Rabbi El'azar ben Rabbi Shim'on in the story of the sixty sailors in *Bava Metsi'a* [84b], who applied this verse to himself: "She is like the merchant ships [from afar she brings her bread]." Along these lines, the rest of Israel, the masses, are called "the sea" opposite the Torah scholar, who is the ship sailing in their midst, the way a ship does in the heart of the sea. So does it say in *Tanna de-Vei Eliyahu*: "'And his seed shall be in many waters'—These are the householders (*ba'alei batim*) of Israel."[539] And the wicked of Israel are called "the waves of the sea," as Scripture says, "The wicked are like the tossing sea,"[540] for at times they trouble the Torah scholars among them, who are [like] the ship passing between these waves of the sea.

Furthermore, we find that the collective nation of Israel … is called a "ship" opposite the numerous nations of the world who surround her from every side.

"SEAFARERS"

Those wise men who engage in investigating the worlds—whether it be the deeds of mortal men and the affairs of this world, referred to as the "sea"; or the depth of the *kelipot* ("husks" or "shells," i.e. the forces of impurity), also called "the depths of the sea"—such [sages] are termed by Rabbah bar Bar Ḥannah "seafarers" (*yoredei ha-yam*), just as the Sages, of blessed memory, coined the term "Descenders of the Chariot" (*Yoredei Merkavah*),[541] which is to say that they descend in their intellect to the depth of the matter. In the same vein, they said of Rabbi Meir that his colleagues did not "descend" to the limit of his opinion.[542] Likewise, "Rabbi Nathan … descended to the depth of the law" (*naḥit le-'omka de-dina*).[543]

There are also people who are knowledgeable of the deeds of men, good and evil, because they themselves once committed this very sin. And now that they have returned from their evil path, they are familiar with the nature of the wicked for "There is none as wise as the master of experience." Such people too are referred to effectively as "seafarers." The reason being, that when they sin they lower the sparks of their souls into the the midst of the *kelipot*, called the "depths of the sea," God protect us. Thus, [these people] are called "seafarers." And when they rise up from there, they recount their former deeds, following the example of Rabbi Akiva who said, "When I was an ignoramus, etc."[544]

Now after they beheld all this, the aforementioned wise men dressed those things in parable, as is the wont of all riddlers, who hide their meanings and communicate by way of story and clue. However, the parables and figures of speech are communicable only to a wise man capable of comprehending on his own "the words of the wise, and their riddles."[545] By this, I mean one who has himself paid attention to the affairs of the world. Or, has himself made the rounds of the world, [visiting] many places and lands, and observing many goings-on, be they good or evil. Someone who has these qualifications will easily comprehend the underlying meaning of a given riddle or parable, for he is conversant with the nature of the world and the deeds of the generation ....

This is the import of Rabbah bar Bar Ḥannah's statement, "Seafarers related *to me*." Specifically "to me." Which is to say: That language, that narrative, in which the wise men referred to as "seafarers," dressed their intentions, is worthy of me specifically, because I too grasp the affairs of the higher worlds. Like them, "the pathways of heaven are familiar to me."[546] "I applied my heart to seek and to search out by wisdom"[547] the affairs of the creations that obtain in this lowly world. In addition, I actually wandered to distant seas and deserts, and "I have seen all the works that are done under the sun."[548] Today, I am on a par with them. Therefore, they recounted to me and to no other, for I *hear*.[549]

[534]See above note 6.

[535]Source not found.

[536]*Darkhei No'am* 59b.

Par contre, another Kabbalist, Meir Leibush Malbim, was most intolerant of Gersonides' naturalistic philosophy. See for example, Malbim's reaction to Gersonides' attempt to provide a scientific explanation for one of Elisha's miracles, in his commentary to 2 Kings 6:6.

[537]I.e. the *Zohar*.

[538]Proverbs 31:14.

[539]Numbers 24:7; *Tanna de-Vei Eliyahu Rabbah*, chap. 21 (in *Seder Eliyahu Rabbah*, ed. M. Friedmann, Vienna 1904, p. 117).

[540]Isaiah 57:20.

[541]The term "*Yoredei Merkavah*" arose with the ancient *Hekhalot* literature. See Gershom G. Scholem, *Major Trends in Jewish Mysticism* (New York, 1971), pp. 46-47; Elliot R. Wolfson, *Through a Speculum That Shines* (Princeton, New Jersey, 1994), pp. 82-83; idem, "*Yeridah la-Merkavah:* Typology of Ecstasy and Enthronement in Ancient Jewish Mysticism," in *Mystics of the Book: Themes, Topics, and Typologies*, ed. Robert A. Herrera (New York, 1993).

[542]*b. 'Eruvin* 13b. It seems that Rabbi Samuel of Kalvaria has misquoted the passage in the Talmud. There, the metaphor is *standing* rather than *descending*: "His colleagues were unable *to stand* on the limit of his knowledge (*la'amod 'al sof da'ato*)."

[543]*b. Bava Kamma* 53a.

[544]*b. Pesaḥim* 49b.

[545]Proverbs 1:6.

[546]*b. Berakhot* 58b.

[547]Ecclesiastes 1:13.

[548]Ecclesiastes 1:14.

[549]*Darkhei No'am*, 3a-4a.

Appendix 9

A Kookian Midrash on the Name "David"

In London, in 1917, Rav published an esoteric work, *Resh Millin*, an independent Kabbalistic *midrash* on the letters of the Hebrew alphabet. (In 2003, there was published in Jerusalem a supplement to the book, where the author goes beyond individual letters to interpret whole words employing his original method.)

Explicating the significance of the fourth letter of the Hebrew alphabet, *dalet*, Rav Kook writes:

> The *dalet* also uplifts and draws the sap of life from the springs of the higher Deep: *"Daloh dalah"* ("Drew").[550]

The term *"ha-Tehom ha-'Elyon"* ("the higher Deep") is pregnant. In the story of the Flood we read, "On this day, all the springs of the great Deep (*Tehom Rabbah*) split open."[551]

There are truly *two* Deeps, the higher Deep (*Tehom ha-'Elyon*) and the lower Deep (*Tehom ha-Taḥton*).[552] They are alluded to in the verse: "Deep calls unto deep."[553]

At the conclusion of his commentary to the Legends of Rabbah bar Bar Ḥannah, Rav Kook referenced the Talmudic story of David digging down into the foundations of the future Temple, at which time the waters of the Deep threatened to flood the world. But that is only one half of the story. If we follow Rav Kook's interpretive method as laid out in *Resh Millin*, David draws from the lower Deep and the higher Deep *at once*.

In Hebrew, the name "David" is constituted by two letters *dalet* with the letter *vav* between. One letter *dalet* would signify "drawing" from the Deep below, while the other signifies "drawing" from the Deep above. The letter *vav* in this, as in all instances, is the "hook" or connector between the two elements.[554]

In a *pensée* written in St. Gallen, Switzerland, a year or two earlier (1915-1916), Rav Kook expanded upon this theme of the two Deeps:

> We are placed between the two great currents:
>
> All the mountains of spiritual light and fire that are above consciousness surround us; they are forever shocking, and they set off great soul-shocks in our midst.

> And those profound deeps (*tehomot*) that are below consciousness, they too are forever tumultuous, roaring and flooding; their breakers and waves strike us, and we tremble and are swept away with them.
>
> And all these great movements do not cease; they are forever active with great excitement, with a mighty seething, and with a swell of powerful life.
>
> We must constantly prepare our receptacles, all the conduits of life established in us, [in order] that they be ready to receive the good, the pleasant, the straight, the pure, the holy and the luminous—that flow from these two currents together.
>
> And when we are prepared for this, there will flow upon us from above and from below only flows of purity, love, strength and glory; higher waters and lower waters will kiss; and "deep calls unto deep"[555] with strength.
>
> And we can be made of might, to be the conduits that combine the heights and the depths; to raise the abysmal light up to the highest heights; and to lower mighty rays of light down to the deepest depths; to flood with light and life ....[556]

For Rav Kook, it is clear that the Deep above and the Deep below symbolize the supraconscious and subconscious realms respectively.

*

In regard to the two Deeps, the one above and the one below, there is a remarkable teaching of the Rebbe of Izbica (pronounced Izhbitsa) as transmitted by his grandson, Rabbi Gershon Ḥanokh of Radzyn.

> My grandfather, the holy Gaon, of blessed memory,[557] explained the reason that it does not state in Psalm 148, "the waters that are below the earth,"[558] is because at the time that man praises the Lord, blessed be He, there truly is no difference between the upper and lower waters ... Thus, the waters that are below the earth are also included in "the waters that are above the heavens" [verse 4].[559]

On another occasion, Rabbi Gershon Ḥanokh explained this teaching at greater length:

> If man ascends in his [divine] service, then there ascend with him the "lower waters" and become themselves "upper waters" ... All the "lower waters"

become "waters that are above the heavens." Thus, when King David dug the foundations—which is to say that he dug down [into himself] with all kinds of analyses (*birurim*) until he was able to say, "My heart is hollow within me"[560]—*ipso facto*, from his perspective, all are "upper waters" . . . For in truth, there are not two [sets of] waters. There are only "upper waters." All the "lower waters" resulted only from the concealment [of divinity]. So after the great *birurim* (self-analyses) of King David, all the concealments were nullified, and there was revealed that all are "upper waters."[561]

[550]Exodus 2:19. The context is Moses' having drawn water from the well for the daughters of Jethro.

Parenthetically, according to Rabbi El'azar ha-Kalir (or so Rabbi Joseph Kara construed a line in his poem *"Akashtah kesel va-kerev,"* inserted in the Prayer for Rain recited on *Shemini 'Atseret*), the original act of the Creator separating the waters and uplifting the "upper waters" (*"mayim 'elyonim"*) constituted an act of "drawing." Rabbi Joseph Kara adduces the verse in Exodus 2:19: *"Daloh dalah."* The line in the poem reads: *"Tikken ve-khal u-mad ve-gazar ve-dalah mayim."* See Abraham Grossman, "Praises of Rabbi El'azar b. Qilir in R. Joseph Qara's Commentary on *Piyyutim*" (Hebrew), in *Knesset Ezra: Literature and Life in the Synagogue* (Studies Presented to Ezra Fleischer), ed. S. Elizur, M.D. Herr, G. Shaked, A. Shinan (Jerusalem: Ben-Zvi Institute, 1994), pp. 295-296.

[551]Genesis 7:11. See Rabbeinu Baḥya ben Asher, Exodus 15:1, s.v. *ki ga'oh ga'ah* (Chavel ed., p. 126). Baḥya writes that "*Tehom Rabbah*" in Genesis 7:11 refers to the higher *Tehom* and the lower *Tehom*.

[552]In *b. Ta'anit* 25b this is expressed in Aramaic: *"Tehoma 'ila'ah"* and *"Tehoma tata'ah."* And so in *Zohar* III, 32b. See also *Commentary on Talmudic Aggadoth* by Rabbi Azriel of Gerona, ed. Isaiah Tishby (Jerusalem, 1982), Tractate *Ḥagigah*, 52a, line 25 (p. 164): *"Tehom ha-'elyon u-Tehom ha-taḥton."* Tishby (n. 21) points out that this is evidently a variant of *Genesis Rabbah*, whereby the two *Tehomot* substitute for *"ru'aḥ"* of our version to achieve a total of six elements. See *Genesis Rabbah* 1:8-9.

Of interest is the passage in *Masekhet 'Atsilut* (attributed to "Yeroḥam be Yosef") and the accompanying commentary of Rabbi Yitsḥak Eizik Ḥaver, *Ginzei Meromim*, pp. 63-64. (*Masekhet 'Atsilut* may or may not be of medieval provenance. See above note 34.) See too ibid. pp. 75-76.

[553]Psalms 42:8; *b. Ta'anit* 25b and Ps.-Rashi ad loc., s.v. *Tehom el Tehom kore'*: *"mayim 'elyonim u-mayim taḥtonim* (upper waters and lower waters)."

[554]The meaning of the Hebrew word *vav* is "hook." Indeed, the shape of the letter *vav* is that of a hook.

Also, as a part of speech, *vav* is the conjunction "and." See *Resh Millin*, *vav*.

[555]Psalms 42:8.

[556]*Shemonah Kevatsim* 6:97.

[557]Rabbi Mordechai Joseph Leiner, Rebbe of Izbica.

[558]Rabbi Gershon Ḥanokh rules out the possibility that verse 7 refers to the waters below the surface of the earth:

The “deeps” (*tehomot*) stated there do not refer to the water, rather the vessel that contains the water is called “deep.” However, the lower waters themselves are not reckoned there.

(*Sod Yesharim, Sukkot* [Warsaw, 1903], *Leil Sheni de-Sukkot*, par. 77 [39a])

[559]Rabbi Gershon Ḥanokh Leiner, *Sod Yesharim, Sukkot, Leil Sheni de-Sukkot*, par. 59 (30d).

[560]Psalms 109:22; *y. Berakhot* 9:5; *b. Berakhot* 61b; Rabbi Shneur Zalman of Liadi, *Tanya* I, 1 (5b). (The passage in *Tanya* appears to be a conflation of the *Bavli* and the *Yerushalmi*.)

[561]*Sod Yesharim, Sukkot, Leil Sheni de-Sukkot*, par. 77 (39a-b). Cf. the Ḥabad master, Rabbi Aharon Halevi Horowitz of Staroselye, *'Avodat ha-Levi*, Deuteronomy (Warsaw, 1866), *Derushim le-Simḥat Beit ha-Sho'evah*, 14d-15a. The Staroselyer discusses the uniting of the *Tehom ha-'Elyon* (*Binah*) and the *Tehom ha-Taḥton* (*Malkhut*).

Appendix 10

Rav Kook, the Messiah and the Vatican

Before Rav Kook died on the third of Ellul, 5695/1935, Rabbi Yitsḥak Greenblatt of Brisk went to visit the very frail and weak saint. Rabbi Greenblatt asked the soft-spoken Chief Rabbi, known for his tolerance and love of all people, if he thought the Messiah would come in the upcoming year. He responded in the negative: "The Messiah cannot come until the very foundations of the Vatican are uprooted from the ground."

Rabbi Greenblatt's grandson, Rabbi Yoel Greenblatt of Memphis, Tennessee, provided this background information:

> Rabbi Yitsḥak Greenblatt of Brisk, was a *talmid* (student) of Rabbi Ḥayyim Brisker [i.e. Rabbi Ḥayyim Soloveichik]. Rabbi Ḥayyim married my grandparents. My *zeide* (grandfather) was very close with Rabbi Moshe Soloveichik [son of Rabbi Ḥayyim] as they learned together in Brisk and were the same age.
>
> When my *zeide* came to Erets Yisrael in 1930, he immediately became very close with Rav Kook, as they had many friends in common from the Torah World in *Lita* (Lithuania).
>
> My *zeide* of course went to visit the Rav in 1935 because he was dying of cancer. The reason my *zeide* asked Rav Kook such a crazy question about *Mashiaḥ* coming, was because they were both talking about how wonderful things were in 1935 in (then) Palestine. You see, there was a wave of immigrants that were able to come from Eastern Europe to then Palestine. There were literally thousands of *frume Yidden* (religious Jews) and *b'nei Torah* (Torah students) coming in 1935, and people in Yerushalayim were giggling from joy and beginning to say that maybe *Mashiaḥ* is coming. So my *zeide* said to Rav Kook that maybe the *Mashiaḥ* is on his way because of the *kibbuts galuyot* (ingathering of exiles). That was when Rav Kook told him that it was impossible for the *Mashiaḥ* to come because the Vatican was still standing and *Mashiaḥ* could not come until the Vatican was uprooted from its very foundations.

> My uncle, Rabbi Avraham Barukh Greenblatt [father of Rabbi Ephraim Greenblatt of Memphis, Tennessee] studied under Rabbi Moshe Sokolovsky in Brisk and then my *zeide* sent him from Brisk to study under Rav Kook in Mercaz Harav. Around 1932, my uncle asked Rav Kook if he would learn with him *be-ḥavruta* (one-on-one), and Rav Kook said that the only time he had available was around 2 a.m. I don't know what they learned, but my uncle told my family that at 2 a.m. Rav Kook would start learning with him until they would sit on the floor and Rav Kook would talk about how the *Shekhinah* was in *galut* (exile). They would cry together over the *ḥurban beit ha-mikdash* (destruction of the Temple) and after a while, Rav Kook would say: "Let us now learn."
>
> My grandfather died in 1950, years before I was born. I only know the Vatican story because my grandfather told it over to my father [Rabbi Nota Greenblatt of Memphis, Tennessee] many times because he was so surprised by Rav Kook's response about the Vatican, and my father has told me the story many times, and in fact, I think I have it on tape from him.

COMMENTARY

In his prognostication, Rav Kook may have been drawing on his own independent vision. On the other hand, it is possible that Rav Kook's enigmatic remark was inspired by various Jewish apocalyptic texts over the ages. Closest in time to Rav Kook is Malbim's commentary to the Book of Daniel, *Yafe'aḥ la-Kets*. Malbim, in turn, quotes Abrabanel's earlier commentary, *Ma'yenei ha-Yeshu'ah*, whereby the "little horn" that arose on the fourth beast with "eyes like the eyes of a man, and a mouth speaking great things" (Daniel 7:8) refers to the emergence of the papacy in Rome. Abrabanel adheres to the rabbinic interpretation of the fourth beast as Imperial Rome.[562] Abrabanel's original contribution is that the "little horn" refers to the popular notion that about the time that Roman Emperor Constantine converted to Christianity in 337, he raised up Sylvester, a hitherto undistinguished cleric, and established him as pope in Rome.[563] This would be the beginning of the Christian Roman Empire and pontifical rule of Rome. What does the future hold in store for that mighty empire? Daniel prophesied:

> … his dominion shall be taken away, to destroy and to perish unto the end. And the kingdom and the dominion, and the greatness of the kingdoms under the whole heaven, shall be given to the people of supernal saints … .[564]

In the centuries that followed, more than one aspirant Messiah would confront the pope in Rome in a showdown of civilizations. In 1280, Abraham Abulafia attempted to convert Pope Nicholas III to Judaism. (Luckily, before the Pope had time to burn Abulafia at the stake, Nicholas suddenly died of apoplectic stroke.) In 1530, Solomon Molkho (a.k.a. Diogo Pires) had an audience with Pope Clement VII. (Prior to their meeting, Molkho sat for thirty days at the bridge over the Tiber in close proximity to the Pope's fortress, Castel Sant'Angelo, wearing rags and sharing the company of the beggars and the infirm[565] —no doubt in conformity to the Talmudic legend concerning the Messiah, who sits at the entrance to Rome among the lepers.[566]) On that occasion, the young visionary Molkho actually found favor in the pontiff's eyes; later in Mantua in 1532, he was burnt at the stake by Holy Roman Emperor Charles V.

If the symbolism of the fourth beast and the "little horn" of Daniel's vision were still open to interpretation, in the apocalyptic works that followed, the fate of Imperial Rome was quite explicit.

In the fifth and final prophecy of *Nevu'at ha-Yeled* (*Prophecy of the Child*),[567] an Aramaic quatrain, we read:

'Ir le-tel titpenei
ve-tuv lo titbenei
de-nafkat kiyyunei
ve-kula yifnei.[568]

A city will be laid waste
and will not be rebuilt
for it produced idols.
All shall be wasted.

The stanzas of *Nevu'at ha-Yeled* proceed in alphabetical order. The letter following *'ayin* is *peh*. Thus, the very next stanza of the poem begins "*Pipus de-Romaya ...*" The Polish *maskil* (enlightened Jew) Isaac Satanow translated this into Hebrew: "*Ha-Apif[y]or shel Romi*" (The Pope of Rome).[569]

[562]See *Genesis Rabbah* 76:6; *Yalkut Shim'oni*, chap. 1064 (to Daniel 7:8); and *Ḥiddushei Ramban, Ketubot* 51b.

[563]*Ma'yenei ha-Yeshu'ah, ma'ayan* 8, *tamar* 5.

The story of Constantine granting to Sylvester sovereignty over Rome is the stuff of fiction. It is contained in the *Donation of Constantine*, an eighth-century forgery. (Earlier, one of the sixth-century Symmachian forgeries, the *Vita beati Silvestri*, paints a charming picture of Sylvester's close relationship to Emperor Constantine.) Abrabanel assumed Constantine's empowerment of Sylvester to be historical fact.

Gersonides (cited by Abrabanel) had no need of the legend of Sylvester. To account for the transition from pagan Rome to Christian Rome, Gersonides simply assumed that the "little horn" seen by Daniel symbolizes Constantine. Unable to abide this symbolism (primarily because there was nothing "little" about Constantine the Great), Abrabanel substituted the hitherto insignificant Sylvester for Constantine as the transitional figure of Daniel's apocalyptic vision. Gersonides would have responded that the "littleness" of the horn refers to the relative insignificance of Christianity until Emperor Constantine lent it his aegis. (An additional problem inherent in Gersonides' exegesis was his portrayal of Constantine as the eleventh emperor when according to Abrabanel he was actually the thirty-ninth.)

Both Gersonides and Abrabanel believed that the thought of the "little horn" to change the times and the religion *("ve-yisbar lehashnaya zimnin ve-dat")* in Daniel 7:25 alludes to Christianity's shifting of the dates of the festivals and its abolition of the *mitsvot* or commandments of the Torah. (Indeed, at the First Council of Nicaea, convoked by Constantine in 325, it was decided that the Christian observance of *Pascha* would no longer be determined by the Jewish calendar but would be independent thereof.)

Abrabanel found supposed support for his equation of the "little horn" with Christianity in the Midrash's identification of the "little horn" with Ben Natsur. (See the note above.) However, there is no truth to Abrabanel's contention that Ben Natsur is a veiled reference to *Yeshu'a ha-Notsri* or the Nazarene.

[564]Daniel 7:26-27.

[565]Solomon Molkho, *Ḥayyat Kaneh* (Amsterdam [1765]), 3b-4a.

[566]*b. Sanhedrin* 98a.

[567]*Nevu'at ha-Yeled* is attributed to Naḥman Ḥatufa (Katufa). The exact date of its composition is unknown. Maimonides' grandson Rabbi David ha-Nagid (1222-1300) allegedly penned a commentary to *Nevu'at ha-Yeled*, so certainly it was known by his time.

As pointed out by Rabbi Abraham Halevi in his commentary, *Nevu'at ha-Yeled* shares certain themes in common with other apocalyptic literature such as [*'Atidot*] *Rav Hai Gaon, Nistarot Rabbi Shim'on ben Yoḥai, 'Asarah 'Otot* [*ha-'Atidim*], and *Nevu'at Zerubavel.* (That may be said as well for the material found at the end of the thirtieth chapter of *Pirkei de-Rabbi Eliezer;* see *Pirke De Rabbi Eliezer,* ed. Gerald Friedlander, London, 1916, p. 222, n. 3. That additional material is not found in Rabbi David Luria's edition of *PDRE.*) See Rabbi Abraham Halevi, *Sheloshah Ma'amrei Ge'ulah,* ed. Amnon Gross (Jerusalem, 2000), pp. 63, 92, 93, 95. Those apocalyptic works were assembled in Yehudah Even-Shmuel (Kaufman), *Midreshei Ge'ulah* (Giv'atayim-Ramat Gan: Mosad Bialik, 1968). Cf. ibid. pp. 134, 191, 316 (*"ha-'ot ha-shevi'i,"* lines 35-36), 79 (and *variae lectiones* at the end of the volume).

Most blatant are the common themes in the fifth prophecy, such as Armilus (Romulus) "born of Satan and Stone, who is the tenth horn" (*"Kam min sitna ... yelid avna, de-hu 'asiri karna"*). See Even-Shmuel, p. 53, n. 70 and p. 80, lines 97-98 of *Sefer Zerubavel;* and p. 195 (*Nistarot shel Rabbi Shim'on ben Yoḥai*). The symbol of the tenth horn or tenth king (of Rome) comes from the Book of Daniel 7:7, 20, 24. See Even-Shmuel, p. 76.

The previous stanza which tells how Israel, exiled to the desert, shall eat briny plants and *retama* roots for forty-five days (*"Tsimḥei meluḥin ve-shorashei retamin, akhlin mem-he yomin"*), is also to be found in *Nistarot shel Rabbi Shim'on ben Yoḥai* (Even-Shmuel, p. 195).

[568]For my transcription of the fifth prophecy, I have utilized the superior version of *Nevu'at ha-Yeled* accompanied by the commentary of Rabbi Abraham Halevi (1517), published in Gross's collection, *Sheloshah Ma'amrei Ge'ulah.* See ibid. pp. 84, 93-94.

[569]*Nevuat ha-Yeled* with commentary of Isaac Halevi Satanow (Berlin, 1789), Fifth Prophecy [p. 19]. The word "pope" is derived ultimately from the Greek πάππας *(páppas)* or "father."

Nevu'at ha-Yeled was highly regarded in Ḥasidic circles: Breslov, Lubavitch, Nadvorna. See Rabbi Samuel Halevi Horowitz, *Avaneha Barzel,* in *Kokhvei 'Or* (Jerusalem, 1998), pp. 437-438, Rabbi Menaḥem Mendel Shneurson of Lubavitch, *Derekh Emunah / Sefer ha-Ḥakirah* (Poltava, 1912), 50a; and Rabbi Mordechai Leifer of Nadvorna, *Ma'amar Mordekhai* (M. Sighet, 1900), 40b. See further Bezalel Naor, *From a Kabbalist's Diary* (Spring Valley, NY: Orot, 2005), pp. 145-150.

As for the high regard in which Rav Kook held Rabbi Menaḥem Mendel of Lubavitch, author of Responsa *Tsemaḥ Tsedek,* see *Igrot ha-Rayah* (Jerusalem, 1961), p. 290 (Letter 682).

Appendix 11

The Mysterious *Nunim* of Psalm 107

In the *TaNaKh*, or Bible, there are two places where there appear in the spaces between verses the Hebrew letter *nun*. The most famous occurrence is in the Pentateuch in *Parashat Beha'alotekha* (Numbers 10:35-36), where traditionally the two verses are bracketed by a letter *nun* before and after:

> נ וַיְהִי בִּנְסֹעַ הָאָרֹן, וַיֹּאמֶר מֹשֶׁה: קוּמָה ה׳, וְיָפֻצוּ אֹיְבֶיךָ, וְיָנֻסוּ מְשַׂנְאֶיךָ, מִפָּנֶיךָ. וּבְנֻחֹה,
> יֹאמַר: שׁוּבָה ה׳, רִבְבוֹת אַלְפֵי יִשְׂרָאֵל. נ

> And it was, when the Ark traveled, [that] Moses said: "Rise up, O LORD, and let Your enemies be scattered; and let them that hate You flee before You." And when it rested, he said: "Return, O LORD, [unto] the ten thousands of Israel."

In that case, two eminent *tanna'im* (sages of the Mishnah) disagreed as to the significance of the *simaniyot* or signs. According to Rabbi [Judah the Prince], the marks come to distinguish these verses as a separate book, apart from the rest of the Book of Numbers. Thus in reality, there are not *five* Books of Moses but *seven*! (Numbers itself compartmentalizes into three books: the portion before the two verses; the two verses discussed; and the portion after the two verses.) The other *tanna*, Rabbi Shim'on [ben Gamliel], was of the opinion that the two *nunim* signify dislocation. The two verses do not belong here but somewhere else (in the portion of the *Degalim*, the banners or standards).[570] The reason they were inserted here? To provide a break between one punishment (*pur'anut*) and another; a breather between one calamity and the next. The first calamity is the Children of Israel distancing themselves from the "Mountain of the Lord," i.e. Mount Sinai. The second calamity is their base desire for meat.[571]

There is one other place in the *TaNaKh* where we find these *simaniyot*: the verses of the "*yoredei ha-yam*" (seafarers) in Psalms 107:23-28. According to Masoretic tradition, each of these six verses is preceded by a letter *nun*.

> נ יוֹרְדֵי הַיָּם, בָּאֳנִיּוֹת;   עֹשֵׂי מְלָאכָה, בְּמַיִם רַבִּים. נ הֵמָּה רָאוּ, מַעֲשֵׂי ה׳;   וְנִפְלְאוֹתָיו,
> בִּמְצוּלָה. נ וַיֹּאמֶר--וַיַּעֲמֵד, רוּחַ סְעָרָה;   וַתְּרוֹמֵם גַּלָּיו. נ יַעֲלוּ שָׁמַיִם, יֵרְדוּ תְהוֹמוֹת;
> נַפְשָׁם, בְּרָעָה תִתְמוֹגָג. נ יָחוֹגּוּ וְיָנוּעוּ, כַּשִּׁכּוֹר;   וְכָל-חָכְמָתָם, תִּתְבַּלָּע. נ וַיִּצְעֲקוּ אֶל-ה׳,
> בַּצַּר לָהֶם;   וּמִמְּצוּקֹתֵיהֶם, יוֹצִיאֵם.

> Those who go down to the sea in ships; who do work in many waters.
> They saw the deeds of the LORD, and His wonders in the deep.
> For He commanded, and raised the storm wind, which lifted up [the sea's] waves.
> They ascended to the heavens, they descended to the depths; their soul melted away because of trouble.
> They reeled to and fro, and staggered like a drunken man; and all their wisdom was swallowed up.
> They cried unto the LORD in their trouble, and He brought them out of their distress.

As opposed to the verses concerning the travels of the Ark in the wilderness, where the sages provided clear-cut explanations for the *simaniyot*, here, on the "high seas," things are rather sketchy. There is a brief discussion in the *Talmud Bavli*, *Rosh Hashanah* 17b, but essentially, the signs remain a mystery.[572]

Our guide throughout this work, Rav Kook, of blessed memory, does not discuss the *nunim* of the Psalm, but he does discuss in some depth the earlier, more famous signs of Numbers. With the reader's permission, I shall apply Rav Kook's method of interpretation to the verses of the *"yoredei ha-yam ba-'oniyot,"* the sea voyagers.

In a discourse devoted to *Parashat Beha'alotekha*, preserved in Rav Kook's own hand in one of the *Eight Journals* (*Shemonah Kevatsim*),[573] the Rav differentiated between two lights: the Light of Moses (*'oro shel Moshe*) and the Light of Messiah (*'oro shel Mashi'aḥ). T*hough they were once united in the "supernal splendor of the First Man" (*zihara 'ila'ah de-Adam ha-Rishon*),[574] unfortunately they have since come apart.

Rav Kook's opens his discourse with this salvo:

> Moses our Teacher includes all of the souls of Israel from the aspect of the Torah; and Messiah includes them in and of themselves, from (the aspect of) "the thought of Israel" that precedes all.[575] Is not the soul of Israel the root of the Torah and its inwardness (*penimiyut*)? The Torah was created for Israel.[576] Therefore, it is said of the Messiah, "He shall be very high," even higher than Moses.[577] Yet, from the aspect of the revelation of the Torah, Messiah merely comes close to the level of Moses.[578]

The prerequisite for the Torah of Moses is *bushah*, shame. At Mount Sinai there was instilled a sense of shame, as it is written, "In order that His fear be upon your faces."[579] This was interpreted by the sages, of blessed memory, to refer to "shame."[580] The hallmark of Messiah's Torah is the exact opposite: *ḥutspah*, impudence. "In the footsteps of Messiah, *ḥutspah* shall increase."[581]

Moses cannot abide the impudent. In the words of Rav Kook, Moses "cannot illuminate within the *ḥutspah*." That is precisely the point at which Messiah enters the picture.

Within the entire Torah there is a single incursion of the Messianic dimension, a single brilliant flash of the Light of Messiah—the two verses of *Vayehi bi-neso'a ha-'aron* ("And it was, when the Ark traveled ..."):

> That is the light that shines in the portion of *Vayehi bi-neso'a ha-'aron*, which was written in the middle between one calamity and another; the Light of Messiah that fears not *ḥutspah*, whether it be that of abandonment of the Torah[582] and "fleeing the school"[583] [alluded to] in the verse "They traveled [away] from the Mountain of the Lord,"[584] or grumbling[585] and debasement to the desire of meat.[586]

Messiah has "broad shoulders." Moses is incapable of shedding a ray of light on a landscape grown so dark that the Torah has been forsaken and the people hanker for meat. On this dark horizon, there explode the pyrotechnics of Messiah, capable of countenancing *ḥutspah* of epic proportions.

As a lifelong student of Rav Kook, the thought occurs to me that he might treat the enigmatic *nunim* of the Psalm of the seafarers in a similar fashion.

In the Ḥasidic tradition, at the afternoon service on the eve of the Sabbath, Psalm 107 is recited. The custom was instituted by the Ba'al Shem Tov himself.[587] Ostensibly, the reason for this custom is that at this time, the souls assigned to Gehinnom are released for the duration of the Sabbath. At the conclusion of the Sabbath, they must return to purgatory. This Psalm describes the process whereby the souls are raised from the depths.[588] In the commentary ascribed to the Ba'al Shem Tov,[589] a focal point is the cluster of verses of the *yoredei ha-yam*. A great soul descends to the depths of the sea to raise up and redeem "the oppressed souls" (*neshamot ha-'ashukot*).[590]

Lo and behold, this lifeline extended to the drowning, this Messianic beacon of light flashing a ship lost at sea, is indicated by the appearance of telltale *simaniyot* in the form of *nunim*.

One asks: What has all of this to do with the legends of Rabbah bar Bar Ḥannah? It was none other than the illustrious Vilna Gaon who observed at the onset of his commentary to the legends that they are based on the passage of the *"yoredei ha-yam,"* the sea voyagers, in Psalm 107!

[570]The medieval commentators were divided as to the exact location within the Book of Numbers. See Saul Lieberman, *Hellenism in Jewish Palestine* (New York: JTSA, 1994), p. 40.

[571]See *Sifra, Beha'alotekha*; and *b. Shabbat* 115b-116a. Cf. *Shabbat* 104a: *"Simanin 'aseh ba-Torah."* For a lengthy treatment of the subject, see Lieberman, op. cit., pp. 38-43.

For the practical application of the law (*halakhah le-ma'aseh*), see Rabbi Solomon Ganzfried, *Keset ha-Sofer* (Ungvar, 1871), 15:7, 8 (29a); and the appended *Lishkat ha-Sofer, ḥakirah* 17 (64a-d).

[572]See further the commentaries of Rashi and Rabbi Yedidyah Norzi, *Minḥat Shai* to Psalm 107; Rabbi Nathan of Rome, *'Arukh*, s.v. *akin ve-rakin*; Rav Hai Gaon, quoted in *Ḥiddushei Rashba, Shabbat* 103a. A comprehensive discussion may be found in Rabbi Eliyahu Katz, Responsa *Be'er Eliyahu, Orah Ḥayyim* I (Be'er Sheva, 2003), no. 118 (pp. 139-144). (The latter source was brought to my attention by Rabbi Moshe Zuriel *shelit"a*.)

[573]This discourse was first published in the booklet *Ginzei Rayah* 2: *Ḥodesh ha-Aviv* (n.p., n.d.), pp. 26-28, under the title "Moses and Messiah." Today it is available in *Shemonah Kevatsim* 8:157.

[574]The term comes from the *Zohar*. See *Zohar* I, 36b. Cf. *Ra'aya Mehemna* in *Zohar* III, 83; and the explication of the discourse in Rabbi Ḥayyim Vital, *Sha'ar Ma'amrei Rashbi* (Jerusalem, 1898), *Kedoshim*, 37a. And see the sources provided by Rabbi David Cohen (the Nazirite) to *Orot ha-Kodesh*, vol. I, p. 279 (*"Zihara 'Ila'ah"*); published in vol. 2, pp. 597-598.

[575]*Genesis Rabbah* 1:4.

[576]See *Seder Eliyahu Rabbah*, chap. 14:

> There are two things in the world that I totally love: Torah and Israel. But I do not know which comes first. I said to him: "My son, it is the way of men to say that the Torah comes first, for it is said, 'The Lord possessed me, the beginning of His way' [Proverbs 8:22]. But I say, Israel come first, for it says, 'Israel is holy to the Lord, the beginning of His harvest' [Jeremiah 2:3]."

See *Seder Eliahu Rabba*, ed. M. Friedmann (Vienna, 1902), chap. 15 (p. 71).

Rav Kook quotes this passage in a halakhic responsum to Rabbi Zalman Pines, penned in St. Gallen, Switzerland on 19 Tevet, 5676 (1916). See *Mishpat Kohen*, no. 144:6 (327a). Rav Kook argued that saving the Jewish People from physical destruction (*hatsalat Kelal Yisrael*) comes under the rubric of preserving the fabric of the Torah (*le-migdar milta*).

For the unique halakhic situation of *"hatsalat Kelal Yisrael,"* see the earlier responsa of Rabbi Joseph Colon, *She'elot u-Teshuvot Mararik*, no. 167; and Rabbi Ezekiel Landau, *She'elot u-Teshuvot Noda' bi-Yehudah Tinyana, Yoreh De'ah*, no. 161.

[577]Isaiah 52:13; *Midrash Tanḥuma, Toledot* 14. See Rabbi Ḥanokh Zundel ben Yosef, *'Anaf Yosef* there, who quotes Rabbi Samuel Laniado's commentary to Isaiah, *Keli Paz* (Venice, 1657). (Rabbi Laniado, in turn, quotes Don Isaac Abrabanel.) And see *'Arpalei Tohar* (Jerusalem, 1983), p. 17 = *Shemonah Kevatsim* 2:35.

[578]Maimonides, *MT*, *Hil. Teshuvah* 9:2. See Rabbi Ḥayyim Kanievsky, *Kiryat Melekh* (B'nei Berak, 1983), ad locum.

[579]Exodus 20:16.

[580]*b. Nedarim* 20a.

[581]*m. Sotah* 9:15; *b. Sotah* 49b. In *Orot*, Rav Kook writes: "Without the insolence of 'the footsteps of Messiah' (*ha-ḥutspah de-'ikva di-Meshiḥa*), it would be impossible to explain mysteries of the Torah openly." See *Orot ha-Teḥiyah* (Lights of Renascence), chap. 39; in *Orot*, ed. Naor (2015), p. 363.

[582]*b. Ta'anit* 29a; *Shabbat* 116a.

[583]According to the Midrash, they were "as a child fleeing from school" (*ke-tinok ha-bore'aḥ mi-beit ha-sefer*). *Midrash Yelamdenu*, quoted in *Tosafot, Shabbat* 116a, s.v. *pur'anut rishonah vayyis'u*. (In Naḥmanides' commentary to Numbers 10:35 [Chavel ed., p. 231] it is referred to as an anonymous *Aggadah*.) Earlier, we have an Aramaic version of this *derash* in *y. Ta'anit* 4:5 in the name of Rabbi Zechariah, the son-in-law of Rabbi Levi (*"le-'ilein talayya de-mitpenei min sifra ve-nafkin lon bi-kefarei"*).

[584]Numbers 10:33.

[585]Numbers 11:1.

[586]Numbers 11:4. Rav Kook's great-grandfather, Rabbi Dov Baer Jaffe of Utian, arrived at an ingenious halakhic connection between the decampment from Sinai and the sudden craving for meat, based on *b. Zevaḥim* 60b and the opinion of Rabbi Ishmael in *b. Ḥullin* 17a. This insight was recorded by his son, Rabbi Mordechai Gimpel Jaffe, *Tekhelet Mordekhai* [supercommentary to Naḥmanides] (Jerusalem: Levin-Epstein, n.d. [1954]), Numbers 10:35, s.v. *Vayehi bi-neso'a ha-'aron* (125b-126a).

[587]One may consider authoritative the statement to this effect by Rabbi Menaḥem Naḥum Twersky of Chernobyl in *Me'or 'Eynayim, Beshallaḥ*: "This is [the reason] the Besht, of blessed memory, instituted saying every Eve of the Sabbath Psalm 107…" See *Me'or 'Eynayim* (Slavuta, 1798), 57b.

Rabbi David Yitsḥak Eizik Rabinowitz (1898-1979), the Skolyer Rebbe of Vienna and Brooklyn, inherited the *niggun* (tune) of the Ba'al Shem Tov to Psalm 107. According to family tradition, it was transmitted in an unbroken chain from the Ba'al Shem Tov. The Skolyer was a direct descendant of Rabbi Barukh of Mezhbizh, grandson of the Ba'al Shem Tov. (This *niggun* was brought to my attention by my dear friend Rabbi Naḥman Schneider.)

[588]See Rivka Schatz, "The Commentary of R. Israel Ba'al Shem Tov to Psalm cvii—The Myth and the Ritual of 'The Descent to She'ol'" (Hebrew), *Tarbiz*, Tishri-Adar 5733 [1972-1973], pp. 154-184.

Rabbi Abraham David Lavut of Nikolayev has a different explanation for the recitation of Psalm 107 at this time. It serves a retroactive rather than proactive purpose. Rather than relating to the forthcoming salvation of souls from Gehinnom for the duration of the Sabbath, this is an utterance of thanksgiving for our having survived and not succumbed to the material challenges of the past week (i.e. the struggle to make a living). Thus, it is conceived as a sort of *birkat ha-gomel* (cf. *b. Berakhot* 54b). For that reason, Rabbi Lavut advocates that it be recited before a quorum of ten! See Rabbi A.D. Lavut, *Sha'ar ha-Kollel*, appended to *Siddur Torah 'Or 'al pi Nusaḥ ha-Ari zal* (Vilna: Romm, 1935), 17:2 (22d).

[589]Though Rivka Schatz (see previous note) was convinced that the commentary was composed by the Besht, of late, Chaim Elly Moseson has deconstructed her supposed proofs. See Chaim Elly Moseson, *From Spoken Word to the Discourse of the Academy: Reading the Sources for the Teachings of the Besht* (Ph.D. dissertation, Boston University, 2017), pp. 140-148. In Moseson's opinion, it is unlikely that there issued from the pen of the Besht other than personal communications (ibid., pp. 148-149). Moseson concludes: "The fact that the Besht was known to have encouraged the recitation of this Psalm on Friday afternoon for Kabbalistic reasons similar to those expounded in the commentary, probably contributed to its association with him, to the point that, whether it first occurred in print or already in manuscript, it came to be attributed to him directly" (ibid., p. 148). I thank Dr. Moseson for sharing his yet unpublished dissertation.

I might add that Schatz ("The Commentary of R. Israel Ba'al Shem Tov to Psalm cvii," p. 159) mistakenly accepted at face value the attribution to Rabbi Menaḥem Mendel Shneurson of Lubavitch (author responsa *Tsemaḥ Tsedek*) of a teaching contained in Rabbi Ḥayyim Liebersohn, *Tseror ha-Ḥayyim* (Bilgoray, 1913). It has since been established that the teaching is by Rabbi Jacob Perlow of Novominsk (author *Shufra de-Ya'akov*). See Rabbi Yosef Perlow, *"Emet le-Ya'akov," Heikhal ha-Besht* 35 (Tishri 5774), pp. 131-148; and the new edition of *Shufra de-Ya'akov*, ed. Rabbi Yosef Perlow (Jerusalem, 2016), Introduction, p. 9; and *Balak*, s.v. *yizzal mayim mi-dalyav* (448b-449a). (At some future date, I may demonstrate that there is overlap between that particular *ma'amar*—as well as other *ma'amarim* of the same curious provenance—and the Ḥabad *ma'amarim* of Rabbi Aharon Halevi Horowitz of Staroselye, printed in his work *'Avodat ha-Levi*, but that is a separate discussion.)

[590]See above note 68.

Kabbalistic Chart

'Olamot	***Partsufim***	***Sefirot***	**5 Levels of Soul**	**3 Dimensions of *Sefer Yetsirah*[591]**
Adam Kadmon	*Arikh Anpin*	*Keter*	*Yeḥidah*	
Atsilut	*Abba*	*Ḥokhmah*	*Ḥayah*	
Beri'ah	*Imma*	*Binah*	*Neshamah*	*'Olam* (Space)
Yetsirah	*Ze'ir Anpin*	*Vav Ketsavot*[592]	*Ru'aḥ*	*Nefesh* (Soul)
'Asiyah	*Nukva*	*Malkhut*	*Nefesh*	*Shanah* (Time)

[591]Based on the system of the Vilna Gaon in *Likkutei ha-Gra* appended to *Be'ur ha-Gra* to *Sifra di-Tseni'uta*. See above Appendix 2.

[592]*Vav Ketsavot* or "Six Extremities" is shorthand for the six *sefirot* of *Ḥesed, Gevurah, Tif'eret, Netsaḥ, Hod* and *Yesod*.

Lexicon of Kabbalistic Technical Terms

Bat Kol (Divine voice) – *Malkhut*

'Elohim Ḥayyim ("Living God," a cognomen of the divinity) – *Binah*

'Emet (Truth) – *Tif'eret*

'Erets (Earth) – *Malkhut*

Ḥakal Tapuḥin (Aramaic, Apple Orchard) – *Malkhut*

Levanah (Moon) – *Malkhut*

Mayim (Water) – *Binah*

Melekh (King) – *Tif'eret* (or *Ze'ir 'Anpin*)

Nahar ha-yots'e me-'Eden ("the River that issues from Eden") – *Binah*

'Olam ha-Ba (also in Aramaic, *'Alma de-'Atei,* the World to Come) – *Binah*

Peh (Mouth) – *Malkhut*

Reḥovot ha-Nahar (the Expanses of the River) – *Binah*

Sdeh Tapuḥim (Hebrew, Apple Orchard) – *Malkhut*

Shamayim (Heaven) – *Tif'eret*

Shekhinah (Divine Indwelling) – *Malkhut*

Shemen (Oil) – *Ḥokhmah*

Shemitah (the seventh or Sabbatical year) – *Malkhut*

Yovel (the fiftieth or Jubilee year) – *Binah*

Bibliography of Works Cited by Rav Kook

Arama, Isaac. *ʿAkedat Yitsḥak* (Commentary to Pentateuch)

Buzaglo, Shalom. *Mikdash Melekh* (Commentary to *Zohar*)

Cordovero, Moses. *ʾOr Neʿerav*

Elijah ben Solomon (Vilna Gaon). Commentary to Proverbs

_____. Commentary to *Tikkunei Zohar*

Ḥaver, Yitsḥak Eizik. *Beit ʿOlamim* (Commentary to *ʾIdra Rabba*, section of *Zohar*)

Ḥayyim ben Isaac (of Volozhin). *Nefesh ha-Ḥayyim*

Luzzatto, Moses Ḥayyim. *ʾAdir ba-Marom* (Commentary to *ʾIdra Rabba*, section of *Zohar*)

_____ (attributed to—). *KaLaḤ Pitḥei Ḥokhmah*

Naḥmanides, Moses. Commentary to Pentateuch

Paquda, Baḥya ibn. *Ḥovot ha-Levavot* (*Duties of the Heart*)

Shneur Zalman ben Barukh (of Liadi). *Likkutei Torah* (commentary to Leviticus, Numbers, Deuteronomy and Song of Songs)

Vital, Ḥayyim. *Sefer ha-Gilgulim* (*Book of Reincarnations*)

General Bibliography

Aaron Hakohen of Apta (Opatów). *Keter Shem Tov.* Part Two. Zolkiew, 1795; Brooklyn, 1981.

Abraham ben Eliezer Halevi. *Peirush Nevu'at ha-Yeled.* In: *Sheloshah Ma'amrei Ge'ulah.* Ed. Amnon Gross. Jerusalem, 2000.

Aḥdut, Eli. "Jewish-Zoroastrian Polemics in the Babylonian Talmud" (Hebrew). *Irano-Judaica* 4 (1999), 17-40.

Alfasi, Isaac. *She'elot u-Teshuvot Rabbeinu Yitsḥak Alfasi*. Livorno, 1781.

Alster, Yitsḥak. *'Olat Yitsḥak*. 2 vols. Jerusalem, 2003-2005.

Alter, Judah Aryeh Leib. *Sefat Emet.* 5 vols. Piotrków—Cracow, 1905-1908.

Arieli, Isaac. *'Eynayim le-Mishpat*. Tractate *Kiddushin*. Jerusalem, 1936.

Arzy, Shaḥar, and Idel, Moshe. *Kabbalah: A Neurocognitive Approach to Mystical Experiences.* New Haven, 2015.

Ashlag, Judah Leib. *Ha-Sulam*. Commentary to *Zohar.* 10 vols. London, 1970-1971.

Avidor, Shmuel Hakohen. *Ha-Ish neged ha-zerem*. Tel-Aviv, 1962. New edition with marginalia of Tsevi Yehudah Hakohen Kook. Tel-Aviv, 2002.

Aviner, Shelomo. *Tsevi Kodesh.* (Biography of Rabbi Tsevi Yehudah Hakohen Kook.) vol. 1. Beit El, 2005.

Aviner, Shelomo, and Neuman, Ze'ev (Ed.). *Rabbenu: Harav Tsevi Yehudah Hakohen Kook* (pictorial album). Jerusalem, 2004.

Avivi, Yosef. *Kabbalat ha-Gra*. Jerusalem, 1993.

_____. *Kabbalat ha-Rayah*. 4 vols. Jerusalem, 2018.

_____. *Zohar Ramḥal*. Jerusalem, 1997.

Azriel of Gerona. *Commentary on Talmudic Aggadoth*. Ed. Isaiah Tishby. Jerusalem, 1982.

Ba'al Shem, Israel. *Ba'al Shem Tov 'al ha-Torah.* Ed. Shim'on Menaḥem Mendel [Wodnik] of Gowarczów. Lodz, 1938.

Baḥya ben Asher ibn Ḥalawa. Commentary to Pentateuch. Ed. Charles B. Chavel. 3 vols. Jerusalem, 1968.

Baḥya ibn Pakuda. *The Book of Direction to the Duties of the Heart* (*Al-Hidaya ila Fara'id al-Qulub*). Trans. and ed. Menaḥem Mansoor. Oxford, 1973.

Barg, Mordechai Gimpel. *Be'er Mordechai.* Jerusalem, 1926.

Bedersi, Yedayah ("Ha-Penini"). *Beḥinat ha-'Olam.* Mantua, 1478.

Ben-Arza, Sarah Friedland. *"Shekhenut ve-Korat Gag."* In *Me'at la-Tsaddik.* Ed. Gershon Kitsis. Jerusalem, 2000.

Benayahu, Meir. *Kabbalistic Writings of R. Moshe Ḥayyim Luzzatto* (Hebrew). Jerusalem, 1979.

_____. *Toledot ha-Ari.* (Biography of Rabbi Isaac Luria.) Ramat-Gan, 1967.

_____. *Yosef Beḥiri.* (Biography of Rabbi Joseph Karo.) Jerusalem, 1991.

Ben-Naïm, Joseph. *Malkei Rabbanan.* Jerusalem, 1931.

Berlin, Naftali Tsevi Yehudah. *Ha'amek Davar.* Commentary to Pentateuch. Vilna, 1879.

Bialik, Ḥayyim Naḥman. *"Metei Midbar."* Odessa, 1902. Available at http://benyehuda.org/bialik/metey.html

Blaser, Isaac. *'Or Yisrael.* Vilna, 1900.

Blau, Moshe. *'Al Ḥomotayikh Yerushalayim.* Tel-Aviv, 1946.

Bornstein, Samuel (of Sokhatchov). *Shem mi-Shmuel.* Jerusalem, 1974.

Brown, Benjamin. *The Ḥazon Ish: Halakhist, Believer and Leader of the Ḥaredi Revolution* (Hebrew). Jerusalem, 2011.

Buzaglo, Shalom. *Mikdash Melekh.* Amsterdam, 1750.

Chajes, J.H. *Between Worlds: Dybbuks, Exorcists, and Early Modern Judaism.* Philadelphia, 2003.

Cohen, David. *Tikkunim be-Sifrei ha-Tur*. Brooklyn, 1995.

Cohen, David ("the Nazirite"). *Ḥug ha-Rayah: Shi'urei Rabbenu David Cohen, HaRav Ha-Nazir ... 'al 'Orot ha-Kodesh*. Ed. Harel Cohen. vol. 1. Jarusalem, 2018.

_____. *Kol ha-Nevu'ah*. Jerusalem, 1979.

_____. *Mangeinot ha-Tikkunim*. Commentary to *Tikkunei Zohar*. Ms. excerpted in *Pitḥei ha-Pardes*.

_____. *Pitḥei ha-Pardes*. Commentary to *KaLaḤ Pitḥei Ḥokhmah*. Jerusalem 2009.

Cordovero, Moses. *'Or Ne'erav*. Venice, 1587.

_____. *Pardes Rimonim*. Munkatsh [Mukachevo], 1906; photo-offset Jerusalem, 1962.

_____. *Shi'ur Komah*. Warsaw, 1883.

Dov Baer of Linitz (Illintsi). *Shivḥei ha-Besht*. Ed. Avraham Rubinstein. Jerusalem, 2005.

Dov Baer of Mezritch. *Maggid Devarav le-Ya'akov*. Ed. Solomon of Lutzk. Koretz, 1781; Brooklyn, 1986.

_____. *'Or Torah*. Ed. Isaiah of Dinowitz. Koretz, 1804; Brooklyn, 1986.

Eisenstein, Judah David. *The Tales of Rabbah bar-bar Ḥannah*. New York, 1937.

Eliach, Dov. *Avi ha-Yeshivot*. (Biography of Rabbi Ḥayyim of Volozhin.) Jerusalem, 2011.

_____. *Ha-Gaon*. (Biography of Vilna Gaon.) 3 vols. Jerusalem, 2002.

Elijah ben Solomon Zalman (of Vilna). *Aderet Eliyahu*. Commentary to Pentateuch. With super-commentary of Yitsḥak Eizik Ḥaver. *Be'er Yitsḥak*. Ed. Samuel Luria. Warsaw, 1887.

_____. *Be'ur ha-Gra* to *Sifra di-Tseni'uta*. Ed. Jacob Moses of Slonim. Vilna and Horadna, 1820. Ed. Samuel Luria. Vilna, 1882. Ed. Bezalel Naor. With *variae lectiones* and glosses of Moses Solomon of Tolochin from the manuscript of the Library of Congress, Washington, DC. Jerusalem, 1997.

_____. Commentary of Gra to *Sefer Yetsirah*. Ed. Menaḥem Mendel of Shklov. Horadna, 1806. Ed. Samuel Luria. Warsaw, 1884.

_____. *Likkutei ha-Gra*. Appended to *Be'ur ha-Gra* to *Sifra de-Tseni'uta*. Ed. Samuel Luria. Vilna, 1882.

_____. *Likkutei Torah me-ha-Gaon Rabbeinu Eliyahu mi-Vilna*. Ed. Yisrael Ḥayyim Mikhel Levensohn. Warsaw, 1899.

_____. *Peirush 'al Kamah Aggadot*. Including *Aggadot Rabbah bar Bar Ḥannah*. Vilna, 1800.

_____. *Peirush 'al Yonah*. Commentary of the Vilna Gaon to the Book of Jonah. Vilna, 1800.

_____. *Sefer Mishlei 'im Be'ur ha-Gra*. Commentary to the Book of Proverbs. [Ed. Menaḥem Mendel of Shklov]. Ed. Moshe Philip. B'nei Berak, 1985.

_____. *Tikkunei Zohar* with commentary of Vilna Gaon. Vilna, 1867.

_____. *Yahel 'Or*. Commentary of the Vilna Gaon to *Zohar*. Ed. Naftali Herz Halevi Weidenbaum (of Bialystok). Vilna, 1882.

Eliashov, Shelomo. *Leshem Shevo ve-Aḥlamah: Hakdamot u-She'arim*. Piotrków, 1909.

_____. *Ḥelek ha-Be'urim*. Jerusalem, 1935.

_____. *Sefer ha-De'ah*. Piotrków, 1912.

Epstein, Aryeh Leib. *Halakhah Aḥaronah ve-Kuntres ha-Re'ayot*. Koenigsberg, 1859.

Epstein, Isidore. *Avraham Yitzhak Hacohen Kook: His Life and Works*. n.p. [London], 1951.

Epstein, Perle. *Pilgrimage: Adventures of a Wandering Jew*. Boston, 1979.

Eshed, Eli. *"Sefer Kol ha-Tor—Aggadah Rivlina'it o Moreshet ha-Gra?"* In *Be-Ḥadrei Ḥaredim, Forum: Sefarim ve-Soferim*, Dec. 11, 2009. Available at the blogspot: bhol.co.il

Even-Shmuel (Kaufman), Yehudah. *Midreshei Ge'ulah*. Giv'atayim-Ramat Gan, 1968.

Eybeschuetz, Jonathan. *Luḥot 'Edut*. Altona, 1755.

Ezra of Gerona. *Commentary to Song of Songs*. In *Kitvei Ramban*, vol. 2. Ed. Charles B. Chavel. Jerusalem, 1968.

Feldman, Aharon. *The Juggler and the King: The Jew and the Conquest of Evil: An Elaboration of the Vilna Gaon's Insights into the Hidden Wisdom of the Sages*. Israel, 1990.

Fisher, Shelomo Yehonatan Yehudah. *Beit Yishai: Derashot*. Israel, 2004.

Fishman, David E. *Russia's First Modern Jews: The Jews of Shklov*. New York, 1995.

Forshlager, Michael. *Mikha'el be-Aḥat*. (Biography of Rabbi Forshlager.) Ed. Ben Zion Bergman. Ashdod, 2013.

Frankel, Yonah. *Darkhei ha-Aggadah ve-ha-Midrash*. vol. 1. Giv'atayim, 1991.

Gabbai, Meir ibn. *'Avodat ha-Kodesh*. Warsaw, 1891; photo-offset Jerusalem, 1973.

Ganzfried, Solomon. *Keset ha-Sofer*. Ungvar, 1871.

Gikatilla, Joseph. *Sha'arei Orah*. Ed. Joseph Ben Shlomo. 2 vols. Jerusalem, 1970.

_____. *Sha'arei Orah. Gates of Light*. Trans. Avi Weinstein. San Francisco, 1994.

Ginzburg, Simon. *Rabbi Moshe Ḥayyim Luzzatto u-V'nei Doro*. Tel-Aviv, 1937.

Goldberg, Hillel. "Rabbi Isaac Hutner: A Synoptic Interpretive Biography." *Tradition* 22 (4), Winter 1987, pp. 18-46.

Gordon, Hirsch Loeb. *The Maggid of Caro*. New York, 1949.

Gottlieb, Efraim (Ed.). *Hebrew Writings of the Author of Tiqqunei Zohar and Ra'aya Mehemna*. Jerusalem, 2003.

Grossman, Abraham. "Praises of Rabbi El'azar b. Qilir in R. Joseph Qara's Commentary on *Piyyutim*" (Hebrew). In *Knesset Ezra: Literature and Life in the Synagogue* (Studies Presented to Ezra Fleischer), pp. 293-308. Ed. S. Elizur, M.D. Herr, G. Shaked, A. Shinan. Jerusalem, 1994.

Ḥarlap, Ya'akov Moshe. *Leḥem Abirim*. Jerusalem, 1993.

_____. *Mi-M'ayenei ha-Yeshu'ah*. Jerusalem, 1981.

Ḥaver (Wildman), Yitsḥak Eizik . *Afikei Yam*. 2 vols. Jerusalem, 1994.

_____. *Beit 'Olamim*. Warsaw, 1889.

_____. *Ginzei Meromim* (commentary to *Masekhet 'Atsilut). Masekhet 'Atsilut 'im Be'ur Ginzei Meromim.* Johannisburg, 1864. Ed. Yonatan Meir. Jerusalem, 2000.

_____. *Magen ve-Tsinah.* Koenigsberg or Johannisburg, 1855; Jerusalem, 2005.

_____. *Pitḥei She'arim.* Warsaw, 1888; photo-offset Tel-Aviv, 1964.

Ḥayyim of Volozhin. *Nefesh ha-Ḥayyim.* Vilna and Horadna, 1824.

Heilman, Ḥayyim Meir. *Beit Rabbi.* 3 vols. Berdichev, 1902.

Hershkowitz, Isaac. "Innovative Aspects in the Research of *Kol HaTor*" (Hebrew). *Da'at* 79-80 (2015), 163-182.

Hillel, Moshe. *'Over la-Soḥer: R. Yitsḥak ben R. Michael Copio: Bein Me'arat Sdeh ha-Makhpelah le-'Arba Me'ot Shekel Kesef.* Jerusalem, 2016.

Hirschensohn, Ḥayyim. *Motsa'ei Mayim.* Budapest, 1924.

Horowitz, Aharon Halevi (of Staroselye). *'Avodat ha-Levi.* Vol. 1. Genesis-Exodus-Leviticus. Lemberg, 1861. vol. 2. Numbers-Deuteronomy. Warsaw, 1866.

Horowitz, Isaiah Halevi. *Shnei Luḥot ha-Berit.*Amsterdam, 1648-1649.

Horowitz, Samuel Halevi. *Avaneha Barzel.* In *Kokhvei 'Or.* Jerusalem, 1998.

Horowitz, Shabtai Sheftel Halevi. *Nishmat Shabtai Halevi.* Prague, 1616.

Horowitz, Shmuel Shmelke Halevi (of Nikolsburg). *Divrei Shmuel.* Lemberg, 1862.

Hurwitz, Pinḥas Elijah (of Vilna). *Sefer ha-Berit.* 2 parts. Brünn, 1797.

Huss, Boaz. "Demonology and Magic in the Writings of R. Menaḥem Ziyyoni," *Kabbalah* 10 (2004), 55-72.

Hutner, Isaac. *Paḥad Yitsḥak: Igrot u-Ketavim.* Brooklyn, NY, 2016.

_____. *Paḥad Yitsḥak—Yom ha-Kippurim.* New York, 2004.

Ibn Shu'aib, Joshua. *Derashot Rabbeinu Yehoshua ibn Shu'aib.* Ed. Ze'ev Metzger. 2 vols. Jerusalem, 1992.

Ibn Tsur, Moshe. *Me'arat Sdeh ha-Makhpelah.* Jerusalem, 1910.

Idel, Moshe. *Golem: Jewish Magical and Mystical Traditions on the Artificial Anthropoid.* Albany, 1990.

_____. *Ḥasidism: Between Ecstasy and Magic.* Albany, 1995.

Igra, Abraham Joseph. *Toledot Avraham Yosef.* Cracow, 1938; photo-offset Brooklyn, n.d. [1980].

Ilan, Aharon. *'Eynei Yitsḥak.* (Biography of Rabbi Isaac Arieli.) Jerusalem, 2018.

Isaac ben Ḥayyim of Volozhin. *Peh Kadosh.* On Genesis and Exodus. Warsaw, 1890. On Pentateuch. Ed. Dov Eliach. Jerusalem, 1995.

Isaac of Acco (Acre). *Me'irat 'Eynayim.* Ed. Ḥayyim Aryeh Erlanger. Jerusalem, 1993.

Jacob Joseph of Polnoye. *Toledot Ya'akov Yosef.* Korets, 1780.

Jacobs, Louis. *The Jewish Mystics.* Reading, England, 1990.

Jaffe, Mordechai Gimpel. "Kabbalistic Ideas Written by Rabbi Mordechai Gimpel Jaffe" (Hebrew). Winner's Auction, Winner's Unlimited No. 105 (Wednesday, February 21, 2018). Lot 516.

_____. *Tekhelet Mordekhai.* Supercommentary to Naḥmanides on Pentateuch. Jerusalem, n.d. [1954].

Joseph Ḥayyim (of Baghdad). *Ben Yehoyada'.* 4 vols. Jerusalem, 1898-1904.

Judah Leib of Kremnitz. *Ziz Sadai.* Lublin, 1634.

Kanievsky, Ḥayyim. *Kiryat Melekh.* B'nei Berak, 1983.

Kanievsky, Ya'akov. *Ḥayyei 'Olam.* Tel-Aviv, 1967.

Karo, Joseph. *Beit Yosef, Orah Ḥayyim.* Venice, 1550.

_____. *Maggid Meisharim.* Vilna, 1875.

Katz, Ben-Zion. *Rabbanut, Ḥasidut, Haskalah.* Parts 3-4. Tel-Aviv, 1958.

Katz, Eliyahu. Responsa *Be'er Eliyahu.* 3 vols. Be'er Sheva, 2003.

Kempinski, Menaḥem. *Me-Ruzhin le-Tsiyon.* (Biography of Rabbi Meir Yeḥiel Shapira of Drohobycz.) Har Berakha, 2010.

Kiperwasser, Reuven. "Rabba bar bar Ḥana's Voyages" (Hebrew). *Jerusalem Studies in Hebrew Literature* 22 (2008), 215-242.

Kohut, Alexander. *Aruch Completum.* 10 vols. Vienna, 1878—New York, 1892.

Kook, Abraham Isaac Hakohen. *'Arpalei Tohar.* Ed. Yitsḥak Shilat (Greenspan). Jerusalem, 1983.

_____. *"Derekh ha-Teḥiyah." Ha-Nir* 1 (1909). Reprinted in *Ma'amrei ha-Rayah*, vol. 1.

_____. *'Eyn Ayah.* Ed. Ya'akov Filber. 4 vols. Jerusalem, 1987-2000.

_____. *Ginzei Rayah.* Ed. [Ben-Zion Shapira]. vol. 3: *Ge'ulah u-Malkhut* (*Le-Yom ha-'Atsma'ut*). n.p. [Jerusalem], n.d. [1985].

_____. *Ginzei Rayah.* vol. 2: *Ḥodesh ha-Aviv.* n.p., n.d.

_____. *Halakhah Berurah.* Tractate *Beitsah.* Jerusalem, 1940.

_____. *Haskamot ha-Rayah.* 2nd edition. Ed. Ari Chvat, Tsuriel Ḥallamish and Yoḥanan Fried. Jerusalem, 2017.

_____. *"Ḥiddushei ha-Rayah le-Yad ha-Ḥazakah le-ha-Rambam."* In Moshe Zuriel, *Otserot ha-Rayah.* vol. 3. pp. 9-66. Rishon-LeZion, 2002.

_____. *Igrot ha-Rayah.* Ed. Tsevi Yehudah Hakohen Kook. vol. 1: 1888-1910. Jerusalem, 1961. vol. 2: 1911-1915. Jerusalem, 1961. Vol. 3: 1916-1919. Jerusalem, 1965. vol. 4: 1920-1921. Ed. Ze'ev Neuman. Jerusalem, 2018.

_____. *Igrot la-Rayah.* Ed. Ben Zion Shapira. Second expanded edition. Jerusalem, 1990.

_____. *'Ikvei ha-Tson.* Jerusalem, 1906. Reprinted with notes of the author's son Tsevi Yehudah Kook. Jerusalem, 1967.

_____. *'Ittur Soferim.* vol. 1. Vilna, 1888; photo-offset Jerusalem, 1974.

_____. *Kevatsim mi-Ketav Yad Kodsho*. Ed. Boaz Ofen. 3 vols. Jerusalem, 2006 -2018.

_____. *Kitsur Mesillat Yesharim*. In Tsevi Yehudah Kook. *Li-Sheloshah be-Elul*. vol. 2. pp. 23-31. Jerusalem, 1947. Reprinted in *Ma'amrei ha-Rayah*. vol. 2. pp. 273-276. Jerusalem, 1984. And in Moshe Zuriel. *Otserot ha-Rayah*. vol. 2. pp. 297-300. Rishon le-Zion, 2002.

_____. *Koren Rav Kook Siddur*. Commentary by Bezalel Naor. Israel, 2017.

_____. *Li-Nevukhei ha-Dor*. Ed. Shaḥar Raḥmani. Tel-Aviv, 2014.

_____. *Ma'amrei ha-Rayah*. vol. 1. Ed. Elisha Langenauer and David Landau. Jerusalem, 1980. vol. 2. Ed. Elisha Aviner-Langenauer. Jerusalem, 1984.

_____. *Metsi'ot Katan*. Ed. Harel Cohen. Israel, 2018.

_____. *Mishpat Kohen*. Ed. Tsevi Yehudah Hakohen Kook. Jerusalem, 1937.

_____. *Orot*. Ed. Tsevi Yehudah Hakohen Kook. Jerusalem, 1920. Expanded edition with additional material. Jerusalem, 1950. Ed. Bezalel Naor. Bilingual Hebrew-English edition. Israel, 2015.

_____. *Orot Ha-Kodesh*. Ed. David Cohen. 3 vols. Jerusalem, 1985. Vol. 4. David Cohen and Yoḥanan Fried. Jerusalem, 1990.

_____. *Orot ha-Teshuvah*. Ed. Tsevi Yehudah Hakohen Kook. Jerusalem, 1925. 5th edition. Expanded edition with additional material. Jerusalem, 1970.

_____. *Pinkesei ha-Rayah*. vol. 3. Ed. Levi Yitsḥaki. Jerusalem, n.d. [2011]. vol. 4. Ed. Z.M. Levin and B.Z. Kahana-Shapira. Jerusalem, 2017.

_____. *Rav A.Y. Kook: Selected Letters*. Trans. Tzvi Feldman. USA, 1986.

_____. *Resh Millin*. London, 1917. Expanded edition with additional material. Jerusalem, 2003.

_____. *Shabbat ha-'Arets*. Jerusalem, 1910.

_____. *Shmonah Kevatsim*. 2 vols. 2nd edition. Jerusalem, 2004.

_____. *Shmu'ot Rayah: Bereshit-Shemot*. Ed. Yeshayahu Hadari. 2nd edition. Jerusalem, 2015.

_____. *Siddur 'Olat Re'iyah*. Ed. Tsevi Yehudah Hakohen Kook. vol. 1. Jerusalem, 1939. vol. 2. Jerusalem, 1949.

_____. *"Te'udat Yisrael u-Le'umiyuto."* In *Ha-Peless* 1 (1901), 45-52. Reprinted in Moshe Zuriel. *Otserot ha-Rayah*. Vols. 1-2. pp. 693-733. Tel-Aviv, 1988.

Kook, Tsevi Yehudah Hakohen. *Li-Netivot Yisrael*. vol. 1. Jerusalem, 1967. vol. 2. Jerusalem, 1979.

_____. *Li-Sheloshah be-Ellul*. (Biography of Rabbi Abraham Isaac Hakohen Kook.) vol. 1. Jerusalem, 1938. vol. 2. Jerusalem, 1947. vols. 1 and 2 photo-offset Jerusalem, 1978.

_____. *Pe'amim: Siḥot Rabbeinu Tsevi Yehudah Hakohen Kook*. Ed. Ilan Tor, Shlomo Aviner and Ḥayyim Vidal. Jerusalem, 2007.

_____. *Tsemaḥ Tsevi: Letters of Rabbi Tsevi Yehudah Hakohen Kook*. vol. 1. Ed. David Landau, Ze'ev Neuman and Shaḥar Raḥmani. Jerusalem, 1991.

Laniado, Samuel. *Keli Paz*. Commentary to Isaiah. Venice, 1657.

Lavut, Abraham David. *Sha'ar ha-Kollel*. Appended to *Siddur Torah 'Or 'al pi Nusaḥ ha-Ari zal*. Vilna, 1935.

Leifer, Mordechai. *Ma'amar Mordekhai*. M. Sighet, 1900.

Leiman, Shnayer Z. "The Adventure of the Maharal of Prague in London: R. Yudl Rosenberg and the Golem of Prague." *Tradition* 36:1 (2002), 26-58.

_____. "Did a Disciple of the Maharal Create a Golem?" *The Seforim Blog*, Thursday, February 8, 2007.

_____. "The Letter of the Maharal on the Creation of the Golem: A Modern Forgery." *The Seforim Blog*, Sunday, January 3, 2010.

Leiman, Sid Z. "When a Rabbi is Accused of Heresy: The Stance of the Gaon of Vilna in the Emden-Eibeschuetz Controversy." In *Me'ah She'arim: Studies in Medieval Jewish Spiritual Life in Memory of Isadore Twersky*, pp. 251-263. Ed. Fleischer, Blidstein, Horowitz, Septimus. Jerusalem, 2001.

Leiner, Gershon Ḥanokh of Radzyn. *Sod Yesharim, Sukkot*. Warsaw, 1903.

Leiner, Mordechai Yosef. *Mei ha-Shiloʾaḥ*. Part One. Vienna, 1860. Part Two. Lublin, 1922.

Leiner, Yeruḥam. *Tifʾeret Yeruḥam*. Brooklyn, NY, 1967.

Levin, Joshua Heschel. *ʿAliyot Eliyahu*. Vilna, 1856.

Lieberman, Saul. *Hellenism in Jewish Palestine*. New York and Jerusalem, 1994.

_____. *Tosefta Ki-Fshutah*. Part 7: *Seder Nashim*. Third Printing. Jerusalem, 2007.

Liebes, Yehuda. *"Masekhet ʾAtsilut: Ḥibbur Kabbali Psevdo-Epigraphi me-ʾet ha-Gaʾon mi-Vilna bi-Tseʿiruto?"* In Liebes, Yehuda. *Li-Tsevi u-le-Gaʾon*. Tel-Aviv, 2017.

Lifschitz, Ḥayyim. *Shivḥei ha-Rayah*. Jerusalem, 1995.

Lifshitz, Joseph Isaac. "*Nefesh HaḤayyim* and its Sources in Ḥasidei Ashkenaz" (Hebrew). *Daʿat* 79-80 (5775/2015), 77-93.

Lintop, Pinḥas Hakohen. *Beʾer Yisrael* (ms.).

_____. *Kanaʾuteh de-Pinḥas*. Ed. Bezalel Naor. Spring Valley, NY, 2013.

_____. [Article in] *Knesset ha-Gedolah*, Year 1 (Warsaw, 1890). Ed. Isaac Suvalsky.

_____. *Netivot ha-Shalom* (ms.).

Löw, Judah ben Bezalel (Maharal of Prague). *Derekh Ḥayyim*. Cracow, 1589. Jerusalem, 1971; photo-offset of London, 1961.

_____. *Gevurot Hashem*. Cracow, 1582. Jerusalem, 1971; photo-offset of London, 1954.

_____. *Netsaḥ Yisrael*. Prague, 1599. Jerusalem, 1971; photo- offset of London, 1957.

_____. *Tifʾeret Yisrael*. Venice, 1599. Jerusalem, 1970; photo-offset of London, 1955.

Luzzatto, Moses Ḥayyim. *Adir ba-Marom*. Ed. Samuel Luria. Warsaw, 1886. Ed. Yosef Spinner. Jerusalem, 1990. Ed. Mordekhai Chriqui. Jerusalem, 2018.

_____. *Daʿat Tevunot*. Ed. Samuel Luria. Warsaw, 1889. Ed. Ḥayyim Friedlander. Second Edition. B'nei Berak, 1975. Ed. Yosef Spinner. Jerusalem, 2012.

_____ (Misattributed to—). *Derekh ʿEts Ḥayyi*m. Addendum to *Mesillat Yesharim*. Zolkiew, 1766.

_____ (Attributed to—). *KaLaḤ Pitḥei Ḥokhmah.* Koretz, 1785. Ed. Yosef Spinner. Jerusalem, 1987.

_____ (Attributed to—). *KaLaḤ Pitḥei Ḥokhmah* with commentary *Pitḥei ha-Pardes* by David Cohen. Jerusalem, 2009.

_____. *La-Yesharim Tehillah.* Amsterdam, 1743.

_____. *Ma'amar ha-Ge'ulah.* Ed. Samuel Luria. Warsaw 1889. Uncensored version. Ed. Ḥ. Touitou. n.p. [Israel], 2002.

_____. *Pitḥei Ḥokhmah ve-Da'at.* Ed. Samuel Luria. Warsaw, 1884.

_____. *Secrets of the Redemption* [*Ma'amar ha-Ge'ulah*]. Trans. Mordechai Nissim. Jerusalem, 2004.

_____.*Takt"u* [515] *Tefillot.* Ed. Shalom Ullman. Israel, 1979.

Maimonides, Moses. *Commentary to the Mishnah.* Ed. Joseph Kafaḥ. 3 vols. Jerusalem, 1963-1968.

_____. *The Guide of the Perplexed.* Transl. Shlomo Pines. Chicago, 1964.

_____. *Moreh Nevukhim.* Transl. Michael Schwarz. Jerusalem, 2002.

_____. *Teshuvot ha-Rambam.* Ed. Joshua Blau. 3 vols. Jerusalem, 1957-1961.

Malbim (Wisser), Meir Leibush. *Mikra'ei Kodesh.* Commentary to Prophets and Writings. Warsaw, 1874.

Mandelbaum, Alexander Aryeh (Ed.). *Kiryat Arba': Torat Talmidei ha-Gra.* Jerusalem, 1995.

Margaliyot, Reuven. *Kuntres NaRaN.* In idem. *Sha'arei Zohar.* ff. 129-135. Jerusalem, 1957; photo-offset Jerusalem, 1994.

_____. *Nitsutsei 'Or.* On Talmud. Second printing. Jerusalem, 2002.

Mark, Zvi. *Mysticism and Madness in the Work of R. Nahman of Bratslav* (Hebrew). Tel Aviv, 2003.

Menasseh ben Israel. *Nishmat Ḥayyim.* Amsterdam, 1652.

Midrash Mishlei. Ed. Solomon Buber. Vilna, 1893.

Midrash Tanḥuma. Ed. Solomon Buber. Vilna, 1885.

Midrash Tehillim. Ed. Solomon Buber. Vilna, 1891.

Migash, Joseph ibn. *Ḥiddushei ha-Ri Migash, Bava Batra*. Ed. Politansky and Dahan. Beit Ḥilkiyah, 2014.

Molkho, Solomon. *Ḥayyat Kaneh*. Amsterdam [1765].

Moseson, Chaim Elly. *From Spoken Word to the Discourse of the Academy: Reading the Sources for the Teachings of the Besht*. Ph.D. dissertation, Boston University, 2017.

Naḥman ben Simḥah (of Breslov). *Shir Na'im/Song of Delight*. Ed. David Sears. Spring Valley, NY, 2005.

_____. *Likkutei Moharan*. Part One. Ostraha, 1808. Part Two. Mohilev, 1811.

Naḥmanides, Moses. Commentary to Pentateuch. Ed. Charles B. Chavel. 2 vols. Jerusalem, 1969.

_____. *Ḥiddushei ha-Ramban*. vol. 3. Tractate *Shavu'ot*. Ed. Moshe Hershler and Eliyahu Lichtenstein. Jerusalem, n.d.

_____. *Kitvei Ramban*. Ed. Charles B. Chavel. 2 vols. 3rd printing with additions. Jerusalem, 1968.

_____. *Milḥamot Hashem*. Defense of Alfasi against criticisms of Zeraḥyah Halevi, *Ha-Ma'or*. In Vilna edition of Talmud.

_____. *Sha'ar ha-Gemul*. Final chapter of *Torat ha-Adam*. In *Kitvei Ramban*, vol. 2.

_____. "*Torat Hashem Temimah*." In *Kitvei Ramban*, vol. 1.

Naor, Bezalel. *Be-Mayim 'Azim Netivah*. n.p., 1988.

_____. *From a Kabbalist's Diary: Collected Essays*. Spring Valley, NY, 2005.

_____. "*Gilgulei ketav-Yad 'Adir ba-Marom' le-Ramḥal*," *Sinai*, Tishrei-Ḥeshvan 5759 (1999), 53-62.

_____. *The Limit of Intellectual Freedom: The Letters of Rav Kook.* Spring Valley, NY, 2011.

_____. *Maḥol la-Tsaddikim.* Monsey, NY and Jerusalem, 2015.

_____. *Of Societies Perfect and Imperfect: Selected Readings from Eyn Ayah, Rav Kook's Commentary to Eyn Yaakov Legends of the Talmud.* New York, 1995.

_____. "Plumbing Rav Kook's Panentheism." In Naor, Bezalel. *From A Kabbalist's Diary: Collected Essays.* And in *Engaging Modernity: Rabbinic Leaders and the Challenge of the Twentieth Century*, 79-89. Ed. Moshe Z. Sokol. Northvale, NY, 1997.

_____. *When God Becomes History: Historical Essays of Rabbi Abraham Isaac Hakohen Kook.* New York, 2016. Revised edition 2017.

Neriyah, Moshe Tsevi. *Bi-Sdeh ha-Rayah.* Tel-Aviv, 1991.

_____. *Likkutei ha-Rayah.* Tel-Aviv, 1990.

_____. *Siḥot ha-Rayah.* Tel-Aviv, 1979.

_____. *Tal ha-Rayah.* Tel-Aviv, 1993.

Nevuat ha-Yeled. Ed. Isaac Halevi Satanow. Berlin, 1789.

Papo, Eliezer. *Pele Yo'ets.* Constantinople, 1825.

Patai, Raphael. *The Children of Noah: Jewish Seafaring in Ancient Times.* Princeton, 1998.

_____. "Exorcism and Xenoglossia Among the Safed Kabbalists," *Journal of American Folklore* 91 (1978), 823-835.

Perlow, Jacob (of Novominsk). *Shufra de-Ya'akov.* Ed. Yosef Perlow. Jerusalem, 2016.

Perlow, Yosef. *"Emet le-Ya'akov." Heikhal ha-Besht* 35 (Tishri 5774), pp. 131-148.

Philipson, David. *Max Lilienthal, American Rabbi: Life and Writings.* New York, 1915.

Pinso, Abraham. *Katit la-Ma'or.* Ed. Ya'akov Moshe Hillel. Jerusalem, 1995.

Pirke De Rabbi Eliezer. Ed. Gerald Friedlander. London, 1916.

Preschel, Tovia. *"Berakhah 'al Kiddush Hashem." HaDo'ar*, no. 37 (24 Elul 5730/1970).

Rabbinovicz, Raphael Nathan Nata. *Dikdukei Soferim, Bava Batra*. Munich, 1881.

Rabinowitz, Zadok Hakohen (of Lublin). *Dover Zedek*. Piotrków, 1911.

_____. *Komets ha-Minḥah*. Lublin, 1939; photo-offset B'nei Berak, 1967.

_____. *Maḥshevot Ḥaruts*. Piotrków, 1912; photo-offset B'nei Berak, 1967.

_____. *Takkanat ha-Shavin*. Piotrków, 1926; Beit El, 1988.

Recanati, Menaḥem. *Piskei Halakhot*. Bologna, 1538.

Reines, Alvin Jay. *Maimonides and Abrabanel on Prophecy*. Cincinnati, 1970.

Rivlin, Shelomo Zalman. *Midrash Shelomo: Derashot*. Jerusalem, 1953.

Roi, Biti. "'And They Were Watering the Torah': The Gaon of Vilna and his Affinity to *Tiqqunei ha-Zohar*" (Hebrew). *Da'at* 79-80 (5775/2015), 31-76.

Rosen, Joseph. *She'elot u-Teshuvot Tsafnat Pa'ane'aḥ ha-Ḥadashot*. vols. 1-3. Modi'in 'Ilit, 2010-2017.

Rosman, Moshe. *Founder of Ḥasidism: A Quest for the Historical Ba'al Shem Tov*. Berkeley, CA, 1996.

Rubinstein, Moshe Nathan Halevi. *Kelilat ha-Menorah*. Berdichev, 1892.

Samuel ben Eliezer (of Kalvaria). *Darkhei No'am*. Koenigsberg, 1764.

Schatz, Rivka. *"Peirusho shel ha-Besht le-Mizmor 107"* ("The Commentary of R. Israel Ba'al Shem Tov to Psalm cvii—The Myth and the Ritual of 'The Descent to She'ol'"). *Tarbiz* 42 (1972-1973), 154-184.

Schick, Barukh. *Euclides*. The Hague, 1780.

_____. *Tif'eret Adam*. Berlin, 1777.

Scholem, Gershom G. "*The Idea of the Golem*." In idem. *On the Kabbalah and Its Symbolism*. New York, 1970.

_____. *Major Trends in Jewish Mysticism.* New York, 1971.

_____. *On the Kabbalah and Its Symbolism.* New York, 1970.

_____. "*Tselem*: The Concept of the Astral Body." In idem. *On the Mystical Shape of the Godhead.* New York, 1991.

Schorr, Gedalia. *'Or Gedalyahu.* 3 vols. Genesis—Deuteronomy. Brooklyn, 1986-1998.

Schwarz, Ḥayyim Avihu. *Mi-Tokh ha-Torah ha-Go'elet.* 4 vols. Jerusalem, 1989-1991.

Seder Eliahu Rabba. Ed. M. Friedmann. Vienna, 1904. Photo-offset Jerusalem, 1969.

Sefer ha-Ḥinukh. Anonymous. Ed. C.B. Chavel. Fourth edition with additions. Jerusalem, 1960.

Sefer Yetzirah. Ed. Aryeh Kaplan. York Beach, Maine, 1997.

Shapiro, Moshe. "*Be'urim ba-Aggadot Rabbah bar Bar Ḥannah.*" *Yeshurun* 37 (Ellul 5777/2017), 439-509.

Shilo, Elchanan. "*Parshanut Harav Kook le-Kabbalat ha-Ari: Hofa'at Neshamot Ḥadashot ve-Tikkun ha-'Olam*" in *'Iyunim bi-Tekumat Yisrael*, vol. 18 (2008), 55-75.

_____. "Rabbi Isaac Eisik Ḥaver's Influence on Rabbi Kook's Interpretation of the Kabbalah" (Hebrew). *Da'at* 79-80 (5775/2015), 95-117.

Shneur Zalman ben Barukh (of Liadi). *Likkutei Torah.* Vilna, 1904; photo-offset Brooklyn, 1965.

_____. *Ma'amrei Admor ha-Zaken*: *Et-halekh Liozna.* Brooklyn, 2012.

_____. *Siddur 'im DAḤ.* Brooklyn, 1971.

_____. *Tanya.* Vilna, 1900.

_____. *Torah 'Or.* Vilna, 1899; photo-offset Brooklyn, 1972.

Shneurson, Menaḥem Mendel (of Lubavitch). *Derekh Emunah / Sefer ha-Ḥakirah.* Poltava, 1912.

_____. *Derekh Mitsvotekha.* Poltava, 1911; photo-offset Brooklyn, 1953.

Shneurson, Shelomo Zalman. *Magen Avot.* Berdichev, 1902.

Shtamler, Ḥagay. *Eye to Eye: The Thought of Rav Zvi Yehuda Kook* (Hebrew). Jerusalem, 2016.

Slifkin, Nosson. *Mysterious Creatures.* Israel, 2003.

Spira, Nathan ("Ha-Yerushalmi"). *Matsat Shimurim*. Ed. Moshe Zuriel. Jerusalem, 2001.

Spira, Nathan Nata (of Cracow). *Megalleh 'Amukot, Mahadura tinyana 'al ha-Torah*. Ed. Shalom Weiss. Jerusalem, 1998.

Spira, Tsevi Elimelekh (of Dynów). *B'nei Issachar.* Part 2. Zolkiew or Lvov, 1850.

Teshuvot ha-Ge'onim. Ed. B. Musafia. Lyck, 1864.

Teshuvot ha-Ge'onim, Sha'arei Teshuvah. Ed. Israel Moshe Ḥazan. Livorno, 1869.

Tikkunei Zohar. With commentary of Vilna Gaon. Vilna, 1867.

Tikkunei Zohar. Ed. Reuven Margaliyot. Jerusalem, 1940.

Tosafot Ḥadashim. Commentary to *Mishnah.* Included in *Mishnah.* Ed. Israel Jaffe. Kopyst, 1813.

Tosephta. Ed. M.S. Zuckermandel. Pasewalk, 1881; photo-offset Jerusalem, 1963.

Tsemaḥ David he-Ḥadash. Part III. Warsaw, 1871.

Twersky, Menaḥem Naḥum (of Chernobyl). *Me'or 'Eynayim.* Slavuta, 1798.

Twersky, Y.M., and Novoseller, Zishe (Ed.). *Admorei Malkhut Beit Chernobyl/Grand Rabbis of the Chernobyl Dynasty*. Bilingual edition. New York, 2003.

Uriel, Ya'ir. *Be-Shipulei ha-Gelimah*. (Biography of Rabbi Tsevi Yehudah Hakohen Kook.) Israel, 2012.

Valle, Moshe David. *Sefer ha-Likkutim*. Ed. Yosef Spinner. 2 vols. Jerusalem, 1998.

Vekshtein, Naftali Aharon. "*Vayityaldu.*" In Torah supplement to *Hamodi'a, Mishpatim*, 23 Shevat, 5771 (2011).

Vital, Ḥayyim. *'Ets Ḥayyim.* 3 parts. Jerusalem, 1910; photo-offset Tel-Aviv, 1975.

_____. *Ketavim Ḥadashim le-Rabbeinu Ḥayyim Vital.* Ed. Ya'akov Moshe Hillel. Jerusalem, 1988.

_____. *Otserot Ḥayyim.* Tunis, 1913; photo-offset Jerusalem, 1981.

_____. *Peri 'Ets Ḥayyim.* Dubrovna, 1804.

_____. *Sefer ha-Derushim*, Ed. Ya'akov Moshe Hillel. Jerusalem, 1996.

_____. *Sefer ha-Gilgulim.* Ed. David Greenhut. Frankfurt am Main, 1684.

_____. *Sefer ha-Ḥezyonot.* Ed. Netanel Moshe Mansour. Jerusalem, 2002.

_____. *Sefer ha-Likkutim.* Jerusalem, 1913; photo-offset Tel-Aviv, 1975.

_____. *Sha'ar ha-Gilgulim.* With commentary *B'nei Aharon* by Shim'on Agasi. Jerusalem, 1990.

_____. *Sha'ar Ma'amrei Rashbi.* Jerusalem, 1898; photo-offset Jerusalem, 1988.

_____. *Sha'ar Ma'amrei Razal.* Appended to *Sha'ar Ma'amrei Rashbi.* Jerusalem, 1898; photo-offset Jerusalem, 1988.

_____. *Sha'ar ha-Pesukim.* Jerusalem, 1912; photo-offset Tel-Aviv, 1975.

Weidenbaum, Naftali Herz Halevi. *Luḥot ha-Berit.* Commentary to Anonymous. *Berit 'Olam.* Part 2. Jerusalem, 1937.

Weinberg, Yeḥiel Ya'akov. *Pinui 'Atsmot Metim.* Berlin, 1926.

_____. "Ha-Yeshivot Be-Russia." In *Collected Writings of Rabbi Yeḥiel Ya'akov Weinberg* (Hebrew). Ed. Marc B. Shapiro. vol. 2. Scranton, PA, 2003.

Werblowsky, R.J. Zwi. *Joseph Karo: Lawyer and Mystic.* Oxford, 1962.

Wolberstein, Hilah. *Ish Ki Yafli: Ha-Rav Ha-Nazir.* (Biography of Rabbi David Cohen.) Israel, 2017.

Wolfson, Elliot R. *Through a Speculum That Shines.* Princeton, New Jersey, 1994.

_____. "*Yeridah la-Merkavah:* Typology of Ecstasy and Enthronement in Ancient Jewish Mysticism." In *Mystics of the Book: Themes, Topics, and Typologies.* Ed. Robert A. Herrera. New York, 1993.

Yolles, Ya'akov Tsevi. *Kehillat Ya'akov*. Lemberg, 1870.

Yom Tov ben Abraham Asevilli. *Ḥiddushei ha-Ritba, Bava Batra*. Ed. Moshe Yehudah Hakohen Blau. New York, 1977.

Zacuto, Moses. *Peirush ha-RaMaZ la-Zohar ha-Kadosh*. Genesis-Deuteronomy. 6 vols. Jerusalem, 1998-2005.

Zeitlin, Hillel. *Sifran shel Yeḥidim*. Ed. Aaron Zeitlin. Jerusalem, 1979.

Zemaḥ, Jacob (attributed to—). *Leḥem min ha-Shamayim*. Munkatsh, 1905.

Zevin, Shelomo Yosef. *Le-'Or ha-Halakhah*. Jerusalem, n.d. [c. 1980].

Zilberberg, Yehoshua 'Uziel. *Malkhut Beit David*. B'nei Berak, 1991.

Zimmels, H.J. *Magicians, Theologians, and Doctors: Studies in Folk Medicine and Folklore as Reflected in the Rabbinical Responsa*. London, 1952; photo-offset Northvale, NJ, 1997.

Ziyyoni, Menaḥem. *Sefer Ziyyoni*. Cremona, 1560.

Zohar. Ed. and transl. Daniel Matt. Vols. 1-2. Stanford, California, 2004.

Zohar. Ed. Reuven Margaliyot. With commentary *Nitsutsei Zohar*. 4th corrected edition with additions. 3 vols. Jerusalem, 1964.

Zohar Ḥadash. Ed. Reuven Margaliyot. 3rd printing. Jerusalem, 1994.

Zuckier, Shlomo. "Of Divine Nostrils and the Primordial Altar." *Lehrhaus*, March 8, 2018.

Zuriel, Moshe. *Otserot ha-Rayah*. First edition. 4 vols. Tel-Aviv, 1988-1992. Second expanded edition. 5 vols. Rishon LeZion, 2002.

Zussman, Yosef Leib. *Mi-Beḥirei Tsadikayya: Ma'amarim ve-igrot, reshamim ve-zikhronot… Harav Yosef Leib Zussman*. Jerusalem, 2007.

Indexes

Index of Sources

Bible

Genesis

1:1 185
1:9 124n275
1:16 157n398
1:27 119n289
2:7 120n314
2:10 120n307, 121n316
24:1 188n432
25:16 39n51
25:22 126n287
27:27 106n231, 106n233
32:16 137n347
36:6 40n57
36:31-39 159n388
45:27 121n322
46:26 45n57
49:23 194n464

Exodus

2:10 84n178
2:19 230n550
3:14 27, 28n41, 35n42
7:28 69n138
14:29 122n273
16:7 87n178
18:20 100n207
20:2 95n191
20:16 137n349, 242n579
34:28 95n192

Leviticus

19:4 42n80
19:26 168n411
22:31 225n531
25:17 78n154

Numbers

5:23 174n418
10:33 242n584
10:35-36 240
11:1 242n585
11:4 242n586
12:7 190n454
14:9 55n101
14:35 141n332

16:3 158n385, 164n404

16:30 161n396

16:30-34 161n396

21:9 145n357

23:2 144n352

24:7 227n539

25:6 144n351

25:7 137n350

27:18 120n305, 176n418

Deuteronomy

1:44 40n63, 45n65

4:4 136n331

4:6 110n254

8:15 155n381

12:20 185n447

14:1 68n134

17:9 75n162

21:12 225n532

28:58 223

29:8 223

29:17 41n78

31:17-18 28n30

32:8 40n52

33:2 155n380

33:9 66n135

Joshua

14:15 100n209

Judges

14:14 192n459, 194n466

1 Samuel

2:6 162n403

8:13 110n256

15 65n133

2 Samuel

14:14 194

14:20 121n329

1 Kings

5:11 136n330

2 Kings

6:6 229n536

Isaiah

2:22 42n89

3:9 120n311

5:12 110n260, 111n264

7:7 221n523

8:8 42n88

9:1 99n205

11:3 127n295

11:9 34n36, 40n61, 149n370, 192n460

19:5 219n522

34:14 52n95

40:26 94n191

42:6 111n268

42:21 101n229

43:7 44n54

44:13 119n300

49:6 111n268

52:13 241n577

57:20 227n540

58:11 162n402

66:1 162n400

66:23 120n304

Jeremiah

2:2 141n332

2:3 244n576

5:22 39, 43

9:22-23 181

15:19 192n458, 194n465

31:21 184n436

36:20 58n117

48:10 65n132

51:44 113n255

Ezekiel

31 36n44

32:27 120n310

41:13 196n469

Hosea

4:14 194n472

Amos

8:12 101n228

Jonah

1:1 78n154

1:4 77n154

Micah

7:20 156n394

Zechariah

9:9 131n324

Psalms

8:9 85n186, 107n245

14:7 169n415

16:8 86n176

25:14 99n202, 121n325, 139n367

27:2 41n67

27:4 99n204

36:11 121n327

37:10 29n47

37:29 29n4832

42:8 230n553, 231n555

45:14 109n248

48:2 74n160

50:11 99, 101n233

50:5 139n366

53:7 169n415

68:35 58n119

84:12 119n298

88:6 86n172

89:10 100n222

91:11 128n299

92:13 162n403

107:23 28n37, 74n154

107:23-28 240

107:26 16n5, 51, 176n418, 195n456

107:33 192n456

107:35 192n456

109:22 232n560

113:9 104n215

118:12 40n64

119:89 29n46

120-134 173n418

121:1 174n418

124:3 41n77

144:8 42n79

144:11 42n79

Proverbs

1:6 228n545

1:20 109n247

2:6 173n421

3:6 47-48n85

3:13-14 137n343

3:14 118n282

3:18 69n136

3:32 121n326

4:18 118n288, 170n406, 169n416

8:22 244n576

8:30 185n453

9:5 118n280

10:2 53

10:25 103n213

11:17 68n130

11:19 53n107

12:27 40n60

14:4 118n279

16:4 118

18:1 59n123

18:2 59n122

18:20 167n407

20:5 9, 173n420

21:20 111n263, 80n165

24:4 92n189

26:23 215n515

29:3 57

30:28 41n74

31:14 118n283, 125n280, , 137n344, 227n538

31:26 21n16

Job

14:8-9 74n153

14:11 40n61*, 216, 219n522

19:26 119n290

28:17 73

31:24 51n92

33 196n469

Song of Songs

2:9 168n409

3:7 69n143

5:14 122n272

6:8 66n143, 79n161

7:2 109n249

Ruth

3:7 121n318, 130n320

3:8 130n319

3:13 194

Ecclesiastes

1:3 118n284

1:9 118n284

1:13 228n547

1:14 228n548

1:15 43n90

6:7 102n240, n243

7:10 184n443

7:14 39n50
8:8 53n102
8:9 41n66
8:14 42n81
12:1 28n29

Daniel

7:7 239n567
7:8 236, 238n562
7:20 239n567
7:24 239n567
7:25 238n563
7:26-27 236n564
9:24 27n28, 150n374
12:3 198

1 Chronicles

1:48 120n306
2:6 136n330

Rabbinical Literature

Mishnah

Zera'im

Berakhot

5:1 158n382
9:5 164n404

Mo'ed

Sukkah

5:4 174n418

Hagigah

2:1 123n274

Nashim

Yevamot

16:3 78n155

Sotah

9:15 188n433, 193n461, 242n581

Nezikin

Makkot

3:16 106n229

'Eduyot

1:5 155n384
2:9 138n355

Avot

1:13 59n125
2:14 109n252
3:9 139n364
5:6 42n83, 161n396
6:1 101n230, 111n266

Toharot

Parah

8:9 162n402

Tosefta

Berakhot

7 118n287

Demai

2 163n404

Ta'anit

1 177n418

Sanhedrin

13 141n332

Talmud Yerushalmi

Zera'im

Berakhot

4:4 89n181, 95n191

5:1 194n474

9:1 118n287, 170n405

9:2 177n418

9:5 234n560

Pe'ah

2:4 79n163

Mo'ed

Shabbat

1:2 86n173

Ta'anit

4:5 242n583

Hagigah

2:1 29n43, 73n150

1:7 52n97

Nashim

Sotah

7:5 58n116

Nezikin

Sanhedrin

10:1 163n404

10:2 74n152, 175n418

Talmud Bavli

Zera'im

Berakhot

3a 78n154

5a 215n513

6a 143n337

7a 131n324, 136n341

9b 28n42

10b 168n412

13b 136n336

20b 210

32a 84n183

33a 158n382

34b 41n73

35b 140n333

43b 74n156, 119n296, 127n295

54b 44n53, 195n456, 246n588

56b 122n269

57a 109n246

57b 144n353

58a 54n96, 118n287

58b 228n546

61b 234n560

64a 118n278, 125n279

Mo'ed

Shabbat

11a 83n173

13a 125n283*

30a 86n172

30b 146n361

31a 163n404

33b-34a 86n174

63a 59n121

75a 110n254, 110n260

104a 244n571

112b 138n 354

115b-116a 240n571

116a 242n582

119b 36n45

138b 101n228

139a 100n225

151b 28n29, 86n172

152b 45n55, 80n168

156b 53n106

'Eruvin

13b 100n216, n218, 102n238, 227n542

22a 67n148

55b 44n53

64a 57n115

65a 136n334

Pesahim

49b 228n544, 61n114

50a 48n91

53b 66n138

53b-54a 177n420

87b 109n250

93b-94a 44n49

Yoma

71a 83n175

75b 44n53

77a 70n144

86a 58n117

Sukkah

28a 99n203

49a 177n419

49b 21n16

53 173n418, 177n419

Beitsah

28b 79n161

Rosh Hashanah

17a 51n94, 162n399

17b 241

21b 100n219, 142n335

25b 75n162

35a 86n173

Ta'anit

5b 77n149

23a 159n387

25b 230n552, 230n553

29a 242n582

29b 101n231

Megillah

2a 155n384

7a 128n299

7b 207n487

9b 112n253

19b 79n163

29a 57n110, 58n120

Mo'ed Katan

16 109n249

Hagigah

5b 31n27

12b 103n213, 189n435

13a 170n405

15a 66n144, 73n151

15b 75n166, 74n157, 81n171, 194n471

16a 157n400

27a 60n109, 81n171

Nashim

Yevamot

62a 188n433

63b 145n358

120a 78n155

Ketubot

110a 55n104

111a 150n377

Nedarim

20a 137n349, 242n580

38a 156n393

Sotah

11a 143n342

22a 60n109

37b 58n116

49b 188n433, 242n581

Gittin

57a 31n26

57b 54n96

87b 16n1

Kiddushin

17a 52n100

25a 87n178

31a 157n400

36a 66n134

82a 137n345

Nezikin

Bava Kamma

17a 78n158

53a 227n543

119a 54n93

Bava Metsi'a

83b 67n148*

84a 54n96

84b 227

85a 121n328

85b 70n144

59a 54n94

Bava Batra

8a 54n96

10b 48n91

25b 41n69

36a 54n93

73b 60n108

74b 70n147

161b 16n1

Sanhedrin

5b 40n53

7a 44n54

26b 59n123

33a 106n232

39a 47n85, 54n96, 143n341

42a 118n279

43b 58n116

46a 80n168

65b 123n 274, 206n487, 207n487

75a 74n157

98a 237n566

99b 102n240

100b 185n445

104b-105a 74n152

110 161n396

110a 122n269, 157n393, 161n396

110b 141n332, 200

Makkot

23b 184n438

Shavu'ot

9a 161n398

29a 96n193

'Avodah Zarah

3a 157n398

5a 140n330, 184n433

5b 138n356

11b 28n35

17a 42n86, 53n105

27b 158n383

Horayot

14a 118n278, 118n279

Kodashim

Zevahim

113b 60n108

60b 245n586

Menahot

29b 29n43

Hullin

17a 245n586

57b 54n96

60b 161n398

Bekhorot

30b 163n404

Temurah

4b 54n96

Toharot

Niddah

20b 120n309

61b 86n172

Halakhic Midrashim

Mekhilta

Yitro 1 117n276

Sifra

Metsora‘ 162n402

Emor 9 223n531, 107n242

Beha‘alotekha 244n571

Sifre

Matot 96n193

Shofetim 75n162

Ve-Zot ha-Berakhah 58n118

Aggadic Midrashim

Genesis Rabbah

1:1 185n452, n453

1:4 241n575

1:8-9 233n552

3:7 159n388

5:5 124n275

5:8 160n396

9:2 159n388

11:6 225n532

12:10 29n43

47:6 52n98

64:7 88n180

76:6 236n562

76:7 137n348

Exodus Rabbah

6:2 168n414

21:6 124n275

40:3 188n433

Leviticus Rabbah

4:6 40n57

9:1 136n330

34:3 65n130

Numbers Rabbah

2:13 40n62

18:21 74n161

Canticles Rabbah

Parashah 5 (5:14) 122n272

6:8 74n161

Lamentations Rabbah

Petihata 2 52n97

Ecclesiastes Rabbah

7:8 73n150, 73n151

Zohar

Zohar I

1b 100n220
5b 201
5b-6a 125n277
11b 145n357
29b 121n323
30a 100n220
36b 241n574
51a 35n40
81a 188n431
117a 123n274
129a 184n432
137a 101n235
142b 101n231
143b 101n231
154a 104n215
217b 53n101
224b 101n231
227a 53n101
243a 66n137

Zohar II

5b 61n114
12b 101n231
17b 74n159
25a 93n195
32b 58n119
43a 132n327
46b 142n335
51b 66n144
60b 101n231
61b 101n231
66b 66n144
69a 137n342
70a-78a 119n293
79b 101n232
81a 155n379
83b 142n335
84a 155n380
84b 101n231
85a 119n301
85b 101n232, 142n335
88a 101n231
95 40n56
95a 125n277
100b 84n179
108b 45n59
111b 136n337
112a 40n59
112b 136n337
139a 137n353
150b 161n398
151a 80n168
152 137n353
157a 120n304
166b 155n380
170 150n373
176b 157n396
199a 77n154

215a 126n288

235a 74n160

Zohar III

5a 74n160

13b 53n101

25a 12n15

29a 86n174

29b 40n55

32b 230n552

58a 30n23

60a 66n144

70a 12n15

80b 66n137

83 244n574

84a 101n231

99b 121n323

120b 143n338

124b 150n375

126 168n413

127b 101n232

128b 101n231

129a 170n406

135b 101n231

136a 92n189

136b 69n142

137b 30n23, 74n155

144b 88n178

145a 86n174

150b 219n522

170b 45n59

175 35n40

183b 100n208

245a 139n362

262a 142n335

263b 66n144, 93n195

270b 66n144

272a 137n351

288a 101n231

289b 92n189, 121n316

290b 121n316

292b 101n231

293a 69n142

296a 92n189

Zohar Hadash

Midrash Ruth 88a 130n319

Ra'aya Mehemna and Tikkunei Zohar

Ra'aya Mehemna

Zohar II, 25a 93n195

Zohar II, 43a 132n327

Zohar III, 29a 86n174

Zohar III, 83 244n574

Zohar III, 124b 150n375

Zohar III, 175 35n40

Zohar III, 245a 139n362

Zohar III, 263b 66n144, 93n195

Tikkunei Zohar

(Pagination refers to the Vilna 1867 edition)

Introduction 95n192, 102n241, 103n213, 156n391, 219n522

Tikkun 1 156n391

Tikkun 12 155n379

Tikkun 18 185n454

Tikkun 20 100n210

Tikkun 21 (42a) 155n382

Tikkun 21 (43a) 123n275

Tikkun 21 (43b) 117n273

Tikkun 21 (50a) 130n320

Tikkun 21 (60a) 85n185, 128n299

Tikkun 21 (f.60) 30n25, 74n154

Tikkun 30, netiv tinyana 31n26, 216n520

Tikkun 32 142n335

Tikkun 60 131n324

Tikkun 69 184n434, 186

Maimonides

Commentary to the Mishnah

Introduction 16n2

Introduction to Sanhedrin, chap. 10 (Perek Helek) 205n483

Introduction to Avot (Shemonah Perakim), chap. 5 55n103

Introduction to Avot (Shemonah Perakim), chap. 8 43n91

Mishneh Torah

Hilkhot Yesodei ha-Torah

2 95n191

2:1 110n258

4:12 110n258

10:4 152n368

Hilkhot Teshuvah

5-6 43n91

8:2 119n303

9:2 149n369, 241n578

Hilkhot Mikva'ot

11:12 28n36

Hilkhot Mamrim

2:1-4 22n20

Hilkhot Melakhim

12:4, 5 149n369

12:5 34n36

Guide for the Perplexed

III, 49 132n327

III, 52 83n176

Writings of Lurianic Kabbalah

'Ets Hayyim

Introduction 215-216n520

3:1 41n75

9:1 97n198

32:1 136n330, 136n335

Likkutei Torah

Shelah 136n332

Devarim 136n335

'Otserot Hayyim

212n503

Peri 'Ets Hayyim

Sha'ar ha-Tefillin 41n75, 96n193

Sefer ha-Gilgulim

121n320

206n483

Chap. 1 188n433

Chap. 6 76n171

Sefer ha-Hezyonot

Chap. 22 183n424

Sefer ha-Likkutim

Va-'Ethanan 76n170

Psalms 92:13 162n403

Sha'ar ha-Gilgulim

121n320

Hakdamah 4 76n171

Hakdamah 36 139n362

Sha'ar Ma'amrei Rashbi

Noah 121n320

Kedoshim 241n574

Sha'ar Ma'amrei Razal

Ma'amar Pesi'otav shel Avraham Avinu

136n337

Sha'ar ha-Nevu'ah

3:5 125n277

Sha'ar ha-Pesukim

Vayyeshev 66n141

Shemot 136n330, 136n335

Shelah 136n330, 136n332

Psalms 92:13 162n403

Index of Names

A

Abaye, 99, 101, 142

Abrabanel, Don Isaac, 236, 238n563, 245n577

Abulafia, Abraham, 237

Adam, 119, 188n433

Adret, Solomon ben Abraham (Rashba), 69n134, 211

Ahdut, Eli, 54n96, 77n149

Alfasi, Isaac (Rif), 170n405

Alkabets, Shelomo Halevi, 204n480, 204n481

Alter, Judah Aryeh Leib (of Gur, *"Sefat Emet"*), 128-129n299

Anav, Raphael, 183n424

Arieli, Isaac, 105n225

Asevilli, Yom Tov ben Abraham (Ritba), 30n24, 54-55n96

Ashi, 91, 93, 99, 102

Auerbach, Hayyim Leib, 123n274

Auerbach, Shelomo Zalman, 123n274

Avidor, Shmuel HaKohen, 96n194

Aviner, Shlomo (Shelomo Hayyim HaKohen), 10

Avivi, Yosef, 33n33, 187n430

Azariah, 66, 69n138

Azulai, Hayyim Yosef David (Hida), 129n304, 212

B

Ba'al Shem Tov, Israel, 21n13, 31n26, 45n68, 88n180, 195n456, 220n523, 242, 245-246n587, 246n589

Barg, Mordechai Gimpel, 94n191

Barukh of Mezhbizh, 246n587

Bedersi, Yedayah (*"Ha-Penini"*), 190n449

Benayahu, Meir, 211

Ben Natsur, 238n563

Berlin, Naftali Tsevi Yehudah (Netsiv), 17n6, 132n327, 140n330, 217n512

Bialik, Hayyim Nahman, 146n358

Blaser, Isaac (*"Itzeleh Peterburger"*), 214, 217n506, 217n509, 218n514, 218n515, 218n517

Bloch, Joseph Leib, 221n525

Bornstein, Abraham (of Sokhatchov, *"Avnei Nezer"*), 89n181, 96n193, 176n418

Bornstein, David (of Sokhatchov, *"Hasdei David"*), 175n418

Bornstein, Samuel (of Sokhatchov, *"Shem mi-Shmuel"*), 89n181, 95n191, 175n418

Buzaglo, Shalom, 86n172

C

Charles V (Holy Roman Emperor), 237

Chriqui, Mordekhai, 211

Clement VII (Pope), 237

Cohen, David ("the Nazirite"), 122-123n274, 209

Constantine (the Great, Emperor), 236, 238n563

Copio, Isaac, 213n503

Cordovero, Moses, 46n75, 57, 60n113

D

Daniel, 236, 237, 238n563

David (King of Israel), 131n324, 173, 177n419, 232

David ha-Nagid, 238n567

Dessler, Eliyahu, 170n405, 221n525

Dimi, 91

DiPoce, Eli, 128n299

Dov Baer of Mezritch, 88-89n180, 128n299,

E

Edels, Samuel (Maharasha), 106n234, 200, 207n487

El'azar ben Rabbi Shim'on, 227

Eliach, Dov, 18n6, 114n255, 124n275

Eliashov, Shelomo ("*Leshem*"), 123n274, 187n430, 209

Elijah ben Solomon Zalman (Elijah Gaon of Vilna) (Gra), 9, 10, 16n5, 17n5, 17n6, 18n6, 19n9, 20n10, 34n34, 61n124, 78n154, 78n155, 89n181, 103n213, 106n232, 110, 113-114n255, 115n265, 117, 118, 123-124n275, 126n287, 128n299, 131n324, 140n330, 143n337, 144n352, 156, 158n379, 158n382, 159n387, 160n396, 182n422, 184-191, 195n456, 199, 204n482, 208n488, 209, 217n511, 220n523, 226, 243, 249n591

Elijah of Brisk, 211

Elisha ben Abuyah ("*Aher*"), 73, 75, 77n151, 80n166, 80-81n171, 194, 196n471

Emden, Jacob, 17n6, 200, 207n487

Epstein, Aryeh Leib, 17-18n6

Epstein, Isidore (Yehezkel), 105n225

Epstein, Perle, 97n200, 207n487

Even-Shmuel (Kaufman), Yehudah, 239n568

Eybeschuetz, Jonathan, 17n6

F

Feldman, Aharon, 16n5

Felman, Raphael, 19n9, 48n91

Finkel, Nathan Tsevi ("*Alter fun Slabodka*"), 216, 217n508, 221n524

Fisher, Shelomo, 144n352

Fisher, Ya'akov, 80n166

Fishman, David E., 114n255, 209

Forshlager, Michael, 89n181, 176n418

Friedlander, Hayyim, 33n33, 221n525

Friedman, Israel (of Chortkov), 87n177

Friedman, Israel (of Ruzhin), 87n177

Friedman, Moshe (of Boyan-Cracow), 87n177

G

Geffen, Shem Tov, 35n42

Gersonides, 226, 229n536, 238n563

Gikatilla, Joseph, 30n23, 104n220, 221n525
Gilboa, Hayah, 146n358
Glasner, Moshe Shmuel, 31n27
Gordon, Hirsch Loeb, 204n478
Gordon, Yekutiel, 200, 204n478, 206n484, 209, 211
Greenblatt, Avraham Barukh, 236
Greenblatt, Ephraim, 236
Greenblatt, Joel, 235
Greenblatt, Nota, 236
Greenblatt, Yitshak, 235
Greenspan, Nahman, 202n476
Gruber, Shmuel, 203n476

H

Hagiz, Moses, 200
Halevi, Abraham, 239n567, 239n568
Hamnuna Saba, Rav, 87-88n178
Hananel ben Hushiel, 54n96, 88n178
Hananiah, 66, 69n138
Harlap, Ya'akov Moshe, 10, 115n265, 131n324, 179, 217n505
Haver (Wildman), Yitshak Eizik, 17n5, 18n7, 34n34, 144n352, 156, 158n385, 187n430, 201, 208n488, 233n552
Hayyim of Volozhin, 19n9, 61n119, 124n275, 130n321, 142n333, 182n422, 217n511, 218n514, 218n518, 219n519, 222, 224n527, 224-225n530
Hillel, 68n130, 135, 139, 146n361, 147n363, 163-164n404
Hillel, Moshe, 213n503
Hirschensohn, Hayyim, 54n96, 145n358, 192-197
Hisda, 174n418
Horowitz, Aharon Halevi (of Staroselye), 87n178, 176n418, 234n561, 247n589
Horowitz, Isaiah Halevi (*"SheLaH"*), 68n131
Horowitz, Shabtai (Sheftel) Halevi, 44n54, 45n55.
Horowitz (Lider), Shim'on Tsevi, 123n274
Horowitz, Shmuel Shmelke Halevi (of Nikolsburg), 128n299, 147n362
Hurmin (Hurmin bar Lilitha), 16n5, 51-55, 77n149, 176n418
Hurwitz, Pinhas Elijah (of Vilna), 206n483
Hutner, Yitshak, 20n10, 30n25, 79n162, 163n404, 217n508

I

Ibn Ezra, Abraham, 95n191, 114n257, 194
Ibn Tsur, Moshe, 212, 213n503
Isaac of Acco, 96n193
Isaac (*"Itzeleh"*) of Volozhin, 17n6, 19n9, 124n275, 219n519, 224n528, 225n530
Ishmael, 32n27, 39, 122n269
Ishmael, Rabbi (*tanna*), 141-142n333, 245n586

J

Jacob, 45n57, 121, 130n322, 144n352, 156, 160n394
Jacob ben Meir of Ramerupt (Rabbeinu Tam), 54n96, 142n333
Jacob Joseph of Polnoye, 35n40
Jacob Moses of Slonim, 187n430
Jaffe, Dov Baer (of Turetz, Karelitz and

Utian), 19n9, 203n476, 222, 224, 245n586

Jaffe, Israel, 147n362

Jaffe, Mordechai (of Karelitz), 203n476

Jaffe, Mordechai (of Prague, *"Levush"*), 203n476

Jaffe, Mordechai (of Vienna), 200

Jaffe, Mordechai Gimpel, 19n9, 61n123, 103n206, 107n242, 112n251, 202, 203n476, 222-225, 245n586

Jaffe, Ya'akov, 203n476

Jethro, 143n342, 144n352, 233n550

Job, 143n342, 144n352

Jonathan Hakohen of Lunel, 114n256

Joseph Hayyim of Baghdad (*"Ben Ish Hai"*), 124n277, 145-146n358, 176n418, 207n487

Joseph Zundel of Salant, 218n514

Joshua ben Hananiah, 31-32n27

Joshua ben Korhah, 95n192

Judah Halevi, 95n191, 205n483, 218n518

Judah Leib of Kremnitz, 106n233

Judah the Prince, Rabbi, 240

K

Kagan, Israel Meir, 179

Kanievsky, Ya'akov Yisrael, 182n422

Karelitz, Abraham Isaiah (*"Hazon Ish"*), 182n422, 199-200

Karo, Joseph, 44n55, 81n171, 103n214, 105n225, 199-200, 204n483, 206n483,

Katz, Ben-Zion, 18n6

Katz, Eliyahu, 244n572

Kiperwasser, Reuven, 70n148, 77n149, 195n456

Knobloch, Meyer Yechiel, 203n476

Kohut, Alexander, 54n96

Kook, Dov Hakohen, 105n225

Kook (neé Jaffe), Freida Batyah, 202n476

Kook, Nahum Hakohen, 202n476

Kook, Samuel Hakohen, 159n387

Kook, Shelomo Zalman Hakohen, 18n7

Kook, Tsevi Yehudah HaKohen, 10, 13, 17n6, 20-21n10, 35n42, 60n109, 68n131, 69n134, 87n177, 96n194, 97n200, 103n208, 105n225, 112n253, 113n255, 141n332, 175n418, 179, 203n476, 206-207n487, 213n497, 217n509, 218-219n518, 219n522, 224n527

Kronglass, David (*"David Kobriner"*), 221n525

L

Lavut, Abraham David, 246n588

Leah, 140n332, 143n338

Leiman, Shnayer (Sid Z.), 17n6, 208n487

Leiner, Gershon Hanokh (of Radzyn), 176n418, 231, 233n558

Leiner, Mordechai Joseph (of Izbica), 79n162, 176n418, 205n483

Leiner, Yeruham (of Radzyn), 16n2

Leshem, Zvi, 206n485

Levi bar Hama, 214

Levin, Joshua Heschel, 17n6, 187n430, 190n444

Levovitz, Yeruham, 216, 221n525

Lieberman, Saul, 60n109, 105n225

Lifshitz, Joseph Isaac, 224-225n530

Lilienthal, Max, 219n519
Lilith, 51, 52, 54n95, 55, 176
Lintop, Pinhas Hakohen, 12, 20-21n10, 159n388, 209, 213n492, 220n523
Löw, Judah (Maharal of Prague), 18n7, 31n27, 70n145, 199, 207-208n487, 218n518
Luria, David, 188n433, 239n567
Luria, Isaac (*Ari*), 86n174, 88n178, 119, 127n294, 136, 142n335, 160n396, 204n483
Luria, Samuel, 34n34, 47n85, 209
Luzzatto, Moses Hayyim (Ramhal), 10, 19-20n10, 31n26, 32-33n33, 33-34n34, 47n85, 118, 126n288, 141n332, 159n386, 167, 170n406, 200, 204n478, 209-212, 213n497, 221n525

M

Maimonides, Moses, 16n2, 33n34, 34n36, 48n91, 55n103, 86n176, 95n191, 105n225, 114n256, 132n327, 170n405, 205n483, 226, 238n567
Malbim, Meir Leibush, 196n467, 229n536, 236
Margaliyot, Asher Zelig, 182n422
Margaliyot, Reuven, 80n168, 106n232, 161-162n398, 187-188n431
Medan, Meir, 213n497
Meir, Rabbi (Tosafist), 54n96
Meir, Rabbi (*tanna*), 68n134, 75, 80n166, 194, 196n471, 227
Menahem Mendel of Shklov, 126n287, 187n430, 208n488
Menasseh ben Israel, 182n422, 183n428
Mendelssohn, Moses (of Dessau), 219n519
Mindes, Noah, 209
Mishael, 66, 69n138
Molkho, Solomon (a.k.a. Diogo Pires), 237
Mordechai ben Hillel, 161n398
Morgenstern, Menahem Mendel (of Kotzk), 89n181, 95n191
Moses, 14, 35n42, 76, 79n163, 87-88n178, 95n192, 117, 122n273, 155, 156, 157, 163n404, 190n454, 205n483, 223, 233n550, 240, 241, 242, 244n573
Moshe Ha-Darshan, 144n352
Moshe Hayyim Ephraim of Sudylkow, 88n180

N

Nahman of Breslov, 122n274, 123n274, 126n290, 161n398
Nahman Hatufa (Katufa), 238n567
Nahman of Kosov, 88n180
Nahmanides, Moses, 19n9, 32n29, 46n75, 55n101, 96n193, 119, 126n292, 129n303, 161n396, 194, 196n469, 222, 245n583
Najara, Israel, 194
Nathan, Rabbi, 227
Nathan ben Yehiel of Rome, 54n96, 145n358
Neriyah, Moshe Tsevi, 18n7, 80n166, 141n352, 202n476, 217n505, 217n508, 221n525
Nicholas III (Pope), 237

O

Orenstein, Yesh'ayah, 20n10, 145n357

P

Pappa bar Samuel, 65, 67

Pardo, David, 152n368

Patai, Raphael, 16n1

Paul (Saul of Tarsus), 35n38, 164n404

Perlow, Ya'akov (of Novominsk), 176n418, 246n589

Perlow, Ya'akov (of Novominsk-Brooklyn), 89n181

Pharaoh, 137, 143n342, 144n352

Pines, Zalman, 244n576

Pinhas, 144n351

Pinso, Abraham, 152n368

Polonsky, Shimshon Aharon (of Teplik), 30n25

R

Rabinowitz, Alexander Ziskind (*Azar*), 159n387

Rabinowitz, David Yitshak Eizik (of Skolye-Brooklyn), 245n587

Rabinowitz, Jacob Isaac (of Pshyskha, "*Ha-Yehudi ha-Hakadosh*"), 94n191

Rabinowitz, Zadok Hakohen (of Lublin), 16n2, 77n151, 204-205n483

Rahel, 140n332, 143n338

Rashi, 35n42, 44n53, 45n57, 47n85, 54n93, 54n94, 54n96, 55n99, 55n104, 60n109, 61n121, 70n144, 79n162, 80n168, 86n173, 89n183, 106n231, 106n233, 112n249, 112n253, 122n269, 125n283*, 129n309, 137, 140n329*, 140n330, 141n332, 142n334, 143n346, 143n348, 144n352, 163n404, 175-176n418, 177n419, 178n420, 188n433, 189n435, 190n446, 206n487, 213n500, 219n519, 244n572

Rava, 51, 54n94, 99, 101, 128n299, 206n487

Recanati, Menahem, 46n75, 68n131, 96n193

Reizes, Pinhas, 114n255

Rivlin, Shelomo Zalman, 113n255

Rivlin, Yitshak Tsevi, 113n255

Roi, Biti, 61n124, 88n179, 122n273

Roke'ah, El'azar, 224-225n530

Rosen, Joseph (of Rogatchov, "*Tsafnat Pa'ne'ah*"), 177n419

Rosenberg, Shalom, 160n392

Rosenblatt (Veitzel), Mordechai (of Ashmina and Slonim), 198

S

Salanter, Israel, 123n274, 146n361, 214-221

Samuel ben Eliezer of Kalvaria, 9, 18n6, 19n7, 106n233, 127n294, 226, 229n542

Samuel ben Meir (Rashbam), 54n96, 60n108, 70n148, 77n149, 122n269, 161n398, 170n405, 195n456

Schatz (-Uffenheimer), Rivka, 46n68, 195n456, 206n485, 246n588, 246n589

Schick, Barukh (of Shklov), 112n255, 113-114n255, 115n265, 209

Schiff, Maharam, 30n24

Schneider, Nahman, 246n587

Seidel, Moshe, 171n408, 210

Shabtai Tsevi, 17n6, 21n13, 31n26

Shammai, 135, 138-139, 146n361, 147n363, 163-164n404

Shapiro, Moshe, 16n5, 162n399, 170n405, 182n422

Shar'abi, Shalom Mizrahi (Rashash), 212

Shim'on ben Gamliel, 240

Shim'on ben Lakish, 192, 214

Shim'on ben Menasya, 141n332

Shim'on ben Yohai, 24, 83, 84, 85, 86n173, 86n174, 87n178, 141-142n333, 182n422, 198, 227

Shim'on ha-Tsaddik, 197n475

Shmuel (*amora*), 128n299

Shneur Zalman of Liadi (*"Alter Rebbe"*), 10, 20, 32n31, 48n91,79n161, 80n164, 80n165, 84, 87n178, 103n210, 104n215, 105n226, 112n253, 114n255, 122n270, 126n290, 128n299, 140n332, 143n340, 147n362, 189n433, 206n483, 218n518, 234n560

Shneuri, Dov Baer (of Lubavitch, *"Mitteler Rebbe"*), 114n255

Shneurson, Menahem Mendel (of Lubavitch), 19n9, 48n91, 80n165, 239n569, 246n589

Shneurson, Shelomo Zalman (of Kopyst), 19n9, 48n91

Shochet, Immanuel, 35n40

Simhah Bunim of Pshiskha , 94-95n191

Slonim, Shneur Zalman (of Jaffa), 220n523

Sokolovsky, Moshe, 236

Solomon ibn Gabirol, 193

Soloveichik, Aharon Halevi (of Chicago), 132n327

Soloveichik, Moshe Halevi, 235

Soloveichik, Hayyim Halevi (of Brisk), 214, 235

Soloveitchik, Joseph Baer Halevi (of Boston), 218n514

Souissia, Isaac, 212

Spinner, Yosef, 211, 213n501

Spira, Hayyim El'azar (of Munkatsh), 208n487

Spira, Nathan (*Yerushalmi*), 143n338

Spira, Tsevi Elimelekh (of Dynów), 176n418, 208n487

Sternharz, Nathan (of Nemirov), 122n274

T

Thaddeus Man of Rome, 69n138

Twersky, Abraham (Trisker Maggid), 202-203n476

Twersky, David (of Tolna), 48n85

Twersky, Menahem Nahum (of Chernobyl), 47-48n85, 202-203n476, 245n587

Twersky, Mordechai (of Chernobyl), 203n476

Twersky, Yohanan (of Rachmistrivka), 203n476

Twersky, Ze'ev (of Rachmistrivka), 203n476

V

Valle, Moshe David, 31n26

Vekshtein, Naftali Aharon, 203n476

Vital, Hayyim, 46n75, 69n141, 80n170, 81n171, 96n193, 97n198, 125n277, 130n320, 140n330, 140n332, 142n335, 142-143n337, 147n362, 162n403, 183n424, 188n433, 212, 215-216, 219n520, 244n574

Vital, Samuel, 130n320

W

Wasserman, Elhanan Bunem, 179, 182n422

Weinberg, Yehiel Ya'akov, 80n168, 219n519

Weiss, Yitshak Eizik (of Spinka), 208n487

Weissbord, Abraham Hakohen, 123n274

Wilovsky, Jacob David (Ridbaz), 131n324, 145n357

Y

Yanover, Yehezkel (Hatskel), 19n9, 48n91

Yehudah, Rabbi (*tanna*), 68n134

Yehudah, Rav (*amora*), 86n173, 192

Yehudah, Rav, the "Hindu" (*amora*), 70n147

Yeiva Saba, Rav, 125n277

Yohanan, Rabbi (*amora*), 44n49, 86n172, 86n173, 141n332, 174n418, 177n419, 178n420, 192, 200

Yolles, Ya'akov Tsevi, 17n6

Yosé be-Rabbi Yehudah, 163n404,

Yosef, Rav (*amora*), 118, 125n279, 177n420

Z

Zeide, Shpoler (Aryeh Leib or Yehudah Leib of Shpola), 122-123n274

Zeira, 206-207n487

Zeitlin, Hillel, 131n324

Ziv, Simhah Zissel ("*Alter fun Kelm*"), 216, 221n524, 221n525

Ziyyoni, Menahem, 9, 55n96

Zuckier, Shlomo, 177n419

Zuriel, Moshe, 9, 86n174, 214, 244n572

Zussman, Yosef Leib, 10

Index of Subjects

'Adir ba-Marom, 19n10, 20n10, 33, 126n288, 167, 170n406, 209-210, 213n492

akhla-tina (mud-eater), 73, 74, 78

'Alma de-'itgalya (revealed world), 122n270

'Alma de-'itkasya (concealed world), 122n270

antelope (*'orzila*), 16n5, 57, 58, 61n118

Apple Orchard (*sdeh hakal tapuhim*), 101, 102, 106n231

'arevut (mutual responsibility), 58, 59

'AShaN (*'akrav* - scorpion; *saraf* - fiery serpent; *nahash* - snake), 155

'Asiyah (World of Doing). *See* Four Worlds

'Atsilut (World of Emanation). *See* Four Worlds

'avodah be-gashmiyut (Hasidic doctrine of serving God through the corporeal), 89

awe of the sublime (*yir'at ha-romemut*), 138, 215, 218n517, 220n523

bat kol (divine voice), 78n154, 99, 101, 107n235, 149, 150

Bedouin (*tay'a*), 9, 117, 119-121, 122n269, 124-125n277, 127n294, 131n324, 135-138, 149, 155, 156, 167-169, 170n405, 198, 200, 201

bees, 40-41

beit din (court of law), 79n162, 155

Beri'ah (World of Creation). *See* Four Worlds

be'ur (explanation), 13, 22n17

Binah (Understanding). *See* Ten *Sefirot*

Birur Halakhah (synopses of the *sugyah* or Talmudic discussion), 105n225

bittul (self-nullification), 87n178

bones, 73, 76, 80n167, 120,

breadbasket, 167-168

breath (*hevel*), 42, 47n84

Camp of Israel, 40, 44n53

character traits. *See middot*

chariot (*merkavah*), 52, 53, 55n98

Christianity, 27, 31, 32n27, 35n38, 164n404, 236, 238n563

commandments, 28, 59, 68n131, 85, 88, 95n191, 100, 136, 143n340, 145n357, 157, 205n483, 223; abolition of, 35n38, 83, 164n404, 238n563; angels produced by, 204n483; derision of, 163n404; exemption from, 83, 86n172; knowledge of, 99; mysteries of 101; negative, 160n391, 184; positive, 137, 156, 160n391, 163n404, 189n437; practical, 28, 83, 84, 101, 140n332, 164n404; revealed, 14

conversion to Judaism, 109, 163n404, 237

cruelty, 16n5, 65-67

cupidity, 51

Da'at (Knowledge). *See* Ten *Sefirot.*

dalet. See letters

Darkhei No'am, 9, 18, 106, 127, 226-229

"David" (midrash on the name), 230-234

day and night (symbolism), 92, 95n192

Death of the Kings (*mitat he-melakhim*), myth of, 156, 159n388

deeds (*'uvdin*), 100, 102, 103n208, 136, 143n342

Deep, 173-177, 230, 231, 234

demons, 42, 47n84, 55n96, 143n337

dinim (judgments), 66, 67, 156, 160n392

derush. See Four Levels of Interpretation

desert , 9, 12, 40, 44n53, 109, 111, 117, 120, 135-142, 143n346, 146n358, 146n359, 170, 198, 200, 228, 239n567

devekut (cleaving), 24, 88, 101, 136

divine "oath," 25, 149, 150, 152n368

divine inspiration (*ru'ah ha-kodesh*), 92, 94n190, 126n287, 137, 193, 196n462, 204n483

divine voice. *See bat kol*

donkey(s), 125n277, 131n324, 135, 138, 145n356, 149, 150, 201. *See also* white donkey

Doppelgänger, 189n435

dybbuk (spirit possession), 179-183, 204-205n483

Earth (*'erets*), 25, 29, 103, 155, 157, 160n396, 161n397, 167-171

Edom (Christendom), 32n27

Ehyeh asher Ehyeh, 27-29, 35n42

emet. *See* truth

Erets Yisrael, 91, 123n274, 194, 222, 235

esoteric wisdom (*hokhmat ha-nistar*), 106n234, 122-123n274

evil, 11, 27, 29, 31n26, 33n33, 33n34, 34n34, 40-42, 45n56, 51, 53, 112n253, 121, 159n387, 194, 228; fear, 145n357; inclination, 43, 86n172, 214-215; thought, 74

exile, 23, 25, 27, 28, 29, 33-34n34, 35n42, 130n319, 149, 150, 152n374, 216, 236, 239n567

Exodus, 9, 28, 95n191, 142n335

exorcism, 10, 179-183

exoteric wisdom (*hokhmat ha-nigleh*), 106n234, 122-123n274

fear of God (*yir'ah*), 160n391

fear of punishment (*yir'at ha-'onesh*), 138, 145n357, 215, 218n517, 220n523

fish, 18-19n7, 23, 30n24, 73, 74, 77n149, 78n157, 78n158, 83, 84, 87n178, 88n178, 89n182, 91, 92, 93; single-finned, 91; two-finned, 91, 93

fool, 59, 62n126, 97n200, 135, 138, 146n358, 149, 152n368

Four Levels of Interpretation (*PaRDeS*): *derush*, 9, 57, 59, 60n111, 60-61n114, 61n124, 226; *peshat*, 9, 57, 59, 60n111, 60-61n114, 61n124, 192, 219n519, 226; *remez*, 9, 57, 59, 60n111, 60-61n114, 61n124, 192, 226; *sod*, 9, 57, 59, 60n111, 60-61n114, 61n124, 226

Four Worlds: *'Asiyah* (Doing), 40, 41, 44n54, 46n72, 120; *'Atsilut* (Emanation), 41, 44n54, 61n124; *Beri'ah* (Creation), 40, 41, 44n54, 46n72; *Yetsirah* (Formation), 40, 41, 44n54, 46n72, 46n75

free will, 23, 39, 42, 43, 182n422

frog(s), 65-67, 69n138

gadlut ("greatness"), 24, 93

gated communities, 23, 51

"gatherers of the field" ("*mehatsdei hakla*"), 101, 106n232, 118

Generation of the Desert (*Dor ha-Midbar*), 135-142, 146n358, 146n359, 200

Gevurah (Stern Judgment). *See* Ten *Sefirot*

gevurot (rigors), 66, 69n143, 70n145, 93, 138, 139

gilgul (reincarnation), 76, 80-81n171, 89n181, 188n433

gilui Eliyahu (revelation of Elijah), 198, 202n476

glass, 73

golem (humanoid), 188n433, 206-208n487

good, 11, 22n18, 24, 31n26, 33n33, 33-34n34, 47n85, 65, 67, 68n130, 111, 121, 131n324, 144n353, 151, 159n387, 164n404, 168, 171n408, 194, 228, 231; deeds, 42, 52 55n99, 120; inclination, 214,

good and evil, 33n33, 41, 228

goose (geese), 24, 109, 111

Guarded Wine (*yayin ha-meshumar*), 41

Hagronya, fort of, 65, 66

Halakhah, 9, 13, 14, 16n2, 21n10, 68n131, 68-69n134, 75, 79n161, 79n162, 99-102, 104-105n225, 135, 147n363, 176n418, 178n420, 211, 220n523, 244n571, 244n576, 245n586; halakhic decisor, 123n274, 182n422; halakhic work, 96n193, 104n219, 183n429, 244n576

Halakhah Berurah, 100, 104-105n225

Hanhagat ha-Mishpat (Governance of Justice), 32-33n33

Hanhagat ha-Yihud (Governance of Unity), 32-33n33

hasadim (loves), 93, 138, 139, 156, 157, 160n392; *hasadim de-'Atik* (loves of the Ancient of Days), 25, 156, 158n385, 163-164n404

Hasidism, 20, 89, 216; Breslov, 69n140, 122-123n274, 126n290, 161n398, 239n569; Gur, 128-129n299; Habad, 10, 19n9, 20n10, 48n91, 80n165, 114n255, 208n489, 216, 220n523, 234n561, 239n569, 246-247n589; Izhbitsa-Radzyn, 16n2, 79n162, 158n385, 176n418, 231, 233n557; Kotsk, 89n181, 95n191, 170n405; Lublin, 16n2, 77n152, 204-25n483; Pshiskha, 79n162, 94n191; Ruzhin, 87n177; Sokhatchov, 86n174, 89n181, 95n191, 96n193, 175-176n418

haskamah (approbation), 9, 17-18n6, 226

hayah. *See* soul (five divisions of)

heavens (symbolism), 102, 107n245, 161n397, 168

hesed (lovingkindness), 23, 65, 67, 68n130, 150, 159n387, 160n392; *ba'alei hesed* (masters of lovingkindness), 149

Hesed (Lovingkindness). *See* Ten *Sefirot*

hillul ha-shem (desecration of the Name), 23, 58

hirhur (thought), 210, 211

Hod (Splendor). *See* Ten *Sefirot*

Hokhmah (Wisdom). *See* Ten *Sefirot*

hora'at sha'ah (ad hoc ruling), 14, 79n162

hurmana de-malka (royal authority), 52, 54n96

hutspah (impudence), 188n433, 242, 245n581

'ibbur ("impregnation"), 86n172, 89n181, 201, 208n489

'ikul ha-basar (decomposition of flesh), 80n168

intellect, 11, 74, 75, 83, 85, 92-94, 100, 102, 111, 113n255, 119, 120, 127n295, 132n327, 138, 173, 185, 187n430, 193, 198, 199, 202n476, 207n487, 216, 220n523, 227; practical, 91, 93; theoretical, 91, 93

Ishmael (Islam), 32n27

Jubilee (*yovel*), 100, 104n215, 104n219, 142n335

Kabbalah, 17, 18, 20n10, 32n33, 57, 60n113, 97n200, 99, 112n251, 123n274, 158n385, 159n386, 209, 212, 219n520, 221n525, 222, 223, 225n530, 225n533, 226 ; practical (*kabbalah ma'asit*), 123n274

KaLaH Pithei Hokhmah, 19-20n10, 33n34, 159n386, 160n390, 206n485, 209-211, 213n499

kame'ot (amulets), 17n6

katnut ("smallness"), 24, 88n180, 93

Kelal Yisrael. See Knesset Yisrael

kelipot ("husks"), 21n16, 23, 40, 42, 45-46n68, 112n253, 130n320, 227, 228

Keter (Crown). *See* Ten *Sefirot*

King (symbolism), 41, 46n75, 96n193

Knesset Yisrael (*Ecclesia Israel*), 30n25, 130n319, 171n410

Korahism, 25, 155, 156, 158, 163-164n404

liars, 155, 157

letters, of Hebrew alphabet, 105n225, 230; of the Name, 206n487; *dalet*, 230; *he*, 29; *vav*, 230; *yod*, 29

love of God (*'ahavat Hashem*), 160n391, 215, 218n517, 220n523

lovingkindness (*hesed*), 23, 65, 67, 68n130, 149, 150, 159n387, 160n392

maggid (astral guide), 199, 200, 204n477-482, 204-206n483, 210

magic, 54n96, 60n109, 143n342, 207-208n487

Malkhut (Royalty). *See* Ten *Sefirot*

Maskilim (enlightened Jews), 113n255, 217n506

material possessions, 23

materialism, 24, 83, 84

meat, 155, 157, 185, 240, 242, 245n586

mehatsdei hakla ("gatherers of the field"), 101, 106n232, 116, 118

Mehoza (city), 51, 52, 54n93, 54n94

Messiah, 127n295, 131n324, 202n476, 235, 237; days of, 28, 119; donkey of, 131n324; failed Messiah(s), 21n13, 31n26; generation of, 131n324, 199; "heels of" ("footsteps of"), 115n267, 188n433, 242, 245n581; light of, 220n523, 241, 242; Moses and, 241, 242, 244n573; *shofar* (ram's horn) of, 34n34; son of David, 188n433; Torah of, 242

middot (character traits), 23, 24, 59, 65, 117, 119-121, 132n327, 145n357, 193

Motsa'ei Mayim, 54n96, 146n358, 192-197

Mount Sinai, 14, 24, 58, 79n163, 94n191, 95n192, 118, 125n279, 142n335, 149, 205, 240, 242, 245n586

Mount Tabor, 57-59

music, 55n103, 174n418

Mussar (ethics), literature, 145n357; movement, Rav Kook's critique of, 214-221

mustard, 39, 41

mysticism, 189n435, 207n487

nations of the world, 24, 48n87, 110, 115n265, 149, 227

nefesh. *See* soul (five divisions of)

neshamah. *See* soul (five divisions of)

Netsah (Eternity). *See* Ten *Sefirot*

nevu'ah. *See* prophecy

Nukva. *See partsuf*

oil, fish, 73, 75; goose, 24, 109, 111; scorpion, 197n475; as a symbol of wisdom, 75, 80n165, 111

'Olam (Space), 185, 186, 190n451, 190n455

Oral Torah (*Torah she-be-'al-peh*), 91, 92, 94n188, 95n192, 100, 102, 107n235, 107n241, 155, 156. *See also* Written Torah

Orot (1920), Rabbi Hayyim Hirschensohn on, 192-194, 196n463, 197n475

orthodoxy, 163n404

orthopraxy, 163n404

Palace of the King (*heikhal ha-melekh*), 41

Pardes. *See* Four Levels of Interpretation

parasang(s), 39, 40, 44n49, 44n53, 57, 59, 91, 93, 117, 121, 130n320, 130n323

partsuf: of *Nukva*, 100, 103n208; of *Ze'ir Anpin*, 41, 46n75, 96n193, 140n330

Paul (Saul of Tarsus), 23, 35n38, 164n404

personality, kabbalistic theory of, 198-208

perush (commentary), 13, 22n17

peshat (simple meaning). *See* Four Levels of Interpretation

physiognomy (*hokhmat ha-partsuf*), 24, 119, 127n294

pilpul (dialectic), 75, 92, 99-102, 103n214, 105n225, 156, 224n527

planetarium, 170n405

pomegranate, 80n166

Primordial Kings (Seven), 156, 157, 159n388, 160n395

prophecy (*nevu'ah*), 14, 94n191, 126n287, 204n483, 205n483, 237, 239n567, 239n568, 239n569; Ezekiel's, 103n203, 196n469

Psalm 107, 45n68, 195n456, 240-246

pushkantsa (female raven), 16, 70n147, 70n148

raven, 65, 67

RBG (*rosh, beten, geviyah;* head, belly, chest), 189n441

redemption, 25, 28, 111, 113n255, 122n273, 150, 196n469, 220n523

remez – *See* Four Levels of Interpretation

Resh Millin, 105n225, 162n403, 230, 233n554

revelation, 210; of Elijah, 198, 202n476; of God's glory, 27; of God's unity, 33n33; of Maggid, 200, 206n483, 210; of Torah, 192, 241; reason versus, 94n191; Sinai, 205n483; to Vilna Gaon, 220n523

"root of the soul" ("*shoresh ha-neshamah*"), 24, 126n287, 126n288, 127n297, 159, 208n489

ru'ah. *See* soul (five divisions of)

ru'ah ha-kodesh (divine inspiration), 94n190, 126n287, 137, 193, 196n462, 204

salamander, 60n109

sand (*hol*, symbolism of), 39, 42, 43, 83, 84

saraf (fiery serpent), 155, 156, 158n381

scorpion (*'akrav*), 24, 74, 148, 149, 150, 155, 158n382, 194, 197n475

sea (symbolism), 19n7, 117, 227

Sea of Talmud (*Yam ha-Talmud*), 122n272

Sea of Torah (*Yama de-'Oraita*), 117, 122n273, 123-124n275

Sea of Wisdom (*Yam ha-Hokhmah*), 30n23, 34n36, 40, 91, 92, 101

seafarers (*nehutei yama, yoredei ha-yam*), 9, 27, 39, 40, 42, 51, 78n154, 198, 227, 228, 240, 242

sefirah. See Ten *Sefirot*

serpent (*tanina*), 11, 65-67, 70n147; copper (*nehash ha-nehoshet*), 145n357; fiery (*saraf*), 155, 156

seven [worldly] wisdoms, 24, 109-111, 113n255

Shanah (Time), 185, 186, 190n451, 190n455

"shattering of the vessels" ("*shevirat ha-kelim*"), 159n387, 159n388, 160n390, 192, 194

Shekhinah (divine presence), 143n341, 157, 162n400, 224n530, 236

shemitah (sabbatical year), 104n219

ship (symbolism), 19n7, 28, 30n25, 74, 77-78n154, 83-85, 89n182, 100, 227

Sinai Desert, 9, 198, 200

Sitra Ahera (Other Side), 28, 33n34, 40, 143n342

six extremities (*shesh ketsavot*), 66, 70n145, 75, 92, 93, 249n592

snake (*hivya, nahash*), 74, 155, 156, 158n383

sod. See Four Levels of Interpretation

sod ha-yibbum (mystery of levirate marriage), 194, 196n469, 196n470

Sod ha-Yihud (Secret of Unity), 23, 28, 32-33n33, 65

soul (five divisions of), 188n431; *hayah*, 188n431; *nefesh*, 21n13, 41, 46n72, 78n155, 91, 92, 102, 125n277, 128-129n299, 129n300, 184-186, 187-188n431, 189n435, 189n440, 189n441, 190n450, 190n451, 190n455; *neshamah*, 21n13, 41, 46n72, 78n155, 91, 92, 121, 128-129n299, 129n300, 184, 185, 187n430, 187-188n431, 189n435, 189n440, 189n441, 190n450, 190n451; *ru'ah*, 21n13, 46n72, 78n155, 91, 92, 120, 121, 128-129n299, 130n322, 184-186, 187n430, 187-188n431, 189n435, 189n440, 189n441, 190n450, 190n451, 190n455, 208n489; *yehidah*, 188n431

souls of Israel, 23, 40, 44n55, 241

spear (*romah*), 135, 137, 144n351, 155-157

spiritualism (communing with spirits), 183n429

stars (symbolism), 40

sun (symbolism), 61n398

supersessionism, 27, 32n27, 33n34

symbolism: Bedouin, 24; boat, 77n154, 83; breath, 47n84; cup of wine, 53; David digging the foundation, 175n418; day and night, 92; Deep (*Tehom*), 174, 176n418, 231; dove, 78n154; dry land, 117, 122n270; earth, 25, 157, 160-161n396, 161n397, 168, 170n405; Ecclesia Israel (*Knesset Yisrael*), 30n25; fire, 93, 156; fish, 19n7, 23, 74, 78n158, 89n182; fourth beast of Daniel's vision, 237; frog, 67; front and back, 84; goose, 24, 109; heavens, 102, 107n245, 161n397, 168, 170n405; Jethro, Bil'am and Job, 143n342; king, 41; Kings of Edom, 159n388; knee, 136; leg, 111; "little horn" of Daniel's vision, 238, 239; lying on back, 136; moon, 161n398; mouth, 102; oil, 75, 80n165, 111; ones, tens, hundreds, 40, 41, 75; Rachel and Leah, 140; river, 121, 129n307; salamander, 60n109; sand, 42; sea, 78n154, 103, 117, 122n270, 227; seafarers, sea voyagers, 19n7, 74, 78n154, 89n182, 227, 228; serpent, 67; ship, 19n7, 27, 28, 30n25, 77-78n154, 83, 227; *shofar*, 131n323; sinking the ship, 27, 28, 39, 83, 100; sitting, 143n338; sixty districts, 75; Song of Ascent, 175n418; standing, 136, 143n338; stars, 40; sun, 61n398; *tekhelet*, 137, 145n357; "tenth horn" of Daniel's vision, 239; throat, 66; *tsitsit*, 139, 147n363; water, 93, 101, 106n234, 121, 156; waves, 227; white, 28, 150, 152n372; white donkeys, 25; window of heaven, 168; windpipe, 70n145; wine, 136; wool, 156, 158n385; *Yah*, 29; *YHVH*, 36n44

Tay'a (Bedouin), 9, 117, 119-121, 122n269, 124-125n277, 127n294, 131n324, 135-138, 149, 155, 156, 167-169, 170n405, 198, 200, 201

tefillin (phylacteries), 88n180, 132n327, 143n338

tekhelet (blue), 35n40, 137, 140n329*, 144n353, 145n357, 163n404

Ten *Sefirot* (Ten Attributes): *Binah* (Understanding), 41, 75, 96n193, 100, 102, 103n213, 104n215, 104n219, 104n220, 119-121, 129n300, 129n303, 129n306, 129n307, 129n308, 130n320, 130-131n323, 136, 142n335, 176n418, 190n450, 220n523, 234n561; *Da'at* (Knowledge), 75, 92, 93, 140n330, 220n523; *Gevurah* (Stern Judgment), 70n145, 75, 92, 93, 100, 102, 121, 129n308, 130n323, 144n352, 155, 160n394, 249n592; *Hesed* (Lovingkindness), 25, 70n145, 75, 92, 93, 100, 102, 104n215, 104n219, 121, 129n308, 130n323, 144n352, 152n372, 157, 160n394, 249n592; *Hod* (Splendor), 70n145, 75, 92, 93, 100, 102, 136, 137, 144n352, 249n592; *Hokhmah* (Wisdom), 41, 75, 96n193, 129n307, 176n418, 220n523; *Keter* (Crown), 160n396; *Malkhut* (Royalty), 30n25, 41, 70n145, 74, 91, 92, 94n188, 95n192, 100-102, 103n212, 104n215, 104n219, 106n231, 107n235, 107n241, 120, 129n300, 129n304, 129n308, 130n320, 157, 160n396, 161n397, 161n398, 162n400, 163n404, 176n418, 190n450, 234n561; *Netsah* (Eternity), 70n145, 75, 92, 93, 100, 102, 136, 137, 144n352, 249n592; *Tif'eret* (Beauty), 36n44, 41, 46n75, 70n145, 75, 91-93, 94n188, 95n192, 100, 102, 103n211, 107n245, 119, 121, 129n300, 129n308, 130n322, 130n323, 144n352, 160n394, 161n397, 161n398, 249n592; *Yesod* (Foundation), 70n145, 75, 92, 93, 100, 102, 136, 137, 142n335, 144n353, 176n418, 249n592

teshuvah (return), 47n85, 115n265, 161n398, 177n419; *teshuvah gufanit* (bodily return), 47n85

theology (*Hokhmat Elohut*), 110

Throne of Glory *(Kisse ha-Kavod)*, 44n55

Tif'eret (Beauty). *See* Ten Sefirot

tikkun (correction), 25, 73, 76, 118, 149, 150, 162n403, 167; *ha-guf* (the body); 47n85; *ha-Kavod* (of the Glory), 223; *ha-kelal* (of the collective), 25; *ha-nefulim* (the fallen), 21n16; *ha-neshamah* (of the soul), 10, 12, 21n13, 31n26; *ha-'olam* (the world), 115n267, 156; *ha-perat* (of the individual), 25; *kilkul ve-tikkun* (corruption and correction), 160n390

Torah: bread (symbol), 118; bride (symbol), 61n114; completeness of, 65; dialectic (*pilpul*) of, 156; dry, 215, 216, 219n520; esoteric, 102, 117; exoteric, 84, 102, 117; generalities (*kelalim*), 79n162; giving of, 149, 205; holiness of, 58, 74, 76, 78n158, 110, 118, 125n285; intellectual part of, 75; inwardness (*penimiyut*), 145n357; *Knesset Yisrael Torah*, 30n25; light of, 58, 74, 223; lodging (*akhsanya*), 121; love of, 59; main attribute of (*hesed*), 23, 65; mysteries of, 21n16, 27, 101, 102, 107n245, 123n274, 145n357, 150, 198, 202n476, 216, 245n581; novellae, 14, 75; obligation of knowing, 99; of Messiah, 243; of Moses, 243; practical portion of, 75, 101, 102, 220; revelation of, 241; rigor(s) (*gevurah, gevurot*) of, 66, 155; root of, 119, 120, 241; Sea of Torah, 122, 123; secrets of, 24, 99, 101, 102, 103n202, 216; simple sense of, 84, 123; soul (*nishmat*) of, 222, 223; specifics (*peratim*), 79n162; spiritual portion of, 215, 220n523; toiling in (*'amelut ba-Torah*), 14, 59, 75, 107n240; Torah from heaven (*Torah min ha-shamayim*), 205; Torah of love, 21n16; Torah of truth, 121; Torah scroll, 73; Tree of Life, 69n136; *Tushiyah* (synonym), 61n123; water (symbol), 78n158; way of, 89n181, 95n191, 118; wisdom of, 24, 99, 111, 113n255, 120; with labor (*derekh erets*), 141n333. *See also* Oral Torah, Written Torah

Torah scholar (*talmid hakham*), 16, 19n7, 23, 58, 60n109, 73-76, 77n152, 78n158, 80n167, 80n169, 81n171, 83, 86n174, 88n178, 107n236, 118, 145n357, 227, 235

Torah study, 23, 57, 59, 83, 85, 86, 110, 117, 118; *li-shemah* (for its own sake), 23, 57-59, 60n113; *she-lo li-shemah* (ulterior motivated), 23, 57-59; versus *Derekh Erets* (earning a livelihood), 141-142n333

truth, 155-157, 162n402; *pilpul* of truth, 100, 105n225; Torah of truth, 121; Wisdom of Truth (*Hokhmat ha-Emet*), 223; World of Truth (*'Olam ha-Emet*), 10

tsaddik (righteous), 32n32, 86n173, 87n178, 88-89n180, 103n213, 115n267, 125n277, 131n324, 162n403, 188n433, 201, 208n489

"tsipor shamayim" ("bird of the heavens"), 107n245

tsitsit (ritual fringes), 35n40, 139, 147n363, 163n404

Vatican, 164n404, 235, 236

water(s), 9, 28, 45-46n68, 62n127, 73, 74, 77n149, 78n158, 84, 87-88n178, 91, 93, 99, 100, 101, 102, 106n234, 120, 121, 124n275, 155-157, 173, 195, 216, 227, 231, 232, 233n550, 241; libation (*nisukh ha-mayim*), 174n418; lower, 101, 175-177n418, 231, 232, 233n553, 234n558; "lying waters" (*mayim mekhazvin*), 162n402; masculine, 176-177n418; of *Halakhah*, 101; of knowledge, 34n36; of opinions, 34n36; of the Deep, 173, 174-177n418, 177-178n420, 230-232, 233-234n558; of the sea, 28, 34n36, 78n158; supernal waters, 120; symbol of Torah, 78n158; upper (higher), 176-177n418, 231, 232, 233n550, 233n553

waves, 9, 11, 30n24, 39, 40, 43, 91, 92, 100, 227, 231, 241

white donkeys, 25, 149-150

wine, 51, 53, 77n149, 83, 207n487; guarded (*yayin ha-meshumar*), 41; symbolism of, 136, 142n334

"wings of love and fear," 24, 100, 103n210, 110, 111

wisdom, 24, 28, 57, 74, 84, 91, 92, 96n193, 100, 102, 112n253, 118-121, 129n309, 137-139, 143n342, 144n352, 147n364, 150, 159, 163, 168, 173, 181, 192, 193, 199, 216, 220n523, 228, 241; esoteric, 106n234, 117; exoteric, 106n234, 117; oil of, 75, 80n165; of the body, 117-120; of the soul, 117, 118, 120; of the Torah, 99; Sea of Wisdom (*Yam ha-Hokhmah*), 27, 30n23, 34n36, 40, 91, 92, 101, 198; Wisdom of Kabbalah (*Hokhmat ha-Kabbalah*), 60n113, 103n206, 150, 219n520, 222, 223, 225n533; Wisdom of Truth (*Hokhmat ha-Emet*), 223, 225n533; wordly, 24, 60n113, 109-111, 113n255, 114n256, 115n265, 115n267

wise men, 30n24, 118, 127n294, 138, 184, 227, 228; "agriculturalist," 24, 117, 118; "merchant," 24, 117, 118, 120, 122n269, 125n283*, 137, 198; "seafarer," 27, 78n154, 198, 227, 228

wool, 155, 156, 158n385

World of Chaos (*'Olam ha-Tohu*), 144n352, 157, 159n388, 162n401, 176n418

World of Establishment (*'Olam ha-Tikkun*), 159n388, 162n401

worldly wisdom, 24, 109-111

Work of Creation (*Ma'aseh Bereshit*), 123n274

Work of the Chariot (*Ma'aseh Merkavah*), 99, 103n203, 123n274

World of Speech (*'Olam ha-Dibbur*), 140n332

World of the Female (*'Alma de-Nukva*), 136, 143n338

World of the Male (*'Alma di-Dekhura*), 136, 143n338

World of Thought (*'Olam ha-Mahshavah*), 140n332

World to Come, 28, 29, 32n32, 48n91, 52, 74, 81n171, 109, 111, 121, 124n277, 130n323, 140-141n332

Written Torah (*Torah she-bi-khetav*), 91, 92, 94n188, 95n192, 100, 155, 156. *See also* Oral Torah

Yah, 27, 29, 35n42

yashar (straight, upright), 121, 132n327

yehidah. *See* soul (five divisions of)

Yeshu (Jesus), 27, 30-31n26, 164n404

Yesod (Foundation). *See* Ten *Sefirot*

Yetsirah (World of Formation). *See* Four Worlds

Yoredei Merkavah (Descenders of the Chariot), 227, 229n541

ziz sadai (sea bird), 99, 102, 106n233

לזכות

מוהר"ר יעקב בן דבורה שליט"א

לזכות

רבי שלמה ד"ר פליישנר שליט"א

לז"נ

יחזקאל צבי בן יעקב ז"ל
אסתר שיינדל בת שלום ע"ה

הונצח על-ידי בתם

רייזא עטל בת יחזקאל צבי ואסתר שיינדל שתחי'

לז"נ

אהרן שמואל בן יחזקאל

הונצח על-ידי בנו

צבי בערל בן אהרן שמואל ורחל לאה שיחי'

לז"נ

לב אברהם בן שלמה מיכאל

הונצח על-ידי בן-חורגו

צבי בערל

הנטלף

לזכות

הרב מנחם נחום ב"ר אהרן טברסקי שליט"א

נו"נ לאדמו"ר מטאלנא זצ"ל

לזכות

הרב שאול סייטלר שליט"א

לזכות

רבי משה אייזיקסון שליט"א

לזכות

שלמה בן שושנה שיחי'

אהובה בת שרה שתחי'

זאב אליהו בן אהובה שיחי'

מעין חוה בת אהובה שתחי'

ליכטנשטיין

לז"נ

החתן

דוד אברהם הכהן הי"ד

בן בנימין נתן וברכה הדס

וייס

יא"צ כ"ח כסלו

הונצח על-ידי אחיו רבי דניאל שלום הכהן וייס שליט"א

"מים רבים לא יוכלו לכבות את האהבה ונהרות לא ישטפוה..."

לעילוי נשמת

הרב יצחק ברוך בן אריה ע"ה

נלב"ע ג' תשרי תשע"ח

הונצח על-ידי בנו

הרב נחמן שליט"א

שניידר

ציון לנפש חיה
האשה החשובה והצנועה
עטרת בעלה תפארת משפחתה

מרת שרה סטפנסקי ע"ה

אשת הרב אליעזר שליט"א
בת הרב חיים אורי זצ"ל
למשפחת **ליפשיץ**
נו"נ לבעל האריה דבי עילאי
ולמעלה בקודש

שמן תורק שמה
רואה בטוב עינה
הוי גולה לתורה במסירות קיימה.

שמחת החיים מהותה
רוח נשברה החזיקה
הוי מקבל את כל אדם לימודה.

שמרה לפיה כל ימיה
רכב על דבר אמת בלבבה
השתתפה בשמחת וצרת זולתה.

שלשלת קודש גידלה
רצון בעלה עשתה
הוי מי יתן תמורתה.

נפטרה לשמי מרומים
בשנת ע"ד לחייה
ביום כ"ב כסלו תשע"ח לפ"ק
תנצב"ה

לעילוי נשמת אשת חיל

הדסה ע"ה

בת הרב צבי הירש הכהן וסאדא **לינפילד**

נכדת הרב המקובל רבי פינחס הכהן **לינטופ** זצ"ל

אשת ד"ר אברהם **וינגרטן** שיחי'

נלב"ע בכ"ח בסיון ה'תשע"ח

תנצב"ה

פעלה למען ארץ ישראל

וקיבוץ בניה לתוכה

במסירות נפש

לעילוי נשמת

הרבנית הצדקת

חיה רחל

בת טויבא ואברהם

למשפחת **סילבר**

אשת הרב שלום **לידר** זצ"ל

נלב"ע ראש חודש מנחם-אב ה'תשע"ח

"עוז והדר לבושה ותשחק ליום אחרון"

בעלה

הרב **שלום** ב"ר יצחק אריה וחנה **לידר** זצ"ל

יא"צ י"ב אדר שני

לעילוי נשמת

אברהם בן סלחא ז"ל

נלב"ע בי"ג בכסלו ה'תשע"ט

תנצב"ה

רודף צדקה וחסד

נושא עול הציבור באמונה

מקים יהדות המזרח

לגאון ולתפארת

הונצח על-ידי בנו

הרה"ג רבי אליהו שליט"א

אלן

הרב אברהם יצחק הכהן קוק

ביאור

אגדות רבה בר בר חנה

הוגה מכי"ק על ידי

בצלאל נאור

KODESH PRESS

אורות
OROT

אורות/קודש

ניו-יורק

תשע"ט

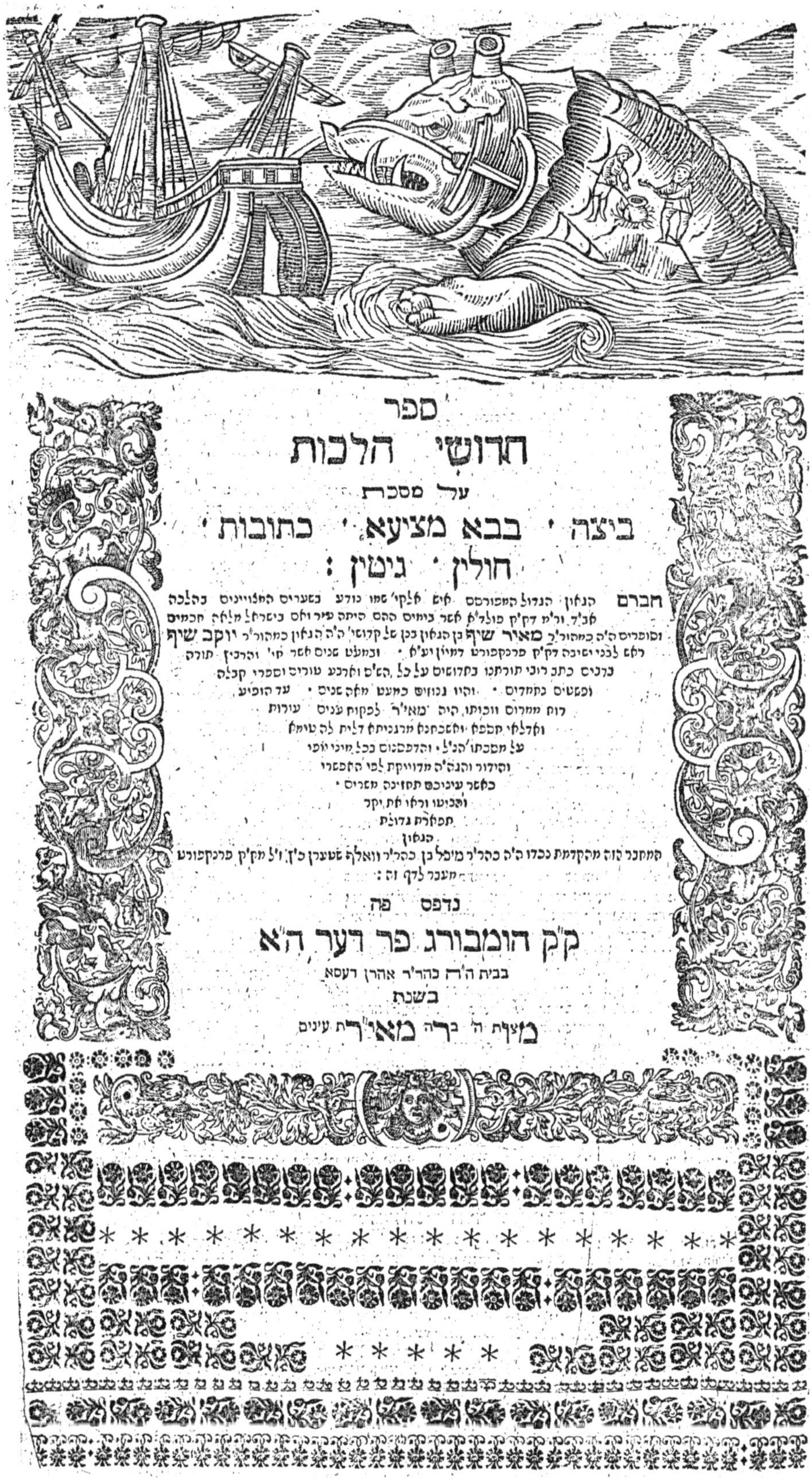
ספר

חדושי הלכות

על מסכת

ביצה · בבא מציעא · כתובות ·

חולין · גיטין :

חברם הגאון הגדול המפורסם איש אלקי' שמו נודע בשערים המצויינים בהלכה
אב"ד ור"מ דק"ק פולד"א אשר בימים ההם היתה עיר ואם בישראל מלאה חכמים
וסופרים ה"ה כמהור"ר מאיר שיף בן הגאון בכן של קדושי' ה"ה הגאון כמהור"ר יעקב שיף
ראש לבני ישיבה דק"ק פרנקפורט דמיין יע"א · ובמעט שנים אשר חי' והרבין תורה
נכנים כתב ידי תורתנו בחדושים על כל הש"ס וארבע טורים וספרי קבלה
ופשטים נחמדים · והיו גנוזים כמעט מאה שנים · עד הופיע
רוח ממרום וזכותו היה "מאיר" לפקוח עינים עורות
ואלמלי קפפא ואשכחנא מרגניתא דלית לה טימא
על מסכתות הנ"ל · והדפסנום בכל מיני יופי
והידור והגה"ה מדוייקת לפי האפשרי
כאשר עיניכם תחזינה מישרים ·
והביטו וראו את יקר
תפארת גדולת
הגאון
המחבר בזה מהקדמת נכדו ה"ה כהר"ר מיכל בן כהר"ר וואלף שטערן כ"ץ ז"ל מק"ק פרנקפורט
מעבר לדף זה :

נדפס פה

ק"ק הומבורג פר דער ה"א

בבית ה"ה כהר"ר אהרן דעסא

בשנת

מצות ה' ברה מאירת עינים

שער ספר **חדושי הלכות** מאת מהר"ם שיף (הומבורג, תצ"ז). האיור למעלה מיוסד על האגדה השביעית של אגדות רבה בר בר חנה ("זימנא חדא הוה אזלינן בספינתא וחזינן ההוא כוורא דיתבא חלתא אגביה וקדחא אגמא, סברינן דיבשתא היא, ונחתינן ואפינן ובשלינן אגביה..."). כנראה, שם המחבר, "שיף", שמשמעותו בלשון אשכנז "ספינה", הוא הנימוק לאיור הדמיוני.

כתב-יד ביאור הראי"ה ל"אגדות רבה בר בר חנה"

חסדי השם, לפני צאתי לדפוס, ניתן לי לעיין בכתב-היד של ביאור הראי"ה מתוך אחד מפנקסיו. את המקור עצמו לא חזיתי, אלא צילום הימנו. על-ידי העיון בו, נודע לי שישנם אי-אלו שינויים בין הנוסח המקורי לזה שנדפס במאמרי הראי"ה, חלק ב (ירושלים, תשמ"ד), עמ' 419-448. על שינויים אלה ומשמעותם, אעמוד בהמשך.

תיאור כתב-היד

בכתב-היד, משתרע הביאור על-פני שלושים-ותשעה עמודים, 15 שורות לכל עמוד.

הביאור מופיע בתוככי פנקס (שם הוא תופס דפים הממוספרים 2124ב-2143ב). גודל העמוד: 7.75 אינץ' רוחב ו-6 אינץ' גובה.

בראש כתב-היד מתנוססת הכותרת: "דרושים לביאורי מאמרי רבב"ח דפ[רק] הספינה". ובאותה השורה משמאלה, בכתב-יד בן המחבר, רבי צבי יהודה הכהן קוק, נכתבו המלים הללו: "טוב ראיה ב[בא] בת[רא]".[1]

לפני ביאוריו, העתיק הראי"ה את האגדות עצמן. כך רשם כסדרן, אגדה וביאורה, אגדה וביאורה, עד שהשלים את חמש-עשרה אגדות רבה בר בר חנה.[2] בסיומן, חתם בברכה: "אברך את ד' אשר יעצני ועד כה עזרני להתחיל ולגמור הרהורי לבבי..."

יש מקומות שנוסח האגדה ביד הראי"ה מתאים לנוסח התלמוד ויש מקומות שהוא חופף את נוסח עין יעקב, ויש מקומות שהוא חורג משניהם. אינו מן הנמנעות שהרב ז"ל כתב את האגדות מתוך הזכרון. ידוע היה הראי"ה בזכרונו הפנומנלי. ידוע גם כן שאת הגהותיו על הש"ס, "הלכה ברורה", המכילות לשונות הרמב"ם ושלחן ערוך, הוא כתב מתוך הזכרון. אם נכונה הנחתנו, הרי מוסבר כיצד נוסח הראי"ה אינו חופף לא את נוסח התלמוד ולא את נוסח עין יעקב. המלאך הממונה על השכחה עשה את שלו.[3] פחות מתקבלת על הדעת היא האפשרות האחרת, דהיינו שהרב במודע ובמכוון יצר נוסח אקלקטי משלו.

שינויי נוסח

יש לעמוד על שינוי נוסח משמעותי בקטע מסויים מהאגדה הששית.

בכתב-היד הנוסח כדלהלן:

> כי יש בתורה ב' אלה הבחינות:
>
> ישנם דברים שהם ראוים לקיום עולם. ע"כ [=על כן] נמצאים הרבה הלכות שלא ישתנו מקביעותם מפני שע"כ [=שעל כן] כך דרך תיקונם שיהיו ברית כרותה לעולם.
>
> ישנם הלכות שמשתנים בהוראתם בדור ודור לפי פרנסיו, וכפי אשר יראה לדיין ושופט שבימיך.
>
> וכ"א [=וכל אחד] העמל בתורה ומחדש בה ע"כ [=על כן] יש לו חלק ונחלה בב' הבחינות.

בנדפס במאמרי הראי״ה חלו שינויים:

כי יש בתורה ב׳ אלה הבחינות:
ההלכות שלא ישתנו מקביעותם, שכך דרך תיקונם שיהיו ברית כרותה לעולם.
ויש גם הלכות שמשתנות בהוראות השעה של חכמי התורה, פרנסי דור ודור, ״השופט אשר בימיך״.
וכ״א [=וכל אחד] העמל בתורה ומחדש בה, ממקור חיי עולם אשר נטע ד׳ בתוכנו והראהו למשה מסיני,
יש לו חלק ונחלה בב׳ הבחינות האלה.

אתה שואל את עצמך: מה המשמעות של התמורות הללו? אין אלה תיקוני או שיפורי לשון הנהוגים בעריכת ספר. כנראה שהאחראים להדפסת הביאור פחדו שמא יבואו רבנים רפורמים ויגלו פנים בתורה שלא כהלכה. לכן העורכים עשו סייג לדברי הרב ז״ל: א) רק ל״חכמי התורה״ הסמכותיים יש כח להורות הוראת שעה; ב) לא כל ״בעל מחדש״ יש לו חלק ונחלה, רק מי שמחדש ״ממקור חיי עולם אשר נטע ד׳ בתוכנו והראהו למשה מסיני״, להוציא מי שמזייף ועושה את התורה פלסתר.

בדומה, בספר ערפלי טוהר שהוצא לאור בשנה הקודמת (תשמ״ג), ״נוטרל״ כביכול משפט שעלול היה להתפרש כמגמה אנטינומיסטית בכתבי הרב, חלילה. במקור כתב הרב:

> ...רק כשהנבואה שרויה בישראל אפשר לתקן ענין כזה על-ידי הוראת שעה, ואז נעשה בדרך היתר ומצוה בגלוי. ועל-ידי סתימת אור הנבואה, נעשה תיקון זה על-ידי פרצה ארוכת זמן, שמדאבת את הלב מצד חיצוניותה, ומשמחת אותו מצד פנימיותה.[4]

ואילו במהדורת תשמ״ג הושמטו המלים ״ארוכת זמן״, והוחלפה המלה ״חיצוניותה״ במלה ״עצמה״, והמלה ״פנימיותה״ במלה ״תכליתה״.[5]

כבר דובר רבות בספרות המשנית מסביב לכתבי הראי״ה על נסיון זה ונסיונות דומים למתן את בשורת הרב ולהאהיל על האורות שלא ייזוקו הבריות מרוב זוהרם. אין סיבה לחזור על הישנות.

יש מקומות שצילום כתב-היד היה דהוי ביותר ובהם לא יכולתי לאמת ולוודא את הנוסח הנדפס במאמרי הראי״ה. כאמור, בירורתי עד מקום שידי מגעת, וברוך השם, בדיקת המקור והשוואתו לנדפס—עבודה מייגעת כידוע למדקדקים—הניבו פירות. כפי שציפיתי, התברר שרובם ככולם של מראי-המקומות המדוייקים סופקו על-ידי העורכים ולא על-ידי המחבר עצמו.

כל הכתוב בסוגריים מרובעים נתוסף על ידי.

ב״נ

---

[1]כנראה שהרצי״ה הועיד את הביאור שלנו לספר המעותד על הש״ס בשם טוב ראיה.

[2]במקומות שלא רשם הרב את האגדה כולה כי-אם תחילתה, השלמתי את המשך האגדה בסוגריים מרובעים. במקרה כזה, שחזרתי את נוסח האגדה של הרב מהדיבורים הפזורים על-פני ביאורו.

[3]דוגמא בולטת ביותר היא שיוך המימרא בסוף האגדה החמישית (״אקרוקתא״) לרב שמואל בר יצחק! למיטב ידיעתנו, אין נוסח כזה. בעל המימרא הוא רב פפא בר שמואל.

[4]שמונה קבצים (ירושלים, תשס״ד), קובץ ב, פיסקא ל.

[5]ערפלי טוהר (ירושלים תשמ״ג), עמ׳ טו.

א

אמ[ר] ר[בה]: אישתעו לי נחותי ימא, האי גלא דמטבע לספינתא, מתחזי כי צוציתא דנורא חיוורתא ברישי[ה], ומחינן עלי[ה] באלוותא דחקיק עליה "אהיה אשר אהיה יה ד' צבאות אמן אמן סלה", ונייח.

יתכן לפרשו כי הולכי ים החכמה האלהית המה נחותי ימא, והעיקר נלע"ד [=נראה לעניות דעתי] שהמה הנשמות שהיו מתגלים [מתגלות] לו ללמדו חידושין ורזין דאורייתא בהנהגה האלהית, או מלאכי השרת, שהם נחותי הים הנודע. והם הודיעו לו מהות כח הטומאה שמטבע לספינתא, שרוצה להטביע ח"ו [=חס ושלום] את כנסת עם ד', והוא מכוון לענין כח הטומאה של אותו האיש יש"ו [=ימח שמו וזכרו], שעיקר הכפירה הי[ה] כי אף שהתחיל השי"ת [=השם יתברך] לגדל את ישראל, מאסם אח"כ ח"ו [=אחר כך חס ושלום]. ובאמת אם הי[ה] כך, הלא השי"ת [=השם יתברך] יודע עתידות, והי[ה] ח"ו כ"ז [=חס ושלום כל זה] רק רע ונקמה כל הגדולה שעשה לנו, אחרי שלא נתקיים בידנו ח"ו [=חס ושלום], רק גרם לנו שנאת העמים וקנאתם, והי[ה] לפי דעתו המובהלת רק מחוץ נראה כחסד, ובאמת הי[ה] עצם הדבר לדין ונקמה. אבל כל עיקר ראיתו הוא מהנראה לעינים כי עזב אותנו השי"ת [=השם יתברך] ביד עמי הארץ, אבל באמת ידענו כי עיקר התכלית וגילוי כבודו ית[ברך] יצא רק מזה אשר ישראל יתפזרו לבין האומות עד יתם פשע, ותתפרסם השגחתו ית[ברך] בגלות ג"כ [=גם כן] על עמו. וגם הגלות מוכרח כדי לכלול ג"כ [=גם כן] ענין עוה"ז [=עולם הזה] בקדושה, שלעת הגאולה יהי[ה] העיקר הרוחניות, וכדברי חז"ל [=חכמינו זכרונם לברכה] "ימים אשר אין בהם חפץ – אלו ימו[ת] המש[יח] שאין בהם לא זכות ולא חובה", ע"כ [=על כן] כאשר רוצה שיוכלל עוה"ז ג"כ [=עולם הזה גם כן] בשלמות, הניח אותנו בהסתר פנים, ונשמור מצוותיו בעסקי עוה"ז [=עולם הזה]. ומשני אלה – דהיינו, השגחתו ית[ברך] בגלות על עמו והגלות דוקא יכין הגאולה, וצירוף עוה"ז [=עולם הזה] עם עוה"ב [=עולם הבא] – זהו סוד יחוד שמו ית[ברך] הכולל כל המדות, ובזה הוא מתגלה כבודו ית[ברך] איך הוא המוציא כל צבא הנמצאים, ועי"ז [=ועל ידי זה] מתאמן שמו ית[ברך] בכל הצדדים, בין בדין בין ברחמים, בין בגשמי בין ברוחני, וגם מתברר שהממשלה לו נצחית, שכל מה שאפשר להיות מהיפוך וסתירה מצד הסט[רא] א[חרא] כבר יצא אל הפועל, ונראה איך שהכל עבדיו. ע"כ [=על כן] כשמתגלה זאת החכמה, שוב לא "אהני לרמאה ברמאותי[ה]", ונייח.

וז"ש [=וזה שאמר] האי גלא דמטבע לספינתא, ובאמת הוא רצה להטביע הספינה, כי החכמה היא המים, מי הים, אבל לנו נמסר לעשות מלאכה במים רבים ע"י [=על ידי] כלים שהם המצות, והרוצה לבטל המצות המעשיות, רוצה להטביע בים כל הספינה. אבל עיקר המצות מיוסדות על בחירת ישראל מכל האומות וזכר יצ"מ [=יציאת מצרים]. ע"כ [=על כן] בא זה הגל הטמא ומתחזי כי צוציתא דנורא חיוורתא ברישי[ה], לומר שרק ברישי[ה] הי[ה] חיוורתא, הנהגה הנוטה ללובן החסד, אבל באמת הי[ה] אש שורף [שורפת] כיון שלא הי[ה] שלמות וקדושה נצחית, כיון שנפלנו לבירא עמיקתא ונתפזרנו באומות להנתן תח"י [=תחת ידיהן]. אבל מחינן עלי[ה] באלוותא דחקיק עלי[ה] אהי[ה] אשר אהי[ה], שהוא

הרב אברהם יצחק הכהן קוק

איך שעיקר הקדושה האלקית [האלהית] מתגלה מהשגחת השי"ת [=השם יתברך] עלינו בגליות, ובזה יתכלל דינא ורחמי, ותתהפך חשוכא לנהורא. י"ה, שהלא "בי"ה ד' צור עולמים" – "עוה"ז [=עולם הזה] בה"א, עוה"ב [=עולם הבא] ביו"ד", ומצד י"ה אנו צריכים ליחד ב' עולמים, וזה א"א כ"א ע"י [=אי-אפשר כי-אם על-ידי] הגלות. ומזכיר שם מלא אח"כ [=אחר כך], לומר שדוקא מאהי[ה] אשר אהי[ה] וי"ה, דהיינו השגחתו עלינו בגלות ותכלית הגלות, שהוא ליחד שמים וארץ, עוה"ז ועוה"ב [=עולם הזה ועולם הבא], הוא סוד השם המלא, המתפאר בענפיו וכלול בכל הקדושות. ועי"ז [=ועל ידי זה] מתגלה ממשלתו על כל צבאות מעלה ומטה. וזהו צבאות, ונודע נאמנותו בעוה"ז ועוה"ב [=בעולם הזה ועולם הבא], וזהו אמן אמן. גם נודע נצחיותו איך שלא ישתנה לעולם, ורצונו לא ישתנה ח"ו [=חס ושלום] כי דברו נצב לעד לעולם. וכאשר יכוהו במטה האלקים [=האלהים] זה, נייח זה הכח הטמא ולא יכול להרע, רק "עוד מעט ואין רשע" ו"צדיקים ירשו ארץ".

ב

אמר ר[בה] ב[ר] ב[ר] ח[נה]: אשתעו לי נחותי ימא, בין גלא לגלא תלת מאה פרסי, ורומא דגלא תלת מאה פרסי. זימנא חדא, הוא אזלינן באורחא ודלינן גלא עד דחזינא מרבעתא דכוכבא זוטא כמבזר ארבעין גריווי דחרדלא, ואי דלינן טפי, הוא מקלינן מהבלא. ורמא לי[ה] גלא קלא לחברתה: חברתי, מי איכא מידי בעלמא דלא שטפתי[ה], דניתי אנא ונאבדי[ה]? א[מרה] ל[ה]: פוק חזי גבורתא דמרך דאפי[לו] מלא חוטא דחלא לא עברית, שנאמר "האותי לא תיראו נאם ה' אם מפני לא תחילו אשר שמתי חול גבול לים חק עולם ולא יעברנהו" [ירמיהו ה, כב].

כבר אמרנו שהגלים הרוצים להטביע הספינות שהולכים [שהולכות] בים, ומבקשים להשחית העולם, הם כוחות הטומאה המתפרצים מאדוניהם ומבקשים לאבד העולם. והנה "זה לעומת זה עשה האלהים", וככח הקדושה לפרטיהם כמו כן כוחות הטומאה הנוגדים אותם, כענין י"ב שבטי י"ה ושנים עשר נשיאים לבית ישמעאל, וכמש"כ [=וכמו שכתוב] "יצב גבולות עמים כמספר [למספר] בני ישראל". והנה מחנה ישראל תלתא פרסי, והוא בעשי[ה]. ונודע שעשי[ה] סוד אחדות, ויצירה עשרות, ובריאה מאות, כי כל מה שיתעלו הדברים בקרבתם לשרשם, כן הוא גודל אורם וריבוי זיום ותפארתם. ע"כ [=על כן] בבריאה, שהוא מקום נשמותיהם של ישראל, הויא שיעור מחנה ישראל תלת מאה פרסי, א"כ ג"כ [=אם כן גם כן] "ז[ה] לעו[מת] ז[ה]", ספי[רות] הסט[רא] א[חרא] וכוחותיהם תלת מאה פרסי. אמנם נודע שהרשעים הם בפירודא, וכמש"כ [=וכמו שכתוב] בעשו "נפשות", כי "יתפרדו כל פועלי און", והשי"ת [=והשם יתברך] לא יניחם להתחבר, ע"כ [=על כן] בין כל בחי[נה] מהם יפסיק כח הקדושה, שלא יתחברו יחד לטשטש העולם. וז"א [=וזה אמרו] בין גלא לגלא תלת מאה פרסי, כי הקדושה הכללית של כל מחנה ישראל מפסקת ביניהם, ומעכב[ת] על ידם שלא יצליחו ו"לא יחרוך רמי[ה] צידו", ורומא דגלא תלת מאה פרסי, שזהו שיעור רוממותו וקומתו בשרשו. והנה כוחות הרע רוצים לצוד נפשות ישראל, אותם [אותן] הנשמות העשוקות הנופלים [הנופלות] בידם, ועי"כ [=ועל-ידי כן] יבא להם שפע וקיום. ואמר זימנא חדא הוא אזלינן באורחא, לא אמר "אזלינן בספינתא", שהכונה שלא נחת בים החכמה, כי להבחין עניני הסט[רא] א[חרא] אין צריך לים החכמה, כי הם בתכלית השפלות נגד הקדושה, ובחינותיהם יתחילו אחרי כל מעלות הקדושה, ונמצא ששם במקומם אין המקום מלא "דעה...כמים לים מכסים". רק אזלינן באורחא, במקום שהנהר נחרב ויבש, לדעת ענינם וכוחותיהם. וחזינא מרבעתא דכוכבא זוטא, כי ישראל נמשלו לכוכבים, והשיג מעלת נפש א[חד] מקטני ישראל שנשבו ע"י [=על-ידי] הקליפות, וראה כי ממנו להם די שפע וקיום כל בחינותיהם. כי נודע שהכוחות הרעות [הרעים] נמשלו לדבורים, וכמש"כ [=וכמו שכתוב] "[וירדפו אתכם] כאשר תעשינה הדבורים", וכה"א [=וכן הוא אומר] "סבוני כדבורים", וכדחז"ל [=וכדברי חז"ל] שהדבורה מתה בנשיכתה, כמ"כ [=כמו כן] עליהם נאמר "אשר שלט האדם באדם לרע לו", כי עי"ז

[=על-ידי זה] "המה כשלו ונפלו", רק שהם שמחים בהצלחתם לשעתם, והחרדל הוא מזון לדבורים כדחז"ל [=כדברי חז"ל] בפ[רק] לא יחפור, "הרחק דבוריך מחרדלאי שהם [שהן] באות ואוכלות לגלוגי חרדלאי". וכלל כוחות הרע המה ד' מדריגות, כנגד ד' מעלות אבי"ע [=אצילות, בריאה, יצירה, עשיה], וכנגד חו"ב תו"מ [=חכמה ובינה, תפארת ומלכות] כנודע. וראה שע"י [=שעל-ידי] נפש קטן מישראל יש להם מקום שפע לכל מחנותיהם, דהיינו כמבזר ארבעים גריווי דחרדלא, נגד כל ד' בחינותיהם, שכל א[חד] כלול מעשרה. ואע"פ [=ואף על-פי] שמתחילה דיבר במאות, מ"מ [מכל מקום] כשבא לדבר נגד בחי[נת] הנפש הנופלת בידם, אין הנפילה לנשמה שהיא בבריאה, כי שמה לא יגיע יד זרים, והוא סוד היין המשומר, רק ביצירה, שהוא סוד טו"ר [=טוב ורע], שמה יוכלו לקנן ולהשליך חכה. וז"ס [=וזה סוד] היכל מלך, כי מלך הוא בחי[נת] ז"א [=זעיר אנפין] המקנן ביצירה, ומכש"כ [=ומכל שכן] כשרוצים לחוטפו למזון להם. ובחי[נת] המזון היא מדרגה אחת פחותה מהניזון, שהם רוצים לבלע חיים, כמש"כ [=כמו שכתוב] "אזי חיים בלעונו", לא בדרך יניקת שפע שהמניק קיים ומעולה מהיונק, רק בליעה ממש באופן שהוא יהי[ה] לחמם, ע"כ [=על כן] באמת משפילים אותו לערך יצירה כשהם עסוקים בבחי[נת] בריאה שלהם, וכענין שכ[תב] העקידה בפ[רשת] המן שענין המזון הוא במדרגה אחת פחות מהניזון, ע"כ [=על כן] הוא ממש עשרות נגד המאות, ויש בו ארבעים גריווי דחרדלא למזונם, אבל הוא רק מקום מוכן לזריעתם, לזרוע ראש ולענה, ולא שפע מוכן, כי הנופל בידם הוא רק נותן להם חיות אם יוסיף טומאה וחטאים שהם מזונות מרים שלהם לקיומם, או כשיוחלט ברשע, אז אפי[לו] מצותיו להם נתנו, להוסיף להם עצמה ב"ימין שקר".

והנה באו לראות בתמונה הטמאה כדי להבין ענינם ואיך להשמר מהם, אך צריך לשמור שלא ידבקו בו ח"ו [=חס ושלום]. ע"כ [=על כן] ביארו החכמים ז"ל [=זכרונם לברכה] שצריך לעבור במרוצה במקום מחזה הקליפות, שלא ידבקו בו ח"ו [=חס ושלום]. והנה ראה ראשית מלאכתם איך יצודו ברשתם, ועוד להם דברים רבים מה שיעשו מהעשוקים כשלא ישתדלו עצמם לצאת ממאסרם, אך שיער כי אין להסתכל יותר בהם ולא לפנות אל האלילים, כי אש זרה מהבל ביש שלהם שורף [שורפת] ומכלה. וע"כ [=ועל כן] אמר אי דלינן טפי הוא מקלינן מהבלא, כסוד "יש הבל אשר נעשה על הארץ", כי כל ענינם הוא רק הבל, וענין הבל הוא רק הכנה לדיבור, כי לא נשלם הדיבור בהם, שכל ענינם הוא מפני שלא נשלמו מקדושת השבת, כנודע דחז"ל [=דברי חז"ל] שע"ש ביה"ש [=שערב שבת בין השמשות] נבראו המזיקין, ולא נשתכללו, ופגומים הם, ובהבל יסודם.

ורמא לי[ה] גלא קלא לחברתה: חברתי, מי איכא מידי בעלמא דלא שטפתי[ה], דניתי אנא ונאבדי[ה]? א[מרה] ל[ה]: פוק חזי גבורתא דמרך דאפי[לו] מלא חוטא דחלא לא עברית. זה נודע כי גם הנשמות הנופלות בידם, מ"מ כ"ז [=מכל מקום כל זמן] שהם בתוך הגוף אינם שולטים בהם ממש, כי הם קשורים בענין הבחירה, ויוכל לשוב בשעה קלה בתשובה אמיתית, אז מוציא מהם כל אשר גזלו. ובאמת הוא דבר נפלא כי עם תוקף גבורתם ועזות פניהם, שהם מנצחים דברים גדולים מופשטים בחומר [מחומר] ופוגעים בם, מ"מ [=מכל מקום] אינם יכולים להיות למפגע להשוכנים בתוך הגוף. והנם [והנה] נמשל הגוף ליבשה הגלוי[ה], ואמר מי איכא מידי בעלמא דלא שטפתי[ה], כי "שטף... עד צואר יגיע", מ"מ [=מכל מקום] אולי נשאר מה בעלמא, דהיינו הבחירה שבנפש שבתוך הגוף, וניתי ונאבדיה. אך משיבה שהיא רק גבורת השי"ת [=השם יתברך], דמלוא חוטא חלא, שהוא חול ועפר

הגוף וכוחותיו, אשר "במה נחשב הוא", ומ"מ [=ומכל מקום] לא יעברנהו, וזש"ה [=וזה שאמר הכתוב] "האותי לא תיראו נאום ד', אם מפני לא תחילו, אשר שמתי חול גבול לים", שהוא מדבר ממש בים הגשמי, ורומז ג"כ [=גם כן] לדברים עליונים מזה, שעיקר הנפילה הוא ע"י [=על-ידי] יאוש שאומר לו היצה"ר [=היצר הרע] כי א"א [אי-אפשר] לו לתקן את אשר עותו אחרי אשר כ"כ [=כל כך] נפל בידו וגבר עליו, אבל באמת "שמתי חול גבול לים חק עולם", ששמתי החק ע"י [=על-ידי] כח הבחירה, שהוא עיקר החק הכולל לעולם, "ולא יעברנהו". א"כ [=אם כן] ראוי להתחזק תמיד ביראת ד', ואפי[לו] הרבה לפשע, כי יש תקוה לברח אל היבשה כ"ז [=כל זמן] שהאדם בחיים, ולא יוכלו גלי הים [ה]זועף להשיגו, כשיברח לחסות בצל הבחירה, כי ע"ז [=על זה] לא ניתן להם כח ושליטה.

ג

אמר ר[בה] ב[ר] ב[ר] ח[נה]: לדידי חזי לי הורמין בר ליליתא דהוא רהיט אקופי דשורא דמחוזא, והוא רהיט פרשא רכיב גמלא מתתאי ולא יכיל לי[ה]. זמנא חדא, הוא מסרגין ליה תרתי כודנייתא וקיימין אתרי גשרי דדונג, ושוור מהאי להאי ומהאי להאי, ונקיט תרי כסי דחמרא בידיה, ומוריק מהאי להאי [ומהאי להאי] ולא נטיף נטפא לארעא. ואותו היום "יעלו שמים ירדו תהומות" [תהלים קז, כו] הוה. שמעו בי מלכותא וקטלוהו.

בא לומר מה שראה כח הרע הבא מתשוקת ההמונים לשום זהב כסלם, וכל תשוקתם אינה כ"א [=כי-אם] לבנות בתי חומה, ולקמץ בממונם שלא לתן לכל דבר צדקה, והם מחשבים שהמה בוטחים במה שישימו על עפר בצר, ויבצרו העיר אשר דרים בה בחומות גדולות. ובאמת, זה הוא עיקר חורבנם. ולא יועיל להם שום הצלה לעת פגע, כי כח המשחית מוכן בזה גופי[ה] שהם מסירים בטחונם מה', ושמים מבטחם בכח ידם. ונודע כי מיושבי מחוזא העשירים היו אנשים כאלה נמצאים, כדאמרי[נן] בר"ה [=בראש השנה] "ופניהם דומין לשולי קדרה, אמר רבא: ואינון משפירי שפירי בני מחוזא ומקרי בני גיהנם". אמר שאף שהלילית עצמה עיקר משכנה במקום חורבן ושממון, כדכתיב "שם הרגיעה לילית", ואין רצונה בישוב העולם, אך ישוב המביא לידי חורבן כחורבן דמי, ועל ישוב כזה היא שמחה.

אמר כי הורמין בר ליליתא, דהיינו מורשה אחד מכוחותי[ה], לשון הורמנא ורשות, הוא רהיט אקופי דשורא דמחוזא, כי משכנו על ראשי החומות הגבוהות, אשר בני מחוזא הטפשים הרימו מגדליהם לתלפיות, וסוברים כי הם מישבי עולם ואינם כ"א [=כי-אם] חרובי קרתא, כי עי"ז [=על-ידי זה] השגחת השם ית[ברך] והצלתו נמנעת מהם, ולא די שלא יועילו להם מבצריהם, עד שלא יצטרכו לשום עזר בבא עליהם אויב, אלא שגם חילים ורוכבי סוסים ג"כ [=גם כן] לא יוכלו למלט נפשם, תחת אשר אם לא שמו מבטחם בארמונות ומבצרים היו נשמרים ע"י [=על-ידי] ההשגחה האלהית, ועתה גם כי רהיט פרשא מתתאי ורכיב גמלא או סוסיא לא יכל לו לגרש כח המבחיל השורה דוקא במבצריהם. ומספר איך שנותנים כח לחבל בין בכלל בין בפרט, כי יש שכ"כ [=שכל כך] גדלו בתאות חמדת הממון עד שאין להם שום רצון אחר כ"א [=כי-אם] להרבות הון בלא תכלית, ואפי[לו] אם יהי[ו] חשוכי בנים שאין לו מה לדאוג לבניו אחריו, וגם כשיהי[ה] לעת זקנותו וחלישות כוחו, שכבר עומד הוא על פתח קברו, ורואה שקרבו ימיו לעבור את העולם לעולם אחר, עכ"ז אע"פ [=עם כל זה, אף על-פי] שהוא מלא שפע המספיק לו כהנה וכהנה עד שאין לו מקום להחזיק כל עשרו, עכ"ז [=עם כל זה] הוא מדקדק על פרוטה שלא ליתן לצדקה לעניי ארץ. וכ"כ [=וכל כך] גובר עליו כח הטומאה עד שאפי[לו] ביום מותו לא יניח כלום לשום דבר שבצדקה, להחיות נפשו העלובה בעוה"ב [=בעולם הבא]. והאנשים האלה המה מרכבה להורמין בר ליליתא, שע"י [=שעל-ידיהם] הוא מתחזק להרבות בבנין ע"מ [=על מנת] לסתור ולהחריב את אשר נתישב, כדי שיגדל השממון והחורבן. והנה

ביאור אגדות רבה בר בר חנה

אנשים כאלה, כשהם חשוכי בנים, יש להם לדאוג לנפשם, שאם אין ברכה להם מצד גופם, יראו עכ"פ [=על כל פנים] שלא תהי[ה] נפשם עקורה מפרים של צדיקים. אבל כשגם פירות של מע"ט [=מעשים טובים] אינם איתם, נמצא שהגוף גם הנשמה שניהם עקורים כפרידה שאינה יולדת ואין בה סי[מן] ברכה כדחז"ל בפ"ק [=כדברי חז"ל בפרק קמא] דקדושין. וז"ש [=וזה שאמר] זמנא חדא הוא מסרגאן לי[ה], מוכנים לרכיבתו, תרתי כודנייתא, היינו חשוכי בנים, שהוא ריקן מכל מצוה, והנשמה שלו ג"כ [=גם כן] כודנייתא דלא ילדה. וקיימין אתרי גישרי דדונג, הכונה שעומדים לעבור מעולם לעולם, ושניהם מרגישים כי כוחות הגוף מתמוטטות [מתמוטטים] והנפש ג"כ [=גם כן] סר צילה ממנה, כדברי הזוהר, "ואין שלטון ביוה"מ [=ביום המות]", והם מלאים עושר ושפע, אשר זה עצמו משכרתו [משכרו?] ביין גאונו. וזהו דנקיט תרתי כסי דחמרא בידי[ה], שהשפע הוא יותר ממה שיוכל לקבל, וא"צ [=ואין צריך] כלל למילואו, ומוריק מהאי להאי, ותחילה אמר ושוור מהאי להאי ומהאי להאי, שכח שולטנותו מקפת את הגוף ואת הנפש, כי לפעמים יחזק כח קמצנותו ע"י [=על-ידי] מה שאומר לו שצריך לחזק גופו הנחלש מזקנה, ולפעמים אומר לו שצריך לפזר זהב וכסף על שרים ושרות לשמח בהם נפשו העגומה, ולמה יתן לצדקה אחרי שמוכרח הוא להוצאות אחרות. וכמו כן תרי כסי דחמרא הכונה שעסקיו פי שנים מצרכיו, ומוציא כסף על עסקיו כדי להרבות עוד הון, ומחשב בדעתו שהוצאתו רבה כי צריך הוא למשרתים ובנינים לעסק זה ולעסק זה, ולוקח ממון מעסק זה ונותן בעסק זה, ולפעמים מהפך מטרתא. אך לא נטיף נטפא לארעא לזולתו, לעניי ארץ, רק בכוסו אשר יתן עיניו בו, ואותו היום "יעלו שמים", שהוא יוה"מ [=יום המות], שהנפש תעלה שמים, והגוף "ירד תהומות", ועכ"ז [=ועם כל זה] לא תסור קמצנותו ממנו, יען הורגל בה כל ימיו ואביק בה כמינות דמיא. ויען כי לא יתן צדקה פדיון נפשו, ע"כ [=על כן] שמעו בי מלכותא של מעלה וקטלוהו, כי לו עסק בצדקה הוסיפו לו חיים, כדחז"ל [=כדברי חז"ל] "וצדקה תציל ממות – ולא ממיתה משונה כ"א [=כי-אם] ממיתה עצמה", "כן-צדקה לחיים".

ד

אמר ר[בה] ב[ר] ב[ר] ח[נה]: לדידי חזי לי ההוא ארזילא בר יומא דהוי כהר תבור. והר תבור כמה הוי? ארבע פרסי. ומשכא דצווארי[ה] תלתא פרסי, ובי מרבעתא דרישיה פרסא ופלגא. רמא כופתי[ה] וסכריה לירדנא.

הנה יסוד התורה הוא ללמוד אותה לשמה וללמוד בקביעות, לא דרך מקרה. והלומד בקביעות לומד לשמה, משא"כ [=מה שאין כן] הלומד שלא לשמה לומד רק דרך מקרה, כדי שידע להזדיין בפני הבריות בתלמוד תורה. והנה אמרו חז"ל [חכמינו זכרונם לברכה] שהר תבור הי[ה] עליו תלמוד תורה רק לשעה כדאי[תא] במגילה. והנה דרך הלומד תורה שלא לשמה, שהוא מעיין לפי שעה בכל ד' חלקי התורה, שהם פרד"ס [=פשט, רמז, דרוש, סוד], כדאי[תא] באור נערב להרמ"ק ז"ל [=להרב משה קורדובירו, זכרונו לברכה] בכת החוטאת שמגובה לבבו אומר שלו יאתה להיות שלם ג"כ [גם כן] בקבלה, כדרך שמשלים עצמו באיזה חכמה. אבל כיון שאין כונתו כ"א [=כי-אם] להתיהר, ע"כ [=על כן] תמיד כשקורא בקול ומדבר בדברי תורה לא יעסוק בחלק הפשט, שהפשט הוא דבר השוה ורגיל בכל אדם ואין לו מקום להתיהר עי"ז [=על-ידי זה]. ע"כ [=על כן] עיקר עסקו הוא רק לפרסם עצמו בג' חלקי דר"ס [=דרוש, רמז, סוד], ומהפשט יסיח דעתו. משא"כ [=מה שאין כן] העוסק בתורה לשמה, שהתורה עצמה חביבה עליו, אז כל עניני התורה שוים לו, דרוש ופשט ורמ"ס [=ורמז, סוד]. והנה גם בג' חלקים שהוא עוסק להתיהר, לא יעסוק בכללותם. וכדברי חז"ל ע"פ [=חכמינו זכרונם לברכה על פסוק] "ורועה זונות יאבד הון", ש"האומר שמועה זו נאה וזו אינה נאה מאבד הונה של תורה". וזה העוסק בתורה להתיהר לגמרי אינו עוסק כ"א [=כי-אם] באותם החלקים שמשער שעי"ז [=שעל-ידי זה] יהי[ה] לו תפארת וכבוד בין הבריות, ועי"ז [=ועל-ידי זה] אין התורה מקדשת מעשיו, ועי"ז [=ועל-ידי זה] מתחלל שם שמים, שלא די שאינו גורם לקדש שם שמים, ולתקן את אחרים, רק אדרבא, אחרים מוסיפים סרה בראותם דרכיו מקולקלים. והנה משעברו ישראל את הירדן קבלו את הערבות בשלמות, כדברי חז"ל [חכמינו זכרונם לברכה] בסוטה, וענין הערבות שכ"א [=שכל אחד] יראה לתקן את חבירו. וזה שע"י [=שעל-ידי] התורה הוא מקלקל לאחרים – כדברי חז"ל [=חכמינו זכרונם לברכה] ביומא: "ה"ד [=היכי דמי] חילול השם? ... וכדה"כ [=וכדברי הכתוב] 'באמור להם עם ד' אלה ומארצו יצאו'" – הוא מנגד לתכלית ברית הערבות המיוחס לירדן.

והנה אמרו חז"ל [=חכמינו זכרונם לברכה], "הראם קרניו נאות ואין כוחו גדול", והיינו שההולך רק אחר שיחה נאה ויופי ולא יראה לחזק כח קדושת נשמתו בכח דברי תורה אמיתי ויראה, והיינו ארזילא שלומד רק מה שהוא תפארת ונוי לפני הבריות, ולא מה שיוסיף כח נצחי לנשמתו בכח וחוזק אמיתי, כדכתיב "תנו עוז לאלהים", להוסיף כח בפמליא של מעלה. ויש רמז בלשון ג"כ [=גם כן] שאור התורה מזולזל אצל עצמו – שהלומד תורה לשמה מכיר מעלת התורה ויקרת ערכה, ויודע איך שמגעת את האדם לשלמות המופלא[ה] שאין למעלה הימנה, ע"כ כ"ד [=על כן כל דבר] שבתורה חביב ויקר בעיניו, ות"ח [=ותלמידי חכמים] יקרים בעיניו, כי יודע ערכם וכבודם, ע"כ [=על כן] אור יקר הוא בעצמו מצד תורת אלהיו שבלבו – אבל זה הלומד להתיהר, ואין התורה אצלו כ"א [=כי-אם] כקישוט חיצוני להטעות את הבריות, לא יכיר חמדת

התורה וקדושתה, ע"כ [=על כן] היא זילא בעיניו, אע"פ [=אף על-פי] שיודע קצת מאורה, וזהו אור זילא. דהוי כהר תבור, פי[רוש] שהוא בר יומא כי יעמוד בשקידתו, כי מהרה יזנח דברי תורה כיון שאינו דבק בתורה מצד קדושתה. והוא כהר תבור שרק לפי שעה בא ללמוד תורה, ואין הקדושה מתקיימת בו. וזה אינו לומד בהדרגה להיות עמל בתורה, להיות יגע בתורה, בתחילה למגרס והדר למסבר, מתחילה פשט ואח"כ [=ואחר כך] רמז, דרוש וסוד, כי "לא יחפוץ [כסיל] בתבונה כ"א [=כי-אם] בהתגלות לבו", שהוא יודע דברי תורה הרבה, ו"בכל תושיה יתגלע". והר תבור כמה הוי? ד' פרסי, שאע"פ [=שאף על-פי] שלומד רק באקראי, הוא קופץ ובולע בלא ישוב הדעת והדרגה מכל ד' חלקי התורה פרד"ס [=פשט, רמז, דרוש, סוד]. אבל כיון שאינו לומד כ"א [=כי-אם] להיות לו חן וכבוד בעיני העולם, ע"כ [=על כן] בי משכי[ה] דצוארי[ה] – פי[רוש] קולו שהוא מתיחס לצוואר – אינו נותן קולו כ"א [=כי-אם] בג' פרסי, דהיינו בדרוש רמז וסוד, שבו יתנשא לומר שהוא חכם גדול, אבל הפשט ישליך אחר גיוו, כי אין לו תפארת בזה. ע"כ [=על כן] לא ידע מקרא ומשנה כצורתה, וכל מה שלומד מפשט אינו כ"א [=כי-אם] כדי שיוכל להיות מתנשא עי"ז [=על-ידי זה] בג' החלקים [ה]אחרים להיות קורא בגרון להיות נגיד שמי[ה]. וגם מאלה הג', לא בכולם יעסוק, כדברי החסיד בחוה"ל [=בחובות הלבבות] בהקדמה שהכסיל לא יעסוק כ"א [=כי-אם] באותן החלקים שיזדיין לפני בנ"א [=בני אדם] לפי ענין חבורתו ודורו, ע"כ [=על כן] עיקר מעינו אינו כ"א [=כי-אם] במחצית מאותם שלמד מהג', ובי מרבעתי[ה] דרישיה, עיקר עיון רישיה ושכלו אינו כ"א [=כי-אם] פרסא ופלגא, כפי ענין הנצרך לבריות. ודימה שהתורה, כל חלק שבה, יש בו ענין הניכר תועלתו לפני בנ"א [=בני אדם] וענין שהוא רק מועיל לאוהבי השי"ת [=השם יתברך] ושוקדי תורתו באמת. והעוסק בתורה לשמה, אין חילוק בעיניו, כי גם הדברים הנצרכים לבריות יעסוק בהם לשם שמים, משא"כ [=מה שאין כן] זה האור זילא יברור רק הנצרך לבריות, ובהם ישים מגמתו, וע"כ [=ועל כן] לא תועיל לו התורה להעמידו על דרך טובה ולקדש דרכיו, רק דרכיו ומדותיו מקולקלים. לא די שלא יקיים את תכלית הערבות שנכרת בירדן להועיל לזולתו בתורת ד' וקיום מצותיו, רק אדרבא, כשרמא כופתי' ותתגלה בהתתי[ה] בבואו לידי איזה נסיון, ויראו הכל סרחונו וקלקול מדותיו, גורם להחטיא את הבריות, וסכרי[ה] לתועלת הירדנא, כי המחטיא הוא הפך הערבות.

ה

ואמר רבה ב[ר] ב[ר] ח[נה]: לדידי חזי לי ההיא אקרוקתא דהוא כאקרא דהגרוניא. ואקרא דהגרוניא כמה הוא? שיתין בתי. אתא תנינא, בלעה. אתא פישקנצא בלעה, וסליק ויתיב באילנא. תא חזי כמה נפיש חילי[ה] דאילנא! אמר רב פפא בר שמואל: אי לאו דהואי התם, לא הימני.

הנה עיקר מדת התורה היא חסד, כמש"כ [=כמו שכתוב] בנוסח התפילה, "כי באור פניך נתת לנו תורת חיים ואהבת חסד". אמנם שלמות התורה ושורש האמונה שיהיו כל המדות כלולים [כלולות] בה בסוד האחדות, וגם מדת האכזריות כשמשתמשים ממנה לקדושה, היא דבר המשלים התורה. והנה שורש החסד, מתחילה פועל לאהוב את עצמו, שזהו ג"כ [=גם כן] חסד, כדחז"ל [=כדברי חז"ל] על שמירת הגוף, "באו נגמול חסד להדא עלובתא וכדכתיב 'גומל נפשו איש חסד'". אבל כשע"פ [=כשעל-פי] התורה מזדמן שצריך למסור נפשו למ[י]תות [?] אכזריות כדי לקדש שם שמים. אך אצל איש בעל מדות טובות הוא דבר קל למסור נפשו ועצמו במקום הצריך. אבל להיות אכזרי על אחרים הוא דבר יותר כבד ומנגד למדות הטובות. אך כשמזדמן שהשעה צריכה לכך, נאמר ע"ז [=על זה] "ארור מונע חרבו מדם", ושאול נכשל בחמלתו על עמלק. אך כ"ז [=כל זה] אינו כבד כשהאכזריות היא על גוים. אבל לפעמים צריך להתאכזר ג"כ [=גם כן] על פושעי בני ישראל, שהם נחשבים בנים ממש לכל ירא ד', וע"ז [=ועל זה] נאמר "ואת אחיו לא הכיר ואת בניו לא ידע", וזאת היא האדירה שבמדת האכזריות, ועכ"ז [=ועם כל זה] לא נמנעת מחק השלמים, ואינו מתרחק עי"ז [=על ידי זה] מהשלמות, אדרבא בזה הוא מעטר שלמותו ועולה ומתחזק בעץ החיים. ומזה אנו יכולים להכיר כח הגבורות הקדושות הנכללות בתוה"ק [=בתורתנו הקדושה], שאורייתא בגבורה איתיהיבת. ובאמת, הרואה מרחוק אדם מתנהג במדת אכזריות אינו יכול לצייר שעוצם עיקר כוונתו לקדושה ולחסד אמיתי, רק מי שמגיע למעלה זו הוא בא למקום איש כזה ורואה איך כל מחשבותיו [מחשבתו] היא רק לחסד, הוא מאמין שהוא אחוז בעץ החיים שהוא מקור החסד והרחמים ע"י [=על-ידי] מדת אכזריותו.

וז"ש [=וזה שאמר] לדידי חזי לי ההיא אקרוקתא, צפרדע, דהצפרדעים מסרו נפשם על קידוש השם במצרים, וכדאמרי[נן] בפסחים שחנניה מישאל ועזרי[ה] למדו ק"ו [=קל וחומר] מצפרדעים למסור נפשם על קדושת השם לכבשן האש. דהוי כאקרא דהגרוניא, דהיינו שנכללת בכל מיני גבורות, ש"ששים המה מלכות" [="ששים גבורים סביב לה"?], סוד שתין פולסי דנורא, סוד הגבורות הנכללים [הנכללות] בו"ק כ"א [=בו' קצוות, כל אחד] כלול מעשר, וענין אקרא דהגרוניא מלשון גרון, שהגרון בו רמוזים הדינים, ע"כ [=על כן] סוד השחיטה מהצואר, שמגירים ומוציאים ממנו הדינים ועי"כ [=ועל-ידי כן] הותר. ואקרא דהגרוניא כמה הוי? שתין בתי, רומז לס' בתי דינים, והיינו שיש בחי[נה] זו בנפש, שכל מדות הרוח מתלהטים [מתלהטות] בדינים, ומתאכזר עצמו במס"נ [=במסירות נפש] על קידוש השם. אבל כ"ז [=כל זה] אינו כ"א [=כי-אם] אכזריות על עצמו, אבל גדולה מזו כשמתלבש באכזריות על אחרים

ביאור אגדות רבה בר בר חנה

לצורך קידוש השם, להנקם מאויבי ד', וזהו אתא תנינא – שהוא אכזר – בלעה, שבטל[ה] מדת אכזריות של עצמו נגד מדת אכזריות על אחרים, שהיא אכזריות יותר גדולה. אך כ"ז [=כל זה] הוא כאין כ"ז [=כל זמן] שאינו צריך להתאכזר על בניו. אבל לפעמים אתא פושקנצא, דהיינו עורב נקבה מלאה דינים ואכזריות על בני[ה], כעורב שהוא אכזרי על בניו, ובלעה עד שלא נודע שבא אל קרבו מדת אכזריות לגבי עצמו והזרים ממנו, נגד מדת אכזריות על בניו. ועכ"ז [=ועם כל זה] סליק יתיב באילנא, בעץ החיים, להפריח פרי חסד וטובה בעולם, כי כל מגמתו הי[תה] חסד וטובת העולם כולו במה שמבער קוצים מהכרם. (אר"ש בר יצחק) [אמר רב פפא בר שמואל]: אי לאו דהואי התם, שבאתי לכלל מדה זו לקיימה בעצמי, לא הימני[ה] שכ"ז [=שכל זה] יעשה מצד חסד וקדושה. וע"ז [=ועל זה] אמר תא חזי כמה נפיש חילי[ה] דאילנא, כי כל הדינים הללו הוא [הם] לתכלית חסד, אנו יכולים ללמוד כמה גדול כח החסד עד שכל הדינים הללו בטלים לגבי[ו] ונכללים בו, והמה נחשבים ג"כ [=גם כן] על גורל החסד.

ו

אמר ר[בה] ב[ר] ב[ר] ח[נה]: זימנא חדא, הוא אזלינן בספינתא, חזינן ההוא כוורא דיתבא ליה אכלה טינא באוסיה, ודחוהו מיא ושדיוהו לגודא, וחרוב מני[ה] שתין מחוזי, ואכלו מני[ה] שתין מחוזי, ומלחו מני[ה] שיתין מחוזי, ומלאו מחד גלגלא דעיני[ה] תלת מאה גרבי משחא. וכי הדרן לבתר תריסר ירחי שתא, חזינן דהוי מנסרי מגרמיה מטללתא, ויתבי למבני הני מחוזי.

יודיע ענין ת"ח שאע"פ [=תלמיד חכם, שאף על-פי] שקלקל מ"מ [=מכל מקום] יש לו תקנה, אע"פ [=אף על-פי] שגדול מאוד הקלקול בת"ח [=בתלמיד חכם] שסרח, כדאשכחן באחר, שמ"מ [=שמכל מקום] אמרה תורה, "מצילין את אחר בשביל תורתו", כהא דמצילין תיק הספר עם הספר, וכדאמר שם בחגיגה ע"פ [=על פסוק] "'לא יערכנה זהב וזכוכית' – מה [כלי זהב וכלי] זכוכית אף ע"פ [=על-פי] שנשבר, יש לו תקנה, כך ת"ח אע"פ [=תלמיד חכם אף על-פי] שסרח, יש לו תקנה". ודימה ענין תקנתו לזכוכית שנשבר להורות על ענין גודל קלקולו, כי באמת זהב ג"כ [=גם כן] יש לו תקנה כשנשבר, ולמה צריך להורות על זכוכית? אלא ששבירת הזהב אינו מגרע אותו כ"כ [=כל כך] ממעלתו, דמ"מ [=דמכל מקום] דהבא הוא, אבל זכוכית, עיקר שלמותו היא צורתו, וכשנתקלקלה צורתו, נפסד לשעה לגמרי, מ"מ ע"י [=מכל מקום על-ידי] מלאכה והיתוך יש לו תקנה. וזה יורה שאפי[לו] נתקלקל הרבה מאד, מ"מ [=מכל מקום] כח נפלא יש בקדושת התוה"ק [=התורה הקדושה], שמעלתו מתהומות הארץ ומחזירתו אל הקדושה, ואפי[לו] דואג ואחיתופל לסוף באים לחיי עוה"ב [=עולם הבא], והיינו שקדושת התורה חופפת ואינה מנחת שהקלקול ישלוט לגמרי בנפש עדי אובד, ואע"פ [=ואף על-פי] שיגבר הרבה ע"ע [=על עצמו] כח הטומאה ח"ו [=חס ושלום], מ"מ [=מכל מקום] פנימית הקדושה שנשאבה בנפשו מאור התורה, פועלת להמציא לו אחרית ותקוה. וגם כי "יזקין בארץ שרשו ובעפר ימות גזעו, מריח מים יפריח".

ואמר שבהליכתו בספינתא לשוט בעניני הנשמות שהמה המהלכים בתוך הים, אלא שהנשמות שהם בגוף נקראים "הולכי הים באניות", והמשוללים כבר מהגוף המה נמשלים לדגים. ועתה מדבר ממצב הנשמה של ת"ח [=תלמיד חכם] שקלקל דרכיו הרבה. ונודע שעיקר האדם הוא החוטם שבו החיות תלוי, וכדברי הזוהר, "בחוטמא אשתמודע פרצופא". גם כח הריח הוא כינוי לאור החכמה, שהריח הוא ג"כ [=גם כן] יותר רוחני מכל חושי הגוף, וכדחז"ל [=וכדברי חכמינו זכרונם לברכה] "איזהו דבר שהנשמה נהנית ממנו ואין הגוף נהנה ממנו? הוי אומר זה הריח". ואירע בת"ח [=בתלמיד חכם] אחד שעלתה טינא בלבו ע"י [=על-ידי] מחשבה רעה שקננה בשכלו. וזהו דאכלה טינא באוסיה, ששרץ נכנס בחוטמו ונתקלקלו מעשיו עי"ז [=על-ידי זה] עד שנדחה מקדושת התורה ודחוהו מיא ושדיוהו לגודא, כדברי הזוהר דמי שאינו ראוי לאור התוה"ק [=התורה הקדושה] איכא כמה נחשים ועקרבים דעוקצים לו, מאותן השומרים את דרך עץ החיים, ומי שנתקלקל הרבה, נדחה מהתורה, וממילא עי"ז [=על-ידי זה] נתקלקל הרבה עד שכל המעשים

שלו נתקלקלו. ונודע שכל מסכתא יש לה ענין מעשים מיוחדים הכלולים בה, וגבול קדושה לעצמה, וכשלומד האדם התורה ומקיימה, הוא מיישב העולם נגד כל מס[כתא] בחלק קדושתה, וכשמתקלקל בדרכיו, נחרבו אותם שתין מחוזי, ומחוז הוא יותר מעיר, שבחי[נת] מלכות נקראת "עיר אלקים [אלהים]", דהיינו המשנה כצורתה, וכשהגדיל מעשיו בפלפול וחידושי תורה הרבה, נעשה מכל עיר מחוז, ונחרבו כולם. מ"מ [=מכל מקום] התורה שלמד כבר וחידש הרבה דברים, יש מהם שהם נאותים רק לפי שעה, ויש מהם דברים נצחיים נאותים לכל דור ודור, הוא דבר שאי-אפשר להאבד, רק שכח החיים ניטל מהם. מ"מ [=מכל מקום] אכלו מני[ה] שתין מחוזי, היינו מאותן עניני תורה שהם מחודשים לשעה. ומלחו מני[ה] שתין מחוזי, מאותן ד"ת [=דברי תורה] שהם ראויים לקיום לדורות. כי יש בתורה ב' אלה הבחינות: ישנם דברים שהם ראוים לקיום עולם. ע"כ [=על כן] נמצאים הרבה הלכות שלא ישתנו מקביעותם מפני שע"כ [=שעל כן] כך דרך תיקונם שיהיו ברית כרותה לעולם. ישנם הלכות שמשתנים בהוראתם בדור ודור לפי פרנסיו, וכפי אשר יראה לדיין ושופט שבימיך. וכ"א [=וכל אחד] העמל בתורה ומחדש בה ע"כ [=על כן] יש לו חלק ונחלה בב' הבחינות. והנה זה הוא בחלק המעשי שבתורה, שכללו הוא שש קצות שנכללים [שנכללות] בשתא סדרי, ופרטם שתין מסכתא שהם שתין מחוזי, אך חלקי העיון בעיונים שכליים הם בג' בחי[נות] חב"ד [=חכמה, בינה, דעת], למעלה מו"ק [=מו' קצוות]. ואע"פ [=ואף על-פי] שהסיר עינו האחת והביט בה על תאות העוה"ז [=העולם הזה], מ"מ [=מכל מקום] מטבע החכם ג"כ [=גם כן] להשכיל בחכמה מצד הנטי[ה] הטבעית. גם מזה הי[תה] תועלת, דמלאו מחד גלגלא דעיני[ה] תלת מאה גרבי משחא, להורות על שמן החכמה שמילא בכל ג' בחינות שבכללות הדעת, שהם ג' מאות, כיון שמדבר במעשה בבחי[נת] עשרות שהם שתין, כשמדבר בדרכיו העיונים שהם בחי[נה] למעלה מהמעשה, חוזר ובא למספר המאות. אבל כ"ז [=כל זה] הוא רק מה שעכ"פ [=שעל כל פנים] הועיל לאחרים אע"פ [=אף על-פי] שקלקל לעצמו, כהא דאחר, דמ"מ [=דמכל מקום] גמר ר"מ [=רבי מאיר] תורה מפיו. אבל אמר דקדושת התורה הועילה עליו ג"כ [גם כן] עד שא"א [=שאי-אפשר] שיודח לגמרי, רק אחרי שנצרף, פועלת פנימיותו ועצמותו שיחזור בגלגול, ואותו הכח העצמי שנכלל בו ע"י [=על-ידי] תורתו, פועל עליו בגלגול עד שחוזר לתקן כל מה שהחריב, דכוחותיו מ"מ [=מכל מקום] גדולות [גדולים] המה. וחזי אחרי י"ב חודש שנצרף מעט בכור עוני, וחזר לעולם, או שלמעלה סדרו דרכי תיקונו שע"י [=שעל-ידי] עצמות קדושת התורה שנשתאבה בו, יטרח לתקן ולבנות כל מה שהרס. וזה דנסרי מגרמוהי מטללתא, ובנו הני מחוזי, שחוזר בגוף, או בכמה ניצוצות, כפי דרכי ההנהגה העליונה, ומתקן כל מה שהחריב. ומצינו דוגמא לזה, אע"פ [=אף על-פי] שאינו דומה, ברע"מ [=ברעיא מהימנא] שחוזר לתקן ענין ע"ר [=ערב רב], ועיי[ן] בספר הגלגולים שת"ח [=שתלמיד חכם] מתגלגל ביותר מפני שאינו רואה כ"כ [=כל כך] הגיהנם, ומ"מ י"ל [=ומכל מקום יש לומר] שהי[ה] צריך תריסר ירחי שתא לעכל זוהמא, כדי שתתעורר קדושת התורה בתר עיכול הגוף.

ז

אמר רבה ב[ר] ב[ר] ח[נה]: זימנא חדא, הוא אזלינן בספינתא, וחזינן ההוא כוורא דיתבא חלתא אגביה וקדחא אגמא. סברינן דיבשתא היא, ונחתינן ואפינן ובשלינן אגבי[ה]. וכד חם גבי[ה], אתהפיך. ואי לאו דמקרבא ספינתא, הוא טבעינן.

הנה לעיל במאמר ראשון גבי "ההוא גלא דמטבע לספינתא" בארתי ענין הטבעת הספינה, שהוא הביטול ממצוות מעשיות, להיות נטבע רק בשכל ועיון לבדו, וזהו ראשית חטאת. אמנם אי[תא] במקדש מלך דיש נשמות גדולות העסוקות הרבה בעיון כרשב"י [=כרבי שמעון בן יוחאי] וחביריו שהם פטורים מהמצוות, כדאמרי[נן] בפ"ק [=בפרק קמא] דשבת, "אבל כגון אנו מפסיקים [לקריאת שמע ולתפילה]". למדנו מזה שאפשר שיהי[ה] אדם גדול שאין ללמוד ממדרגתו ומדרכיו. והנה מזדמן לפעמים שאדם אחד רואה דרכיו של האדם הגדול כשמתנהג בעניני הגשמיות ומשוטט במחשבתו בענינים גבוהים, ועושה הכל לשם שמים, וכל ימיו עוסק רק בעשיית נחת רוח ליוצרו, עד שנמצא בחי[נה] שכל ימיו כקדושת שבת, ומותר לו להנות מעוה"ז [=מעולם הזה] כענין "הרוצה לנסך יין ע"ג [=על גבי] מזבח, ימלא גרונם של ת"ח [=תלמידי חכמים] יין". אך צריך לדעת כי הוא משוטט במחשבה אחת מתחתית מדרגות עניני החומר ומדבק מחשבתו בהשי"ת [=בהשם יתברך], ואין דבר חוצץ בפניו, משא"כ [=מה שאין כן] שאר בנ"א [=בני אדם] כשיהנו מעוה"ז [=מעולם הזה] יתלכלכו בעניני החומר ולא יוכלו לעלות. ועיי[ן] בלקו"ת להגרש"ז [בלקוטי תורה להגאון רבי שניאור זלמן] דברים קרובים בענין זה של מעלת קדושים כאלה, ומדמה אותם לדגים המשוטטים שלא בהדרגה, ועיי[ן] בפ[רשת] משפטים בסבא. וזהו הכוורא, אין ללמוד ממנו מדרכיו כשהם ניכרים לעין כל שהילוכו בקדושה ועבודה גדולה שאי-אפשר להדמות לו, רק לפעמים ע"י [=על-ידי] שצריך ללמוד עם תלמידיו הוא משפיל מדרגתו מעט, ונראה בו עניני עוה"ז [=עולם הזה] וחומריות, ועי"ז [=ועל-ידי זה] בא אדם שלא כמעלתו להתנהג כדרכיו, לתקן עצמו ע"פ [=על-פי] מנהגיו, אבל הוא נופל בעניני עוה"ז [=עולם הזה]. וגם כשלא יהי[ה] זריז במצות מעשיות, ואין כחו יפה לאחוז בחכמה, הוא מסוכן לאבד את קדושתו, לכן צריך לחזור למדרגתו ולעבוד בעבודת הגוף בתורה הנגלית וכ"ע [=וכל עניני] תורה כפי מעלתו, ולהזדרז במצות ע"פ [=על-פי] מצב גופו. אמר דזימנא חדא הוא אזלינן בספינתא, לעיין בעניני החכמה בהלבשת החומר כמש"כ [=כמו שכתבתי] כמה פעמים, וחזינן ההוא כוורא, היינו אדם קדוש וגדול בענקים כרשב"י [=כרבי שמעון בן יוחאי] וחביריו, דיתבא לי[ה] חלתא אגבי[ה], כי יש בחי[נות] פנים ואחוריים, ואחוריים הם ענין בחי[נת] השפלה הנצרך להשלמת זולתו, וראה מצד בחי[נת] אחוריו קצת עניני חומריות בהנהגתו, אבל באמת מחשבתו היתה בענינים גבוהים לתקן בעבודת הקודש כפי ענין החכמה הגלוי[ה] לו. אך סברינן דיבשתא היא, ועושה הדברים כפשוטן, ועשינו גם אנו כמעשיו וסלקינן, עלינו במעלה לפי מחשבתינו ואפינן ובשלינן אגביה, עסקנו בעניני החומר. גם לא עסקנו כ"כ [=כל כך] במצות המעשיות כמו הוא שעקר ענינו בתורה וחכמה. אבל כד חם גביה, ונתעוררה אשתא דגרמי בו מקדושה העליונה שבלבבו, אתהפיך תיכף לאיש אחר, שזהו מדתם של קדושי עליון הללו, שאינם צריכים

לשום הדרגה, כי כל מעשיהם בדבקות קדושת השי"ת [=השם יתברך]. אז ראינו שאין אנו יכולים ללכת ע"פ [=על-פי] הנהגתו ששגבה מאתנו, ואבדנו דרך, ואי לאו דמקרבא ספינתא, כי לא הרחקנו ללכת להסיח דעתנו מעניני פשוטי התורה ומעשי המצות בזריזות ועבודת [נסמך, כנראה שחסרה כאן מילת "הגוף", וצריך לומר "ועבודת הגוף"—ב"נ] שעמדה לנו להיות למגן בעדנו משטף מים, הוא טבעינן בתוך ים המים, כי הקדושים העליונים הם נמשלים לדגים שבים שאין צריכים כלים לשוט, ע"כ [=על כן] הם משוטטים ע"י [=על-ידי] חכמתם וקדושתם גם אם ממעטים במעשים ע"י [=על-ידי] שקידתם בתורה ועיון שכלי כרשב"י [כרבי שמעון בן יוחאי] וחביריו, אבל כגון אנו צריכים להשלים עצמנו בכלי הגוף ועבודתו, שהם לנו כספינה לעבור ארחות ים, וזאת שעמדה לנו שלא הרחקנו הרבה.

ח

אמר ר[בה] ב[ר] ב[ר] ח[נה]: זימנא חדא, הוא אזלינן בספינתא, וסגאי ספינתא בין שיצא לשיצא דכוורא תלתא יומי ותלתא לילותא. איהו בזקיפא ואנן בשיפולא. וכי תימא, לא מסגי ספינתא טובא, כי אתא רב דימי אמר: כמיחם קומקומא דמיא מסגי שתין פרסי, ושדי פרשא גירא וקדמא ליה. ואמ[ר] ר[ב] אשי: ההוא גילדנא דימא הוא, דאית לי[ה] תרי שיצי.

אמר שהיו מהלכים בים החכמה ובחנו נשמה אחת בדרכי התפשטות חכמתה. ונודע שיש ב׳ בחינות שכל – שכל עיוני ושכל מעשי – שהנשמה, אחרי השלימה חוקה בתורה וחכמה בעוה״ז [=בעולם הזה] מושלמת בשתיהן. ודרך עיונם הי[ה] על ההתפשטות שבנשמה ההיא מראש שכל עיוני שלה עד שכל המעשי שלה, בכל ג׳ בחינותיה דנפש, רוח ונשמה, ובכל א[חת] מהם בב׳ בחינותיה, בבחי[נת] השגתה בתפארת ומלכות, דהיינו סודות תורה שבכתב ותורה שבע״פ [=שבעל-פה]. אך יש השגה כללית בלא פרטים, ויש השגה פרטית, ויש השגה בכל מדה דחסד וגבורה מצד עצמה, ויש השגה בהדעת המחבר המדות, שבו ״חדרים ימלאו״. וכשמשיג בחיבורי המדות השגה פרטית, ע״כ [=על כרחו] צריך להשיג מקודם השגה פרטית בכל מדה בפ״ע [=בפני עצמה], וזהו מופת כשמשיג בחיבור המדות לפרטיהם ודאי כבר עלו בידו ההשגה הפרטית בענין תוכן המדות מצד עצמם [עצמן], והדעת היא הכולל הו״ק [=הו׳ קצוות], ומתפשט בכולם. ויש השגה מצד השכל האנושי בטבע ע״י [=על-ידי] פלפול ודרכי השכל, והשגה מצד רוה״ק [=רוח הקודש] ושפע אלקי [=אלהי]. אך בעצם ההשגות תתחלקנה: יש משיג מהמאוחר אל הקודם, וזו היא השגה הדרגית מחויבת לבעלי חומר, ויש השגה עצמית הולכת מהקודם אל המאוחר, כחכם שמציע לפני תלמידו את הידוע לו.

ואמר שהלכו בין שיצא לשיצא, היינו בין ההתפשטות של ב׳ מיני השכל שכלולים בנשמה ההיא, שעל-ידם היא פורחת ושטה בים החכמה, הלכו תלתא יומי ותלתא לילותא, פי[רוש] בכל ג׳ בחינות דנר״ן [=דנפש, רוח, נשמה] בהשגתם בתושב״כ [=בתורה שבכתב] דעקרה בת״ת [=בתפארת] שהיא בחי[נת] יום, ומצד השגתה במל[כות], תורה שבע״פ [=שבעל פה] בחי[נת] לילה. וכי תימא לא מסגי ספינתא טובא, היינו שהיתה השגתם רק בדרך כלל, וזו היא השגה מועטת כענין דברי זוה״ק [=זוהר הקדוש] בענין ידיעת השגת אלקות [אלהות], דהמדרגה הקטנה היא הידיעה בדרך כלל, והגדולה בדרך פרט, ע״ז [=על זה] השיב דכד מיחם קומקומא דמיא, כי המים הם חסדים, והאש גבורות, והחום שהמים מתחממים ע״י [=על-ידי] האש היינו חיבור חו״ג [=חסדים וגבורות], ומקום מציאותם בחיבור הוא בסוד הדעת המחבר. מסגי שיתין פרסי, היינו ידיעה פרטית בו״ק [=בו׳ קצוות] דג׳ יומי וג׳ לילותא הנ״ל [=הנזכרים לעיל] בכל מדה בפרטיותיה דהם יו״ד, וזהו לענין כמות הידיעות. ואמר עוד דאיכות הידיעה הי[ה] כ״כ [=כל כך] גדול ועמוק, עד שהפרשא, שהוא החכם דשדי גירא, שזורק חיצי השכל בשכל האנושי להשיג, הוא קדמא ליה, שהיתה השגתו מעולה מכל השגה שכלית מהירה, רק דאיהו בזקיפא, דהיינו שהשגת הנשמה

ביאור אגדות רבה בר בר חנה

הנ"ל [=הנזכרת לעיל] – ההוא כוורא – הי[תה] בדרך השגה הגדולה מלמעלה למטה, שזהו בזקיפא, לענין השגת החכמה, ואנן בשיפולא, מלמטה למעלה. וע"ד [=וער דרך] הציור, יש לומר ג"כ [=גם כן] להיפוך, דהליכה בזקיפא הוא מלמטה למעלה, ובשיפולא הוא ממעלה למטה. והיינו, שהנשמה ההיא השיגה השגותי[ה] מצד עצמה, וכשנחקקו ההשגות בה והם השיגו מהותה, נתגלה להם ענייני השגותיה כמו שהם כבר ערוכים בה. והיא השיגה אותם מצד טבע השגותיה, דהיינו כדרך המשיג לחדש דברי חכמה ממטה למעלה; והם שלא הי[ה] ביכולתם לחקור עד מקום שורש החכמות הגדולות החקוקות בה משורשם, רק ע"י [=על-ידי] שמצאו בה, הכירו אותם כמו שהם גמורים וערוכים, הי[ה] מהלך השגתם כרואה דבר ערוך לפניו בשיפולא ממעלה למטה, בהשקפה על כל שיעור הקומה שלה. ואמר ר"א [=רב אשי]: דההוא גילדנא דימא הוא, דאית לה תרי שיצי, פי[רוש] כי יש קטנות וגדלות בהשגה, וכשעולה למעלה גדולה הרבה, אז אין חילוק בין שכל עיוני למעשי, כי הכל במעלת עיוני, שמקור השכל המעשי הוא ג"כ [=גם כן] העיוני. וכשמשתלם בהשגה, עולה המעשי למקור העיוני, ונעשה באחדות א[חת] דבר אחד לגמרי. וכשהנשמה במעלה כזו, ההשגה מנועה לשוכני חומר לגמרי. רק גילדנא דימא הוא בבחי[נת] קטנות, שאז העיוני והמעשי מחולקים לב' בחינות ואית לי[ה] תרי שיצי, ועי"ז [=ועל-ידי זה] מצאו מקום להשגה מפני החלק שנמצא קשור בשכל המעשי.

ט

אמר רבה ב[ר] ב[ר] ח[נה]: זימנא חדא, הוא אזלינן בספינתא, וחזינן ההיא ציפרתא דהוה קאי עד קרסוליה במיא ורישיה ברקיעא. ואמרינן: לית מיא. ובעינן למיחות לאקורי נפשין. נפק בת קלא ואמר לן: לא תחותו להכא, דנפלא ליה חצינא לבר נגרא הכא הא שבע שנין ולא מטיא לארעא. ולא משום דנפישי מיא, אלא משום דרדיפי מיא. אמר רב אשי: ההוא זיז שדי הוא, דכתיב "וזיז שדי עמדי" [תהלים נ, יא].

הנה בחיוב השגת התורה, עיקר החיוב נחלק לב' גדרים: לדעת המצות ופרטי הלכותיהם, וזה חיוב גדול על האדם להשיג ולדעת, אע"ג [=אף על-גב] דאמרו חז"ל [=חכמינו זכרונם לברכה] "דבר קטן הויות דאביי ורבא נגד מעשה מרכבה", מ"מ [=מכל מקום] גדול החיוב לעמול ולדעת חוקי דיני התורה, ולהוסיף לקח ופלפול בחכמה הנגלית שבתורה, והדברים מגיעים עד רום המעלות ומגיעים את האדם להשיג צפונות בנועם ד' כדברי חז"ל [=חכמינו זכרונם לברכה] במדרש ע"פ [=על פסוק] "העם ההולכים בחשך – אלו בעלי תלמוד – ראו אור גדול", אע"פ [=אף על-פי] שנדמה שעוסקים בדברים קטנים, בהלכות ודינים, מ"מ [=מכל מקום] גדול ערכם מאד, אלא שאין זה סוף מעלת האדם, כי האדם נברא לדעת את ד', ולהשיג כפי יכולתו צפונות סתרי תורה ורזי עולם ב"סוד ד' ליראיו". אבל חלק הלימוד לדעת המעשה אשר יעשה הוא ג"כ [=גם כן] עיקר גדול ורחב מאד. והנה נודע שעובדין תלויים במל[כות], נוק[בא], וכל השגות שנוגע למעשים, בה תלויין, והאדם הגדול בענקים המתנשא לראש השגות גדולות ע"י [=על-ידי] גדפין דאהבה ויראה, עיקר עיונו יהי[ה] בהשגות גדולות נעלות מעניני המעשים, והבחינה בנפשו שבה מתעסק בחכמת המעשים הוא מצד חלקים התחתונים שבחכמתו ושכלו, אך מ"מ [=מכל מקום] לא יאמר האדם כי הדברים קלים ומעטים של עניני המעשים, ואין חיובם גדול וחזק, עד שיתרשל מהם, כי הם מתפשטים הרבה מאד. ונודע שסוד ז' ספירות התחתונות, שבהם סוד תורה שבכתב ושבע"פ [=ושבעל-פה], ובבחי[נת] המלכות כל הבחינות בה תלויין בעובדין. אבל יש בחי[נת] התורה בענין הפלפול דקוב"ה [=דקודשא בריך הוא] חדי ביה, ועיקר השמחה הוא בבינה, וסוד "אלו ואלו דברי אלהים חיים" הוא בבינה, וא"כ [=ואם כן] עולה מעלת פלפולה של תורה, להראות פנים לטהור ולטמא, עד הבינה, שהוא סוד היובל, יותר עמוק מסוד השמיטה דכוללת שבע שנים, וכיון שכל השגתינו הוא רק בז' תחתונות, ע"כ [=על כן] אין להשיג איך "אלו ואלו דא"ח [=דברי אלהים חיים]", כי רק "לשאלה קיימא" בינה.

והנה הנגרא הוא העושה מלאכה במים רבים, ומתקן ספינות וכלים ללכת בהם ולעבור "אורחות ימים", שהם דרכי המצות ודיניהם, שע"י [=שעל-ידיהם] עוברים את הים באופן שלא יטבע האדם "בשיא [בשוא] גליו", כמש"כ [=כמו שכתבתי] לעיל כמ"פ [=כמה פעמים] בענין טביעת הספינה. וכח הבנין הוא ע"י [=על-ידי] הפלפול של אמת שמוציא הלכה ברורה. ולפעמים הענין עמוק עד שאי-אפשר להחליט בפלפול ונשאר ספק. ונמצא שאינו משיג עד הסוף מפני שנוגע בסוד "או"א [=אלו ואלו] דברי אלקים [אלהים] חיים",

ביאור אגדות רבה בר בר חנה

בינה סוד החיים, ע"כ [=על כן] גדול החיוב להשיג ולעמול עד שידע דבר על מכונו, "'דבר ד'' – זו הלכה", כפי האפשרי. ובאמת, אע"ג [=אף על-גב] דהשגות דמעשה המצות לכאורה יש להם [להן] קץ ותכלית, שאינם עולים [שאינן עולות] כ"כ [=כל כך] בעניינים גבוהים, אבל מפני שרצון השי"ת [=השם יתברך] להגדיל תורה ולהאדירה, קבע פרטי ההלכות ע"כ [=על כל] הדברים המתחלפים והמקרים ההוים בעולם, וכח התנועה והשינוי הוה בעולם תמיד, ע"כ [=על כן] מזדמן [מזדמנים] תמיד ספיקות ועיונים חדשים, מפני רדיפת המקרים וחילופי העיונים שבאים עי"ז [=על-ידי זה]. ע"כ [=על כן] החיוב גדול לעמול בזריזות גם בחלק המעשי, ועי"ז [=ועל-ידי זה] יבוא למעלה רמה להיות "זוכה לדברים הרבה" בצירוף עיונו בסודות המצות וסתריהם [וסתריהן]. והנה נודע שהמלכות נקראת "שדה חקל תפוחין", שצריכה לעבודה ממחצדי חקלא, וזה החכם העוסק עם עיונו באלקיות [באלהיות], גם בחלקי המעשים, הוא נעבד לשדה, ומ"מ [=ומכל מקום] הוא זז משדה ועולה בהשגתו בגבהי מרומים, ודבק בהשגתו בעניינים אלקיים [אלהיים], אע"פ [אף על-פי] שעיוניו בדברים חומרים.

וזהו שסיפר שבהיותם הולכים בעיון דרכיים החכמה חזו ההיא ציפרתא, ציפור שמים, נפש חכמה העולה בהשגתה ע"י [=על-ידי] גדפין שלה למקום גבוה, ועומד רק עד קרסוליה בבחי[נות] התחתונות שלו, במיא, במים התחתונים, דהיינו השגת ההלכות והדינים, ורישיה ברקיעא, להשיג בדברי סודות ועיונים גדולי ערך ברזי עולם. והרואה איך שעיקר עיונו ועוצם מעלתו תלויה בהשגות רמות ברום עולם, סובר שעניני ההלכות אינם גדולים ורחבים, עד שיגיע לשלמותם גם בלא זירוז גדול, ואמרינן לית מיא, שאינם רבים כ"כ [=כל כך], ובעינן למיחות לאקורי נפשין מעמל הויות דאביי ורבא ופלפול של הלכה. נפק בת קלא, שסוד הבת קול הוא מבחי[נת] מלכות: לא תחותו הכא, שלא תוכלו לרדת כ"כ [=כל כך] בנקל לעומק העיון וסוף הפלפול בעומקא של הלכה. ע"כ [=על כן] אתם צריכים לאחוז גם בזה ביד חזקה ועמל גדול, דנפלה לי[ה] חצינא לבר נגרא שעוסק בפלפול, נפל[ו] לו עיונים גדולים בפלפול, שהוא החצינא, הכלי שבו עושין הספינות כמשכ"ל [=כמו שכתבתי לעיל], הא שבע שנין, היינו בעומק כל חדרי החכמה שבכל המדות, הז"ת [=הז' תחתונות] שבהם [=שבהן] תלוין המעשים והתורה המעשית, ולא נחתא לארעא, שלא השיג לתכלית, מפני שיש מקום עומק עד שמגיע לסוד "אלו ואלו דברי אלהים חיים", סוד הבינה. ולא משום דנפישי מיא, כי באמת, מועטים וקלים העיונים לערך עיונים השכלים שבסודות וסתרי תורה, שאותן הדברים אין להם קץ ותכלית מצד עצמם, אלא משום דרדיפי מיא, מרודפים ע"י [=על-ידי] השינוים של גלגל התנועה המשנה מקרי העולם ומזמין ספיקות רבות שצריך לחתכם ע"פ [=על-פי] דין אמת לאמתה של תורה. ע"כ [=על כן] החיוב גדול לשום "עמל אדם לפיהו", ופי[רוש] "פה" הוא מלכות, תושבע"פ [=תורה שבעל-פה] דעובדין בה תליין, "וגם הנפש לא תמלא", היינו רבותא שהנפש, היא בחי[נת] מלכות, לא תמלא, כי גם חכמת המעשה גדול ונשגב עד מאד. אמר רב אשי: ההוא זיז שדי הוה, אותו ציפרתא שעוסק בב' חלקי התורה הללו, הוא זיז שדי, שדר בשדה דחקל תפוחין, וזז ג"כ [=גם כן] משם לעלות למעלה אל רוממות השגה, שנאמר "וזיז שדי עמדי", היינו עם בחי[נת] ת"ת [=תפארת], שמים, שעולה לשמים ע"י [=על-ידי] מה שייחד שניהם, תורה ועובדין.

ו

ואמר רבה ב[ר] ב[ר] ח[נה]: זימנא חדא, הוא אזלינן במדברא, וחזינן הני אווזי דשמיטן גדפייהו משומנייהו, ונגדי נחלי דמשחא מתותייהו. ואמינא להו: אית לכו מנייכו חולקא לעלמא דאתי? חדא דליא לי אטמא וחדא דליא לי גדפא. כי אתאי לקמיה דרבי אליעזר, אמר: עתידין ישראל ליתן עליהם את הדין.

הנה אווז רומז לחכמה, כדברי חז"ל [=חכמינו זכרונם לברכה] "הרואה אווז בחלום – יצפה לחכמה". אבל ממה שאמר הכ[תוב], שמביאים חז"ל [=חכמינו זכרונם לברכה] שם, "חכמות בחוץ תרונה", נראה דהכונה בהם לחכמות המפורסמות, המשמיעים קולם ותועלתם לרבים, כמו חכמת הטבע, תכונה וכיו"ב [=וכיוצא בזה], ולא כן תוה"ק [תורתנו הקדושה], דעליה נאמר "כל כבודה בת מלך פנימה", ו"חמוקי ירכיך כמו חלאים' – מה ירך בסתר אף ד"ת [=דברי תורה] בסתר". והנה כל החכמות אף שאינם [שאינן] עיקריות, מ"מ [=מכל מקום] ראוי לישראל, ובפרט לחכמי תורה, שידעו אותן, מפני שעי"ז [=שעל-ידי זה] מתקדש שם שמים, ויוכלו להגיע עי"ז [=על-ידי זה] לתכלית שפיזר הקב"ה [=הקדוש ברוך הוא] בעולם את ישראל כדי להוסיף עליהם גרים ולפרסם יחודו בעולם. וזה אי אפשר כ"א ע"י [כי-אם על-ידי] שידעו ישראל החכמות, שעי"ז [=שעל-ידי זה] ידעו מה להשיב לאפיקורוס. והנה אם היו ישראל יודעים גם אותן החכמות, ומתכוונים בלימודם לשם שמים, אזי מתקדש שם שמים, הן ע"י [=על-ידי] שעל ידם יזכו לעוה"ז [=לעולם הזה], להרחיב עניני העוה"ז [=העולם הזה], והי[ה] זה קידוש השם בין אוה"ע [=אומות העולם], כדברי חז"ל [=חכמינו זכרונם לברכה] "איזהו חכמה ובינה שהיא לעיני העמים? הוי אומר: זה חישוב תקופות ומזלות". גם עי"ז [=על-ידי זה] אפשר להוסיף דעת גם בתורה ויראת ד'. וכתוב בשם הגר"א ז"ל [=הגאון רבי אליהו זכרונו לברכה] שכל מה שחסר לאדם מלימוד החכמות, נחסר לו כאלה מאה פעמים מלימוד התורה, כי החכמות רקחות וטבחות הם לתורת ד'. והנה אם היו ישראל יודעים ומבינים בכל חכמה ומדע, היו החכמות עצמם [עצמן] מתעלות, שכל אחת היתה סיבה להגיע לקדושה ולמעלה עליונה, כי היו מאחדים אותם עם קדושת התורה, להשכיל יותר בחכמת השי"ת ע"י [=השם יתברך על-ידי] החכמה הניכרת בברואים. ונמצא שהיו מתעלים עי"ז [=על-ידי זה] עניני האהבה ויראה, ויתר המדות הקדושות, שהם גדפין אל הנשמה להתעלות אל מקום הר מרום בית ד'. גם עניני החכמה שע"י [=שעל-ידי] הרחבת[ם] היו מתרחבים למעלה מהם, שהיו מגיעים להשיג יותר על-ידם בחכמת אלקות [אלהות]. אבל עכשיו שנמסרו אלה החכמות לאוה"ע [=לאומות העולם], הריקים מדעת תורה ויראת ד', נמרטו מהם הגדפין, וע"י [=ועל-ידי] ריבוי חכמתם, מתנשאים להכחיש שרשי הדת, מפני שאינם מבינים עמקי התורה, והחכמות שמתרחבים [שמתרחבות] מהם אינם כ"א [כי-אם] דברי חול, למטה ממדרגת אותן החכמות, ולא יפנו למעלה. אבל באמת, כשנחקור אם יש בהם תכלית לעבודת השי"ת [=השם יתברך], נמצא שבין בכח הפעולה החמרית להגדיל מעשי עוה"ז [=עולם הזה] יש בזה עבודת ד', לקדש שם שמים בהרבות כבודן של ישראל, בין בעניני הרוחניות שהיו מרוממים את ההשגה יותר, כמש"כ בחוה"ל [=כמו שכתוב בחובות הלבבות] בענין הבחינה בברואים, ומי שלא יבחין, נאמר עליו "ואת פעל ד' לא יביטו ומעשה ידיו לא ראו".

ביאור אגדות רבה בר בר חנה

וזה אמר: זימנא חדא הוא אזלינן במדברא, מקום השממון, לעיין בחכמות חיצוניות שאינם [שאינן] חכמות התורה, שהיא עיקר ישובו של עולם, חזינן הני אווזי, חכמות המפורסמות דשמיטן גדפייהו משומנייהו, כי השמן רומז לחכמה, כמש"כ [=כמו שכתוב] "אוצר נחמד ושמן בנוה חכם", וע"י [=ועל-ידי] ריבוי חכמתם טעו באורח השכל, ונשרו מהם הגדפין המביאים את האדם לתכלית נעלה ונשגב, שהם אהבת ד' ויראתו ושרשי האמונה והעבודה שראוי להמשך מכל חכמה, ונגדי נחלי דמשחא, היינו נחלי החכמה מנגדים ונמשכים מתותייהו, שרק בחכמות השפלות של כלים ומכונות והגדלת התאוות יתנו את פרים ולא יביטו את פעל ד' להשכיל באמתתו ית[ברך]. ואמינא להו: אית לכו חולקא בעלמא דאתי? אם מעלות קדושה הגורמות קדוש השם ית[ברך] ג"כ [=גם כן] יש לקנות מהם? חדא דליא לי אטמא, שכח הפעולה המעשית שבהם, יכולים ישראל להשתמש בו, כשישובו בתשובה, ויהי[ה] כבודם של ישראל מתעלה עי"ז [=על-ידי זה], ועי"ז [=ועל-ידי זה] יגדל כבוד השי"ת [=השם יתברך] וכבוד תוה"ק [=תורתנו הקדושה], וחדא דליא לי גדפא, מה שאפשר להוציא מהם דברים קדושים המביאים ליתרון הכשר חכמה, להגיע למעלות גבוהות של קדושה. וכד אתינא לקמיה דר"א, אמר: עתידין ישראל שיתנו עליהם את הדין, כי אם היו אוחזים ביושר תוה"ק [=תורתנו הקדושה] היתה דעתם מתרחבת לזכות לדברים הרבה, והיו מקדשים שם שמים גם ע"י [=על-ידי] אלה החכמות, וכשמונעים הטוב, יתנו ע"ז [=על זה] דין וחשבון, כי עלינו להיות לאור גויים, להמשיך יראת ד' וידיעת אחדותו ית[ברך] בעולם, והכלים הנאותים ע"ז [=על זה] הוא חכמה ובינה שנגד העמים, שהם חשבון תקופות ומזלות, והדברים הדומים להם, כי בזה יתקרב קץ פדות נפשינו וגאולתינו.

יא

ואמר רבה ב[ר] ב[ר] ח[נה]: זימנא חדא, הוה קאזלינן במדברא, ואתלוי בהדן ההוא טייעא, דהוה שקל עפרא ומורח ליה, ואמר דא אורחא לדוכתא פלן, ודא אורחא לדוכתא פלן. אמרינן ליה: כמה מרחקינן ממיא? ואמר לן, הבו לי עפרא. יהבינן ליה ואמר לן: תמניא פרסי. תנינן ויהבינן ליה. אמר דמרחקינן תלתא פרסי. אפכית ליה ולא יכילת ליה.

בכלל אמר תחילה בכל דבריו שהיו הולכים בספינתא. רק במאמר שלפני זה, ובזה המאמר, סיפר שהיו הולכים במדברא. ושורש חילוק הענינים הוא כי הים והיבשה הוא [הם] נגד התורה הנגלית והנסתרת. וחכמות שמדברים [שמדברות] בענינים עליונים ונסתרים, מעניני הנשמה, הם מענין הים, והמדברים [והמדברות] בעניני הגוף, המעשים והמדות, ענינם יבשה. אך מקור התורה במדבר שהוא הפקר לכל, ודברי הגר"א ז"ל [=הגאון רבי אליהו זכרונו לברכה] על דברי התיקונים ד"רעיא מהימנא בקע ימא במטה דילי[ה] ובסוף יומיא יבקע ימא דאורייתא בקולמסא דילי[ה]", דהיינו שהנסתרות יהיו גלויות, ויהפך ים ליבשה להיות בו דרך לעבור ברגל, נח להשיג. והנה ענין הטייעא מצינו ג"כ [=גם כן] בזוהר כמ"פ [=כמה פעמים] שהי[ה] עמהם טייעא, והוא מעלה מיוחדת בחכמה, שמצינו ב' ענינים בתורה ולומדיה: כי חז"ל [=חכמינו זכרונם לברכה] אמרו "הכל צריכים למרי חיטיא" על סיני, "'ורב תבואות בכח שור' קרי רב יוסף אנפשיה". א"כ [=אם כן] דומה ענין פעולת החכם על התורה לפעולת השור העובד ומוציא תבואות מהארץ, להיות לחם להחיות בהם את האדם בלחמה של תורה, ונקראים ג"כ ת"ח [=גם כן תלמידי חכמים] "מחצדי חקלא" בלשון הזוהר. ויש במקרא ג"כ [=גם כן] ענין סחורה על השגת התורה, "כי טוב סחרה מסחר כסף", "היתה כאניות סוחר". והחילוק שבין עובד האדמה לסוחר, כי העובד יושב במקומו, ועובד ומוציא לחם, והסוחר סובב והולך לקנות סחורה המקובצת, והוא נודד ממקומו תמיד. כן יש בחי[נה] בחכמים שהוא עומד במדרגתו ובמקומו, ועוסק בתורה וחכמה, ואינו נד והולך. ויש כת חכמים, שמעיינים בחכמתם ע"י [=על-ידי] סיוע של כל הדברים שרואה תחת השמש, ובכל חילוקי בחינות הנבראים. וגם בוחן הרבה דברי תורה מנפשו, והולך ממדרגה למדרגה לבחון דרכים ונתיבות של תורה. גם הוא מכין [מכון] איך להתנהג בפועל בקדושת התורה, ובאיזה דרכים יגיע על ידה למעלות עליונות, בין ע"י [=על-ידי] התורה שמחדש בעצמו, בין מה שחכמים אחרים מחדשים. והוא דוגמת הסוחר המזמין הסחורה לפני הקונים.

והנה ללמד לכל אדם דרכו ומעלתו, איך יתנהג בעניני שלמותו, הוא לימוד גדול ונורא, כמש"כ הגר"א [=כמו שכתב הגאון רבי אליהו] במשלי כי יש לכל אחד אורח מיוחד לפי ענינו, ואין דרך שלמותו של זה שוה לשל זה, כשם שאין פרצופיהם דומות, ועיי[ן] בדברי הגרמ"ח [=הגאון רבי משה חיים] לוצאטו בפי' לאד"ר ע"פ [=בפירוש לאדרא רבא על פסוק] "ואורח צדיקים כאור נוגה". ויש דרך להבחין מעלת כל אחד מצד ערך נפשו ונשמתו, בין בשורש קדושתה ממקורה וערכה מצד עצמה, בין לפי מצב מעשיו ועניניו. אמנם יש

ביאור אגדות רבה בר בר חנה

חכמה גדולה להכיר ג"כ [=גם כן] מגופו של אדם כל עניניו ודרכי תיקונו, כי הדבר פשוט אחרי אשר בצלם אלהים ובמחוגה אלקית [אלהית] נעשה הגוף, וכשם שיש להשכיל מענין הגוף ג"כ [=גם כן] כמה ענינים בעניני אלקות [אלהות], כמש"כ [=כמו שכתוב] "ומבשרי אחזה אלוה", על אחת כמה וכמה שיש להבחין עניני הנפש על ידו, והמשכיל בזה, כמו בענין "זה ספר תולדות אדם", שכתב הרמב"ן בשם רב שרירא שיש דרך חכמה להכיר בפרצוף האדם כל דרכיו ומעשיו, וכהובא בזוהר פ[רשת] יתרו, וכמסופר בשם האר"י. א"כ [=אם כן] ידע ג"כ [=גם כן] מענין גופו איזה דרך זו ילך לקנות כל המעלות האפשריות לו משלמות וקדושה. ויש חכמה בזה להכיר בריח ממש, ויש ג"כ [=גם כן] בחי[נה] בענין הריח שהוא רומז על השגה גדולה, אבל היא מבוררת הרבה, כמש"כ במ"א [=כמו שכתבתי במקום אחר] כי החוש הוא מבורר אבל אין השגתו בענינים נשגבים, והשכל יש בו לפעמים ספיקות אבל השגתו נתלית בנשגבות, אבל הריח הוא מיוחס לנשמה, והוא הנאה נעלה מאד ומבוררת, שעכ"פ [=שעל כל פנים] הוא חוש. ע"כ [=על כן] החכם הזה ששם דרך מחקרו על שלמות נשמתו של אדם ע"י [=על-ידי] גופו, היו בהשגתו ב' מעלות, שהיתה השגתו קרובה לחוש ומבוררת, ומכ"מ [=ומכל מקום] עלה מתוך השכלת הגוף, שהיא נגלית בערך הנשמה, לענינים גבוהים רבי הערך.

והנה האדם במצבו בגוף הוא רחוק מכל בחי[נת] הקדושה אם לא יקדשהו, ומצד טבעו הוא רחוק מכל מעלה, אלא שאם יכינהו, יזכה למעלה וחן וכבוד, אבל מדת מעלתו של הגוף היא לזכות לסוד הרוח, שהיא עיקר האדם, שבחינתו בתפארת, כמש"כ [=כמו שכתוב] "כתפארת אדם". ועומק החכמה, שורש התורה, "אורייתא מבינה נפקת", שהיא השמינית למדרגה, כנודע מדברי חכמים בכינור של ימוה"מ [=ימות המשיח] שהוא של שמנה נימין. ועיי[ן] מגדל עוז ה[לכות] תשובה פ"ח [=פרק ח] ובשער הגמול להרמב"ן. נמצא שלפי טבעו של גוף האדם, הוא רחוק מקדושת שורש התורה שמונה מעלות, שענין הגוף הוא במלכות דעשיה, ועיי[ן] זוהר תרומה ע"פ [=על פסוק] "יבא כל בשר להשתחוות". רק כשמתכוין לקדש עצמו, יזכה להיות "איש אשר רוח בו", וירחק ג' מעלות ממעלת המים העליונים של רחובות הנהר היוצא מעדן. וזה החכם המכיר כח הנשמה ומעלתה מעניני הגוף וכוחותיו, כח חכמתו גדול להיות "יתיב בתווני דליבא", כי גם אם יערוך איש נגדו מעשים טובים בגלוי, ומדות טובות, מ"מ [=מכל מקום] אם גופו לא נתקדש באמת, יכיר את תוכו כענין "ותהי עונותם על עצמותם". וכמשה"כ [=וכמו שאמר הכתוב] "הכרת פניהם ענתה בם".

וזה שסיפר זימנא חדא הוה אזלינן במדברא, לחקור בחכמות התחתונות מצד הגוף לעלות על-ידם אל חכמה מעולה בעניני הנשמה, ואיתלוי בהדן ההוא טייעא, חכם העמקן בדברים, וחוקר לכל תכלית בחכמת התורה ע"י [=על-ידי] ראיית חושיו בעניני האדם והעולם, ע"כ [=על כן] הוא תר וחופש ונודד לדרכים לראות מעשה ד' ונפלאותיו, והוא יודע דרכי המדות והמעלות ותהלוכותיהם כראוי לכל אדם לפי ענינו, כי שלמות חכמתו להכין התורה היא שתהי[ה] מושגת לכל אדם לפי ערך הנאתו וקירוב תועלתו, כסוחר הזה שמזמין הסחורה ליד הקונה בלא טורח. והי[ה] כשרונו דהוה שקיל עפרא, [מלה בלתי-קריאה] בשכלו התבונן על עניני העפר, הגוף שהוא עפר מן האדמה, ומורח ליה להשיג ע"י [=על-ידו] נפלאות במעלות הנשמה ודרכי קדושתה בהשגה ברורה כענין הריח. והנה אמר הא אורחא לדוך פלן והא אורחא לדוך פלן, על מדרגה שראוי לכל אדם להשתדל להשיגה לפי ערכו, הי[ה] מיעץ לפי הכרתו ע"י [=על-ידי] הגוף להכיר ממנה ג"כ [=גם כן] נפשו ומעלתה, ומראהו איזה דרך יבחר לו לבוא לשלמותו, כי אין הדרכים שוים לכל אדם. והנה לא היה תימא [=תימה] כ"כ [=כל כך] כשמבחין על הדרכים והמדות שבכח

המעשים, שעכ"פ [=שעל כל פנים] נתלים בחומר, אלא שגם הענינים הנתלים במקום גבוה הרבה ג"כ [=גם כן] היה משיג ע"י [=על-ידי] הגוף. והוא דאמרינן לי[ה] כמה מרחקינן ממיא, שיבחין הריחוק של בחי[נת] הנשמה ממים העליונים, שהוא עלמא דאתי, סוד הבינה, שהוא "הנהר היוצא מעדן". (מעל השורה: בזוהר תרומה קע"ה ב' "מים דא בינה".) ואמר לן תמניא פרסי, היינו מתחילה קודם שהורה אותם דרך הקדושה איך להעלות נפשם, היו רחוקים כל המעלות הנמצאות, שהיו בשפל המצב, כמו "ותגל מרגלותיו", דשכיבת לארעא, כמבואר בדברי הזוהר, ועי[ין] ספר הגלגולים. אך אח"כ [=אחר כך] הורה להם דרך בית חייהם, איך לזכות למעלה האפשרית לאדם. אח"כ [=אחר כך] תנינן ויהבינן ליה, והי[ה] ג"כ [=גם כן] כוונתו "תנינן" מלשון משנה, שלמדו דרכיו והלכו בהם ואח"כ [=ואחר כך] חזרו לחקור ממנו מעלתם, כמה רחוקים הם מתכלית שלמות העליון של סוד עוה"ב [=עולם הבא]. ואמר להם תלתא פרסי, כי לבחי[נת] הרוח יזכה האדם בקביעות, כי הנשמה אינה כ"א [=כי-אם] מתנוצצת באדם ומאירה מלמעלה עליו, עיי[ן] בס[פר] נפה"ח [=נפש החיים], ובחי[נת] הרוח היא בת"ת [=בתפארת], "ותחי רוח יעקב אביהם", והוא תלתא פרסי מסוד הבינה לפי סדר המעלות: חג"ת [=חסד, גבורה, תפארת], ובינה על גביהם, לאנקא לבנין. אפכית ליה, היינו להורות על אדם שחיצוניותו טוב ותוכו רע, להכיר ענינו ע"י [=על-ידי] הגוף, וחשב שבו יטעה, ולא יכלית לי[ה], כי "סוד ד' ליראיו", להכיר ע"י [=על-ידי] הגוף את כל תוכן ענינו הפנימי כפי מה שהוא, וכמש"כ [=וכמו שכתוב] "ואת ישרים סודו", שה"ישר" נקרא ההולך בנתיב ישר של מדות טובות, ומטהר גופו להיות "אכסניא של תורה" וחכמה, התורה והקדושה שורים [שורות] עליו להחכימו באור גדול של תורת אמת, וכמש"כ [=וכמו שכתוב] בדוד "ואדוני חכם כ[חכמת] מלאך האלקים [האלהים]".

יב

ואמר רבה בר בר חנה: אמר לי ההוא טייעא: תא ואחוי לך מתי מדבר. אזלי וחזיתינהו ודמו כמאן דמבסמי וגנו אפרקיד, והוה זקיפי בירכיה דחד מנייהו, ועייל טייעא תותיה בירכיה כי רכיב גמלא וזקיפא רומחיה, ולא נגע ביה. פסקי חדא קרנא דתכלתא דחד מנייהו, ולא הוה מסתגי לן. אמר לי: דלמא שקלת מידי מנייהו, אהדריה, דגמירי דמאן דשקיל מידי מנייהו לא מסתגי ליה. אזלי אהדרתיה, והדר מסתגי לן. כי אתאי לקמיה דרבנן, אמרו לי: כל אבא חמרא וכל ב[ר] ב[ר] ח[נה] סיכסא! למאי הלכתא עבדית הכי? למידע אי כב[ית] ש[מאי] אי כב[ית] ה[לל], איבעי לך למימני חוטי ולמימני חוליות.

נראה שזה החכם החכימו בגודל מעלת דור המדבר, שבאמת ענין דור המדבר גבוה מאד, שהיו "דור דעה", ובדברי האריז"ל מבואר שסבת העדר כניסתם לארץ ג"כ [=גם כן] הי[תה] מפני מעלתם, כדאי[תא] על פסוק "ואתם הדבקים בד' אלקיכם [אלהיכם] וגו'", והיה ענינם בסוד גדול עד שהנהגת א"י [=ארץ ישראל], שהיא גלויה, סוד עלמא תתאה, לא הי[תה] ראויה להם מפני דבקותם במקום עליון, שהיתה הנהגתם ראויה בדרך נסים שהיא דרך הסוד, ויין רומז לסוד, כמשחז"ל [=כמו שאמרו חז"ל] "יין ניתן בע' אותיות וסוד ניתן בע' אותיות, נכנס יין יצא סוד". והנה עליהם הופיע אור החירות כי יצאו ממצרים בסוד הבינה, וזהו דמו כמאן דמבסמי מלאים מסוד היין, ודמו כמאן דגנו אפרקיד, שאפרקיד הוא רומז על חירות, ע"כ [=על כן] פרקדן לא יקרא ק"ש [=קריאת שמע] מפני שצריך להורות שיש עליו עול. ואמר שאי-אפשר להגיע כלל לדעת גודל עוצם מעלתם, עד שאפי[לו] הבחי[נה] התחתונה שבהשגתם, שהיא ענין הברך, שהוא סוד נה"י [=נצח, הוד, יסוד] שבהם, שהוא סוף המעלות שבהם, כדהוה זקיפא, הכונה שהיו גם בחי[נות] תחתונות שבהם בסוד עלמא דדכורא, שהוא ענין העמידה, מפני גודל מעלתם, ע"כ [=על כן] הי[ה] עיקר ענינם בתורה שהוא סוד עלמא דדכורא, כי עלמא דנוקבא הוא סוד עובדין, ובאמת היו בידם מעשים מועטים, שכמה מצות היו חסרות להם, אבל גודל מעלתם בתורה הספיק על הכל, וזהו דהוה זקיפא ברכיה דחד מינייהו. ואמר חד מינייהו שלא הי[ה] אפשר בחינה כללית שלהם, שהכלל מתוסף בקדושתו כנודע ענין תפילתם של רבים, רק הסתכל במעלות התחתונות של[הם] דרך הבחי[נות] התחתונות שלהם, וגם זה היה זקיפא בסוד העמידה. ואמר דהוה רכיב טייעא גמלא ונקט רומחיה בידיה ולא נגע בי[ה], שכללות שלמות הקדושה תלויה בג' דברים, כדאי[תא] בזהר דמשפטים בענין ג' יועצי פרעה, וכנגדם בקדושה, דהיינו: דחילו, ועובדין, וחכמה. והנה הטייעא הוא סוחר, מורה ע"ש [=על שם] חכמתו הגדולה, כמו "כי טוב סחרה מסחר כסף" ו"[היתה כאניות סוחר] ממרחק תביא לחמה". גם אמרו חז"ל [=חכמינו זכרונם לברכה] הגמלים רובם צדיקים, שהיינו יראתם גוברת – כמשפירש"י [=כמו שפירש רש"י] – מפני פרישתם למרחקים וסכנות,

הרב אברהם יצחק הכהן קוק

א"כ [=אם כן] יש בגמל ענין דחילו, גם הוא צנוע כדאחז"ל [=כדאמרו חז"ל] ע"פ [=על פסוק] "'ובניהם' – בנאיהם", "מתוך שהוא צנוע בתשמישו, חוסך עלה"כ [עליו הכתוב]". והצניעות באה מכח הבושה שהיא היראה, כדכתיב "'למען [=בעבור] תהי[ה] יראתו על פניכם' – זו הבושה", א"כ [=אם כן] הי[ה] בו דחילו. גם כח עובדין רומז ברומח, כמשאחז"ל ע"פ [=כמו שאמרו חז"ל על פסוק] "ויקח רומח בידו", שקרא ק"ש שי"ב [=קריאת שמע שיש בו] רמ"ח תבות נגד רמ"ח מ"ע [=מצות עשה]. ובכל ג' מעלותיו יחד, לא הי[ה] יכול להשיג אפי[לו] כח ברכיה דחד מינייהו, ואמר ג' מדריגות נגד ג' מדריגות של ברכים שהם [שהן] נה"י [נצח, הוד, יסוד], ולא נגע ביה. פסקי לקרנא דתכלתא דחד מינייהו, היינו שבהיותו משיג אז ברוה"ק [=ברוח הקודש] קצת ממעלתם, רצה לדעת עכ"פ [=על כל פנים] איזה דרך מבחי[נת] יראה שלהם, שהוא רמוז בתכלת, שתכלת היא סוד היראה, כדאי[תא] בזוהר תרומה, דבי[ה] דיינין דנ"פ [=דיני נפשות], ולא הוה מסתגי לן, שא"א [=שאי-אפשר] בשום אופן לנו ללכת ע"פ [=על-פי] דרכיהם, שדרכיהם גבוהים הרבה מדרכינו. ע"כ [=על כן] אמר ההוא טייעא, שראה שנקט בעצמו דרך גבוה כזה שהשיג מהם וא"א [=ואי-אפשר] לו ללכת בו, שמא שקלת מידי מינייהו? ללמוד מהם לענין הנהגה. אמר שזה אי-אפשר דגמירי במעלתם דמאן דשקל מידי מינייהו לא מסתגי לי[ה], שאין בכוחנו ללכת ע"פ [=על-פי] דרך שלהם, שהוא דרך נשגב ונעלה מאוד. ע"כ [=על כן] אהדריה נהלי[ה] להחליט ולגמור בדעתו שדרך כזה רק להם יאתה ולא לנו, וללכת ע"פ [=על-פי] דרך הראוי לנו לפי מצבנו שקטן הרבה לעומתם. אהדרתיה ונקט דעתי[ה] לדרך הראוי לנו, ואז הלך בדרך ד' ועבודתו כפי ערכו, וזהו הדר מסתגי לן. כי אתאי לקמי[ה] דרבנן, וסיפרתי להם מהשגה זו ומעוצם מעלתם, אמרו שרואים שנגד מעלת דור המדבר אין חכמי וקדושי דורנו נחשבים כלל, שאי-אפשר כלל לעמוד על ענינם, כענין מאמרם "אם הראשונים כבנ"א [כבני אדם], אנו כחמורים". והנה יש ב' מעלות בחכמים, מעלת עצמו הוא ענין העבודה בבחירה, וענין חכמה הוא מהדברים שהאב זוכה לבנו. ואמרו כשהראה לדעת שא"א [=שאי-אפשר] להשיג מעלתם, לא בתורה ולא ביראה, ונודע כי היראה מצד הרוממות אינה כעול על האדם רק עטרת תפארת, וכחמור לעול נאמר על קוצר ההשגה שהשיג יראת הרומ[?] העונש, ואמרו שנגד מעלתם, כל אבא, כל גדולי הדור שבערך רבה, חמרא נחשבים, כיראים מעונש, נגד יראת רוממות שלהם, וכל בב"ח [=בר בר חנה] היינו מצד החכמה, שזהו מהדברים שהאב זוכה לבנו, סכסא, שאין אנו חשובים לחכמים כלל נגדם. והביאו ראי[ה] שהשגתם מנועה מאתנו, שהרי עיקר מה שרצה לדעת מדרכיהם הוא איך להתנהג בדרך עבודת ד', שכללותם היא או דרך הגבורות או דרך החסדים, היינו אי כב"ש [=כבית שמאי] דמחמרי, שהם מסוד הגבורות, אי כב"ה [=כבית הלל] המקילים, שהם סוד החסדים, והיה זה אפשר להשיג מהם מצד חכמתם, גם מצד מעשיהם, אחרי שראה ענינם. ובציצית יש חוטין וחוליות, וכלל החוטין ל"ב, מורים על ל"ב נתיבות חכמה, והקשר מורה שהמעשים מאחדים כח החכמה ומקיימים אותה באדם, א"כ [=אם כן] היה לו למימני חוטין, להסתכל בחכמתם, ולמימני חוליות, להסתכל בעובדין שלהם. אלא מדלא השיג מענינם דבר לענין הנהגה ש"מ [=שמע מינה] שהם בכל דרכיהם גבוהים הרבה מערכינו, בין לענין חכמה בין לענין עבודה ומעשים, ע"כ [=על כן] אי-אפשר להשיג מעלתם, שעליהם הכתוב אומר "אספו לי חסידי כורתי בריתי עלי זבח", שהמה מיוחדים, בין בחסידות, דהיינו בעובדין, בין בחכמה, שהוא ענין הברית, כמש"כ [=כמו שכתוב] "סוד ד' ליראיו ובריתו להודיעם", ובהם ב' המעלות נכללים [נכללות] ברוממות גדול.

יג

ואמר רבה בר בר חנה: אמר לי ההוא טייעא: תא אחוי לך טורא דסיני. אזלי וחזאי דהדרן ליה עקרבי וקיימין כי חמרי חיורתי. שמעתי בת קול שאומרת: אוי לי שנשבעתי, ועכשיו שנשבעתי מי מפר לי? כי אתאי לקמי דרבנן, אמרו לי: כל אבא חמרא וכל בר בר [חנה] סיכסא! הוה לך למימר "מופר לך". ור[בה] ב[ר] ב[ר] ח[נה] סבר דלמא משבועתא דמבול קאמר. ורבנן, אם כן, "אוי לי" למה לי[ה]?

הנה הר סיני מקור נתינת התורה, וע"י [=ועל-ידי] נתינת התורה לישראל הם שולטים לע"ל [=לעתיד לבוא] על האוה"ע [=האומות העולם] ומלמדים אותם דרך ד'. אבל כ"ז [=כל זמן] שלא נשלם התיקון, כל האומות נעשו מצירים לישראל ע"י [=על-ידי] שקבלו התורה. נמצא שכעת כל האומות סובבות וכוחות המקטרגים שלהם ומכינים עצמם לעקוץ את ישראל, אבל בפנימיות כוחותם, הם מוכנים להיות משועבדים לעול תורה, וע"י [=ועל-ידי] כן יצאו הם ג"כ [=גם כן] מכח תוקף דיניהם העשוי לחבל, ויחזרו להיות גם המה מכלל בעלי חסד, כדכתיב "לא ירעו ולא ישחיתו בכל הר קדשי". אבל עכשיו, יש בהם ב' כוחות: הם עקרבים שרוצים להשחית את העולם ע"י [=על-ידי] השחתת ישראל ח"ו [=חס ושלום], ומפני שלא נשלם התיקון הראוי ע"י [=על-ידי] ישראל, לא נשלמו אלה הכוחות לצאת מטומאתם, ומ"מ ע"י [=ומכל מקום על-ידי] שישראל עכ"פ [=על כל פנים] מתחזקים בקדושה, ע"כ [=על כן] אי-אפשר להם להשחית את העולם לגמרי, והם עכ"פ [=על כל פנים] נכנעים, ונראה בהם שהם מוכנים לפעול ג"כ [=גם כן] פעולת החסד. ע"כ [=על כן] הני עקרבי קיימין כחמרי, שהוא מורה על השעבוד כחמור לעול המשא, והם חיורתי ג"כ [=גם כן], מורות שלבסוף ישתעבדו ע"כ [=על כרחם] לעשות חסד. ושמעתי ב[ת] ק[ול]: אוי לי שנשבעתי כו', יש לפרש בב' פנים, מפני שמצד הדין, לפי קלקול מעשי העולם, היה ראוי להשחתה וכליון, וזו קשה לפני הקב"ה [=הקדוש ברוך הוא] כדאי[תא] באריכות בזוהר תרומה, על ענין קשה כקי"ס [=כקריעת ים סוף], מצד שהוא נגד הדין, כך אע"פ [=אף על-פי] שראויים להשחתה, והיה ראוי לסלק כח החמרי חיורתי מהעקרבי, וליתן להם רשות לחבל ח"ו [=חס ושלום], אבל כבר נשבע להאריך אף שלא להשחית העולם, או שהיתה הכונה, שהי[ה] ראוי לבטל כח העקרבי ולהכניעם לגמרי, ויהיו ממש חמרי חיורתי, נושאים עול החסד, אלא שנשבע שיהיו ישראל בגלות להתם חטאת, ע"כ [=על כן] אלו הכוחות נצרכים, וענין ההפרה הוא שיזכו ישראל בעבודה ובחכמה, כדאי[תא] בזוהר, שבחכמת סתרי תורה "יפקון ישראל מגלותא". ע"כ [=על כן] התרעמו על גדולי הדור, גם למדו זכות שנסתמו אורות ההשגה מכובד הגלות, עד שאפי[לו] המצוינים א"א [=אי-אפשר] להשיג להם בתו"י [=בתורה ויראה] לזכות את כל הדור למעלה רמה עד שיתוקן הכל, בב"א [=במהרה בימינו אמן]. והוא לא אמר מופר, וחשב ג"כ [=גם כן] שאי-אפשר להשתדל בפורקנא, שאולי לא הגיע הזמן כלל ואסור לדחוק את הקץ. אך רבנן הוכיחו מאמירת "אוי לי". מוכח שהיא מצד המניעה להיטיב, שהוא כביכול צער למעלה. אבל אם היתה הקובלנא רק מצד שאי-אפשר להשלים כפי תביעת מדת הדין, הי[תה] הלשון "קשה לי" ולא "אוי לי", כדמצינו בקי"ס [=בקריעת ים סוף] לשון "קשה".

יד

ואמר רבה בר בר חנה: אמר לי ההוא טייעא: תא, אחווי לך בלועי דקורח. אזלי וחזאי תרי ביזעי דהוה נפיק מנייהו קוטרא. שקל גבבא דעמרא ואמשינה במיא, ואנחיה ברישא דרומחא, ועייליה התם. וכי אפיק, הוה איחרך אחרוכי. אמר לי: אצית! מאי שמעת? ושמעית דהוו אמרין: משה ותורתו אמת והם בדאים. אמר לי: כל שלשים יומין מהדר להו גיהנם להכא כבשר בקלחת, ואמרי הכי, משה ותורתו אמת והם בדאים.

הראה לו סוד מחלוקת קרח וקלקולו, שהיתה כפירתו מתפשטת בתורה שבכתב ובתושבע"פ [=ובתורה שבעל-פה], והם ב' מקורות שמשפיעים חיים לעולם, אע"ג [=אף על-גב] ד"אורייתא מגבורה אתיהיבת", דכתיב "מימינו אש דת למו", מ"מ [=מכל מקום] האש הזאת היא מחיה הכל, והם הפכו שע"י [=שעל-ידי] ב' אלה תושפע עליהם מדה"ד [=מדת הדין] גדול[ה]. והיינו תרי בזעי, פי[רוש] ב' קלקולים שמהם נדונים בעש"ן, סוד ע'קרב ש'רף נ'חש, וי"ל [=ויש לומר] דעקרב רומז על כפירה בתושב"כ [=בתורה שבכתב] שממית ודאי, ונחש סוד הזלזול בתושבע"פ [=בתורה שבעל-פה], אע"פ [=אף על-פי] שלפעמים בי"ד [=בית דין] מבטל דברי בי"ד [=בית דין] חברו, אבל הבא בכפירה, נזוק ומת מלחישת הנחש, ושרף הוא הכולל, מקום יחוד תושב"כ ותושבע"פ [=תורה שבכתב ותורה שבעל-פה], והמחלק ביניהם ומפרידם, נשרף בסוד אש אוכלה. וע"פ [=ועל-פי] דברי סוד ד' אי[תא] בס[פר] בית עולמים להגרי"א [=להגאון רבי יצחק אייזיק] חבר ז"ל [זכרונו לברכה] על האידרא, שסוד צמר הוא חסדים דעתיק, שהיא [=שהוא] למעלה מהנהגת העוה"ז [=העולם הזה] כדאי[תא] בקל"ח [פתחי חכמה] ובדברי הגר"א [=הגאון רבי אליהו], ואסור להגביר החסדים ממקום יותר גבוה שאין העולם סובלו, וזה גרם החורבן במלכין קדמאין ע"י [=על-ידי] רבוי האור. ע"כ [=על כן] שקל צמר ואמשיניה במיא, שמים רומזים לחסדים התחתונים הנמשכים בעולם, והורה שהיה קלקולם שרצו להגביר כח החסדים בסוד הצמר שהוא למעלה מתיקון העולם, והראה שאפילו אם יקיימו כל רמ"ח מ"ע [=רמ"ח מצות עשה] שהם ממשיכים [שהן ממשיכות] החסדים, מ"מ [=מכל מקום] כיון שירצו להפליג הדבר יותר מדאי, יהפך להם לרועץ ותגבורת הדינים, והיינו דאחרך אחרוכי כשהיה ברישא דרומחא, דהיינו בכונת הרמ"ח פקודין. וא"ל [=ואמר לו] ששמע וידוים המורה על קלקולם, ואמרו משה ותורתו, דהיינו סוד תושב"כ [=תורה שבכתב] ותורה שבע"פ [=שבעל-פה], שהתורה המיוחד[ת] לו הוא פלפולא דאורייתא, שהוא כלל עיקר תושבע"פ [=תורה שבעל-פה], אמת, שאע"פ [=שאף על-פי] שהם רצו לעלות למקום יותר גבוה, אבל זה הדרך שמסר לנו משרע"ה [=משה רבינו, עליו השלום] הוא אמת ומתקיים, וסוד הקו האמצעי שהוא "תתן אמת ליעקב", והם בדאין. והנה ע"י [=על-ידי] הגברת החסדים, היה העולם ח"ו [=חס ושלום] חוזר לתוהו, כעת החורבן (וזמן) [וזין] מלכין קדמאין, ואז "ארעא אתבטל[ת]" ח"ו [=חס ושלום], ע"כ [=על כן] סוד המלכות נוקמת מהם על קלקולם הגדול, וענין החדשים של שלשים יום הוא מצד הלבנה, בחי[נת]

מלכות, המאור הקטן, ע"כ [=על כן] כל שלשים יום מהדר להו גיהנם, שמתעוררת עליהם בדינים על שרצו לדחוק רגלי השכינה. וזהו כבשר בקלחת, כי בשר רומז לאודם הדין, והם רצו להגביר החסד יותר מדאי, ע"כ [=על כן] נהפכו עליהם לדין גמור, ורואים שאין קיום לדברי תוהו שלהם, ומתודים: משה ותורתו אמת, ויש קיום בהתמדה לתורת אלהינו, שהיא ברית כרותה לעם, והם בדאים, וכך עונשו של בדאי, אפילו אם אומר אמת, אין שומעין לו, והיינו שאסור ללכת ע"פ [=על-פי] דרך זה המקולקל, אפילו לקיים המצות, דהיינו רישא דרומחא, שעכ"ז [=שעם כל זה] לא יציל כלל, ולא יצילו את נפשם מיד להבה, כדאי[תא] דאחרך אחרוכי, אפילו שהי[ה] טבול במיא.

טו

ואמר רבה בר בר חנה: אמר לי ההוא טייעא: תא ואחוי לך היכא דנשקי ארעא ורקיע אהדדי. אזלי וחזאי דעביד כוי כוי. שקליתא לסלתאי ואנחתיה בכוותא דרקיע. אדמצלינא, בעיתא ולא אשכחיתה. אמרי: איכא גנבי הכא? א[מר] ל[י]: גלגלא דרקיע הוא דהדר. נטר עד למחר כי השתא ומשכחת ליה.

לימד אותו למוד גדול בענין הנהגת השלמות, דהנה כבר ביאר הגרמ״ח [=הגאון רבי משה חיים] לוצאטו בס[פר] אדיר במרום ע״פ [=על פסוק] ״ארח צדיקים וגו׳״ ובענין ״פלוגתא דשערי״, שיש הנהגה כוללת והנהגה פרטית. וצריך ללמוד מדבריו, שיש דרך שהאדם יעסוק בעבודתו ושלמותו לתקנת הכלל, וממילא, מאשר הוא חלק מהכלל, כשיתברך הכלל, יתברך גם הוא בכללם, ויקבל חלק השפע המגיע לו כפי פעלו אשר הכין ואשר הביא בקופת הכלל; ויש הנהגה פרטית, שיעמול לנפשו, ו״מפרי פי איש תשבע בטנו״. והוא הורה לו שב׳ אלו ההנהגות מתאחדות, ואין לחשוב שע״י [=שעל-ידי] עסקו בענין השלמות הכללי לא יבוא לחלקו כ״כ [=כל כך] כאילו עסק בשלמות פרטי, כי לא כן הדבר, שהמה מתאחדים, והכח הפנימי של השלמות הכללי פועל להשלים הפרט הנכלל, שוה ממש ויותר עוד מאילו עסק בשלמות פרטי. ואין לחשוב שהם ב׳ ענינים, ועל הענינים הפרטיים צריך עבודה פרטית במחשבה לעצמו, כי לא כן הוא, רק בכל פרטיו יתברך מהכלל. אמנם יש קצת הפרש, שההנהגה הפרטית סובבת על קוטב סיבות של מצב האיש הפרטי, ויראה לעיניו דרכי סיבותיו איך מתגלגלות לטובתו; ובהנהגה הכללית, ידמה לו שמסובבים סיבות לטובת אחרים, ובאמת אותן הסיבות עצמן שוות לתועלתו הפרטי[ת], רק שצריך לחכות מעט בבטחון על השי״ת [=השם יתברך], ויראה שנשתלשלו הדברים לטובתו הפרטית, כי שבו הפעולות אל הנקודה המרכזית שממנה התחילו לצאת, ומהר יבוא זמן מכוון נגד הפעולות ותצא הכונה הפרטית לאור.

וזה שהורה **היכא דנשקי ארעא**, היא רומזת להנהגה הפרטית, כי הארץ היא הנקודה, וענין הנקודה היא פרטית, **ורקיע** מקיף הארץ וכולל בגלגל הרבה כוכבים ויצורים רבו מספר. למד אותו שב׳ אלה השלמויות ואורחותיהם מתאימים, וא״צ [=ואין צריך] לפנות דוקא לטובתו הפרטית, כי ימצא שלמותו, בכל מיני שלמות, בין גשמי בין רוחני, בכל פרטיו ג״כ ע״י [=גם כן על-ידי] עבודתו לצורך הכלל. וכן עשה, **שקלי לסלתאי**, הכלי שמחזקת [=שמחזיק] מזונותיו, פי[רוש] הכין כלי קבלתו ושפעו נגד מטרת הענינים הכוללים, והיינו **כוותא דרקיעא**, שהוא ית[ברך] משגיח מהחלונות לברך את עמו ונחלתו, ולאחדם כולם וכל יצוריו כולם בברכתו. אלא שעכ״פ [=שעל כל פנים] האדם הוא פרטי, וצריך לפנות מעט לדברים פרטיים שלו, אלא שאין זה עיקר עסקו. וענין חובת התפילה מתיסדת ג״כ [=גם כן] על הפרטיות, שהרי אמרה תורה ״׳לא תאכלו על הדם׳ – לא תאכלו קודם שתתפללו על דמכם״. ובזוהר משפטים, אי[תא] שצריך להתפלל דוקא על מזונו. ונמצא בשעת תפילה והדברים הנתלים, עסק בפרטיות והסתכל ג״כ [=גם כן] בסבותיו הפרטיות איך תבוא לו שלמותו ע״י [=עי-ידי] הכנותיו הכוללות, ולא ראה כ״כ [=כל כך] מהר פרי שלמותו, כמשל ברוחניות, העוסק

בצרכי צבור, מתמעטת חכמתו, ועכ"ז [=ועם כל זה] הוא במעלה עליונה, אלא שאינה ניכרת לפי שעה, ובקרוב ישיב ד' שבותו וימלא אוצרו הפרטי. א"ל [=אמרי ליה] איכא גנבי הכא? היתכן שתמשך משלמות הכללי, מהחלק שעבד העובד לצורך הכלל, ותיסב רק לאחרים ולא לו? א"ל [=אמר לו] שאין הדבר כן, כי כל השלמות יהי[ה] גם לו לבדו, אלא שהסיבות גדולות יותר ומתרחבות, כיון שהם [שהן] סובבות על מרכז הכלל, ע"כ [=על כן] צריך לחכות עד אשר תסובבנה מהלכם [מהלכן] לתקנת הכלל, ויבואו [ותבואנה] לסוף אל הפרטי כפי חלקו. וזהו נטר עד למחר כי השתא, שיהי[ה] סוד הזמן שבו נפעלות הפעולות כפי ערך הראוי להתחלת הפעולות שישובו [שתשובנה] אל מקורם [מקורן], ומשכחת לה, תמצא חלקך הפרטי, יהי[ה] לך לבדך. ובזה מסר לו סוד גדול בעבודה ושלמות. "[ו]אורח צדיקים כאור נגה".

חתימה

אברך את ד׳ אשר יעצני ועד כה עזרני להתחיל ולגמור הרהורי לבבי אודות דברי אלקים [אלהים] חיים, להשכיל בדברי חכמים וחדותם, ולרדת בקוצר דעתי, עד מקום שידי הכהה מגעת, אל קצת מתעלומות חכמת התייר הגדול רבב״ח [=רבה בר בר חנה], שכלל ט״ו למודים במאמריו, לדלות חכמה ממעמקים נגד ט״ו ״שיר המעלות״ שבתהלים שאמר דוד המע״ה [=המלך, עליו השלום], להעלות מים עמוקים שבתהום להרטיב עלמא, כדחז״ל [=כדברי חז״ל] בפ[רק] החליל. כמו כן, אמר ט״ו לימודים גדולים המעלים חכמה ממעמקים, כדה״כ [=כדברי הכתוב] ״מים עמוקים עצה בלב איש, ואיש תבונה ידלנה״. והשי״ת [=והשם יתברך] יאיר עיננו בתורתו, ומפיו יתן לנו ״דעת ותבונה״.

www.ingramcontent.com/pod-product-compliance
Lightning Source LLC
Chambersburg PA
CBHW060501240426
43661CB00006B/873
* 9 7 8 1 9 4 7 8 5 7 1 1 7 *